Inclusive Learning Design in Higher Education

How can you design more inclusive learning experiences and environments? How can you overcome some of the challenges of designing and implementing more inclusive learning?

You will find the answers to these questions and much more in this dynamic new text. Asserting that **good teaching** *is* **inclusive teaching**, it demonstrates how university modules and courses can be designed so that each student, regardless of their complex diversity, is valued equally.

Drawing from the contributions of over 80 experts and colleagues alongside her own extensive experience, Rossi explores how to embed inclusivity at the point of course design and how to set up, run, assess and evaluate inclusive learning environments and experiences. Following a unique 'roots to shoots' journey through an inclusive learning design tree, chapters focus on five dimensions:

- Values
- Context
- Content
- Assessment
- Evaluation

An accessible and practical guide for higher education course design, this book is a must read for higher education educators looking to be more inclusive in the way they design and offer learning experiences.

For further reading, please visit inclusivelearningdesign.com where you'll find extended contributor bios, more case studies, key concepts and background, an 'inclusive learning design' checklist and glossary.

Virna Rossi is a teacher educator based in London, UK. A passionate teacher since 1999, she has worked in all educational sectors: Primary, Secondary, College (FE), Adult Education and Higher Education.

Inclusive Learning Design in Higher Education

A Practical Guide to Creating Equitable Learning Experiences

Virna Rossi

LONDON AND NEW YORK

Designed cover image: Nat Bobinski

First published 2023
by Routledge
4 Park Square, Milton Park, Abingdon, Oxon, OX14 4RN

and by Routledge
605 Third Avenue, New York, NY 10158

Routledge is an imprint of the Taylor & Francis Group, an informa business

© 2023 Virna Rossi

The right of Virna Rossi to be identified as author of this work has been asserted in accordance with sections 77 and 78 of the Copyright, Designs and Patents Act 1988.

All rights reserved. No part of this book may be reprinted or reproduced or utilised in any form or by any electronic, mechanical, or other means, now known or hereafter invented, including photocopying and recording, or in any information storage or retrieval system, without permission in writing from the publishers.

Trademark notice: Product or corporate names may be trademarks or registered trademarks, and are used only for identification and explanation without intent to infringe.

British Library Cataloguing-in-Publication Data
A catalogue record for this book is available from the British Library

Library of Congress Cataloging-in-Publication Data
Names: Rossi, Virna, 1973- author.
Title: Inclusive learning design in higher education : a practical guide to creating equitable learning experiences / Virna Rossi.
Description: First edition. | New York : Routledge, 2023. | Includes bibliographical references and index.
Identifiers: LCCN 2022054343 (print) | LCCN 2022054344 (ebook) | ISBN 9781032136189 (paperback) | ISBN 9781032122298 (hardback) | ISBN 9781003230144 (ebook)
Subjects: LCSH: Inclusive education. | Universities and colleges--Curricula--Evaluation.
Classification: LCC LC1200 .R675 2023 (print) | LCC LC1200 (ebook) | DDC 371.9/046--dc23/eng/20230301
LC record available at https://lccn.loc.gov/2022054343
LC ebook record available at https://lccn.loc.gov/2022054344

ISBN: 978-1-032-12229-8 (hbk)
ISBN: 978-1-032-13618-9 (pbk)
ISBN: 978-1-003-23014-4 (ebk)

DOI: 10.4324/9781003230144

Typeset in Galliard
by SPi Technologies India Pvt Ltd (Straive)

Access the author's website: inclusivelearningdesign.com

Tutti i passi che ho fatto nella mia vita mi hanno portato qui, ora.
Every step I have taken in my life has led me here, now.

                                                          Alberto Garutti

Contents

About me x
Contributors xi
Preface xviii
Acknowledgements xxii
Structure and organisation of the book xxiv

SECTION 1
Learning values—The roots 1

Roots to shoots approach 3
The roots 3
The 'I' root: Intentionally Equitable 5
The 'N' root: Nurturing 9
The 'C' root: Co-created 13
The 'L' root: Liberating 17
The 'U' root: User-friendly 21
The 'S' root: Socially Responsible 26
The 'I' root: Integrative 30
The 'V' root: Values-based 34
The 'E' root: Ecological 38

Co-creation 43

Where are you at now? 59

SECTION 2
Learning context—Set up and engagement 61

1 Ready? Setting up the physical and digital space 65

The physical learning spaces 68
The blended learning spaces 71
The digital learning spaces 76
The mobile learning spaces 81

2 Steady? Needs analysis and orientation — 91

Needs analysis 92
Orientation 99

3 Go! Building community and fostering a support culture — 109

Students' well-being 109
Starting the course 118

SECTION 3
Learning content—Input and practice — 129

4 Using learning thresholds — 135

Learning outcomes 136
Threshold concepts 138
Learning thresholds 141
Big ideas 144
Putting it all together 146

5 Flipped and self-directed — 162

Flipped 162
Self-directed 175

6 Diversified, relevant and creative — 186

Diversified 187
Relevant 206
Creative 215

SECTION 4
Learning assessment—Output and feedback — 231

7 Choice, voice and authentic — 237

Choice 238
Voice 245
Authentic 249

8 Reflective and formative — 261

Reflective and formative assessment 262
Reflective and formative feedback 273

9 Self and peer assessment and feedback — 280

SECTION 5
Learning evaluation   293

10   Lesson evaluation   297

11   Course evaluation   301

Conclusion   309
Index   316

About me

 I have lived the first half of my life in Italy and the second half in the UK. I am a passionate teacher and mother of two boys. I have teaching experience in all UK educational sectors: Primary, Secondary, College (FE), Adult Education, and Higher Education. I started teaching in 1999 and I have worked as teacher educator since 2009. I find it very rewarding to assist colleagues in developing their teaching practices. My motto is 'learn to thrive'.

Contributors

Here are the photos and names of the many colleagues who have contributed narratives to this book, in the order in which they appear in the book. Check the companion website inclusivelearningdesign.com for their biography.

Section 1

Maha Bali, Ezme Hefter, Sakinah Alhadad, Amrita Narang, Charles Wachira, Ashley Jay Brockwell, Carl Gombrich, Kaston Anderson-Carpenter, Sarah Mursal, Paul Kleiman, Kiu Sum, Cassandra Stevenson, Alice Kim, Yfei Liang, Kelly Matthews.

Contributors xiii

Section 2

Sylvia Ashton, Rachel Stone, Stanimira Velikova, Ros Walker, Ashiya Abdool Satar, Zachary Walker, Nokuthula Vilakati, Maida Ali, Belinda Judd, Jennie Brentnall, Nicholas Bowskill, Nina Walker, Godson Gatsha, Gloria Niles, Nomsa Zindela, Pilar Teraan Trueba, Tim Fawns, Derek Jones, Gill Aitken, Era Savvides.

Section 3

Annetta Tsang, Heidi Estrem, Chris Francis, Denise Mac Giolla Rí, Mustapha Aabi, Steven Kolber, Daniel Beneroso, Erin C. King, Seanna Takacs, Arley Cruthers, David Baume, Carole Baume, Tracy Galvin, Jen McParland

Lisa Low, Alexandra Sanderson, Helen Handley, Vicki Dale, Margarita del Pilar Silva Rojas, Joanne Tippett, Edward Windus, Kolton Lee, Rosemary Stott, Camille Dickson-Deane, Aranee Manoharan, Adrienne Baytops Paul, Divya Kapoor, Ourania Varsou, Elaine Fisher.

Section 4

Gustavo Espinoza Ramos, Stephan Hughes, Fionnula Darby, Nellie El Enany, Abd Alsattar Ardati, Mossab Banat, Alessia Bevilacqua, Claudio Girelli, Laura Costelloe, Joanne L. Hall, Asha Rao, Ameena L. Payne, Bonnie Amelia Dean, Kay Sambell, Linda Graham, Chie Adachi, Jo Elliott, Georgeta Ion, Anna Díaz-Vicario, Aleix Barrera-Corominas, Cristina Mercader, Cecilia Inés Suárez.

Section 5

Flower Darby and Xinli Wang.

Preface

Peoples of the Earth was the title of the book my teacher gave me as an exit present at the end of my primary school years. I absolutely loved that book: its illustrations, the stories about the Maya, the Masai, Australian Aborigines and many more. For a ten-year-old curious girl living in a small monocultural town in Central Italy, before the age of the Internet, this was a wonderful window on the diversity in the world. As it turns out, I have been fortunate enough to have indeed connected with many 'peoples of the earth' both through cultural travel and having lived for over two decades in one of the most cosmopolitan cities in the world, London.

In 2020, just before the pandemic, after over two decades of teaching, my interest in human diversity and the ongoing pedagogical challenge of catering for all the different needs that diversity entails, prompted me to embark on the biggest professional project of my life: writing a book to fill a gap – the need for a *practical* guide on inclusive learning design for university practitioners.

Taking account of the changed educational landscape post-pandemic, this book is about things you can design for your course that will make it more inclusive. However, it addresses both 'configuring' *and* 'enacting' the design (Goodyear and Dimitriadis 2013), going from designing and planning to implementing inclusive learning. Hence, through this book I invite you to see yourself as both the architect (with a design and a vision) and a builder (dealing with the practicalities) of more inclusive learning environments and experiences.

This book is an invitation to reflect on what types of choices you intentionally make regarding learning environments, experiences, activities, tasks, assessment and feedback and to what extent they are inclusive (a term I define further down) in terms of inviting the students to bring their whole selves to the course, feeling valued and having their voices heard about their learning. This implies getting away from a procedural focus on inclusivity towards a broader, all-encompassing approach, viewing learning design as a holistic, iterative process.

Why this book

As a teacher educator, my priority has always been to model and embody inclusive teaching because to me **good teaching *is* inclusive teaching**. However, while running the Post-Graduate Certificate in Education, I realised that there is no practical guide to help teachers design more inclusive learning. Yet, there is an urgent need to make our courses more inclusive as the student population grows in numbers and in diversity dimensions.

The writing of this book is the result of many years of designing and redesigning learning experiences; of piloting various teaching approaches to refine my teaching practice; of reading and researching educational theory, including the science of learning; of discussing practice with colleagues and learning from others; of letting my students teach me about inclusivity. Although writing my ideas about inclusivity in a book is part of my own professional growth and development, it also responds to a very real need within the wider UK Higher Education landscape at a time of historical paradigm shifts within education and society. I believe every teacher needs to seriously ask themselves how inclusive their practice is and how they can design more inclusive learning experiences and environments. Inclusivity cannot be left to chance any longer—it needs to be *intentional and paramount*.

My goal in writing this book is to make all educators aware of the critical importance of taking an inclusivity approach to learning design and implementation. Not every teacher knows how to turn inclusive *intentions* into inclusive *practices*. Indeed, this book is about making inclusivity a ***signature pedagogy*** (Shulman 2005)—or hallmark—of the university course you offer or support. This book will help you develop a clearer picture of where you currently stand, what embedding inclusivity in the curriculum design looks like, and your level of readiness to implement change. This book will meet you where you are and provide a practical roadmap to create more inclusive learning.

In this book I hope to demonstrate how inclusive pedagogies are executable (with no budget) across multiple disciplines, and emerge through dialogue with others by sharing how our own teaching practices have developed in relation to our students, social contexts, education and life experiences. I advocate inclusivity as an educational *habit of heart, habit of mind and habit of hand* (Shulman 2005) to cater for each and every student. However, I also propose a realistic appraisal of inclusive approaches by discussing the challenges and logistical issues of designing, implementing and sustaining more inclusive practices.

Through the many case studies presented in the book, you will taste an **international menu** of ideas and examples of inclusive learning design. Some are reminders of practices which have been discussed for decades, such as ways to support dyslexic students; others are newer, surfacing (emergent) inclusivity practices that are easy to implement and are well supported both by research and real-life evidence.

Through the prompt questions at the start of every chapter, and through my narrative, examples and case studies, you will have opportunities to reflect on your own formative experiences and perspectives and to consider a range of new approaches to sustain more inclusive learning environments.

Inclusivity has been talked about for many years, yet it still seems a novel pedagogy—I believe that once people dig a little and grasp the unquestionable necessity of it, it becomes an 'irreversible' threshold concept (Meyer and Land 2006) in that it changes our pedagogical outlook for good.

What does inclusive learning design mean?

In a nutshell:

Inclusive learning design is design that considers the full range of human diversity with its complexity. It is designing learning environments, experiences, activities, tasks, assessment and feedback with students' voice and choice at its heart, so that students can grow academically, culturally and socially.

The phrase is in the right order as inclusivity (first) is the lens through which all learning (second) should be designed (third). It is also useful to define the three terms individually:

Inclusive. It is an educational mindset and ethos. Each student matters is valued equally, treated with respect and provided with real learning opportunities tailored to their individual needs as much as possible.

Learning. The process of acquiring new understanding, knowledge, behaviours, skills, values, attitudes and preferences. This book focuses in particular on the things we put in place to prompt learning within a university course.

Design. The creative, purposeful, deliberate and systematic organization of learning environments and experiences. Design informs plans: it provides a means to gain understanding of the complexity of learning so that appropriate plans can be put in place.

The preceding definitions are my attempt at providing statements of meaning for the key words in this book. However, it is not easy to agree on a universally acceptable definition of inclusive learning design. The three words that make up this phrase are each contentious, so their meanings keep evolving and being redefined. They each can have narrow or broad definitions depending on context and what emphasis is sought. For these reasons, rather than fixed definitions, I favour 'broader understandings' that reflect the complexities of education and that acknowledge that how we define and understand terms is context bound (McArthur 2021). Also, definitions are provisional: they evolve, are reviewed and modified as practice changes, as we change as educators and as the wider world changes.

Who this book is for

This is a book for anyone in education who is interested in more inclusive practices at university. As it is a *practical* guide, it will be of particular interest to university academics such as teachers and lecturers in the UK and other Anglophone countries (faculty in the US), tutors, instructors and similar roles—all those with direct classroom responsibilities.

It will also be useful to:

- Educational developers, academic developers and other teacher educators
- Practitioners such as: third space professionals or 'para-academics' (such as support staff, librarians, technical tutors, study skills tutors, mentors and similar roles)
- Learning designers, instructional designers, e-learning developers and other similar roles
- Quality teams
- Researchers and scholars in: education, learning design and of course inclusivity
- Leaders (such as teaching and learning deans or directors; other programme directors or deans and similar roles)

A note on the way I address you, the reader. As the main audience for this book is university teachers, I have chosen to refer to you as *academics* or as *teachers*, interchangeably. I will often include myself in the discussion by using the term 'we'.

Whether you are new to teaching or have years or decades of experience, this book has something for everyone—something to think about and hopefully something to try out. It is a resource deliberately oriented to practice which showcases a wide variety of learning design responses from diverse contexts while remaining grounded in commitments to inclusivity.

Using the powerful metaphor of a tree with roots and branches, I discuss (1) the values—at the roots—that should inform our inclusive design; (2) the context—how to set up the course and its space and how to engage students; (3) the content—how to provide input and practice in a more inclusive way; (4) the assessment—what outputs to design for students and how to design inclusive feedback; and (5) the critical area of curriculum evaluation. Through the sections of the book and using a plethora of lived examples, I invite you to travel from 'roots to shoots', from the values to the design dimensions and practices.

Head to the companion website inclusivelearningdesign.com to read the *Key concepts and background* chapter where I provide further details about inclusive learning design, why this book is needed and why now, my educational philosophy and my 'show rather than tell' approach in writing this book.

Positionality statement

I acknowledge my cultural and social roots in the Global North. I was born and raised in Italy but have lived the second half of my life in London, UK. As such, my education and professional life and identities have been shaped by European views and values.

I acknowledge that my skin colour and cultural background have given me and continue to give me some privileges both in the Global North and in the Global South. I acknowledge the pain and damage done by various forms of colonisations, of which we are still reaping the effects in both the Global North and in the Global South.

Through cultural travel, learning languages and extensive voluntary work, I have always sought to question my stance and grow in new directions. My life as a cultural nomad in many lands has enriched me enormously and provided me the inspiration to write this book to further the conversation about inclusive educational practices, in an attempt to change the current educational narrative. It is my heartfelt hope that this book might contribute to lifting new faces and new voices alongside more experienced academic 'giants' so that we may, all together, create a better way of teaching and learning for the benefit of all involved.

A note regarding the use of language, acronyms and 'labels': I aim to be as respectful as possible towards all in a rapidly changing socio-cultural landscape, so I apologise for any unintentional mistakes in my use of language, but I would be grateful to be alerted to it to inform future use. You can connect with me on Twitter using my handle: @VirnaRossi or via the companion website.

Bibliography

Goodyear, P. and Dimitriadis, Y. (2013). 'In Medias Res': Reframing Design for Learning. *Research in Learning Technology*, 21. doi: 10.3402/rlt.v21i0.19909

McArthur, J. (2021). The Inclusive University: A Critical Theory Perspective Using a Recognition-Based Approach. *Social Inclusion*, [online] 9(3), 6–15. Available at: https://www.cogitatiopress.com/socialinclusion/article/view/4122/4122

Meyer, J. and Land, R. (2006). *Overcoming Barriers to Student Understanding: Threshold Concepts and Troublesome Knowledge*. New York: Routledge.

Shulman, L.S. (2005). Signature Pedagogies in the Professions. *Daedalus*, 134(3), 52–59. http://www.jstor.org/stable/20027998

Acknowledgements

Overall, I feel this is more a crowdsourced resource than a solo act. The list of people who have supported the writing of this book is very long, but I would like to thank in particular:

- The more than 80 colleagues willing to contribute a case study or other narrative to the book's content.
- The Twitter #lthechat crowd who've inspired and challenged me on a weekly basis.
- The SEDA community through the ongoing, thought-provoking, Jiscmail exchanges.
- My PGCert students, some of whom have written parts of this book. They have been key to my inclusivity practice development, helping me pilot and evaluate various inclusivity approaches.
- The Ravensbourne University London Research Department for supporting this project.
- My more or less formal mentors, who have reviewed drafts and provided general advice: Peter Hartley and John Lea.

The reviewers of sections of the final book draft:

Tracie Marcella Addy, Associate Dean of Teaching & Learning (US); Branko Andjic, Researcher in Educational Science (Austria); Kieran Balloo, Senior Lecturer (UK/Australia); Shirley Bennett, Head of Academic Practice (UK); Joanna Cheetham, Senior Educational Developer (UK); Roisin Curran, Senior Lecturer in HE Practice (Northern Ireland); Rachel Forsyth, Project Manager (Sweden); Xaviera Gonzalez-Wegener (UK); Danielle Hinton, Educational Developer (UK); Donna Hurford, Senior Educational Consultant (Denmark); Jason Kennedy, Instructional coach (US); Madden Tracey, Learning Technology Adviser (UK); Hala Mansour, Associate Professor Education (UK); Lydia Mong, Senior Instructional Designer (US); Teeroumanee Nadan, SFHEA, Researcher in Internationalisation, Inclusive & Digital HigherEd (UK); Ivan Newman, Independent Specialist Study Skills Tutor (UK); Celia Popovic, Associate Professor Education (Canada); Verena Roberts, Educator, Open Learning Designer (Canada); Ruth Smith, Head of Department (Australia); Charlotte Stevens, Senior Educational Developer (UK); Andrea Todd, Senior Lecturer, Director of Pro Bono & Community Engagement (UK); Tünde Varga-Atkins Senior Educational Developer (UK); Steven White, Educational Developer (UK); Victoria Wilson-Crane, Director of Innovative Student Learning (UK).

The early reviewers of the very first draft version in 2020, when I thought I was going to produce an edited volume—their feedback was invaluable in shaping the book as it is now:

Samantha Ahern, Faculty Learning Technology Lead (UK); Maha Bali, Associate professor of practice, Center for Learning and Teaching, American University in Cairo (Egypt); Lindy-Ann Blaize Alfred, AdvanceHE (UK); Kerry Dobbins, Professional Development Advisor, Educational Development (UK); Guillermo García-Coronado, Psychologist, SENCO teacher (Mexico); Kay Hack PFHEA (UK); Mary Kitchener, Educational Developer, Oxford Brookes University (UK); Kathryna Kwok, Educational researcher (UK); Teeroumanee Nadan, SFHEA, Researcher in Internationalisation, Inclusive & Digital HigherEd (UK); Clare Newton, Freelance FE Art and Design educator (UK); Portia Nyaaba, Teacher (Ghana); Jo Peat, Head of Educational Development (UK); Celia Popovic, Associate Professor Education (Canada); Maha Refaat Sakr, Assistant Lecturer of Endodontics (Egypt); Santanu Vasant, Educational Developer and Consultant (UK); Adrian J. Wallbank, Programme Director and Senior Teaching Fellow (UK).

My husband and kids for having the patience with my increased workload to see this project through to completion.

Illustrator

Nat Obour-Awuku (Nat Bobinski)

Instagram: @mr_bobinski
Twitter: @mr_bobinski_
Email: natstone23@gmail.com

It has been a privilege and a great pleasure to illustrate this book with the help of Nat Obour-Awuku (art name Nat Bobinski), a Ghanaian-based illustrator and medical laboratory scientist who has worked on art projects for World Child Cancer, Pediatric Society of Ghana and other organizations across the world. Nat loves traveling and playing video games when he is not working.

Structure and organisation of the book

Reading this book: Roots to shoots

This book is less a recipe and more an invitation to reflect, to listen to a range of global perspectives and to consider what might work for you in your context. For many of us, the act of writing or sketching while engaging with a book can help clarify, make connections and draw implications from our experiences in new ways. So, you may want to keep a pencil at hand to make notes in the margins. This would also make it easier to revisit your thoughts at a later time.

I would also suggest you have some device with Internet connection nearby as there is a constant interplay between the book and the companion website inclusivelearningdesign.com including audio-visual materials.

In which order should you read this book? The roots-to-shoots approach provides a natural journey up the metaphorical inclusive learning design tree: first the roots (values); then the shoots connected to the three areas of context, content, and assessment; and finally the outer evaluation circle. So, you may want to read it in the order in which it is presented, especially if you are new to inclusive practices. However, the various sections can also stand by themselves if you are particularly interested in reading the later sections before the earlier ones, particularly if you consider yourself an inclusivity champion and are most interested in the case studies.

Please take a moment to examine the visual representation of the inclusive learning design tree.

I am aware that there is a lot to take in when you first see this image. There are many elements to it because learning design is *complex* and cannot easily be reduced to a few elements. However, by splitting the image into roots, three branches with their leaves (or fruits) and the outer circle, I hope to provide a logical way to tackle the irreducible complexity of learning design.

This book invites you to travel through five phases of learning design:

1   Values
2   Context
3   Content
4   Assessment
5   Evaluation

These correspond to the sections in this book:

Structure and organisation of the book   xxv

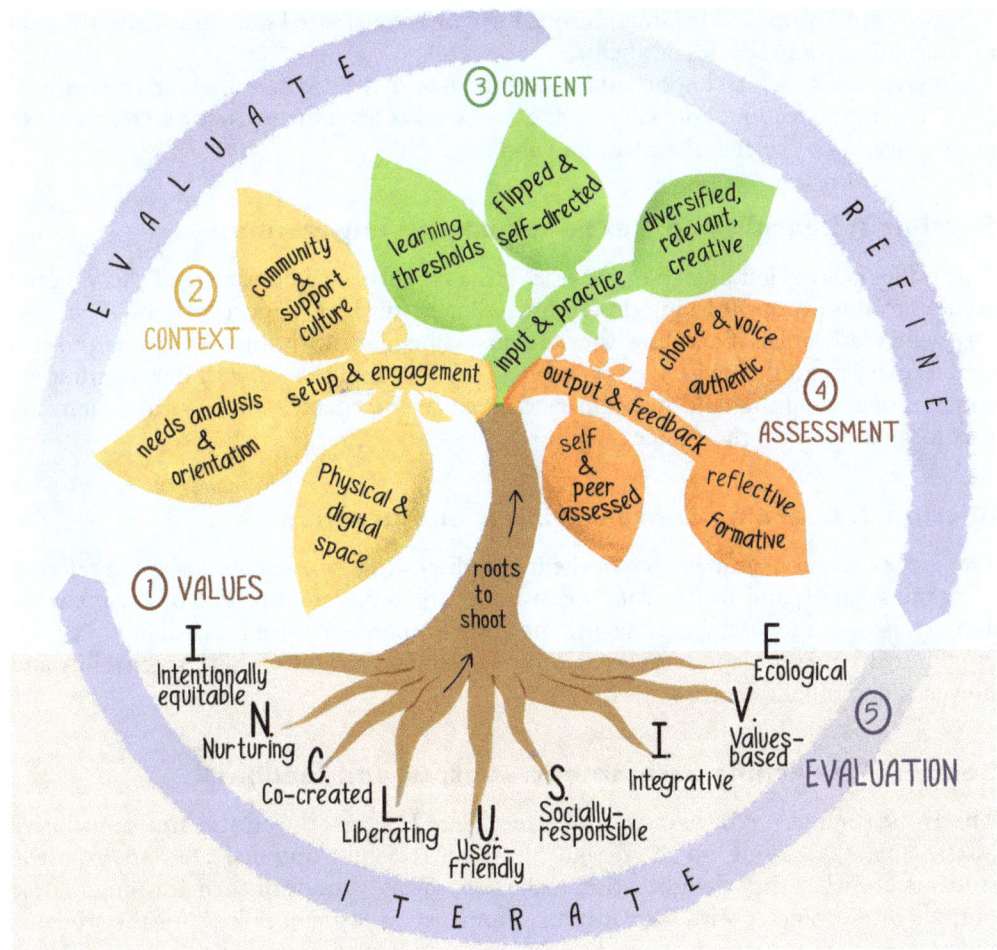

Figure 0.1 The inclusive learning design tree.

Section 1: Values—the roots

Here I introduce the roots-to-shoots tree metaphor to represent my approach to inclusive learning design. The focus of the section is on values which support inclusive learning design represented by the roots of the tree. I use the word 'inclusive' as an acronym for nine further inclusivity values that should drive the learning design process at every stage:

I. Intentionally equitable
N. Nurturing
C. Co-created
L. Liberated
U. User-friendly
S. Socially responsible
I. Integrative
V. Values-based
E. Ecological

For each root I propose a 'stimulus' in the form of a contributed short text from a variety of colleagues from various continents.

Co-creation is such an important inclusivity value that I dedicate a whole chapter to it at the end of the section. You will read the case-studies from the teacher *and the students'* perspective of co-creating their learning and research.

Section 2: Learning context—set up and engagement

This is the (yellow) left branch of the tree. Here I discuss the importance of allowing the context to inform our learning design, including setting up support systems. The context will greatly affect if and how the students will engage with the course at all, so it is vital to carry out a thorough contextual analysis. This is in the sense of our institutional context, of the cultural and disciplinary context of the course, and of all the elements that form and inform the students context.

Section 3: Learning content—input and practice

This is the (green) central branch of the tree. I discuss the course content, often referred to as the syllabus, and which usually consists of the input and practice of key concepts and practices in the discipline. Making the content more inclusive is possible by considering how we present it and how we ask the students to engage with it. Accessibility and universal design take centre stage here.

Section 4: Learning assessment—output and feedback

This is the (orange) right branch of the tree. Here I discuss the critical area of inclusive assessment by focussing on the design of varied, reflective outputs. Outputs from the students are what they design, write, make, do, say as a result of their learning. These outputs often coincide with formative or summative assessment points, for the students themselves, their peers and us, the teachers, to gauge learning progress.

Section 5: Learning evaluation—the outer circle

The circle with the arrows signals an all-important aspect of good teaching and learning: its evaluation is an ongoing effort. The words on the arrows—evaluate, iterate, refine—are the key concepts and practices discussed in this section.

Before starting the roots-to-shoots journey, I invite you to read the 'Key concepts and background' to the writing of this book, on the companion website inclusivelearningdesign.com

Section 1

Learning values
The roots

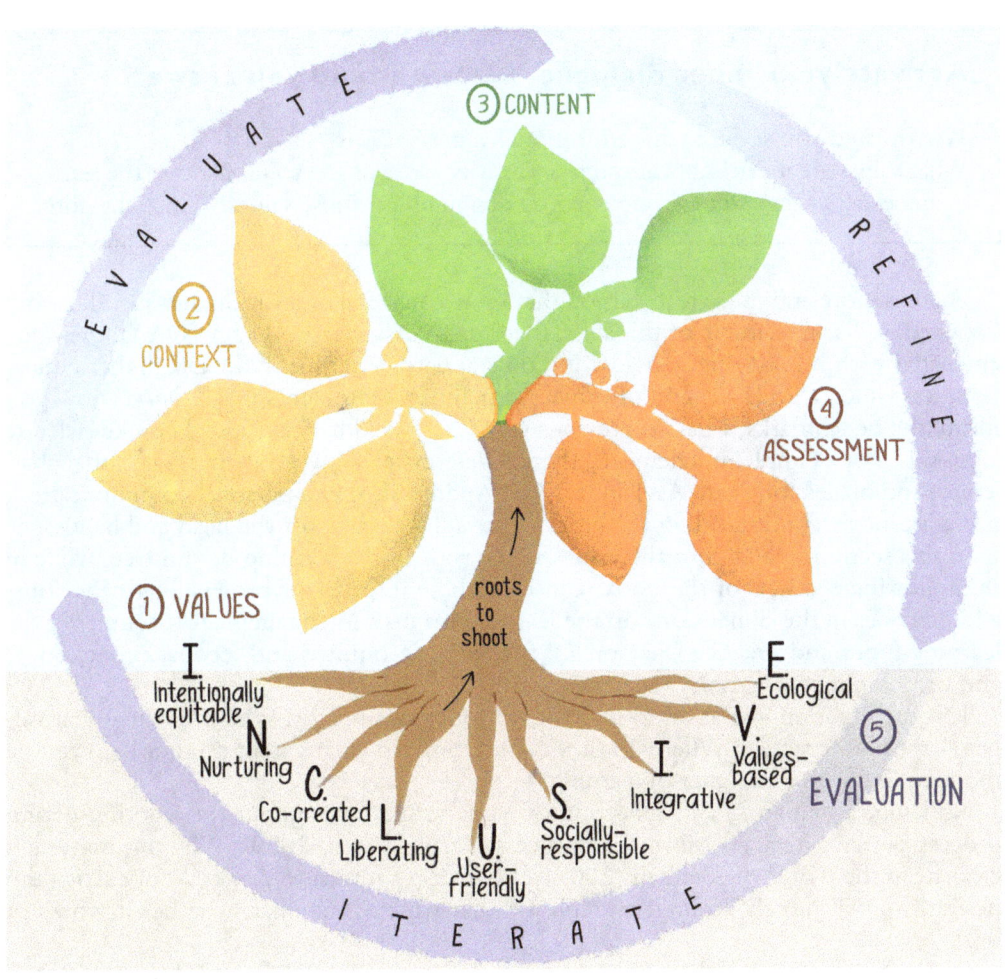

2 Learning values—The roots

Education which does not mould character is absolutely worthless

Mahatma Gandhi

In this section I discuss the 'roots to shoots' tree metaphor to represent my approach to inclusive learning design. The focus of this section is on the *values* represented by the roots of the tree which support inclusive learning design. I use the word 'inclusive' as an acronym for a subset of nine more detailed inclusivity values that should drive the learning design process at every stage. For each root I propose a contributed short text from a variety of global colleagues.

Co-creation is such an important inclusivity value that I dedicate a whole chapter to it at the end of this section where I present further ideas and case studies from the teacher *and the students*' perspective of co-creating their learning and research.

> **Activate your inner dialogue. ... How would you answer?**
>
> What would you say are your educational values?
> What values are inextricably linked to inclusivity for you? Do you think that the learning experiences and environments you design reflect those values? Why/why not?

There is more and more recognition that values matter in education, not just skills and knowledge. As an example of this shift, the Quality Assurance Agency (QAA), the body entrusted with monitoring and advising on standards and quality in UK higher education, has issued a 2022 version of subject benchmark statements where *values* now permeate the benchmarks, whereas previous versions tended to focus mostly on knowledge and skills. For example, in chemistry there is reference to involvement with global challenges and professionalism. As Tunde Varga-Atkins put it in a personal communication, it is a lot more 'about tackling the heart of the subject, not just the head and hands'.

In this section, read about the values at the root of the learning design tree, while in the following sections of the book read how these inform our professional behaviours and practices in the dimensions of: the learning set up and engagement (Section 2), the learning input and practice (Section 3), the learning outputs and feedback (Section 4) and the learning evaluation (Section 5).

This section is an invitation to interrogate your positionality. Who are you? What values shape your practice? Where do they come from? To what extent do they help you be more equitable as a designer of learning?

Noticing, articulating and reflecting on your values throughout the learning design process can be a very transformative process (Anaissie et al. 2020). Why this matters is clear from the words of Kleiman (2009): 'If we don't return to *principles* of curriculum design, we will merely attempt to replicate that which is familiar; whether it works or not'.

As some authors talk of values and others about principles, it is useful to clarify their difference. According to Covey (1989), principles are enduring and fundamental 'guidelines for human conduct' such as fairness or effective communication; values are more akin to *subjective* beliefs regarding specific issues or ideas, and they can change. Principles and values can overlap but what determines our course of actions and goals are not so much universal principles but our *personal values*, because they are our internal drivers.

This also applies in teaching and learning: the educational values we hold directly impact our professional behaviours and practices. For this reason, in this book, I have chosen to focus on values, although many of them overlap with and can also be principles. In my tree metaphor, the values are the roots that feed the entire tree.

For this book, the visualisation of the learning design process as a tree with roots and branches is a very important 'mediating artefact' (Conole 2008), my 'visual learning design representation to document and communicate teaching ideas' (Agostinho 2006). The tree represents the overall inclusive learning design process, which I have defined as:

> Inclusive learning design is design that considers the full range of human diversity with its complexity. It is designing learning environments, experiences, activities, tasks, assessment and feedback with students' voice and choice at its heart, so that students can grow academically, culturally and socially.

Roots to shoots approach

What does 'roots to shoots' mean? This expression is my effort to encapsulate in very few words how each branch of the learning design process—each stage and element—is fed by underlying values, whether these are overt and have been articulated and positioned or not. Roots mean life or death for a tree. Likewise, the values we uphold either support our inclusive learning design or on the contrary (unconsciously?) hinder it.

In the image, the roots of the tree represent the values (1), which feed the dimensions (branches) of: context (2), content (3), assessment (4) and evaluation (5). The leaves are examples of inclusive learning design with a particular focus on the meso-level of *course* design.

My approach is reminiscent of design thinking. It points to the recursive nature of learning design and to the 'additive nature' of each phase of design: the focus on values and context early in the process informs and shapes later phases of content and assessment (Culver et al. 2021).

The roots

Back to the roots. Roots matter. There is something compelling about the use of trees/roots as a metaphor, which explains why they have become like a 'screen' onto which any number of conceptual experiments have been projected (Wampole 2016).

In this book, the roots represent the values which inform inclusive educational practices. As inclusivity has become a contested buzz word, to clarify its meaning, the word 'inclusive' is the umbrella under which I provide nine more values (the nine roots) which are facets of inclusivity and point to its manifestations:

I. Intentionally equitable
N. Nurturing
C. Co-created
L. Liberating
U. User-friendly
S. Socially responsible
I. Integrative
V. Values-based
E. Ecological

4 Learning values—The roots

Figure 0.2 From Unfair to Just and Inclusive.

Of course, these are not all neatly separated values; on the contrary they overlap considerably, and each contribute to enrich my 'show rather than tell' approach to inclusivity. The 'V', for values-based root, is a 'meta-root': it is about the importance of being driven by appropriate inclusivity values which we should clarify and articulate from the outset.

I will now discuss each root-value, one at a time, showing why and how each value affects our inclusive learning design. For each root I will introduce the value it represents and provide some context for the narrative of a contributor which serves as further stimulation, and often provocation, in that area.

The 'I' root: Intentionally Equitable

> **Learning design which is culturally responsive; inclusive 'on purpose' and 'with purpose'.**

> **Activate your inner dialogue. ... How would you answer?**
>
> Why should you cultivate intentional equity? How could you do so?

As teachers, we are the 'hosts' of our own classroom space. Students on a course belong to a cohort which becomes a bit like a family unit. They spend a considerable amount of time in that space, so it is worth asking: is my space hospitable? Who feels welcome and at ease? Who might struggle to belong? How can I achieve a greater sense of equitable hospitality? This is where the word *intentional* is key.

Figure 0.2 uses the image of a tree to clarify and contrast some key terms and concepts in this book, including equity, another contested term with narrow and broad definitions.

The first four frames are based on the 'Addressing Imbalance' illustration series by Tony Ruth (@lunchbreath), based on Shel Silverstein's *Giving Tree* for John Maeda's 2019 Design in Tech Report.

The first one (Unfair), is a *parody* of the apparent ease with which many achieve success: they fit into the 'system' and there are practically no barriers for them to succeed.

The second frame (Fair?), refers to the accommodations and supports institutions often provide which stem from good intentions, but often only support certain types of students, not all.

In the third frame (Equitable), the support is tailored, and the students succeed. Once we reach this frame, we all feel: great, mission accomplished ... or is it? There's still something missing.

In the fourth frame (Just) the tree itself (the system) needs addressing. Many educational systems are like bent (mature) trees, developed over centuries of assumptions and, often, inequalities. Straightening them is challenging and requires sustained multi-directional efforts in the form of restorative practices: an idea derived from ancient and indigenous practices employed in cultures such as Native American and First Nations which promotes a supportive and respectful behaviour to repair any harm caused to others as a result of present or past actions.

Though this seems the best situation, there is still something missing: how about the students' voice and choice?

The fifth and last frame highlights the ideal state: Just and inclusive. In the four previous frames, there was only one type of fruit on offer, with no possibility of choice. Here I am not referring to choice about what institution to attend and what discipline or course to study, but to providing students with real choice and voice *within* whatever institution or course they choose. Get students onboard at the learning design stage to hear how they want their own education shaped, so the tree might grow straighter. This is the level where we can provide justice for all but still cater for individual needs. Of course, it is not easy to provide for all and *at the same time* provide for each. This tension of the collective vs the individual is the hallmark of education nowadays, but I believe inclusivity can help us address both needs.

In order to better understand equity and inclusivity, we need to understand **'intersectionality'**. 'Intersectionality refers to the understanding that social inequalities are not experienced as unitary exclusive phenomenon of race, class, gender, sexuality, disability, and other aspects of social position but as interacting and "reciprocally constructed" phenomenon' (Collins 2015). Although originally the term was specifically about the exclusion of Black women, the racial/gender aspect has now become one of many. Intersectionality is key to understanding the multiple and intersecting barriers faced by students. It challenges well-intentioned inclusivity policies which tend to put students in neat categories.

So, for instance, a visually impaired, Black, female student is likely to experience not one type of barrier only, for example due to the eyesight condition, but also because by being a woman and being Black she might experience additional barriers as these three characteristics can create a compound effect whereby the difficulties multiply. She will have a different and unique experience compared to being visually impaired only or female only or Black only.

Equity conversations are not easy for anyone, mostly because we feel ill-equipped to handle them and there's the fear of blame. Teachers fear that if they speak about unequal access and underserved communities, students whose lived experiences match those would feel singled out. In fact, it usually is quite the opposite: 'talking openly about issues of access and equity normalizes student struggles and counteracts the tendency many students have toward self-blame and isolation' (Saphiro 2020).

The following provocation will help us interrogate our assumptions when it comes to receiving students into our learning spaces. Notice how Maha addresses the question: what does intentionally equitable hospitality mean for us as educators?

Stimulus: Intentionally Equitable Hospitality

By Maha Bali (Egypt)

Do you know that fable about the man, boy and donkey? You can easily find the full story online, but the overall idea is that people kept making fun of this trio—when they were all walking, people made fun that no one was riding the donkey. When the boy rode the donkey, people critiqued the boy for riding but leaving his dad to walk ... when the dad rode instead of the boy, people shamed the man for riding but leaving his son to walk ... when both man and boy rode, they critiqued them for exhausting the donkey ... and on and on ... with the lesson being that you can never please everyone.

However, if we tackle this story from a lens of Intentionally Equitable Hospitality, as a metaphor for our classrooms, we would need to look at it in a more nuanced way. Although we can never please everyone, Intentionally Equitable Hospitality means our values help us to navigate this difficult space to make the choices that would be most hospitable to the most marginalised people in a particular context.

So, taking the story of the boy, man and donkey, we would ask ourselves, in this particular context, whose needs should come first? Who is disempowered in the broader macro system, and in this particular situation? We don't have information on the father's health or boy's age or donkey's situation.

First of all, who is the most marginalised person in this trio? Is it the donkey because it is an animal and does not have a voice to express its preferences? Is it the boy (how old is he?) because he is physically weaker?

> How would your choices differ if:
> The donkey is pregnant? Or sick?
> The boy is diabetic?
> The man needs the exercise to lose weight?

Importantly, who has decision-making power in this context? For example, who speaks for the donkey, who takes care of her/his needs? Whoever said that riding the donkey is a privilege and preferred for all people (example is man wanting to lose weight)? Also, can we assume there is a possibility of switching so everyone gets a break and everyone still gets a turn? Perhaps one person can get a longer turn because of their circumstances and another person a shorter turn because they have a bit more power. Sometimes no one having a turn is also ok.

The obvious connections to teaching and hospitality here is that you need to know a lot and account for a lot to be able to make the right decisions, but you weigh how you make the decisions through a lens of equity first and hospitality second—and remember these things won't happen in practice without intentionality in planning and execution. Instead of assuming the teacher can 'know it all' and plan ahead for all of this, we need to imagine ways of enhancing learner participation in our classes, such that we design our courses 'with' our learners, offering them more and more agency to design their own learning experiences on their own terms, what Nancy Fraser (2005) calls 'parity of participation'. However, we also need to recognise that asking students to work in groups together does not mean there are no power dynamics at play. For example, if donkeys are 'used to being ridden all the time' (metaphor for oppression) they may not choose another situation because they've never been made conscious of it as an option for them—they may reproduce their own oppression even when given the choice.

There will always be power differences amongst students, so how do we promote intentional equity amongst them? How do we ensure that differences in students' cultures are taken into account? For example, if some cultures tend to speak less, or favour particular modes of communication, how is that welcomed into the class? What about if the class is conducted in one language that is some students' native tongue but not others'? How do we ensure that what we present in class and the processes we use in our teaching respect and welcome different cultures, inviting students to share more and more of their own in order to enrich the class and enhance everyone's learning (Figure 0.3)? It is important to differentiate between when you as a teacher need to step back to nurture agency, and when you need to intervene to use your power to nurture agency and promote equity. But most importantly, it is essential not to assume that as teachers 'we already know'—we need to involve students, as individuals and as groups, in the process.

Figure 0.3 How to design a table that addresses people's different needs, rather than ask people to adjust to a pre-designed table.

Bibliography

Fraser, N. (2005). Reframing Justice in a Globalizing World. *New Left Review*, 36, November/December. Available at: https://newleftreview-org.libproxy.aucegypt.edu/issues/II36/articles/nancy-fraser-reframing-justice-in-a-globalizing-world

Gorski, P.C. and Pothini, S.G. (2013). *Case Studies on Diversity and Social Justice Education*. New York: Routledge.

> White, J.A. and Tronto, J.C. (2004). Political Practices of Care: Needs and Rights. *Ratio Juris*, 17(4), 425–453. doi: 10.1111/j.1467-9337.2004.00276.x
>
> **And of course the Intentionally Equitable Hospitality article itself:**
>
> Bali, M., Caines, A., Hogue, R.J., DeWaard, H.J. and Friedrich, C. (2019). Intentionally Equitable Hospitality in Hybrid Video Dialogue: The Context of Virtually Connecting. eLearning Mag (special issue). Available at: https://elearnmag.acm.org/archive.cfm?aid=3331173

Maha has helped us reflect on the way we welcome our students in our learning spaces, whether they must adjust to them or whether we make the effort to adapt them so that each student can succeed. The story of the father and son also brings to light 'generational learning': besides other dimensions of diversity, in today's diverse learning spaces, it is possible that we have pensioners and teenagers learning on the same course. This also needs adaptation from our part, drawing on the strength of each generation and ensuring they can all benefit from each other's unique perspectives. Intentional hospitality is a strong theme throughout this book, and I will address it in more detail in Section 2 about the learning context and building inclusive learning *environments*.

Closely linked to intentional hospitality is the idea of 'nurturing' our students. This is the theme of the next root in the acronym: i.N.c.l.u.s.i.v.e.

The 'N' root: Nurturing

> **Learning design which is holistic; supports well-being; promotes autonomy**

> **Activate your inner dialogue. ... How would you answer?**
>
> In which ways can we 'nurture' our students?
> Why should we aim for a holistic approach to education? How can we achieve it?

To nurture, in the context of this book, means to care for our students while they grow and develop. In a nutshell, it's about our students' 'growing and glowing'. This is similar to 'eudaimonia' in Aristotelian ethics, which refers to the condition of humans flourishing or living well.

As teachers, our primary role is to support students' academic development. However, this is inextricably linked to their general well-being in all aspects of their lives. This does not mean that we need to become their counsellor and carer—that would be unreasonable and beyond our remit as academics. But we do need to engage with the overall well-being of our students *in order to* support their academic growth. As choices of teaching and assessment content and methods influence students' well-being and mental health (Houghton and Anderson 2017), learning design impacts students' well-being. In order to succeed in their studies, students will have to engage with the course and particularly with its assessment, so as teachers we have multiple opportunities to address their well-being *through curriculum design* (Lister et al. 2021).

To nurture students and support them so they can grow and glow, we should promote a **sense of belonging**. It can be useful to think back to a time or place where we felt included, an insider. What helped us feel that way? Belonging is not the same as conformity; quite the opposite. It is the fine balance of providing suitable conditions so each student can be their true self, while respecting others and creating a space where everyone is welcomed and valued because of their diversity, not in spite of it. Because we all have complex identities, we need to remember that boxing students into predetermined categories is not always helpful; rather we need to consider the whole person by taking a multi-identity perspective.

Such broader view of educational well-being—foremost related to our emotional self—has always sat uncomfortably in academic discourse, which privileges rational thought. This might be traced back to the very origins of many militaristic school features that were set up two centuries ago, in post-Napoleonic Europe but still affect the way we 'do things around here' in HE, especially in the Western World. The emotional side of our lives has often been seen as an issue or as a problem to be solved, whereas from neuroscience we have learnt that emotional well-being is key to promoting learning.

In the following narrative, Ezme encourages us to use a holistic lens on all aspects of learning. Notice the four dimensions of holist education that she promotes.

Stimulus: Holistic approaches to educate the 'whole' person

By Ezme Hefte (UK)

Holistic approaches to education aim to nurture the whole person and their holistic relationships with the self, their peers, community, environment and spirituality. Education in this way focuses not only on cognitive development but also affective development, that is, emotional and moral intelligence as well as social navigation, aiming for learners to transition with more ease from the educational setting to society and the working environment with a better understanding of their role within the holistic relationships and how they can enact responsible change within them. To achieve this holistic development in learners a teacher must attend to all four aspects (Figure 0.4) of the 'whole' person throughout learning design and implementation:

Intellectual (Mind)
Physical (Body)
Emotional (Feeling)
Spiritual (Spirit)

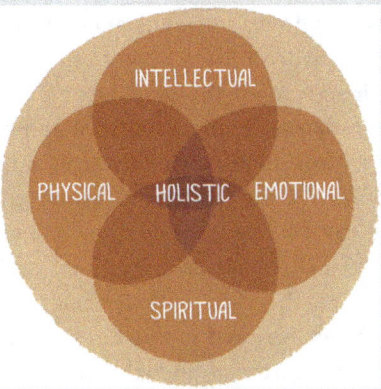

Figure 0.4 The four aspects of self are highly dependent upon each other and often overlap. By taking the holistic approach as educators we can target all aspects at once as shown in the image.

Teaching and learning with this approach manifests itself as highly flexible, student-centred and experiential. For instance, main areas of study should be planned, however lessons themselves should be flexible and fluid enough to accommodate for areas of study in all four aspects and at the students' pace. The goal of holistic education is the process, not the product. Allowing students a choice of topic and a medium to learn through as well as location (indoors, outdoors etc.) whilst ensuring group activities such as discussions are planned around student choice allows for a level of autonomy and self-discipline to be developed whilst simultaneously nurturing the sense of community so vital to holistic approaches and the education of the whole person. Some further tasks to nurture the four aspects include mindfulness and breath work, art-integrated learning, reflective journaling, open-ended discussions, interacting and reflecting upon nature and conflict resolution. Conflict resolution here refers to situations where a conflict occurs within the classroom community: current tasks are put on hold for the group to discuss and work towards a resolution together.

Crucial to taking the holistic approach is establishing the right learning environment where learners feel they are safe and able to express and engage with the emotional and spiritual elements of the whole, make mistakes and be open to discussing mistakes. Art teachers in a 2006 study on holistic approaches found that vulnerability and risk-taking from the teacher themselves aided in inducing this environment, for instance showcasing where the teacher may have struggled or made a mistake and how they approached it, and allowing learners to give feedback on the teacher's work alongside the traditional teacher-to-learner feedback (Lee Carroll 2006). This approach nurtures a sense of community and promotes understanding of holistic relationships through emulation of the real-world environment where mistakes occur and there usually isn't an all-knowing hierarchical figure to turn to for answers when a hurdle is encountered but rather that everyone makes mistakes and learns from them.

In my own experience from running holistic-based extracurricular art and well-being sessions for undergraduates, students described how they had experienced this sense of community. They expressed how the holistic approaches I took towards my teaching had made them feel comfortable very quickly in my presence and that the flexibility of the sessions, inclusion of mindfulness and open discussions helped them feel a part of something. This then contributed to the students describing the sessions as 'breathers' from their regular routines, giving them time and space to look after themselves and explore their creativity.

While the 'holistic environment' can be highly beneficial to both cognitive and affective learning, difficulties surrounding boundaries and safeguarding can arise; therefore, it is vital that teachers and learners set clear boundaries in regards to discussion content as well as have regular signposting reminders and check-ins to ensure practices such as mindfulness do not trigger or cause distress to students.

Bibliography

Lee Carroll, K. (2006). Development and Learning in Art: Moving in the Direction of a Holistic Paradigm for Art Education. *Visual Arts Research*, 32(1), 16–28. Available at: https://www.jstor.org/stable/20715397

Mahmoudi, S. (2012). Holistic Education: An Approach for the 21st Century. *International Education Studies*, 5(2), 178–186. doi:10.5539/ies.v5n3p178

Miller, J.P. (Ed.) (2007). *The Holistic Curriculum* (2nd ed.). Toronto: OISE Press.

Telles Rudge, L. (2008). Holistic Education: An Analysis of Its Pedagogical Application. MA Dissertation, The Ohio State University.

As suggested by Ezme, nurturing students so that they can 'grow and glow' implies we support not only their academic development, but also their social, emotional and even spiritual growth. Of course, this can be sensitive, so according to our level of comfort and the student body we have, some of these dimensions will be more prominent than others.

Mindfulness and meditation practices have become popular in the past few years, but detached from their original religious use, they can be misused and even be counterproductive. On the other hand, some basic 'universal' practices such as deep breathing or stretching to ease tension and gratitude exercises (such as thinking with appreciation about people around us) can be simple to do and can do much to put us and our students in a positive mindset for a better learning experience. There is also a renewed interest in the connection between movement, well-being and learning, with innovative approaches such as walking classrooms where students are asked to engage in learning activities away from their desks (Holmes 2019).

As Ezme has highlighted, key to nurturing is sharing the learning design with the students so they own the learning process as much as possible. This is the theme of the next root.

The 'C' root: Co-created

Students and others as collaborative partners

Activate your inner dialogue. ... How would you answer?

Why should you design learning *with* your students? How can you do so?
Besides your students, who can you partner with in your co-creation efforts?

Co-creation refers to pedagogical partnerships, in particular with students. It is a collaborative, reciprocal process whereby various aspects of teaching, learning and research are developed with students. Co-creation, partnerships and collaboration are part of the current 'sacred' educational vocabulary. As co-creation is a very important inclusive pedagogy, I am going to address it in more depth in a chapter at the end of this section where you will read practice case studies both of teachers and students about students-as-partners initiatives. Here, I will only briefly introduce the key ideas and propose a provocative narrative.

As a value at the root of the inclusive learning design tree, co-creation is an invitation for us all in education to leave traditional ways of siloed, solo working in academia towards much more collegial practices where we create or embrace opportunities to design learning collaboratively: with other internal or external colleagues; with para-academics; with industry 'experts', but above all with our primary stakeholders, our students.

Clearly, the quantity and quality of student partnership that any academic is prepared to engage with depends on their 'partnership readiness' (Gauthier 2020). At times this entails 'helping people to deconstruct their experiences of partnership and oftentimes, 'unlearning' certain ways of knowing and being in partnership with students and other colleagues' (Gauthier 2020).

Engaging students as (real and equal) partners requires a major paradigm shift and rethinking about the very roles of teachers and students. I believe as teachers, there's no better way to keep learning than inviting students to partner with us as we design their learning. Rather than presenting them with the finished and polished version of their course, students should be engaged from the very early stages of learning design, especially when key assessment decisions are made. This is an excellent way to extend intentionally equitable hospitality and to nurture our students - the roots of the tree intertwine and overlap.

In the following provocation, Sakinah provides some very poignant questions about genuine co-creation and invites us to ponder over our 'new possible futures'.

Stimulus: Why genuine co-creation matters

By Sakinah Alhadad (Australia)

> Any situation in which some prevent others from engaging in the process of inquiry is one of violence; ... To alienate humans from their own decision-making is to change them into objects.
>
> —Paulo Freire

Co-creation, at first glance, is the epitome of collaboration with purpose. It is an idea that has its conceptual origins in marketing and design as an innovative means of reconceptualising the economic concept of 'value', with customer empowerment in mind (Ind and Coates 2013). In social sciences, including education, this shift to participatory processes inculcates the similar intent of empowering communities (*minus the capitalism underpinnings*), rather than just documenting information through consultative methods (Rock et al. 2018). This involvement of the community right from the start of the problem-solving process is seen as critical to genuine co-creation. The intent of participatory processes therefore was not only constrained to co-creation of values and understandings *with* the communities of focus, but also of subsequent outputs to be shared within the same communities. Co-creation as democratic practice thus requires a paradigm shift from models preserving privileged information with those in power to equitable collaboration, with shared power (Rock et al. 2018).

While co-creation certainly has multidisciplinary underpinnings and practices, with its nuanced differences, there remain similar challenges, some of which serve as paradox to inclusion principles. Here, I pose key questions to consider as we navigate potential pitfalls, challenges and paradoxes towards possibilities for co-creation as values-based paradigm for inclusive education.

Who gets a seat at the table?

Power inequities are ever-present in any community we name—the consideration of who gets a seat at the table and the whys and the hows of participation in co-creation are critical for potential directions and impact of any co-creation. Conceptually, this is often thought of as 'stakeholders' in the group involved in co-creation. For genuine inclusion and equitable collaboration, and for meaningful co-creation, this group configuration shapes collective articulation, problematisation, design, and co-creation of values, practices and outcomes (Figure 0.5).

Christine Ortiz (2021) highlights the importance of inclusion of *both* the people who are most proximate to the experienced problems as well as those who hold power in the systems that create and perpetuate the issues or inequities. Having these multiple vantage points optimises the outcomes of the co-creation in ways that support the principles of empowerment through meaningful understanding of

Figure 0.5 Teachers and students assemble the learning experience by collaborative co-creation.

the problems to be addressed, with possibilities for co-creation in tangible ways through shared power. While those with more power often *initiate* the co-creation endeavours (Bovill 2019), stakeholder configuration is entangled with power and strategies for power sharing for an intentionally meaningful, inclusive collaboration.

How is dignity and sharing power upheld?

Power and dignity are both complex constructs that have structural, relational, dynamic and multi-layered dimensions, all of which are omnipresent in various contexts in our lives. In the education sphere, it is well acknowledged that any true co-creation requires challenging the status quo of traditional power dynamics (i.e., usually of traditional power asymmetry in student-teacher collaborations). While sharing power is often mentioned in the co-creation literature, *dignity* (Killmister 2017) is less so. I argue here that sharing power without considerations of human dignity can easily become tokenistic. Inequitable power structures and dynamics disproportionately influence individuals' sense of rightful belonging and dignity across places, spaces and time (Sengupta-Irving and Vossoughi 2019). Centering dignity when considering ways to share power, ways of knowing, doing, and being in co-creation raises our approaches to that of human rights and respect as duty to our fellow collaborators. Centering dignity forces us to consider power beyond traditional power dynamics of roles and positions, to that of sociopolitically imposed intersectional inequity, vulnerabilities, historicities and lived experiences (Alhadad et al. 2021). Creating an environment where there is shared trust, dignity is upheld and collective and individual responsibilities established will allow those with less power at initiation of the co-creation work to be more confident in initiating new directions, and for productive, equitable dialogue. Dignity and power are arguably some of the most important considerations for genuine co-creation as any collaboration without intentionally protecting and flourishing people or communities within serves to contradict democratic values of co-creation for rightful futures.

How do we honour ourselves as historical actors, with a past, present and future?

Co-creation enables people and communities to be authors of their own destiny. It has been argued that through partnerships for co-creation, people can develop their values, ways of being and their own sense of self as they become actively involved in constructing knowledge, validating lived experiences and developing capabilities to co-create (Gravett et al. 2020). Co-creation can occur through many methods and methodologies, all with the view to co-construct and co-create new futures.

Truly inclusive co-creation is as hard as it is vital. There will be some who are ambivalent about this, and some who actively oppose the idea of co-creation (Lubicz-Nawrocka 2017), particularly where the requirements for genuine, meaningful co-creation may be seen as 'too challenging'. As inclusive educators, we must remember that the status quo does not change on its own. Every step matters. Do not be afraid to initiate co-creation for meaningful, transformative change from a position of power and privilege, no matter how limited that may be.

Bibliography

Alhadad, S.S.J., Vasco, D., Williams, J.C., Dizon, P., Kapnias, R.L., Khan, S.B., Payne, H., Simpson, B.C. and Warren, C.D. (2021). Learning, Unlearning, and Relearning Together: Unmasking Power in a Students as Partners Program Using Collaborative Autoethnography. *Student Success*, 12(2), 38–50. doi: 10.5204/ssj.1934

Bovill, C. (2019). A Co-creation of Learning and Teaching Typology: What Kind of Co-creation Are You Planning or Doing? *International Journal for Students as Partners*, 3(2). doi: 10.15173/ijsap.v3i2.3953

Gravett, K., Kinchin, I.M. and Winstone, N.E. (2020). More than Customers: Conceptions of Students as Partners Held by Students, Staff, and Institutional Leaders. *Studies in Higher Education*, 45(12), 2574–2587. doi: 10.1080/03075079.2019.1623769

Ind, N. and Coates, N. (2013). The Meanings of Co-creation. *European Business Review*, 25(1), 86–95. doi: 10.1108/09555341311287754

Killmister, S. (2017). Dignity: Personal, Social, Human. *Philosophical Studies*, 174, 2063–2082. doi: 10.1007/s11098-016-0788-y

Lubicz-Nawrocka, T. (2017). Co-creation of the Curriculum: Challenging the Status Quo to Embed Partnership. *Journal of Educational Innovation, Partnership & Change*, 3(2). http://dx.doi.org/10.21100/jeipc.v3i2.529

Ortiz, C. (2021). The Problem with Problems Workbook: A Guide for Using Problem Definition as a Tool for Equity. Available at: http://equitymeetsdesign.com/

Rock, J., McGuire, M. and Rogers, A. (2018). Multidisciplinary Perspectives on Co-creation. *Science Communication*, 40(4), 541–552. doi: 10.1177/1075547018781496

Sengupta-Irving, T. and Vossoughi, S. (2019). Not in Their Name: Reinterpreting Discourses of STEM Learning through the Subjective Experiences of Minoritized Girls. *Race Ethnicity & Education*, 22(4), 479–501. doi: 10.1080/13613324.2019.1592835

Sakinah has proposed provocative questions that each of us in education should ponder on, if we want to move towards more inclusive co-created learning, as the following example illustrates.

Imagine you are (re-)designing a course or a few modules on human geography. Rather than doing it in isolation, why not set up a co-creation learning design forum or workshop and invite a good selection of recent alumni, prospective students (especially from underserved communities), non-government organisations, nomad communities representatives, environmental activists, members of minority religions, refugee workers and anyone else who might be able to contribute ideas to the course content and structure. After discussing what subject benchmarks are expected and what was done well in past iterations, we could open the discussion up to the group we have assembled. The wide range of experiences that each stakeholder offers will greatly enrich the learning experiences, environments and journey we design. We will be in a better position to configure a more inclusive learning experience by collaborative co-creation.

I discuss more examples in the co-creation chapter at the end of this section.

Many of the ideas of the first three roots—intentionally equitable hospitality, nurturing through holistic pedagogies and the key role of student partnerships—point to a radical shift in the way we perceive our role as teachers and the role of our students. This new vision of our respective roles aligns with an overall transformative and liberating view of education. This is the focus of the next root: L for Liberating.

The 'L' root: Liberating

> **Liberating in purpose, mode and content through inquiry**

> **Activate your inner dialogue. ... How would you answer?**
>
> What are some of the things education needs liberating from?
> How do you envisage a liberating pedagogy?
> How can you contribute to a more liberated learning design and practice?

Of the nine root-values of the metaphorical learning design tree, this is probably the most intriguing, probably because the word 'liberating' seems provocative in itself. Liberating can mean so many things to different people in different educational contexts. It can be about a mindset and about practices. It can be applied at the micro, meso and macro levels of education. If we take the broad meaning of 'liberating education', one of the best explanations about what it means comes from Robert A. Scott (2013) in a thought piece written when he was president of the Adelphi University, New York:

> The liberating curriculum is ... a program for citizenship, for civilianship, a civic degree. It is liberal in its form of inquiry. ... This curriculum is a preparation for living, for wondering why. It purports not just to teach one how to earn a living, but

how to live. It offers instruction and experience in both technique and vision—the ultimate combination in education ... to develop in students the capacity to check assumptions and to understand the value-laden choices that await them as consumers, decision-makers, and arbiters of ethical choices.

Such a curriculum does not just happen, however; it must be intentionally designed.

As the preceding quote shows, there are many facets to a liberating pedagogy, because it touches the why, what, how, where and when of everything we do in teaching and learning. And all these aspects can be done in the 'usual way', or we can inject our learning design with some innovative liberating practices that support more inclusive pedagogies. In this book you will encounter many examples of liberating practices, particularly through the diverse case studies.

Liberating pedagogies very much align with critical pedagogies, understood as approaches that are 'fundamentally democratic, informal, non-hierarchical, determined by participants' (Seal and Smith 2021). Taken in this sense, critical liberating learning is the purpose of this book: an attempt to show (rather than tell) what an inclusive liberating pedagogy looks like: how to design, plan, set up and run courses that are inclusive by design and by their very nature liberate both us the academics and our students. Inclusivity is about liberation.

One key facet of liberating the curriculum, as seen by a number of initiatives in many large and small universities in the UK and around the world, is about *decolonising the curriculum*.

Decolonising is one facet of inclusivity. But once more, defining the term decolonising is difficult because this has also become a buzz word in education, it is politically charged and it has acquired broader as well as narrower meanings. It seems that most in academia agree that colonisation is a core aspect of the hidden curriculum in higher education, and that decolonising it is the trickiest threshold concept.

When it comes to learning design, decolonising can refer to different things but it should be aimed at broadening out and enhancing the student experience. The following provocation provides food for thought about what decolonising means, in the context of liberatory practices, in the context of inclusive learning design.

Stimulus: Decolonising

By Amrita Narang (UK)

Today discourse of equality, diversity and inclusion (EDI) in higher education is more visible, supported, and talked about. As universities continue to set their goals to meet the EDI agenda, it is important to note that decoloniality and decolonisation is given its due importance, and is not conflated with the umbrella term EDI. Whilst these are familiar terms amongst academics and policymakers, there is a sense of agreement that decoloniality and decolonisation mean different things to different individuals, often dependent on discipline background, professional values and personal beliefs of both students and academics.

In my previously published article for Advance HE (Narang 2021), I explored decolonisation of pedagogy with respect to curriculum and look at examples of re-imagining curricula designs. In another article published in *Educational Developers Thinking Allowed* (Narang n.d.), I discussed the role of academic developers and shared resources to elicit thinking about decolonisation amongst academics. The current reflective piece dives deep into the ecosystem of knowledge, curriculum and pedagogy using the lens of decoloniality, and analyses ways to prototype a decolonised curriculum.

Whilst sometimes used interchangeably, there is a theoretical difference between decolonisation and decoloniality. In simple terms, the former is mostly considered a political and territorial project, and the latter is primarily engaged with ideological and epistemological ones (Mignolo 2007). In this narrative I will use both terms as means to convey contextual intersections and their implications for knowledge, curriculum and pedagogy in the context of higher education.

Decolonial practice within learning, teaching, assessment and feedback practices is not about diversifying lists of topics or tasks or internationalising the curriculum. It entails creating spaces for critical exploration and meaning making, to question dominant forms of knowledge, and to recognise voices that are at the margins, or absent altogether. These spaces need to be thought of and designed for keeping in mind our students. Locating their perspectives in designing our curriculum is a good place to start with. One would then think about 'What is their viewpoint?', 'What social, cultural, political influences have informed it?' 'What types of experiences do they bring with them?' The key is to think about how best we can integrate their differing worldviews and stories to the knowledge they learn, to build a coherent and meaningful educational experience, as shown in Figure 0.6.

Figure 0.6 Decolonisation is not a patchwork approach to curriculum; instead it is a careful consideration of all different threads of knowledges and practices, bringing them together, woven into a pattern of design that expands the imagination of those who teach and those taught to the possibilities of knowing beyond the centre.

Creating epistemological access (Morrow 2009) to get to the roots of discipline-specific knowledge is one way. Epistemological access is about uncovering histories of debates in the discipline and to understand how your curriculum has come to be what it is—by exposing yourself to debates and contestations in other part of the world, and to assess how similar or dissimilar they are from your experience—and ultimately how theorists and researchers have thought about it and theorised it. A deep-rooted probe of our subject matters is most likely to enable us and our students to question traces of coloniality within the curriculum, whilst promoting reflexivity and affirming agency.

Thinking practically as academics and academic developers, we then need to ask ourselves:

What is the site of knowledge production—that is, where has the discourse of knowledge originated from?
How is knowledge pedagogised into the curricula?

References

Behari-Leak, K. (2019). Disrupting Single Stories through Participatory Learning and Action. In L. Quinn (Ed.) *Re-imagining Curriculum: Spaces for Disruption.* Cape Town: Sun Media.

Centre for Global Higher Education (2021). Towards 'Decolonizing' Curriculum and Pedagogy (DCP) across Disciplines and Global HE Context. [webinar] Available at: https://www.youtube.com/watch?v=UwH9RByQ_tI

Mignolo, W.D. (2007). Coloniality of Power and De-colonial Thinking. *Cultural Studies*, 21, 155–167. doi:10.1080/09502380601162498

Morreira, S., Luckett, K., Kumalo, S.H. and Ramgotra, M. (2020) Confronting the Complexities of Decolonising Curricula and Pedagogy in Higher Education. *Third World Thematics: A TWQ Journal*, 1–18. doi: 10.1080/23802014.2020.1798278

Morrow, W.E. (2009). Bounds of Democracy: Epistemological Access in Higher Education. HSRC Press.

Narang, A. (2021). Expanding Notions of Pedagogy to Empower Change. [Blog] AdvanceHe, Available at: https://www.advance-he.ac.uk/news-and-views/expanding-notions-pedagogy-empower-change

Narang, A (n.d.) Decolonisation of Curriculum. [online article] EDTA. Available at: https://edta.info.yorku.ca/decolonizing-the-curriculum/

Amrita invites us to reflect on ways in which the learning we design and offer might be 'colonised' and ways to move forward towards more decolonised practices, which weave in various knowledge systems to create beautiful new patterns (as evoked by the image).

Decolonisation challenges our professional beliefs, behaviours and practices quite deeply and can be destabilising. It can help to see how others are furthering these changes. Throughout this book, you will encounter the stories of many global colleagues who are moving towards designing less white-Eurocentric learning experiences and environments in an attempt to carve a better future from our past. I hope these will inspire and encourage you in your own personal journey.

Whether real 'total' decolonisation is possible is debatable (Baume 2021), but what we can do is add decolonising efforts to the other enhancements we make towards a more inclusive and liberated learning design. Another way is to free it from standard practices which have been used unquestioned for decades, such as the hegemony of the lecture or of the assessed (5000-word) essay typical of many UK university courses. The next root value is about ways of making our learning design more user-friendly, for instance by favouring variety and choice of learning inputs and outputs.

The 'U' root: User-friendly

Accessible to all

Activate your inner dialogue. ... How would you answer?

How can you make your learning design user-friendly to your students and other stakeholders?
How can Universal Design for Learning support greater accessibility in education?

Something which is user-friendly is foremost accessible to the vast majority of its users. Accessibility is concerned with equity of access, opportunities *and outcomes.* Taking once more a broad meaning, accessibility should address all the dimensions of diversity that could become a barrier to learning: language, digital accessibility/divide, physical accessibility, neurodivergence, disability/ableism, first in family, socio-economic exclusion, immigration/visa privilege, gender and sexuality and intersectionality to name the main ones.

Although there is much talk of accessibility and support for students with additional learning needs, the reality in UK universities is that the onus tends to be on the student who has such needs to make a case, fill the forms, meet the support staff, negotiate the adjustments and so on. Although signposting to relevant centralised support and services is part of our academic role, if we design learning in a universal way, we can dramatically reduce the demand for those services because we have provided a suitably accessible course to the vast majority of our cohorts.

A very effective way of making our course design more user-friendly for our students is by adopting a Universal Design for Learning (UDL) approach. UDL is a *process* about removing barriers that could prevent some students from engaging, by making the whole course by design accessible to all, or nearly all. In this book, UDL is about universal thinking and mindset, whereby we aim to maximise learning for students of all backgrounds and learner preferences, while minimising the need for special (retrofit) accommodations and maintaining academic rigour. A UDL approach should be part of a *wider* inclusivity lens applied to learning design.

As explained on the cast.org website (CAST 2018), the three UDL principles for learning design are:

1. Principle 1: Provide multiple means of representation. Present information and content in different ways.
2. Principle 2: Provide multiple means of action and expression. Differentiate the ways that students can express what they know.
3. Principle 3: Provide multiple means of engagement. Stimulate interest and motivation for learning.

Rather than advocating designing the one ultimate learning experience that will perfectly suit everyone (which is impossible) UDL is about designing multiple, diverse *pathways* by providing students choice of and voice in inputs and outputs.

This is very different from the typical academic mindset, namely, to cater for the 'average' student (in all dimensions: ability, speed, background) and catch the rest (those who need more support or the fast fliers or anyone who is not 'average') through accommodations. By experience this approach makes it more difficult for us teachers, particularly in large cohort, because the quantity and quality of retrofits is on the rise. Rather, by starting from a 'catering for the fringe' position, we can automatically cater for those in the centre. Shelley Moore (2016) uses an excellent analogy: teaching is like bowling. Professional bowlers do not send the bowl down the middle, but they enter at an angle, to hit the hardest pins to hit (the ones on the far right and far left), to give themselves the maximum chance to strike them all at once. As teachers, if we change the aim, and adjust our teaching so it supports the students on the fringe, we will automatically also cater for the others. This is what UDL invites teachers to do: design learning with in-built choice and flexibility as this will be beneficial for *all* students.

However, realistically, even if we adopt UDL learning design principles, *some* students will still require additional adjustments, but these can be negotiated with the individual student themselves, rather than rigidly pre-set. In this case, it is also important to discuss with the rest of the cohort the rationale behind UDL and where that is still not enough, the types of measures taken to support individuals who require additional support, in order to avoid stigma for the few and resentment for the others.

I will now review some critiques to the UDL approach and offer some responses.

UDL is utopian. Yes, to a certain extent it is, like many other valid approaches that are difficult to implement.

UDL places unreasonable demands on learning designers and teachers. Yes, UDL requires more preparation, because university academics are not used to designing learning with learner variability in mind. With a UDL approach, teachers must front-load the needed preparation in order to *design in* the accommodation as a normal part of the course. This ultimately benefits everyone. For example, instead of waiting for the course to start and then finding out that you have a few dyslexic students who find text-dense documents hard to process, you design a text version broken down in chunks and a visual aid that you talk through (perhaps through a screencast shared ahead of class) to provide dual code access to the content (writing/visual and speaking) for everyone. The front-loaded effort pays off later on, when we have fewer accommodations and adjustments to make.

UDL dangerously resembles learning styles (Boysen 2021). I disagree as learning styles, *wrongly* applied to education, means you cater for the preferred style of students, hence, potentially *eliminating* variety and choice. UDL promotes designing for variations, so variety and choice are at the core, in order to cater for various learning *needs*, not simple preferences.

UDL does not have a sound enough scientific foundation. It is true that UDL is based on a simplified view of neuroscience, rather than cognitive science. UDL is interested in the neural networks and their relationship rather than simply in the cognitive mechanisms that make learning possible in the brain. I think we need both, as evidenced in many case studies in this book, because learning is much more than electronic impulses. Learning is also emotional, social and relational, hence the neurological perspective is useful to teachers.

UDL is only concerned with cognitive and physical disabilities, but there are many other 'situational, dispositional, and institutional barriers to learning that have not been well addressed in education or UDL' (Zaloudek 2014). I agree that UDL has so far not been extensively used to address socio-cultural aspects of learning, although educators like Andratesha Fitzgerald present UDL as a tool for anti-racism and 'as an effective framework to teach Black and Brown students' (Fitzgerald 2020). As inclusivity is broad and needs many perspectives, in this book UDL is one of the lenses I propose for inclusive learning design, but not the *only* one; it is *another lens* to invite teachers to ask different questions and examine different perspectives when designing learning.

In spite of the potential drawbacks mentioned above, from experience and reading about the experience of others, I believe UDL is a very useful approach to more inclusive learning design. UDL has gained much traction in the US in the past decade, and that is where Charles, who has contributed the following narrative, is based. He discusses the origin of UDL principles and practices and the key role of UDL in catering for diverse learning needs.

Stimulus: Universal Design for Learning—Designing for Extreme Users

By Charles Wachira (USA)

The Center for Applied Special Technology, CAST (2018) defines Universal Design for Learning as follows: 'Universal Design for Learning (UDL) is a framework to improve and optimize teaching and learning for all people based on scientific insights into how humans learn'. However, a common challenge is that educators and learners do not always comprehend or relate to UDL. Instructors may not appreciate its value because they do not perceive the benefits or simply do not *identify* instances of UDL around them.

Universal design is all around us. Coined by architect Ronald Mace, universal design focuses on designing products and environments that are accessible by all people without adjustments or modifications. Public works, industrial design and infrastructure lead the way in implementing universal design in everyday products. These improvements have been realised through innovation, legislation and litigation. Over the years, we have experienced universal design applications such as curb cuts on raised sidewalks, automated sliding doors in buildings and captioned videos.

A perfect example of universal design in practice is the modification of the sidewalk concept with a lowered or cut curb to allow easier access from the street. Blackwell (2016) writes: 'At last, on July 26, 1990, President George H.W. Bush signed the landmark Americans with Disabilities Act, which prohibits disability-based discrimination and mandated changes to the built environment, including curb cuts'.

The following image (Figure 0.7) represents a curb access without the application of universal design concepts. While still functional, the curb's use is restrictive to users with varied needs.

Figure 0.7 Standard design curb.

Figure 0.8 Universal design curb.

The above image (Figure 0.8) illustrates a design concept that has been extended for general users through universal design. Previously, the curb cut design was located at accessible parking spaces for easy navigation to curbs.

By extending this curb cut design beyond the accessible parking spaces, a wide range of users including parents with baby strollers, injured athletes in crutches and small children are able to easily access the sidewalk.

These improvements, made possible through universal design, may be applied to teaching and learning in an effort to attain equitable use. According to Lieberman, Lytle and Clarcq (2008), 'UDL emerged from the field of architectural design when federal legislation required universal access to buildings and other structures for individuals with disabilities'. A curb cut designated only for accessible parking spaces only addresses a compliance requirement for persons with disabilities. However, application at multiple points of a raised sidewalk entry avails the benefits to a wide range of sidewalk users. The same principle is transferable to teaching and learning through the application of the UDL framework in course design.

Imagine designing a storefront and taking into account the needs of all the users (persons with disabilities, parents with baby strollers, injured athletes on crutches and small children) who will frequent the establishments. In that vein, an instructor applying UDL would reflect on learner variability, realising that all learners are unique in how they learn and thus design a curriculum that allows for easy access and engagement. For example, a common and easily adoptable technique is the use of captioned videos in the classroom. In addition to providing content engagement options to learners with disabilities, captioned videos extend their benefits to a diverse set of users. Learners in noisy environments such as commuter trains and loud households are able to watch videos uninterrupted with the captions enabled. Captions allow for easy note taking as learners have the ability to pause and copy from the screen. In addition, captioned videos provide non-native speakers with a visual option to engage with the content.

Barriers are everywhere. Just as the raised sidewalk presents challenges to pedestrians, learning environments present various learning barriers such as access and exclusion. Through design that considers learner variability, instructors are able to identify and mitigate these barriers. By considering learner variability, the instructor acknowledges that all learners are unique in how they learn and interact with the content. Curriculum design with learner variability at the core allows for easier access and engagement.

References

Blackwell, A.G. (2016). The Curb-Cut Effect. *Stanford Social Innovation Review*, 15(1), 28–33. https://doi.org/10.48558/YVMS-CC96

CAST (2018). Universal Design for Learning Guidelines version 2.2. Available at: http://udlguidelines.cast.org

Lieberman, L.J., Lytle, R.K. and Clarcq, J.A. (2008). Getting it Right from the Start: Employing the Universal Design for Learning Approach to Your Curriculum. *Journal of Physical Education, Recreation & Dance; Reston*, 79(2), 32–39. doi: 10.1080/07303084.2008.10598132

UDL is one of the strongest themes throughout this book. Just like I said regarding inclusivity, to me designing learning in a universal way is a professional competency and behaviour, not a simple technique. In Section 3 in particular, I propose many case studies about universally designed learning solutions which I believe should become our default setting as academics.

Another important lens through which we should design learning is asking ourselves: how can my learning design support positive social impact? This is the theme of the next root-value.

The 'S' root: Socially Responsible

> **Better citizens of the world through service learning**

> **Activate your inner dialogue. … How would you answer?**
>
> What does social responsibility mean to you in the context of university teaching and learning?
> How can you help your students have social impact by the way you design learning?

This root-value is about universities having an orientation to society. It's about us and our students collaborating with and having impact on the wider world *through their learning*. Why is this an inclusivity value? Because equity, nurturing, co-creating, liberating, user-friendly—all the previous values discussed until now do not happen in a vacuum, but they are highly context-specific. University education happens in a local, global, geographical, historical, cultural, social context which shapes its *mission*.

The very raison d'être of universities is linked to their capacity to enhance their 'glocal' context: local ('town and gown' partnership) as well as global. This aligns with the ideas Patrick Blessinger and Mandla Makhanya discuss in a short piece entitled: *Towards higher education in service of humanity* (2018):

> In the final analysis, the main justification for the existence of a higher education institution is that it fulfils its mission by adequately serving the contemporary needs of its constituents. Therefore, colleges and universities must continually assess the relevance of their mission and goals and frequently evaluate their effectiveness in achieving those outcomes.

The current set up of higher education as a big business detracts from this deeper purpose. Universities are often in competition with each other for grants, research, rankings, students and funding. On the other hand, there is a push for international collaboration and wider impact of university education on the local *and* the global realities. University education ideally needs to address the immediate needs of the local context and communities as well as the global challenges of the world, well summarised in the 17 Sustainable Development Goals (SDGs) by the UN (Grau et al. 2017). This also aligns with recognising students' needs and interests: new generations seem to be ethically conscious in a way that many of us were not 20 or 30 years ago; for instance, they feel they have a moral duty towards our environment. So, by providing, at appropriate points, socially responsible learning and assessment opportunities, we can catch more than one bird with one stone: we fulfil the university's deeper purpose, we are more relevant in today's society, we allow students to experience social impact (McArthur 2021) in things they are interested in and we help make the world a better place for all.

This important role of university education has been called many things: service learning, place-based education, community impact, community-engaged learning and similar terms. It can be summed up by: 'bring the community to your class and your class to the community' (Unlu 2021, original text in Italian, my translation). Although these various terms mean slightly different things, they all come under the umbrella of HE for the common good. But what does common good refer to?

> Common goods are those that contribute to the general interest, enabling society as a whole to be reinforced and to function better, as well as individuals to live better. Therefore, common goods must benefit all.
> (Daviet 2016)

This type of civil engaged learning often results in very meaningful and mutually beneficial relationships and partnerships being established between the university and external bodies, communities, industry or charities with remarkable benefits for the students themselves. Besides, civil engagement could help universities survive at a time where they risk becoming 'redundant' (Arvanitakis and Hornsby 2016).

Social responsibility applied to the meso-level of course design means making links between the students' learning experience within the university and the wider world beyond its boundaries. It means creating opportunities for students to be involved with local and global projects and initiatives. It also means, irrespective of the field of study, infusing our courses with the 17 SGDs, which I will address in more detail in the last root-value 'Ecological'. But above all, it means understanding that through the various modules a student studies, they are *becoming*. Inclusive Learning Design which is socially responsible has an impact on our students' *becoming*.

As Robin DeRosa (2021) puts it:

> We need to shift our mindset to think of course design as a series of acts that collectively bring our college or university into being. Therefore, we need to pause in the act of course design and consider: what does my university need to be?

Social responsibility is one aspect of inclusive learning design. It needs to be seen in tandem with efforts to decolonise the curriculum and instill equity. This is highlighted by the following piece, which positions social responsibility within an integrative model with other important inclusivity aspects.

Stimulus: Community engagement and social projects

By Kaston Anderson-Carpenter (USA)

In the current socio-political climate, it is important to understand how educators can promote socially responsible learning through inclusive design. There are three major components that comprise the integration of social responsibility community engagement, global and multicultural perspectives and lifting every voice. These components are not mutually exclusive; rather, they represent an interactive, integrated approach to supporting socially responsible inclusive design.

Figure 0.9 shows the interaction between community engagement, global and multicultural perspectives and lifting every voice.

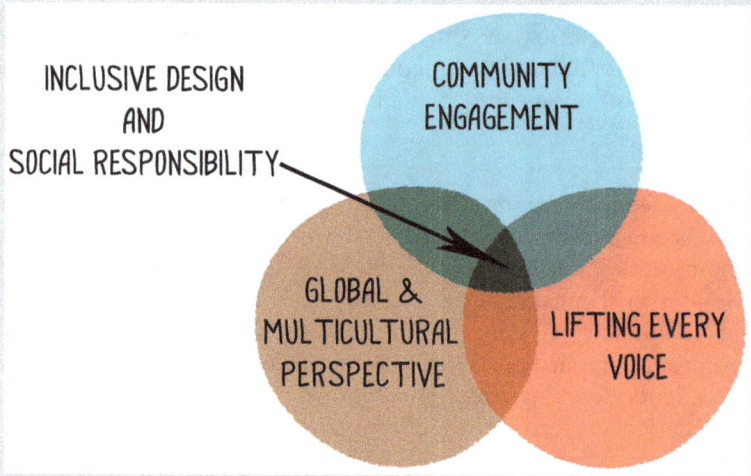

Figure 0.9 An integrative model of promoting inclusive design and social responsibility.

A key element of incorporating community engagement into inclusive design is creating conditions for students collaboratively with other groups to meet or address a common issue. In the wake of pandemic pedagogies (such as increased use of digital tools for emergency remote teaching), achieving this goal may require some nontraditional activities. However, the power and utility that technology provides can actually make community engagement much more feasible than in years or decades past.

This work can be grounded in global and multicultural perspectives. Highlighting global and multicultural perspectives requires educators to ensure that non-Western theories are brought to the forefront throughout the course. More specifically, it requires highlighting non-Western theories, models and frameworks throughout the curriculum. For instance, educators could highlight the models and theories and frameworks that guide community empowerment in Indigenous cultures from across the African continent. Some music educators might lead their classes on a course-long exploration on how music from cultures across the Asian continent have influenced the entertainment industries in Europe and the Americas. Furthermore, senior educational leaders can support educators by striving to incorporate global, multicultural perspectives across the curriculum.

When designing inclusive courses, educators can integrate research articles, books and other materials from different areas of the world. Some educators might also find it helpful to introduce their students to research from scholars with various gender identities, researchers with various disabilities, scholars from diverse subcultures, and also those who are of African, Arab/Middle Eastern, Asian and Indigenous ancestry (Akintola and Chikoko 2016, Elkashef et al. 2019). By introducing a diversity of perspectives to students and reinforcing the theories through application, educators may inspire their students to become innovative, critical thinkers.

The final component is lifting every voice. This component focuses heavily on highlighting the stories from marginalised groups. In inclusive design, it can include bringing people into the (virtual) classroom to share their lived experiences with students. Educators can also lift up the voices of marginalised groups by introducing students to research and community work that prioritises the stories of people who are not traditionally represented in educational materials. For some educators, this may mean including materials on the lived experiences from the Romani, or Roma culture (McFadden et al. 2016). Others may focus on foster parenting or people living with HIV (Rajabiun et al. 2008, Heslop 2016). Still other communities that could be highlighted in curricula include people who are homeless and those who use illicit and/or illegal substances.

It is critical for educators to bring experiences from marginalised communities to the forefront of class discussions. In many cases, however, it can be more effective to recruit and invite individuals from marginalised communities to give virtual lectures about their experiences. In this way, students can gain a much deeper sense and appreciation for what it is like to experience life through another person's perspective. For other students, inviting (virtual) guest speakers can provide them with a better understanding of how people living in certain social conditions or experiencing certain health issues must navigate the world and the barriers they face. By integrating the three areas shown in the image, educators can be proactive in programming for inclusive design and social responsibility. Such strategies can facilitate a deeper learning experience, as well as innovative solutions that improve the human condition.

Bibliography

Akintola, O. and Chikoko, G. (2016). Factors Influencing Motivation and Job Satisfaction among Supervisors of Community Health Workers in Marginalized Communities in South Africa. *Human Resources for Health*, 14. doi:10.1186/s12960-016-0151-6

ElKashef, A., Alzayani, S., Shawky, M., Al Abri, M., Littlewood, R., Qassem, T., Alsharqi, A., Hjelmström, P., Abdel Waheb, M., Abdulraheem, M. and Alzayed, A. (2019). Recommendations to Improve Opioid Use Disorder Outcomes in Countries of the Middle East. *Journal of Substance Use*, 24, 4–7. doi:10.1080/14659891.2018.1489906

Heslop, P. (2016). How I Care: Foster Fathers Recount their Experiences Caring for Children. *Adoption & Fostering*, 40, 36–48. doi: 10.1177/0308575915626378

McFadden, A., Atkin, K., Bell, K., Innes, N., Jackson, C., Jones, H., MacGillivray, S. and Siebelt, L. (2016). Community Engagement to Enhance Trust between Gypsy/Travellers, and Maternity, Early Years' and Child Dental Health Services: Protocol for a Multi-method Exploratory Study. *International Journal for Equity in Health*, 15, 183. doi: 10.1186/s12939-016-0475-9

Rajabiun, S., Rumptz, M.H., Felizzola, J., Frye, A., Relf, M., Yu, G. and Cunningham, W.E. (2008). The Impact of Acculturation on Latinos' Perceived Barriers to HIV Primary Care. *Ethnicity & Disease*, 18, 403.

As the narrative shows, social impact is a complex dimension of learning design. However, irrespective of the field of study or stage of students, there is scope on every course to foster positive community action through the curriculum content, assessment or the way the course is run, with the inclusion of marginalised voices. In the rest of the book there are many case studies linked to social responsibility, advocacy and service learning, particularly in Chapters 6 and 7.

Social responsibility links very well with the next root-value: integrative, an invitation to break the silos in which many university courses operate.

The 'I' root: Integrative

> **Connects learning with research and work; promotes interdisciplinarity**

> **Activate your inner dialogue. ... How would you answer?**
>
> What are important elements that you should 'integrate' in your learning design? How can your learning design support interdisciplinarity?

This root is about connections. An integrated learning design promotes connection between different areas of learning. It connects research and practice; it connects studies and work; it connects different disciplines; it connects different areas of study by cutting across disciplines and more.

Why is this integration important? Firstly, because many students experience their studies as a disconnected series of learning events, carefully separated by 'subject silos'. This situation makes it difficult for students to see the big picture by joining the dots of their learning experience. Students are not able to situate their studies in the bigger picture of the whole field of study, and even less can they situate their learning within the context of wider world issues. In a sense, it's as if they never get to see the whole puzzle, but only the few pieces that *they* put together. Universities and academics need to become 'knowledge integrators' (Bridgstock 2016) for better contextualised learning.

As academics, integration has to do with bringing different things together rather than solely focus on the content of our disciplines. Many teachers strive to offer both depth and breadth of knowledge and understanding to their students. This is sometimes referred to as T-shaped knowledge, where a person has both generalist knowledge and at least one specialism. Considering the time constraints we have at university, how can we maximise both types of learning? This is where integration can be very effective, especially as, after all, we are not just after knowledge or understanding: we are aiming for wisdom (Arvanitakis and Hornsby 2016). Although an integrative learning design refers to many threads being pulled together and although it can be realised in a variety of ways, one key way of realising it is through interdisciplinarity. Hence, for the rest of this root-value discussion I will focus on interdisciplinary approaches.

Of course, it is important for students to develop expertise in an area which they will probably work in, so subjects and disciplines (which are wider than subjects and more akin to fields of study) have their advantages: they provide a space to develop depth of understanding and test the boundaries of various areas of study. Disciplinary knowledge is fundamental to interdisciplinary learning.

Traditionally, students study subjects at school and then choose a field of study at university. However, there is a growing realisation in many universities that rigid subject and discipline silos are becoming more and more irrelevant. Especially if that's all the student experiences from the start to the finish of their university studies. Many academics would like to offer students a broader and richer learning experience which encompasses more than one discipline. This is also in recognition of the fact that we live 'in the age of supercomplexity' (Barnett 2000): our students face a future which is very different from our past or our present. The skills, abilities and attributes they need to face their future are not the remit of only one discipline.

Interdisciplinary means that at least two different disciplines are involved such as art and maths. An integrated learning design has at its heart interdisciplinary approaches that 'lead to student engagement, experiential learning with motivated students becoming self-aware, forming positive relationship and who recognize their own responsibilities in the community' (MacMath et al. 2009).

Interdisciplinarity is looking for ways to combine different ways of thinking to the learning experience, because people from our same discipline tend to have a similar *mindset* to ours. This is important because it is in the 'gaps' between the disciplines that real innovation occurs: 'Disciplinary communities guard their boundaries in competition with other disciplines, yet it is in the gaps beyond disciplinary boundaries—the interdisciplinary areas—that major new insights and research breakthroughs occur' (RSE 2017).

The stimulus piece for this root-value is from the London Interdisciplinary School—a whole university where students only learn in an interdisciplinary way—and it highlights the relationship and commonalities between interdisciplinarity and inclusivity.

Stimulus: Interdisciplinarity and inclusivity: What are the connections?

By Ashley Jay Brockwell and Carl Gombrich (UK)

Interdisciplinary learning, in common with inclusive learning design, is grounded in negotiating diverse world views and perspectives. An interdisciplinary approach is usually applied to address complex questions or broad issues, or solve practical problems that are beyond the scope of a single discipline. Interdisciplinarity can also be associated with theoretical goals such as achieving 'unity of knowledge ... on a limited or grand scale' (Klein 1990:11).

In embedding interdisciplinary thinking in educational programmes, teachers and learners face challenging and often uncomfortable conversations. As Welch (2012:100) explains:

> By situating itself as a means for synthesizing insights from diverse perspectives into a holistic understanding of complex phenomena, interdisciplinarity engages disciplinary thought at the core of its most basic assumptions.

These assumptions, whether they concern ontology (the nature of 'reality'), epistemology (the means by which 'reality' is known), axiology (beliefs about what is valuable or worthwhile) or methodology (specific ways of approaching a topic), are usually implicit rather than explicit in disciplinary teaching. As such, much of the thinking around interdisciplinarity focuses on foregrounding and confronting the unacknowledged, and often problematic, foundations of established disciplines.

Reflexivity is crucial in interdisciplinarity, as a means of seeing beyond the biases and value judgements that are inherent in disciplinary training. In common with the discourse of inclusivity, interdisciplinarity also involves flagging and navigating power differentials. These may arise between disciplines or, on a larger scale, between clusters of disciplines—for example, when science, technology, engineering and mathematics are perceived as more 'valid' or 'important' than the social sciences, arts and humanities.

In relation to power, another key question is how interdisciplinary education is engaging, or might engage, with post-imperial and decolonisation movements in education—and in parallel, how decolonial scholars approach the question of interdisciplinarity. Willinsky (2000) illustrates how the existence of academic disciplines is both an artefact of, and a tool for perpetuating, the imperial mentality of 'dividing the world' along race, gender and culture lines (which was initially used to justify colonisation). If interdisciplinary researchers and educators limit their focus to academic disciplines as conventionally understood, the same gaps and injustices persist (Figure 0.10).

McGregor (2004) and colleagues address this issue by explicitly calling attention to ways of knowing that are found 'across, between, beyond and outside' disciplines. These include, for example, place-bound and community-based stories, songs and spiritualities within Indigenous communities. In other contexts, interdisciplinary and transdisciplinary programmes may integrate non-academic knowledge from industry, non-profits or the arts.

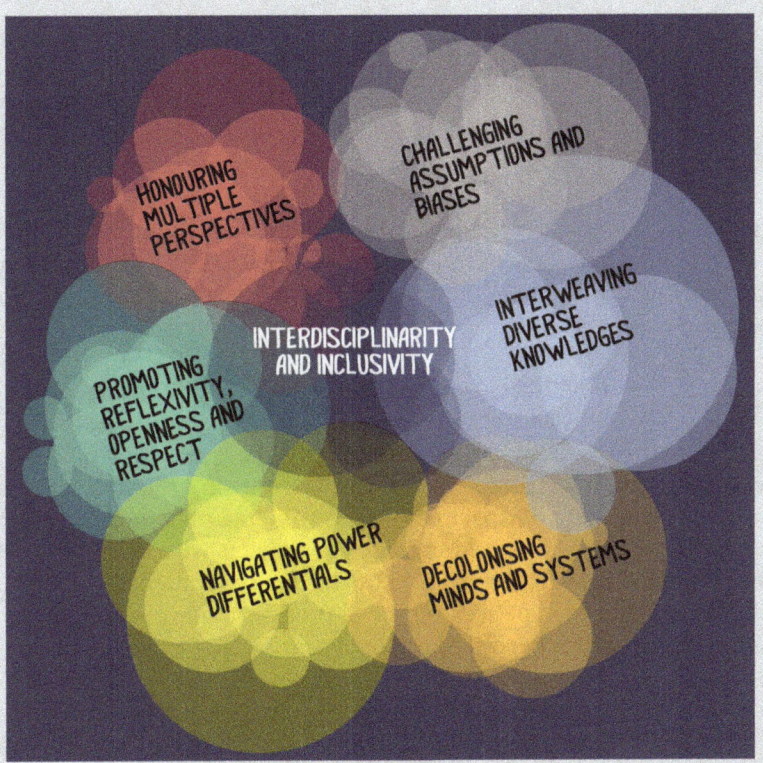

Figure 0.10 Common threads between interdisciplinarity and inclusivity. Image credit: Maria Madero.

At the London Interdisciplinary School, the curriculum for our flagship Bachelor of Arts and Sciences (BASc) degree in Interdisciplinary Problems and Methods is designed by a team that exemplifies considerable diversity in relation to age, gender, ethnicity, political leanings, neurological differences and life experiences, as well as disciplinary backgrounds. This is navigated within the context of widening participation in higher education, with targeted outreach to under-represented groups. We are also keen to work with companies and organisations outside higher education. As such, we would welcome an exchange of ideas with other researchers and educators working at the interfaces of inclusivity and interdisciplinarity.

Bibliography

Klein, J.T. (1990). *Interdisciplinarity: History, Theory and Practice*. Detroit: Wayne State University Press.

McGregor, S.L.T. (2004). The Nature of Transdisciplinary Research and Practice. Working paper. Mount St Vincent University, Halifax, Nova Scotia. Available at: https://www.kon.org/hswp/archive/transdiscipl.html

Welch, J. (2012). Interdisciplinarity and the Question of Being. *Issues in Integrative Studies*, 30, 99–127.

Willinsky, J. (2000). *Learning to Divide the World: Education at Empire's End*. Minneapolis, MN: University of Minnesota Press.

The London Interdisciplinary School is the embodiment of integrated higher education. However, as most of us academics work and operate within disciplinary departments, it can be difficult to envisage how to create bridges that connect our discipline to others, unless there is an intentional support for interdisciplinary learning at institution level.

The message of this book is: interdisciplinarity can be at the macro, meso and micro level of learning design. It does not need to entail a whole overhaul of existing practices, but it could be a matter of identifying where, during the course of a module, you could infuse your discipline with the approaches of another one, in order to enrich the learning experience and provide new perspectives to the students. The next level would be to create some collaboration and shared modules or projects with another discipline. And even further this could lead to the creation of clusters (of students' cohorts) that could learn together for an extended period of time during the academic year. Of course, these learning design interventions need to be carefully considered and student consultation is important.

Interdisciplinarity is an evolving field and a hot topic due to some perceived ongoing issues, for instance around assessment. Academics are experimenting and discussing how integration is attained when assessments are designed, employed, and realised in light of the fact that, ultimately, interdisciplinarity is about embracing (integrating) both discipline knowledge and interdisciplinary knowledge in a coherent way.

All of the previous roots converge into the next one because they all support a values-based learning design.

The 'V' root: Values-based

Helps interrogate your 'why': your purpose and drivers

> **Activate your inner dialogue. … How would you answer?**
>
> Why is it important that you articulate your learning design values?
> How can you do so?

There are some interesting learning design models created by UK universities. JISC (n.d.) has created a family tree to represent some of the best-known ones in the UK, such as Carpe Diem by Gilly Salmon and ABC by UCL, but not many of them focus or highlight values-based education *as part of learning design*. In contrast, all the roots being discussed in this section and indeed the entire book are an invitation to take inclusivity and all its facets as a *value to drive learning design*. Although the expression 'values-based education' is commonly understood in academia as 'social responsibility' (discussed earlier on in this section), I take this root-value as a 'meta' one, to include all the other roots of the symbolical tree and as an opportunity to further highlight how values are at the root of inclusive learning design.

Everyone has values (personal drivers), whether they are overt and have been thought through and articulated or hidden and overlooked. Why is it important to articulate our attitudes and values? Because we academics as well as our students bring to the learning environment a complex set of overlapping values which we do not necessarily *share*. By articulating our values, we situate ourselves in the ethical landscape of personal and professional values; we check our common ground; we can critically examine ourselves and make changes where needed; we have a starting point that we can return to at a later point in time to reassess any changes or progress and we can reflect on whether we have been able to live up to our values in our learning design and deployment (Garman 2005), because we should be coherent by *living* the values we espouse.

What values should we promote? Most higher education institutions have a mission statement which encapsulates what the institution is about and what it cares about. Some institutions do a good job of advertising their mission and values by making them visible on-campus and by using them to drive curriculum decisions. Some institutions are not that proactive and many of their academics might not even be aware of the core 'official' values they are supposed to promote through their work. However, what everyone absorbs is what is commonly called the 'hidden curriculum': all the assumed rules, the *real* values and attitudes that are the daily currency of the institution, though unspoken. The hidden curriculum is often spoken of in a negative way because it is seen as *reproducing* unfair, discriminatory or classist norms (Speirs 2021). However, the hidden curriculum can also be seen in a positive way: it can be used to change the hidden narrative. As the hidden curriculum teaches things to students that are beyond the course content (syllabus), it can be leveraged by teachers to teach positive characteristics such as all the values discussed in this section and additional ones such as dignity, appreciation and humility.

What follows is a provocative narrative about the critical importance of articulating one's values and sharing these with students *before* embarking on learning design.

Stimulus: Check your why: Creating inclusive principles for learning design, *before* designing a course

By Sarah Mursal (UK)

Before we walk into a classroom, we have this notion of *our* world and what we need to teach on a subject or contextualise as per our experiences, references and suggested reading. But, how about we check in with our values and articulate our own principles to shape the delivery of content and to design for an evolving curriculum.

In my experience teaching students at University (level 4–6) in Film Design, I need to check my values and check what informs my rationale. And I need to be more aware of my own world vision, as shown in Figure 0.11. My values and each student's values will be different based on our experiences and abilities. So how do we create an inclusive learning environment? How can our teaching synergise with all learners from diverse backgrounds and different incoming knowledge?

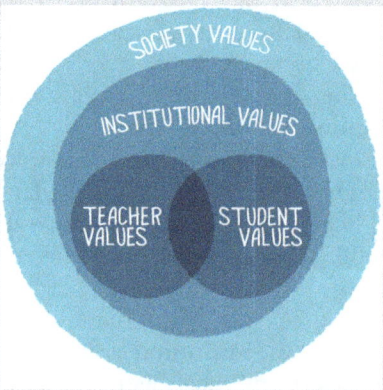

Figure 0.11 The teacher and student values sit within the institutional and society values.

Good principles are the foundation for curriculum design. As Kleiman (2009) suggests, good curriculum design is appreciated by students and it is the foundation for good learning experiences. I have adopted the following three 'universal' principles as my own curriculum design values: Balance, Curiosity and Decolonising.

Balance in this context relates to an understanding between teacher and student that learning is shared, with students taking responsibility for their own learning. In production design for film, balance represents the hands-on experience of students, with the teacher advising as a 'Guide on the side' (McWilliams 2009). Robinson (2006) suggests that this is an 'act of faith': trusting that students will learn through 'doing', 'making' and 'building', will complete tasks and be able to reflect on their own work and learning.

Curiosity encourages students to test and play, and I believe the strongest learning comes from exploring, for instance by challenging students through activities or in unusual locations. Similarly, Sharples (2019) discusses 'learning by making' and 'learning through storytelling'. These approaches are useful as I often use stories to help students learn and keep them curious.

Decolonising as a principle: raising consciousness and addressing issues that may be non-inclusive, or being anti-racist in a global sense. This principle helps review contextual resources for teaching (Bhambra et al. 2018). Decolonising brings up questions starting from the global implications of taking students to visit museums and choosing to focus on specific artefacts (a big picture meaning), to our own preconceptions of assumed knowledge when addressing classes (a close up meaning). Decolonising asks us to consciously move away from labels to define groups in society, challenging us to interact with individuals and their experiences. Within my discipline, this ideology is central to creating an inclusive curriculum and to empowering students who have the ability to change people's attitudes through film production, in an intuitive and creative manner. In practice, I am on the road to decolonise my courses, for example by providing non-Western references in class, such as discussing 'beauty' as a cultural construct and focusing on hidden attitudes.

Balance, curiosity and decolonising are not only broad principles but also the main values which guide my learning design.

To me it is very important that: I acknowledge and articulate my own values every time I begin a new learning design; I share my values with my students so they understand what my drivers are; I encourage them to think about their own evolving values; we reflect and review both my and their values and how they evolve in time. In other words, we make values the subject of open discussion.

Blessinger et al. (2019) discuss the notion of the 'hidden curriculum' and ethical use of knowledge and how to use it in the service of humanity. This was a light bulb realisation for me as we have a responsibility to be aware of our own hidden agendas. Articulating our principles and values before we design our curriculum is key to achieve inclusivity.

Classroom activity idea

You and your students brainstorm your values—mind maps or cut-out images from magazines or digitally. For you this sums up your educational philosophy.

Do this at the start of the course and then review them at the end of the course. Have they changed? Why do you think?

Bibliography

Bhambra, G.K., Dalia, G. and Nişancıoğlu, K. (Eds.) (2018). *Decolonising the university*. Pluto Press

Blessinger, P., Sengupta, E. and Makhanya, M. (2019). Creating Inclusive Curricula in Higher Education. [online] University World News. Available at: https://www.universityworldnews.com/post.php?story=20190422070841869

> Kleiman, P. (2009). *Design for Learning: A Guide to the Principles of Good Curriculum Design*. [ebook] PALATINE (HEA). Available at: http://cielassociates.co.uk/wp-content/uploads/2014/08/KLEIMAN2009DesignforLearning.pdf
> McWilliam, E. (2009). Teaching for Creativity: From Sage to Guide to Meddler. *Asia Pacific Journal of Education*. doi: 10.1080/02188790903092787
> Robinson, A. (2006). Using Formative Assessment to Improve Student Learning through Critical Reflection. In C. Bryan and K. Clegg (Eds.) *Innovative Assessment in Higher Education*. Routledge.
> Sharples, M. (2019). *Practical pedagogy*. London and NY: Routledge.

This narrative reminds us that we all have intersecting values that drive our pedagogical actions.

However, the hot question is: should we 'teach' values? There is no clear agreement about whether we *can* even 'teach' values, or whether we think you 'learn' values. However, no education is values-free, it's just about articulating one's values or not. Directly or indirectly, as teachers we *project* our values onto our students. If we are open about our values, as the preceding narrative suggests, students can appraise them for themselves. But also, we can be intentional in the way we design learning so that our students develop values, for instance providing them with opportunities to advocate for a cause as some case studies in the following sections show.

One very important value that we should all promote is having an ecological ethos in all we do in education. This is the theme of the last root-value.

The 'E' root: Ecological

> **Sustainable; addresses Sustainable Development Goals; optimises the use of resources**

> **Activate your inner dialogue. ... How would you answer?**
>
> Irrespective of your field, how can your learning design have social purpose? How can it address and support ecological practices such as sustainability?

This root-value is about *ecological sustainability*, creating a vision of ecologically responsible education. This is another key role of higher education: to promote learning that will have positive impact on others as well as *on the planet*. This is no trivial matter as David Orr (1992) writes: 'All things considered, it is possible that we are becoming more ignorant of the things we must know to live well and sustainably on the Earth'. Over 30 years since those words were penned, they are more relevant than ever.

Ecological is understood here as the relationship between living organisms and their environment. As it has been the case with other key terms in this book, I am taking 'ecological' to have a broad meaning, one which embraces the efforts to positively impact on all the different ecosystems we are part of. It is a value which should impact behaviours and practices.

Barnett (2018) has written an important book about 'The ecological university', which he calls a 'feasible utopia': it is done with intent, it is an ongoing process and one that will never be finished. Barnett points to seven 'zones' of the ecological university: 'knowledge, learning, culture, persons, society, economy and the natural world' and says that the emphasis on the financial aspect (economy) has detracted from full involvement with the other zones.

He advocates universities to become institutions which have 'an *active* concern for the whole Earth; even the universe (The clue is in the name 'university' with its connotations of universality and universe)' (Barnett 2018).

An ecological university is one that is aware of its place and role in the attainment of the UN 17 sustainable development goals (SDGs), which are:

(1) No Poverty, (2) Zero Hunger, (3) Good Health and Well-being, (4) Quality Education, (5) Gender Equality, (6) Clean Water and Sanitation, (7) Affordable and Clean Energy, (8) Decent Work and Economic Growth, (9) Industry, Innovation and Infrastructure, (10) Reduced Inequality, (11) Sustainable Cities and Communities, (12) Responsible Consumption and Production, (13) Climate Action, (14) Life Below Water, (15) Life On Land, (16) Peace, Justice and Strong Institutions, (17) Partnerships for the Goals.

Each SDG is further broken down into more detailed targets. From the list it is clear that these are not goals simply linked to protecting nature, but they embrace many types of *social* ecologies. Apart from being one of the goals in its own right, education (no. 4) plays a key role if the other SDGs are to be achieved. Target 4.7 is of particular relevance for inclusive higher education:

> By 2030, ensure that all learners acquire the knowledge and skills needed to promote sustainable development, including, among others, through education for sustainable development and sustainable lifestyles, human rights, gender equality, promotion of a culture of peace and non-violence, global citizenship and appreciation of cultural diversity and of culture's contribution to sustainable development.

This book directly supports this target, but it also touches on many others SDGs such as 5, 10, 16, 17.

SDGs realisation requires a set of skills and abilities which have been called 'inner development goals' (there is an international organisation that bears that name) which links to the 'nurturing' root-value discussed earlier.

It is to be expected that a global framework such as this which needs to be embedded and enacted at local level is necessarily contested, however SDGs still provide a good foundation to explore issues of ecological sustainability.

Sustainability can be considered one of the biggest areas of ecological education, yet most students go through their university studies without ever focussing on their potential role in making things better for the whole planet—they never develop ecological literacy. This is literally not sustainable anymore. Students are interested in ecological learning; 'green' jobs and ecological literacy are prized professional and personal abilities for the world of work, so we should all feel the responsibility to integrate inclusive, ecological learning in *all* learning experiences we design.

In the following short text, Paul Kleiman helps us reflect on the multiple meanings of sustainability.

Stimulus: Sustainability—a wicked problem

By Paul Kleiman (UK)

A few years ago, I researched and wrote a book chapter (Kleiman 2010) on how the notion of sustainability manifests itself, or might manifest itself, in the performing arts curriculum. In answer to an email question I sent around, an eminent music colleague provided some fascinating examples of how sustainability might operate in the subject area. Although all the examples provided interesting and potentially valuable avenues to explore further, perhaps the most memorable and relevant of his comments was the final sentence of his email: 'I'm afraid I don't understand the term sustainability at all. My apologies.'

More recently, a discussion on the #creativeHE list around sustainability and creativity and based around the UN's 17 Sustainable Development Goals demonstrated how much of a 'wicked problem' the pursuit of sustainability poses.

The apparent confusion is, perhaps, unsurprising. It is very noticeable—and the more one looks, the more noticeable it becomes—how the words 'sustainable', 'sustainable development' and 'sustainability' have become part of the strategic, operational and everyday discourses and practices of higher education. One of the consequences of their ubiquity, however, has been a multiplicity of definitions, understandings and misunderstandings of what the terms actually mean, and the influences and impact of these various and varied currents and streams of discourse around the notion of sustainability manifest themselves in a plethora of ways in higher education.

What is unarguable is that education is critical in shaping the individual and collective knowledge, skills, values and attitudes that will enable people to move along pathways towards sustainable development. Education is a catalyst for development itself. Education a key determinant of social and economic transformation and an essential precursor to peace, tolerance and sustainability. It equips learners of all ages with the knowledge, skills, values and attitudes needed to be responsible global citizens, such as respect for human rights, gender equality and environmental sustainability.

When it comes to designing a sustainable or ecological curriculum, there are some key design principles that are relevant whatever the discipline. Like most design principles, the principles underpinning a sustainable curriculum are simple and straightforward—at least to state, if not to implement. Good sustainable curriculum design requires:

- Optimal use of resources (time, people, content)
- Minimisation of waste (time, energy, materials)
- Sensitivity to the local environment (educational, economic, social, political) at a micro-, meso- and macro level
- The ability to adapt quickly and easily to a rapidly changing environment

Figure 0.12 Dimensions of the sustainable curriculum.

But behind those principles, the important factor influencing the ability to design a truly sustainable curriculum in accordance with those principles is the actual, lived values of the higher education institution itself—which may differ significantly from what appears in the public-facing, brand-conscious mission statement and espoused values.

Unless there is genuine commitment at the highest institutional level to ensuring that the notion of sustainability flows indelibly through all the activities and outputs of the institution and is embedded in all its systems and processes—including its many and varied curricula—then it is likely that sustainability-focused initiatives will remain piecemeal and short-lived.

Education for sustainability requires designing that education in a way that is sustainable.

Bibliography

Kleiman, P. (2008). *Design for Learning*. Lancaster: Palatine. Available at: https://bit.ly/3iw4EVG

Kleiman, P. (2010). Staging Sustainability: Making Sense of Sustainability in HE Dance, Drama and Music. In P. Jones, D. Selby and S. Sterling (Eds.) *Sustainability Education: Perspectives and Practice across Higher Education* (pp. 155–170). London: Earthscan.

This provocative narrative shows that as academics and institutions, we urgently need to acquire a sustainable, ecological mindset in everything we do in education: in the course content whether directly relevant or creating new links ourselves; in the way we teach the discipline; in the physical and digital spaces and resources we use; in the way we help students become ecological citizens and champions.

Sustainability has deeply intertwined physical *and social* dimensions which converge in inclusive practices. To design and enact ecologically sustainable learning we will need to transcend discipline boundaries (integrate); develop social responsibility and co-create the path with students. Indeed, all the previous values-roots converge into this last one because this whole inclusive learning design is an ecology in itself, and all those elements flow into each other and into the bigger picture.

For instance, in class, you could list the 17 SDGs on a wall and ask students to comment on how they can contribute to each one. Together, you can find obvious and nuanced connections with each SDG. You and your students could also come up with a personal SDGs action plan to improve your personal and professional life in each of the 17 goals. This matters, because if we do not build sustainability and its many facets in our professional teaching practice, 'we run the risk of sending our students out into the world completely unprepared for their future' (Meredith 2022).

Having reviewed the nine root-values that form the I.N.C.L.U.S.I.V.E. acronym, I now return to 'C for co-created' which is key to make inclusive learning design a reality.

Co-creation

As mentioned previously in the 'C for co-creation' root discussion, co-creation refers to pedagogical **partnerships**, in particular with students. It is about creating a strong learning allegiance with our students; a collaborative, reciprocal process whereby various aspects of teaching, learning and research are developed *with* students. In a nutshell co-creation is about living the mantra 'nothing about us without us' applied to students' learning.

> **Activate your inner dialogue. ... How would you answer?**
>
> How can co-creation support a more inclusive learning design?
> Which types of student partnership activities are available to you?
> What barriers make it difficult to engage in co-creation? How can you overcome them?

Co-creation is one of the QAA expectations:

> *Higher education providers take deliberate steps to engage all students, individually and collectively, as partners in the assurance and enhancement of their educational experience.*
>
> (QAA 2012)

Why is pedagogical partnership a valuable inclusive practice? Cook-Sather et al. (2019) point to three ways in which partnerships with students enhance inclusivity:

> The first is through positioning students to bring their identities and lived experiences to bear on developing inclusive classrooms. The second way in which student consultants act as agents to increase inclusivity is by drawing on their experiences to recommend pedagogical approaches that are responsive to a greater diversity of students. The third way in which student consultants can increase inclusivity is by making faculty aware of—and reinforcing—pedagogical practices they already use but may not recognize as fostering inclusivity.
>
> (Cook-Sather et al. 2019)

Despite this, the reality for most academics is that learning design is a solo act. What are the main challenges to learning co-creation? Firstly, it is a question of mindset. Most academics operate within institutions that see the teachers as the 'cooks behind the scenes' dishing out polished courses to the students who are passive recipients/consumers of what's been prepared *for them*. The point of this chapter is promoting the idea that doing that process *with them* is a better way. Co-creation repositions teachers as co-learners. Secondly, unless there is an institutional drive and processes in place to encourage co-creation, there are few opportunities in terms of time, space and resources to engage in co-creation. This means that it is often perceived as additional workload by academics. Finally, in order for co-creation to be an inclusive process, it needs to include a variety of students, internal and external colleagues as well as industry partners, but it is very challenging to source and bring together this cluster of people (Bovill et al. 2016).

One of the best ways we can design more inclusive learning is by setting up a *learning design workshop* a few months before our course is due to start, where we either configure some important aspect of the course together, such as assessment (students as leaders), or at least review our draft planning for the course (students as consultants). Who should join such learning design co-creation effort? Ideally at least three types of stakeholders: students, colleagues and industry partners.

> Students: alumni, current students, potential students. These are the most important stakeholders and the ones necessary for real co-creation to happen. Students are particularly well placed to make suggestions regarding the quality and quantity of assessment, which is an area that often creates much stress to both students and teachers.
> Colleagues: internal, external, with a variety of seniority levels, from or outside our discipline or field of study. Besides academics, we could invite para-academics to join us: colleagues from the library, student services, technical tutors, and learning technologists, just to mention a few.
> Industry partners. There is a delicate balance between inviting industry experts to co-design learning and allowing them to dictate what the curriculum should be for their business needs.

A useful model for course design co-creation is to call the initiative a *hackathon*, because this implies a group of people getting together to find a solution to a problem. This is particularly beneficial for students, as Palmer (2022) notes: 'Not only does the hackathon engage students in university planning and processes, giving them a genuine opportunity to feed into solutions, but also gives senior management a direct line to students willing to share positive solutions'.

Should *all* aspects of a course being designed be open to co-creation? That depends on your partnership readiness, the level of student choice and voice already built into your course(s) and many other contextual factors. It might be better to start small; for instance you could choose to co-create only the assessment regime of a course by inviting just *one or two* students—they are the most important stakeholder. You can then gradually expand your co-creation efforts.

However, we should be aware of the many demands on students' time, so co-creation initiatives should involve students' remuneration. If there is no budget for student involvement, there is enough evidence to show that students in particular benefit in many different ways by being involved in learning design (Cook-Sather et al. 2019); so, if we only ask for a small amount of time, perhaps only a few hours, students will be willing to join us in co-creation.

It is also important to design flexible partnerships so students can 'leave' at any point and give as much as they want to it. If not, we incur the risk of developing the 'tyranny of participation' whereby 'students are expected to be both strategic, instrumental consumers *and* active citizens of their university' and this can be difficult to manage (Barbosa Mendes and Hammett 2020).

The following three case studies explore very different aspects of pedagogical partnerships: students as co-creators; student partnerships in research; and culturally respectful partnerships.

In the first case study, from the UK, Kiu Sum (a student) writes about her first-hand experience of participating in a student partnership programme. Notice the variety of co-creation initiatives she has shared in and what benefits she has clearly reaped.

Including the 'Students' as Co-Creators

By Kiu Sum (UK)

'Partnership in higher education' is no simple topic. If you asked me a few years ago as a new prospective student starting university, I would have perhaps described it as 'contributing equally in a team to experience positiveness and the beneficial outcomes in the project'. However, the journey I have experienced goes beyond just 'contributing equally to a team'. It is the whole holistic self that one experiences journeying through university that is impacted by becoming a student-partner. These ten words are how I can (somewhat) sum up my lived experience of partnerships:

Empowerment
    Inclusivity
        Diversity
            Opportunity
                Student-voice
                    Authenticity
                        Ownership
                            Trust
                                Transformation
                                    Awareness

I was fortunate to be involved in the 'Student as Co-Creators' at the University of Westminster. This programme is a core part of the institution, based in the Centre of Education and Teaching Innovation and bridging across the university, providing opportunities and resources for students and staff to work together on research projects, enhancing learning and teaching. The benefits reaped from this partnership work are multiple. The scheme allows opportunities for prominent topics within education to be addressed through the three distinctive strands: learning and teaching research collaborations (to enhance learning and teaching environment), disciplinary research collaborations (research within a specific discipline or across disciplines), and curriculum design collaborations (develop an aspect of the course of modules).

Concepts of student partnerships have stimulated many theoretical contributions as well as institutional transformation worldwide, consolidating partnership in a wider societal meaning rather than being confined to learning and teaching only (Bovill and Woolmer 2019). On the other hand, there has been a need to continuously overcome challenges experienced while embracing the values developed within partnerships across today's neo-liberal universities (Gravett et al. 2020). Higher education should redefine what education is at all levels, not merely following the institutional norms, but for students to take ownership of what education is. Perhaps it is a difficult concept for new students initially. But it is a concept that should be embedded into the curriculum and the institutions' mission and values. This ensures that staff and students feel valued and inclusive, building a community, breaking down the barriers whilst supporting their health and well-being towards a healthy and energised community to face the ever-evolving societal challenges (Bovill 2017). Partnership requires commitment: taking the time to really understand what it means personally to each of us and how we reform the way we perceive power dynamics in our educational system.

I was very fortunate to participate in several year-long partnership projects at university. One example was a project to evaluate the effectiveness of mobile technology during class in a final year life sciences cohort in a module where several degree courses shared a module. In collaboration with the module leaders, this project was conducted before technology became a norm to facilitate engagement in pedagogical practices. Another project that I worked on was examining the results of the National Student Survey between two faculties, comparing the differences and similarities between life sciences and social sciences. As a result of this interdisciplinary project, members of the Students as Co-Creators team also consisted of academic partners from the represented disciplines. A recent partnership project that I participated in examined the link and engagement between academia and industry for student opportunities during their studies. This project was more student driven; thus, the team consisted of student representatives from each level of study to provide insight into how best to engage students during the pursuit of their university degrees.

Involvement in partnership practice has been an eye opener of how I can contribute as a student. But I'm also taking a step back and observing how the 'Westminster Co-Creators Principles' (Figure 0.13) can apply to me, adding value to the institution as a learner and beyond my degree.

My time in higher education has thus far been very fruitful. And every partnership project I have participated in has had that 'feeling fresh' experience where the

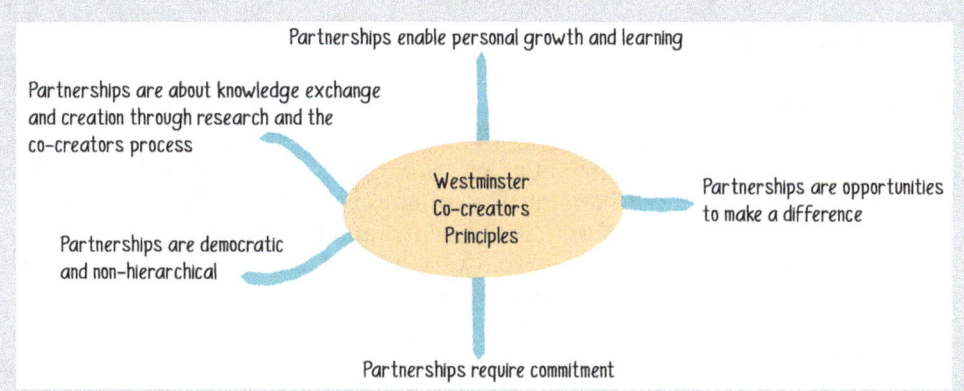

Figure 0.13 Westminster Co-Creators Principles. (available at: http://cti.westminster.ac.uk/student-partnership-2/)

different groups of peers I worked with bring that new energy vibe, all eager to learn—whether students with students or staff with students. It is a transparent and open space where we all have this one collective mind, channelling our aspirations through a single project from different disciplinary lenses or by seeing the same topic from the perspective of different cohorts within the same discipline (Sum et al. 2021). It is about breaking down barriers through questioning our identity (Sum 2021) and our critical approach. To me, partnership empowers me, giving me the voice to build trust and ownership in the learning ecosystem and for me to share that space with other like-minded peers for more inclusivity and diversity to be authentic in raising awareness and transforming the higher education space. It is recognising that learning and teaching is a collaborative process involving everyone to achieve our aspirations.

So, what does partnership mean to you? How can you embed it in your practice?

Bibliography

Bovill, C. (2017). 'Breaking down staff-student barriers: moving towards pedagogic flexibility', in Kinchin, I. M. and Winstone, N. (eds.) Pedagogic frailty and resilience in the university. Rotterdam: Brill Sense, pp.151–161.

Bovill, C. and Woolmer, C. (2019). How Conceptualisations of Curriculum in Higher Education Influence Student-staff Co-creation in and of the Curriculum. *Higher Education*, 78(3), 407–422.

Gravett, K., Kinchin, I.M. and Winstone, N.E. (2020). 'More than Customers': Conceptions of Students as Partners Held by Students, Staff, and Institutional Leaders. *Studies in Higher Education*, 45(12), 2574–2587.

Sum, K. (2021). Navigating My Ethnic Minority Identity in Higher Education: A Student Reflection. *The Journal of Educational Innovation, Partnership and Change*, 7(1), 2055–4990.

Sum, K., Dimitropoulos, L. and Kurik, G. (2021). Enhancing Student Learning and Teaching Experience through a Cross-level Collaboration: A Reflection. *Student Engagement in Higher Education Journal*, 3(2), 4–9.

Inclusivity note

Potential barriers:

1. Students with learning disabilities or with English as additional language might think they do not have much to offer as partners. It might be difficult for them to speak up in a forum with teachers and others.
2. Mindset: students and teachers from very hierarchical cultural backgrounds might find it odd or even inappropriate for teachers to seek partnerships with students.
3. Budget and time issues.

Potential solutions:

1. Create a space as safe as possible where you set out clear expectations and invite the students to have their say in more than one mode: during the live meetings or asynchronously via other channels (emails or virtual walls such as Padlet).
2. To get buy-in from students (and to enhance our own motivation), find a colleague and a student either internally or from another institution and invite them to speak (remotely if more convenient) about the partnership they have been involved with. Ask them to discuss the pros and cons of the partnership projects so everyone can have realistic expectations.
3. For budget and time issues, start small, by inviting just one or two students to join you on one or two occasions to co-create just one aspect of the course (such as assessment).

This case study straight from the voice of a student clearly shows the many benefits of various types of student partnerships, in terms of personal and professional development for the students involved. Indeed, it is hard to tell who benefits more, whether it's the students or the institution itself: partnerships with students are win-win initiatives, if done well.

Whether there is a formal students-as-partners programme in place at your university or not, you can still take practical steps to promote and undertake some co-creation activities with students, for instance in research. The next case study, from Canada, is about 'students as research partners' written by Alice Kim in collaboration with her student Cassandra Stevenson. Notice the four phases of partnership that they discuss.

Students as research partners

By Cassandra Stevenson and Alice Kim (Canada)

What do we mean by 'students as research partners'?

The concept of 'students as partners' views students as co-creators of knowledge in partnership with instructors (Cook-Sather et al. 2018). In our conceptualisation of 'students as research partners', here too students are viewed as co-creators of knowledge, contributing meaningfully to the research process. Importantly, this perspective holds that a student does not only learn by being actively engaged and mentored throughout various phases of research, but also adds value to the research itself through collaboration. In this way, this type of partnership upholds two core principles of inclusive learning: co-creation and collaboration.

This chapter is based on our personal experiences in student-instructor partnerships, both as a student and an instructor.

Benefits of having 'students as research partners'

Having students as research partners can engender positive outcomes for both parties, including the development of new skills and perspectives, and expanded networks. Additionally, when instruction or mentorship is paired with the act of conducting research, what is implicit often becomes explicit and we, as researchers, are likely to be more intentional in both our decisions and actions throughout the research process. In this way, the research itself is strengthened as a result of integrating varied perspectives and enhancing intentionality throughout each phase of the research project.

Trajectory of student-instructor research partnerships

Figure 0.14 represents a generalised trajectory of student-instructor research partnerships, highlighting their continuous nature and potential to carry through multiple research projects. Although all partnerships are unique and may deviate from the figure, it reflects four important phases that are generally part of the research process.

The first phase is to activate the partnership, either for the first time or for a new project with an existing partner. For new partnerships, an open invitation from an instructor about research opportunities at the start or end of class, for example, would help signal to students that the instructor is open to working with them and would encourage students to reach out. In our case, Alice mentioned in lecture that she was open to collaborations, so Cassandra approached her.

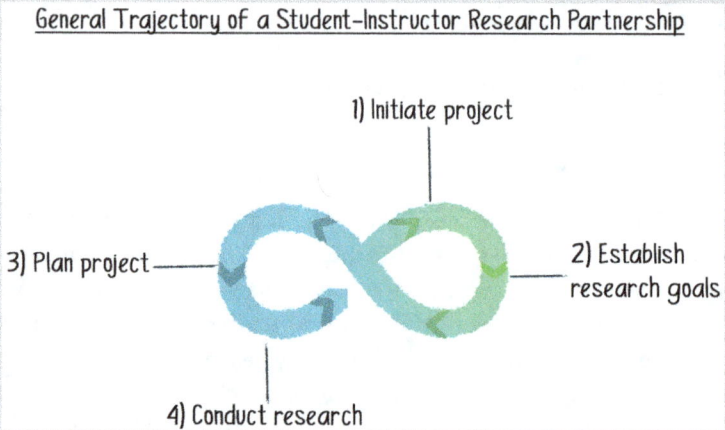

Figure 0.14 The phases of a student-instructor research partnership.

The next phase is establishing a possible research project; instructors can openly discuss the possibility of collaborating on a project and the corresponding expectations for both the student and instructor. In this phase, it should be clarified whether there is opportunity for coauthorship of dissemination pieces, such as published papers and presentations. These conversations should include what is required to be an author, as well as what determines authorship order, especially since these customs vary across disciplines. However, regardless of the discipline one is working in, the project in question should be mutually beneficial and ideally align with both parties' interests. For Alice and Cassandra, this was established through an informal meeting about both of their research interests and career aspirations. Alice presented Cassandra with an archival dataset and told her she could investigate whatever question she liked, provided the data was available. They decided to conduct a study testing the predictive ability of homework and in-class assignments on final exam grades.

Once partners have identified a suitable project, they can begin the planning phase, where they develop concrete goals and a timeline to complete the project. Specific tasks can include developing a research question, and planning and executing data collection and analyses, as well as disseminating the results, all of which can be done collaboratively. Alice walked Cassandra through data processing and analysis procedures, then Cassandra was able to continue independently. Once they had their results, they worked together to research articles for the introduction and they worked on the paper together.

Alice approached Cassandra with the opportunity to present their findings at a conference. They worked on the presentation together, and Cassandra had the opportunity to present the findings herself. This process was collaborative from beginning to end. It's important to maintain a synergistic relationship, which is essential for reaping the many benefits these partnerships can offer (Cook-Sather et al. 2019).

For Cassandra, the greatest benefit was the confidence and agency this experience afforded her. It helped her realise her potential as a researcher and allowed her space to develop ideas in a supportive environment. For Alice, the greatest benefit was the satisfaction of working with a talented student and seeing them grow as a researcher, as well as discussing ideas about pedagogical research with someone with a different/student perspective.

Concluding remarks

In this case study, we have briefly outlined the concept of students as research partners, the potential benefits these partnerships can cultivate, and a generalised trajectory that they may follow. To hear more about our personal experiences and why we feel student-instructor partnerships are so important, please refer to the video corresponding to this chapter.

Bibliography

Cook-Sather, A., Matthews, K.E., Ntem, A. and Leathwick, S. (2018). What We Are Talking about when We Talk about Students as Partners. *International Journal for Students as Partners*, 2(2), 1–9. https://doi.org/10.1513/ijsap.v2i2.3790

Cook-Sather, A., Bahti, M. and Ntem, A. (2019). *Pedagogical Partnerships*. 1st ed. Elon, NC: Elon University Center for Engaged Learning.

Healey, M., Flint, A. and Harrington, K. (2014). *Engagement through Partnership: Students as Partners in Learning and Teaching in Higher Education*. York: The Higher Education Academy.

Inclusivity note

Potential barriers:

1 The risk of attracting only the more capable and academic-minded students, perhaps the students who mirror how we are as academics.
2 Some policies might present an obstacle to research partnerships, for instance in terms of authorship of outputs.

Potential solutions:

1 When we open the call for research partners, we could highlight that students who belong to minorities are particularly welcome to apply. If we are from a white or European background, we could partner with a colleague from a minority group for a joint venture research, so when we invite students as research partners they will feel more at ease to form a cluster where they are not the only representative of a minority.
2 We need to check all the policies regarding student involvement in research, in terms of remunerations and authorship.

This case study builds on the ideas of the previous one: here we see the many benefits of partnerships for *both* students *and* teachers-researchers. It is clear that this was a very positive experience for both parties and one where the typical teacher-student hierarchies were upended. This is not always easy, because both teachers and students bring to the partnership initiative their *cultural* backgrounds and assumptions, which may make it difficult to work as equals on a shared project.

On the companion website inclusivelearningdesign.com (under Section 1) you will find a case study by Yifei Liang and Kelly Matthews (Australia) entitled 'Culturally respectful pedagogical partnership (Asia)'. Rather than a practice case study, this is a more conceptual piece where the authors, following a scoping review, explore factors which foster more culturally respectful partnership practices. The narrative sheds light on a number of important considerations when it comes to setting up intercultural student partnerships: 'learners and teachers engage in ongoing negotiations of power and cultural identity in cross-cultural partnerships' (Zhang et al. 2022). What platforms, language and activities are used set the tone for power relationships and, if done respectfully, can enhance intercultural learning for all involved.

Rather than letting fear of the unknown (cultures) stop us from entering into partnerships with students, open and respectful dialogue among all involved can go a long way in paving the way for fruitful and intentionally equitable co-creation.

Conclusion

This chapter is about the value of co-creation with our students. Indeed, the educational sector is far behind others in getting the 'users' more involved in their processes, in evaluating existing offer and in the development of new offers.

I started the chapter discussing the why and how of various learning design partnerships with students and others; for instance, setting up learning design workshops (or hackathons) with the specific aim of enhancing the learning design of a module or a course, followed by the three case studies highlighted: students as co-creators, student partnerships in research, and culturally respectful partnerships.

At the start of the chapter, I invited you to think about these questions:

Activate your inner dialogue. ... How would you answer?

How can co-creation support a more inclusive learning design?
Which types of student partnership activities are available to you?
What barriers make it difficult to engage in co-creation? How can you overcome them?

My provisional answers, based on the ideas discussed in this chapter are:

Co-creation is a radical act, which makes the students *partners* in, rather than purely recipients of, education. It is about including the students at decision stage, rather than simply presenting them with the finished and polished educational offer without their input in its design. Clearly, the more partnerships we can develop with students, the more we will be able to understand their needs and preferences and refine what we offer them.

Partnerships are also inclusive because they help students develop in a more holistic way (academically, socially and professionally).

Students can be involved as partners in many different aspects of institutional life and systems, though arguably the most impactful on the rest of the student body is to invite them to be *learning* co-creators. This can even extend to becoming co-teachers, for instance leading some classes for their peers.

Besides the practices, I hope the discussion and case studies have shed light on the possibilities that partnerships open up, in terms of reshaping the higher educational narrative: 'Engaging in pedagogical partnership is often positioned as a counter-narrative to the increasingly dominant economic view of higher education as a commodity to be consumed by individuals' (Zhang et al. 2022).

If there are no formal students-as-partners initiatives in your institution, you may be able to start one yourself. Or you may simply involve one or two students in a current project of yours, or in the active review of the course you are teaching them.

Ultimately, co-creation and students as partners boil down to believing in students, in their willingness and *ability* of providing input, and in their abilities to be co-creators of their learning.

Often the main barrier to (more) involvement of students as partners is our own mindset. Once we believe that co-creation is worth the extra effort, we can overcome most practical barriers. Student partnership is a theme that resurfaces in all the following sections because it is a *value* that should inform our practice, not simply a technique.

End note to Section I

In this section, I have discussed the meaning of the roots of the metaphorical learning design tree. By using the word inclusive as an acronym, I reviewed nine important drivers for our learning design, with the help of short narratives by colleagues. I highlighted the 'co-created' root by dedicating to it a chapter with three accounts of co-creation. It is my hope that this overview has provided you with food for thought about the importance of values-based education and what values can support inclusivity.

> **Activate your inner dialogue. ... How would you answer?**
>
> What have your learnt in this section about learning values?
> What are your main take aways for your learning design to be more …
>
> I. Intentionally equitable
> N. Nurturing
> C. Co-created
> L. Liberating
> U. User-friendly
> S. Socially responsible
> I. Integrative
> V. Values-based
> E. Ecological

As this is a roots-to-shoots approach, the focus is on how these values relate to the rest of the tree. In the next sections, we travel up the three branches and discover how these values inform the context (Section 2), content (Section 3), assessment (Section 4) and evaluation (Section 5) of our learning design.

Check the companion website to this book, inclusivelearningdesign.com under Section 1 for further resources about co-creation and the other root-values.

Bibliography

Background

Agostinho, S. (2006). The Use of a Visual Learning Design Representation to Document and Communicate Teaching Ideas. *23rd Annual ASCILITE Conference: Who's Learning? Whose Technology?* Available at: https://citeseerx.ist.psu.edu/viewdoc/download?doi=10.1.1.470.9155&rep=rep1&type=pdf

Anaissie, T., Cary, V., Clifford, D., Malarkey, T. and Wise, S. (2020). Liberatory Design: Your Toolkit to Design for Equity, version 1.0 [card deck]. Stanford k12 lab network. Available at: https://dschool.stanford.edu/s/Liberatory-Design-Cards.pdf

Conole, G. (2008). The Role of Mediating Artefacts In Learning Design. In *Handbook of Research on Learning Design and Learning Objects: Issues, Applications and Technologies*. doi: 10.4018/9781599048611.ch008

Covey, S. (1989). *The Seven Habits of Highly Effective People*. New York: Simon and Schuster.

Culver, K.C., Harper, J. and Kezar, A. (2021). *Design for equity in higher education*. Los Angeles, CA: University of Southern California, Pullias Center for Higher Education.

Kleiman, P. (2009). Design for Learning: A Guide to the Principles of Good Curriculum Design. [ebook] Palatine (HEA). Available at: http://cielassociates.co.uk/wp-content/uploads/2014/08/KLEIMAN2009DesignforLearning.pdf

Turner, C. (2020). #LTHEchat188: The Role of a Systems Approach in Successfully Supporting Learning, Students and Staff with host Prof Colin Turner. [Blog] #LTHEchat Blog. Available at: https://lthechat.com/2020/11/08/lthechat190-the-role-of-a-systems-approach-in-successfully-supporting-learning-students-and-staff-with-host-prof-colin-turner-profcturner/

Wampole, C. (2016). *Rootedness: The Ramifications of a Metaphor*. Chicago, IL: The University of Chicago Press.

Intentionally Equitable

Kapilashrami, A. (2021) Intersectionality-informed framework for tackling racism and embedding inclusion and diversity in teaching & learning. AdvanceHE. Available at: https://www.advance-he.ac.uk/news-and-views/embracing-intersectionality-interrogate-and-action-equality-diversity-and-inclusion

Intentionally hospitable

Shapiro, S. (2020). Inclusive Pedagogy in the Academic Writing Classroom: Cultivating Communities of Belonging. Journal of Academic *Writing*, 10(1), doi: 10.18552/joaw.v10i1.607.

Nurturing

Holmes, R. (2019). Walking Towards a More Embodied Pedagogy. JUICE. Available at: https://juice-journal.com/2019/05/21/walking-towards-a-more-embodied-pedagogy/

Houghton, A. and Anderson, J. (2017). *Embedding Mental Wellbeing in the Curriculum: Maximising Success in Higher Education*. York: Higher Education Academy.

Lister, K., Seale, J. and Douce, C. (2021). Mental Health in Distance Learning: A Taxonomy of Barriers and Enablers to Student Mental Wellbeing, *Open Learning: The Journal of Open, Distance and e-Learning*. doi: 10.1080/02680513.2021.1899907

Molloy, E. and Bearman, M. (2019). Embracing the Tension between Vulnerability and Credibility: 'Intellectual Candour' in Health Professions Education. *Medical Education*, 53(1), 32–41. doi: 10.1111/medu.13649

Co-created

Gauthier, L. (2020). An Evolution of Learning to Support Partnership Readiness. *Teaching and Learning Together in Higher Education*, (29). Available at: https://repository.brynmawr.edu/tlthe/vol1/iss29/4

Liberating

Anaissie, T., Cary, V., Clifford, D., Malarkey, T. and Wise, S. (2020). Liberatory Design: Your Toolkit to Design for Equity, version 1.0 [card deck]. Stanford k12 lab network. https://dschool.stanford.edu/s/Liberatory-Design-Cards.pdf

Baume, D. (2021). Some Possible Accounts of a (partially) Decolonized Curriculum, of a Decolonisation Process, and of What Success Might Look Like. Available at: https://docs.google.com/document/d/1ElaiDODy9OOKTxK1bd_dsmTLU0TQ8Hprs7E_FzJknbM/edit?usp=sharing

Crilly, J., Panesar, L. and Suka-Bill, Z. (2020). Co-constructing a Liberated / Decolonised Arts Curriculum. *Journal of University Teaching & Learning Practice*, 17(2). Available at: https://ro.uow.edu.au/jutlp/vol17/iss2/9

Gopal, P. (2021). On Decolonisation and the University. *Textual Practice*, 35(6), 873–899. doi: 10.1080/0950236X.2021.1929561

Scott, R. (2013). Thoughts on a 'liberating' education. *Liberal Education* (AAC&U), 99(4). [online] Available at: https://www.adelphi.edu/news/liberating-education/

Seal, M. and Smith, A. (2021). *Enabling Critical Pedagogy in Higher Education*. 1st edn. Critical Publishing. Available at: https://www.perlego.com/book/2825784/enabling-critical-pedagogy-in-higher-education-pdf

User-friendly

Boysen, G. (2021). Lessons (Not) Learned: The Troubling Similarities between Learning Styles and Universal Design for Learning. *Scholarship of Teaching and Learning in Psychology*. doi: 10.1037/stl0000280

CAST (2018). Universal Design for Learning Guidelines version 2.2. Available at: http://udlguidelines.cast.org

Fritzgerald, A. (2020). *Anti-racism and Universal Design for Learning: Building Expressways to Success*. Wakefield, MA: CAST Professional Publishing.

Merry, K. (2021). UDL with Kevin Merry. [podcast] Talking Learning and Teaching. Available at: https://anchor.fm/kevin-merry/episodes/Episode-1-UDL-with-Kevin-Merry-ev1iu5

Moore, S. (2016). Shelley Moore: Transforming Inclusive Education. [video] Available at: https://www.youtube.com/watch?v=RYtUlU8MjlY

Nave, L., (2021). Inclusive Instructors Use UDL with Tracie Addy. [podcast] Think UDL. Available at: https://thinkudl.org/episodes/inclusive-instructors-use-udl-with-tracie-addy

Sanger, C.S. (2020). Inclusive Pedagogy and Universal Design Approaches for Diverse Learning Environments. In C. Sanger and N. Gleason (Eds.) *Diversity and Inclusion in Global Higher Education*. Singapore: Palgrave Macmillan. https://doi.org/10.1007/978-981-15-1628-3_2

Zaloudek, J. (2014). Radical Accommodation: Course Design for Extreme Access to Education. *International Conference The Future of Education*. Florence: Libreria Universitaria. Available at: https://conference.pixel-online.net/FOE/prevedition.php?id_edition=6&mat=VDO

Website dedicated to Inclusive UDL practice: https://include.wp.worc.ac.uk/

Socially responsible

Arvanitakis, J. and Hornsby, D. (2016). Are Universities Redundant? In *Universities, the Citizen Scholar and the Future of Higher Education* (pp. 7–20). doi: 10.1057/9781137538697_2

Blessinger, P. and Mandla, M. (2018). Towards Higher Education in Service of Humanity. [online] *University World News*. Available at: https://Www.Universityworldnews.Com/Post.Php?Story=20180130100345559

Daviet, B. (2016). Revisiting the Principle of Education as a Public Good. Education, Research and Foresight: Working Papers. [online] Available at: https://unesdoc.unesco.org/ark:/48223/pf0000245306

DeRosa, R. (2021). Never Forget: Your Course Is Not Only Yours. THE Campus. [online] Available at: https://www.timeshighereducation.com/campus/never-forget-your-course-not-only-yours

Grau, F.X., Goddard, J., Hall, B., Hazelkorn, E., Tandon, R. and Escrigas, C. (Eds.) (2017). *Higher Education in the World 6. Towards a Socially Responsible University: Balancing the Global with the Local*. Global University Network for Innovation (GUNi).

McArthur, J. (2021). The Inclusive University: A Critical Theory Perspective Using a Recognition-Based Approach. *Social Inclusion*, 9(3), 6–15. Available at: https://www.cogitatiopress.com/socialinclusion/article/view/4122/4122

Unlu, V. (2021). Come creare un ambiente inclusivo in Classe. [Blog] Better Learning. Available at: https://www.cupitaly.it/blog/come-creare-un-ambiente-inclusivo-in-classe

Integrative

Arvanitakis, J. and Hornsby, D. (2016). Are Universities Redundant? In *Universities, the Citizen Scholar and the Future of Higher Education* (pp. 7–20). doi: 10.1057/9781137538697_2

Barnett, R. (2000). University Knowledge in an Age of Supercomplexity. *Higher Education*, 40, 409–422. doi: 10.1023/A:1004159513741

Bridgstock, R. (2016). Educating for Digital Futures: What the Learning Strategies of Digital Media Professionals Can Teach Higher Education. *Innovations in Education and Teaching International*, 53(3), 306–315. doi: 10.1080/14703297.2014.956779

MacMath, S., Wallace, J. and Chi, X. (2009). Curriculum Integration: Opportunities to Maximize Assessment as, of, and for Learning. *McGill Journal of Education*, 44, 451–466.

RSE (2017). Pillars and Lintels: The What's, Why's, and How's of Interdisciplinary Learning. [online] Available at: https://rse.org.uk/pillars-lintels-interdisciplinary-learning/

Values-based

DeRosa, R. (2020). A Consistent, Mission-aligned Instructional Framework for the Fall and Beyond (opinion). Inside Higher Ed. [online] Available at: https://www.insidehighered.

com/digital-learning/views/2020/05/13/consistent-mission-aligned-instructional-framework-fall-and-beyond
Garmon, M. (2005). Six Key Factors for Changing Preservice Teachers' Attitudes/Beliefs about Diversity. *Educational Studies: A Journal of The American Education Studies Associaton*, 38, 275–286. 10.1207/s15326993es3803_7
JISC (n.d.). Learning Design Family Tree: Jisc Project Outcomes and Key External Relationships [image]. Available at: https://repository.jisc.ac.uk/6728/1/Learning_Design_Family_Tree_i2.pdf
Speirs, N. (2021a). The Hidden Curriculum and its Impact on Working-class Students. [podcast] Teaching Matters Podcast. Available at: https://www.teaching-matters-blog.ed.ac.uk/podcast-the-hidden-curriculum/
Speirs, N. (2021b). The Hidden Curriculum as Doxa: Experiences of the Working Class. In T. Hinchcliffe (Ed.) *The Hidden Curriculum of Higher Education*. AdvanceHE.

Ecological

A comprehensive resource list of 'Students as partners and change agents' is available on Mick Healey's website: https://www.healeyheconsultants.co.uk/resources
Also, the *International Journal for Students As Partners* has a special issue on 'Partnership in fostering socially just pedagogies', available at: https://doi.org/10.15173/ijsap.v6i1.5129

Barnett, R. (2018). *The Ecological University*. Oxon and New York: Routledge.
Bryan, A. (2021). Academia, Climate Change, and the Future: An Interview with Kim Stanley Robinson. [Blog] Book Club, Available at: https://bryanalexander.org/book-club/academia-climate-change-and-the-future-an-interview-with-kim-stanley-robinson/
Bryant, P. (2021). Be More Cockatoo: Learning Design Ecosystems for a Post-crisis World. [Blog] Peter Bryant: Post Digital Learning. Available at: https://peterbryant.smegradio.com/be-more-cockatoo-learning-design-ecosystems-for-a-post-crisis-world/
Meredith, A. (2022). How to Teach Sustainability. [blog] WonkHE. Available at: https://wonkhe.com/blogs/how-to-teach-sustainability/
Orr, D.W. (1992). *Ecological Literacy: Education and the Transition to a Postmodern World*. Albany: State University of New York Press.

Co-creation chapter

Barbosa Mendes, A. and Hammett, D. (2020). The New Tyranny of Student Participation? Student Voice and the Paradox of Strategic-active Student-citizens. *Teaching in Higher Education*. doi: 10.1080/13562517.2020.1783227
Bovill, C. (2017). A Framework to Explore ROLES within Student-Staff Partnerships in Higher Education: Which Students are Partners, When, and in What Ways? *International Journal for Students as Partners*, 1(1). https://mulpress.mcmaster.ca/ijsap/issue/view/306
Bovill, C., Cook-Sather, A., Felten, P., Millard, L. and Moore-Cherry, N. (2016). Addressing Potential Challenges in Co-creating Learning and Teaching: Overcoming Resistance, Navigating Institutional Norms and Ensuring Inclusivity in Student–Staff Partnerships. *Higher Education*, 71, 195–208. doi: 10.1007/s10734-015-9896-4
Cook-Sather, A., Bahti, M. and Ntem, A. (2019). *Pedagogical Partnerships*. Elon, NC: Elon University Center for Engaged Learning.
Mercer-Mapstone, L. and Abbott, S. (Eds.) (2020). *The Power of Student-staff Partnerships: Students, Staff, and Faculty Revolutionizing Higher Education*. Center for Engaged Learning Open-Access Book Series. Elon University. https://www.centerforengagedlearning.org/books/power-of-partnership/

Page, S., Lewis, E., Cantor, N. and Phillips, K. (2019). *The Diversity Bonus*. Princeton, NJ: Princeton University Press.

Palmer, A. (2022). Repurposing Hackathons to Engage Students as Partners. [Blog] The SEDA Blog. Available at: https://thesedablog.wordpress.com/2022/04/06/repurposing-hackathons-to-engage-students-as-partners/

QAA (2012). The UK Quality Code for Higher Education. Available at: https://www.qaa.ac.uk/docs/qaa/quality-code/quality-code-overview-2015.pdf?sfvrsn=d309f781_6

Zhang, M., Matthews , K. and Liu, S. (2022). Recognising Cultural Capital through Shared Meaning-Making in Cross-cultural Partnership Practices. *International Journal for Students As Partners*, 6(1), 64–80. https://doi.org/10.15173/ijsap.v6i1.4893

Where are you at now?

Before you get into the tree's branches and leaves, I invite you to stop and reflect on your current practice. If you have chosen to read this book, it is likely that you have an interest in inclusivity and you might already have at least some experience in designing inclusive learning environments and journeys for your learners. If that is the case, well done. But, by experience, I find that even very inclusive learning designers need reminders and are eager to further develop their inclusive approaches as educational practices evolve, and policies and institutions change.

The nine-point 'Inclusivity Star' (Figure 0.15) is a simple visual way to take stock of your starting point in inclusive learning design, a self-evaluation tool to gauge where you are at in the areas addressed by this book. Ask yourself how inclusive you feel your learning design is at present in each proposed area and score yourself for each star point. Each star point is a chapter of this book which highlights some key inclusivity areas or approaches. The star points are colour coded according to the three tree branches which correspond to the book sections: yellow for context, green for content and orange for assessment.

Of course, not all the suggested ideas linked to the star points might be entirely clear to you at this stage, but you probably have enough background knowledge to gauge their meaning and score yourself in those areas.

How to use the star

Give yourself a 1 where you feel your learning design in that particular aspect is *not* very inclusive, all the way up to 5 wherever you think your learning design is very inclusive. For example, if the orientation you provide to your students at the start of the course is not very inclusive at this time, you may score yourself 1 or 2 on that star point. If, on the other hand, you feel that the assessment you design for students provides them with choice and voice and is authentic, you may score yourself 4 or 5 on that star point.

Use a pencil to mark your score on each star point and then 'join the dots', literally, to form a web shape. The bigger (closer to the star points ends) and the more regular the resulting web shape is, the better you are doing in terms of inclusive learning design. If the shape is big and full and quite regular, it means you are designing learning in a very inclusive way. This book will be useful to you as it will provide you with food for thought and examples of practice to further expand your inclusive approach.

If the shape is quite irregular, this means that you have identified some areas where your learning design is not as inclusive as you would wish. In this case, you will find the chapters in this book which address those specific low points are most useful to you.

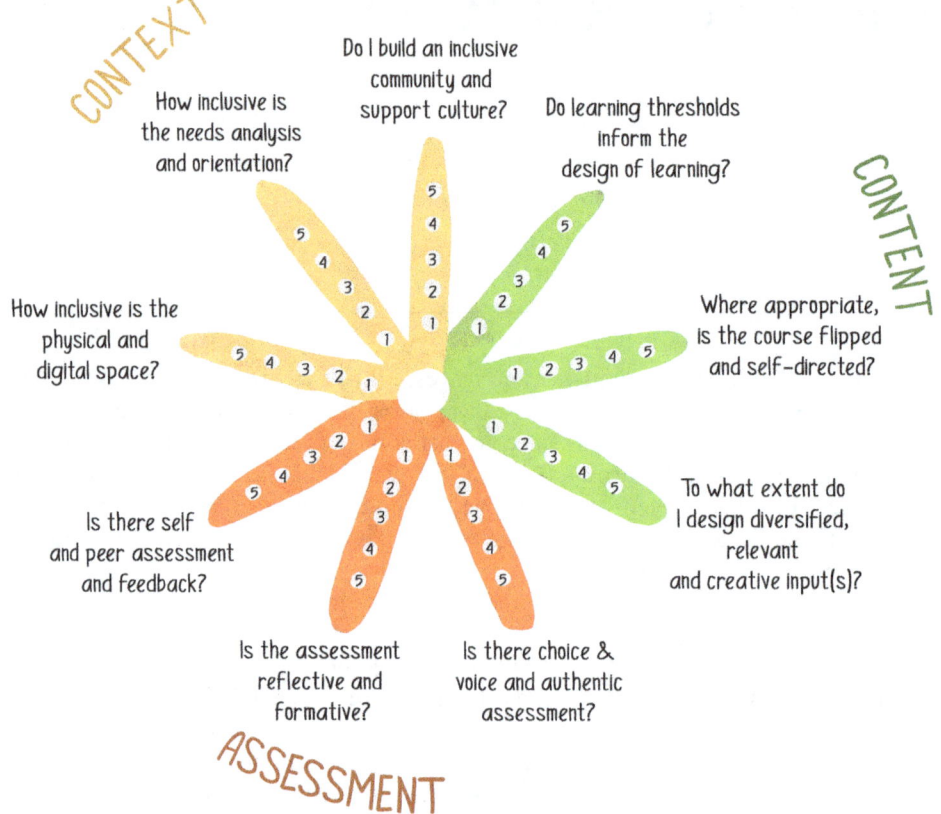

Figure 0.15 The nine-pointed star: a tool for diagnostic self-assessment in the dimensions of context, content and assessment.

If the shape is small (close to the centre) as you have scored yourself low on most areas, take heart as the ideas and examples of practice in this book will support you to develop more inclusive learning design approaches and in future, your inclusivity star shape will grow bigger.

As the chapters of this book do not represent an exhaustive list of possible inclusive learning design, you may want to make note of any other inclusive learning design practices that do not correspond to any of the star points. These could be your current areas of strength or, on the contrary, things you would like to introduce in the future.

This book is a delicate balancing act between an invitation for reflection and a call to action. In the final part of the book, I will invite you to return to this 'Inclusive Star' diagram, when hopefully you will have a clearer understanding of those headings and will have read examples of practice to illustrate them. At that stage you will be able to gauge your progress in your understanding (and perhaps in your practice as well, if you read this book over an extended period of time) of inclusive learning design and you should be ready to create a plan for your future inclusive learning design that makes sense for *your* context.

From the roots addressed in Section 1 I now invite you to travel from 'roots to shoots' by reading Section 2 where I discuss how *context* should inform our inclusive learning design.

Section 2

Learning context
Set up and engagement

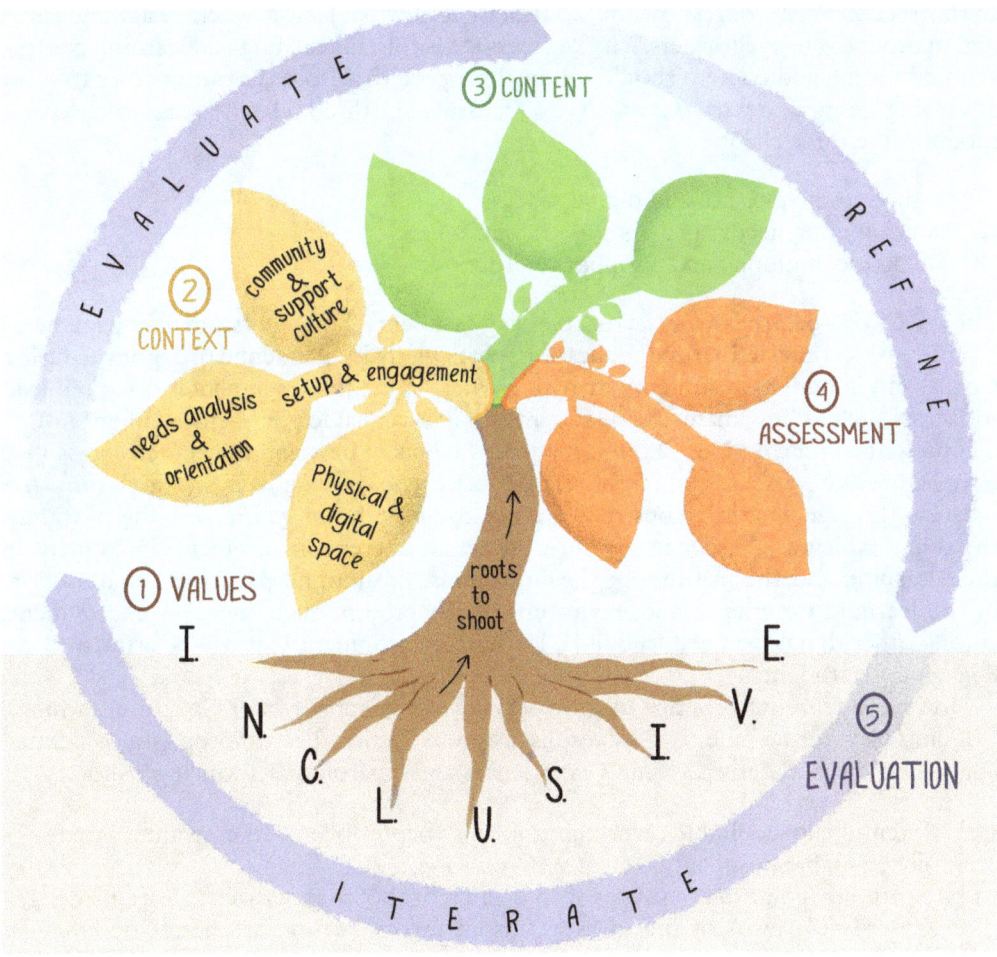

This section is essentially about situational awareness because 'context is a pervasive and potent force in any learning event' (Tessmer and Richey 1997). Many learning design models focus on content and assessment and leave out of the picture values and context. The approach advocated in this book does the opposite: it puts the emphasis on values and context *to determine* content and assessment.

DOI: 10.4324/9781003230144-4

Context has so many facets: there is the immediate, current context and the historical one; there is the local and the global context; the geographical and the social context; there is the personal student context and how it relates to the course *and* institutional context; there is a political and a financial context. Each and every contextual dimension related to a course affects it, more or less directly.

> **Activate your inner dialogue.... How would you answer?**
>
> What are the main contextual factors that affect your practice?
> How can you leverage contextual factors to design more inclusive learning?

In this section I will address the importance of contextual factors when designing learning, in order to engage learners. The key message is this: in teaching and learning context should be king, and content should follow. I propose that from the outset you carry out a learning design *contextual analysis*, by focussing on three related areas which correspond to the three chapters:

(1) setting up the physical and digital spaces;
(2) carrying out a needs' analysis and orientation and
(3) building community and a support culture.

The set-up of a course is a key factor to engage students, however 'student engagement' has become a contested term in education, particularly in 'pandemic pedagogy' (during Covid) and in our era of students' analytics, where student engagement is often reduced to factors such as how many clicks students do in a virtual learning environment (VLE) in a prescribed time period. Though that may help us understand how much access they have had to the platform and might relate to their engagement, it is only a *quantitative* measure. Engagement as a construct is more to do with the *qualitative* side of things, the things which are harder to measure: students' interest, involvement, investment in their learning and the institution; their readiness, meaningful participation and effort in the learning experience and environment. To prompt such (deeper) engagement, among other things we need to build a learning environment that will be attractive and engaging for students.

How can attention to context *at learning design stage* support more inclusive learning?

Going back to the nine root-values discussed in Section 1, an appropriate contextual analysis can help us design learning experiences and environments which are more:

I. Intentionally equitable (everything in this chapter relates to extending intentionally equitable hospitality)
N. Nurturing (contextual analysis will inform a more holistic approach to learning design)
C. Co-created (most of the ideas discussed in this section are better designed in partnership with students)
L. Liberating (the ideas discussed in this section about the use of physical and digital spaces, needs analysis and orientation and community building have the effect of liberating our learning design)
U. User-friendly (we can create user-friendly environments and experiences only if we are aware of who our learners are and what their needs are)

S. Socially responsible (the context from micro to macro will determine in which ways we can promote positive social impact)
I. Integrative (in this section I discuss integrating the physical and the digital, the needs analysis and the orientation, the community building and the support system, and all of these elements with each other)
V. Values-based (the context analysis starts with ourselves, hence checking our drivers is the first step towards values-based course design)
E. Ecological (by carrying out a contextual analysis we can reveal the ways in which we can provide a more sustainable learning experience, in a broader sense)

The contextual analysis we carry out at the start of learning design has the potential to reveal hidden opportunities and is likely to lead us to design more inclusive learning experiences and environments because it enhances our *empathy* for our learners. There are many interacting contextual factors that affect learning, so we need a 360-degree approach to analysing them:

- Ourselves
- Our students
- Our institution
- Our discipline

First, know thyself. A literature review (Van Lankveld et al. 2017) about contextual factors which affect teacher identity and professional development found that there are 'four factors that strengthen or constrain the development of a teacher identity in the university context: the direct work environment, the wider context of higher education, interaction with students, and staff development activities'. We also need to become aware of *our own* personal positionality as academics: we need to see beyond our local contexts and become aware of just how culturally situated our understanding of knowledge, teaching and learning is. We could map our identities and reflect on questions such as: How does my (socio-cultural) background affect my worldview and my professional practice? What are the values that inform my practice *at this time*? It is a good idea to share a positionality statement with students at the start of the course, like the one at the start of this book.

Second, we need to better understand our students and *their* context. We must take time to get to know who our students are, what is their context and how this affects their learning. The most favourable and useful time to do this is just before a course starts or in week 1. We could consider questions such as: Who are my students? What is their background, context and situation? What personal circumstances can potentially support or hinder their learning?

Third, we need to recognise what forces are at play in *our institutions* and what contextual factors have the greatest impact on our learning design. Questions to think about are: What physical and learning spaces are available to me and what are their affordances and limitations? What are the local community and the broader national contexts which affect my institution's priorities, policies and practices? How can I leverage institutional contextual factors (such as priorities, initiatives and policies) to design more inclusive learning?

Fourth, closely linked to this is the *disciplinary context*. What habits of heart, mind and hand do students need to develop to become proficient in my field? What are the big

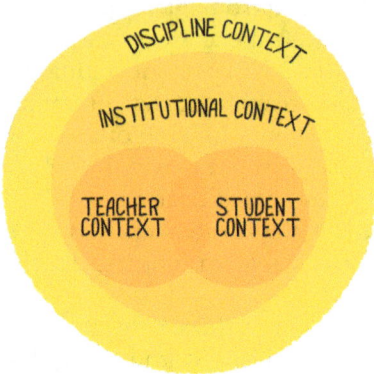

Figure 0.16 Situating teacher and student context within institutional and discipline context.

ideas and thresholds in my discipline? How have they changed in recent years? Are there inherent biases within the knowledge and approaches to learning in the discipline which may serve to reinforce a lack of inclusivity?

These interrelated dimensions are visually represented in Figure 0.16.

It is very important to recognise that all the contextual factors mentioned previously (and in the image) are not fixed; on the contrary, they are in constant flux; they considerably overlap and there can be *tension* among them, with forces pulling in different directions. For example, a student's own context and background might be at odds with institutional policies and practices. Or the institution might not be up to speed with (potentially) fast-changing disciplinary practices. Gaining the big picture of the various factors involved in our professional context can help us understand and negotiate these tensions as we design and enact the curriculum.

There is a two-way relationship between context and learning design: learning design depends on the context; on the other hand, the learning designed affects, changes and can create new contexts. In our busy academic schedule, it pays off to take the time to carry out a contextual analysis at the start of learning design as this is likely to lead us to design more holistic, intentionally inclusive learning experiences and environments where context and content go hand in hand. If we do not carry out an appropriate contextual analysis, we risk ending up with a course that 'misses the mark' for the students', the teachers' or the curriculum's needs (Fink 2013).

I trust that the ideas and case studies presented in this section will inspire you to give more attention to contextual factors that affect the set up and engagement of students on your courses.

Bibliography

Fink, L. (2013). *Creating Significant Learning Experiences: An Integrated Approach to Designing College Courses*. San Francisco, CA: Jossey-Bass.

Tessmer, M. and Richey, R.C. (1997). The Role of Context in Learning and Instructional Design. *ETR&D*, 45, 85–115. doi: 10.1007/BF02299526

Van Lankveld, T. Schoonenboom, J. Volman, M., Croiset, G. and Beishuizen, J. (2017). Developing a Teacher Identity in the University Context: A Systematic Review of the Literature, Higher Education Research & Development, 36(2), 325,342. doi: 10.1080/07294360.2016.1208154

Chapter 1

Ready? Setting up the physical and digital space

> Sometimes the path itself is not set up to let people succeed
>
> Julie Dirksen

> **Activate your inner dialogue. ... How would you answer?**
>
> What impact do physical and digital spaces and places have on learning?
> How can you design the physical and digital spaces more inclusively?

A UNESCO paper (2012) defines the learning environment as 'the complete physical, social and pedagogical context in which learning is intended to occur'. In this chapter I will focus more on the physical and digital learning spaces while Chapters 2 and 3 address aspects of the social space of learning.

University spaces can be seen as containers where various things to do with learning and teaching happen. However, learning spaces are not neutral: even a physical classroom with blank walls gives a message about what was left out, what is not on display and conveys unspoken messages regarding the way learning is supposed to happen and the expected culture of learning within the space. When a space is filled with people, interactions, values and a purpose, it becomes a place.

An important first step to turn a space into an inclusive learning *place* is configuring the physical and digital spaces the course will make use of—with an emphasis on access and accessibility—so they promote inclusive learning, and they support the building of the course as a place for a **community of learning**. Although ineffective learning environments can be enhanced during a course, it is better to give them appropriate attention at learning design stage.

First, think about a personal experience of a learning space or place that 'worked' for you—a time when, either as a student or as a teacher, you felt the learning space supported learning. What did you value in that learning environment? How can you reproduce those success factors in the environments you design for your students?

Second, if you have not done it yet, I invite you to visit a colleague's classroom during a lesson. What captures your attention? What messages do you receive from the set-up of the classroom, the way students interact and the teacher's manner? How have the people in the space created a place for learning? What is the general 'feeling' you get from the learning space and situation? How might all of this impact on the students and their learning?

Space has not been as researched as other aspects of teaching and learning so it is still hard to define the relationship between the space and the learning. Of course, there are physical as well as organisational factors which determine how spaces are organised. But broadly, it seems clear that the way spaces are organised reflects the types of interactions that are valued. So, in a way, paying attention to the way spaces are designed in order to provoke certain exchanges is a form of 'encounter management—using design features to bring people together in settings where mutually beneficial interactions may occur' (Temple 2014). This implies being intentional in the way we design the learning environment, rather than leaving it to chance.

A very interesting AdvanceHE report on 'Future Learning Spaces—Space, Technology and Pedagogy' (Elkington and Bligh 2019) presents a useful conceptualisation and vocabulary to talk about learning spaces: 'space is understood to be transparent, enabling, stimulating, associative, cognitively integrated and socially integrated'. I believe that as teachers we have the power to make learning spaces all of those things, depending on how we configure and enact learning design. In a nutshell, learning spaces need to be intentionally '[designed with] appropriate pedagogies in mind, be multi-functional and ideally also multi-sensory' (Krajewski and Khoury 2021).

Even before the pandemic, but much more since the seismic changes it has accelerated in higher education, university spaces are undergoing considerable changes: lecture-based learning is not as central to university life as it has historically been, but institutions are also moving towards more hands-on, active, flexible and informal spaces, where social and cross-disciplinary interactions are valued (Adams Becker et al. 2017). Today teachers design, re-design, and re-purpose not only analogue, but also more and more technology-enhanced learning materials and activities. And these materials and activities are increasingly situated within *wider digital spaces*, usually virtual learning environments (VLEs) which have become the new home base for many courses, even when the course is run on site.

Technology is a valuable ally, not a simple tool. Since the forced adoption of more digital forms of learning due to the pandemic, when rather than technology in classrooms, we have seen the reality of 'classrooms in technology' (Hillman 2022), many have realised that to use technology in a 'transformative sense' (Hattie 2015) they should view online and on-site learning on a continuum of learning modes where what really matters is not the place or tool but the pedagogical intention. However, it is even better to move beyond this dichotomy of pedagogy vs technology, towards a vision of a more complex 'entangled pedagogy that encapsulates the mutual shaping of technology, teaching methods, purposes, values and context' (Fawns 2022).

When discussing learning spaces, we need to address the question: **is learning 'situated'?** This is an important question because since the seminal work of Lave and Wenger (1990) on situated learning over three decades ago, there has been a lively debate regarding the validity of this theory. In a nutshell the theory states that knowledge should be learned in the same place as it is used, that it is a social process and that it best happens within communities of practice, for instance as apprenticeship. Although apprenticeships are very valuable for some types of learning, they are not the *only* way to acquire a particular skillset and are also very difficult to implement on a large scale within HE systems. Other weaknesses of the situated learning theory are the fact that learning can very well happen independently through cognitive processes and also that creative thinkers can disrupt existing communities of practice rather than simply be assimilated in them.

There are also those who say that although on the one hand, learning environments matter, on the other hand we should remember that good learning design is based on principles that are 'space agnostic' (Bryant 2021), in the sense that what really matters are 'the types of activities, relationships, and engagements we build, not on the placement of desks and chairs, the size of the teaching desk or whether cameras are on or off'.

I believe the best approach is a middle ground between situated learning and space agnostic learning. Ultimately, we should seek to establish more meaningful, positive, happy relationships within the spaces we operate in. Through the case studies in this chapter, you will read about ways to improve your use of spaces to make them more inclusive, by aligning the use of the learning space with your pedagogical values and purposes.

As 'space has social dimensions, as well as the more obvious material ones' (Temple 2014), what **barriers** can students face in their learning journey through physical and digital spaces? Some possible difficulties students can have include hearing difficulties, visual difficulties, physical mobility difficulties, information processing difficulties, language difficulties, low internet bandwidth, cultural difficulties, digital literacy, social impairment and more. Keeping these potential difficulties in mind, reflect on how the way you set up and use physical and digital spaces helps you achieve learning that is more:

I. Intentionally equitable
N. Nurturing
C. Co-created
L. Liberating
U. User-friendly
S. Socially responsible
I. Integrative
V. Values-based
E. Ecological

Like all other aspects of learning design, co-creation is very important for learning spaces: we should involve students in the decisions about how to configure and use the various spaces we have access to. This will help us build a better place for everyone involved.

The concept of 'safe space' has become very popular in the context of making spaces welcoming for groups of students who have been traditionally 'underserved' in higher education. However, we need to be realistic: we cannot guarantee that a space will always be totally safe for every user. What we *can* do is talk about ways in which we are planning to make the spaces as safe as possible, but also provide warning when something in the course might be a trigger for some due to their lived experiences. This has been called a 'principled space' (BARC n.d.) and is based on establishing ground-clearing practices such as recognising privilege and active listening. This applies to all types of learning spaces.

As this book is aimed at the 'meso' level of course design, I am not going to discuss the broader university-wide decisions about facilities and building spaces. The discussion and case studies in this chapter address various types of spaces and how we can leverage the affordances of each type of space (and of their blends) to create more inclusive learning environments. In this chapter I invite you to read practical ideas about the setup and use of four interrelated types of learning spaces:

- physical
- blended
- digital
- mobile

The physical learning spaces

The post-pandemic rebalancing of the digital and physical estate of each institution has meant hybrid learning solutions have become the norm. As a consequence, our course home base has shifted, and the physical classroom is not the *exclusive* space for group learning it used to be. Even if we are not on campus as much as before, it is vital to ensure that the physical learning spaces we do use are safe and accessible to support students' full engagement with the learning experiences we design. Where possible, the space should also reflect student diversity.

Winston Churchill once said: 'We shape our buildings; thereafter they shape us'. Applying this to educational spaces, the idea is that we create spaces which reflect what type of learning we value. But at the same time, the learning spaces themselves influence the type of learning we value and promote. By *intentionally* setting up the physical space in ways that reflect an inclusive approach to teaching and learning, we are more likely to set up more inclusive experiences.

The physical learning space matters also in terms of addressing sedentarism, a real issue for university students' well-being as they spend most of their time in the university premises sitting down. Injecting some movement in our live lessons, for instance asking students to move around, change seat or group, or use rotating stations, all make learning better because movement activates our brains. In this regard, the study of 'instructional proxemics' is a fascinating field: how one uses the space, how one moves and relates to others within that space (McArthur 2008). While some academics have active ways of relating to their cohort, for some leaving their place behind the large desk in a lecture hall and venturing among the students and interacting with them is a big change and a novel use of space.

In the following case study, read about a number of practical things we can do to improve our physical learning spaces.

Physical learning spaces to promote creative teaching

By Sylvia Ashton and Rachel Stone (UK)

Our case study takes place in a fictitious higher education learning space such as a seminar or a lecture theatre. The ideas are drawn from our book, *An A to Z of Creative Teaching in Higher Education* (Ashton and Stone 2021). Our work is predicated on inclusivity so we're going to assume that any room design takes into account the requirements of every learner and teacher who's going to walk through the door.

In this piece we focus on the physical environment. As McGregor (2007) observes, the design and layout of rooms for teaching and learning convey messages of socialisation that we are often not even aware of. For example, she suggests, a poor learning environment can carry the message that the learners within it, and their learning, are given little value. To truly enable, empower and provide a meaningful identity for students, an environment needs to be created that disrupts these notions (Lippman 2015).

So—let's have a go at creating a great learning space! We'll look at the obvious elements first—is it bright, is it the right temperature, is it spacious? Tanner (2008), researching in 24 schools in the USA, found that optimising these factors led to a significant increase in achievement.

Now let's turn to our room layout. Traditional classroom set-ups reinforce notions of the teacher as the holder of power, knowledge and authority, and the students as passive recipients of that knowledge.

In our imaginary room, we want to maximise active learning. Tables in 'islands' encourage more learner movement and more peer-to-peer interaction and maximise the ability of the teacher to circulate, assess and support individuals as they complete tasks.

Say we find that our imaginary space is too crowded, too dark, too hot and the furniture, in rows, is bolted to the floor. Well, let's see if we can swap to a better room or ask if any adjustments can be made. If that fails, we'll have more breaks, find breakout space if we can and maybe flip our teaching so that more of the work is done by learners outside an inadequate space.

Figure 1.1 What a lesson in an inclusive learning space could look like.

A teacher who puts the learners at the heart of the learning can mitigate the effects of a poor physical learning environment to a certain extent (as evidenced in Heron and Heward 1982). However, the fact remains that a low-quality learning environment can not only restrict the range of possible teaching and learning approaches, it can also impact on student–teacher and student–student interaction, prevent individual needs from being met and be inefficient and costly (McGregor 2007).

For the most part, formal learning spaces in higher education settings are designed on *the assumption that the body has no role to play in cognition* (O'Loughlin 1998, 2006 in Stolz 2015: 475). However, there is a significant and growing body of neurological research that suggests otherwise. In this short case study we have attempted to describe a space which begins to recognise the importance of the physical environment and to show how that space can mirror our approach to teaching and learning.

Bibliography

Ashton, S. and Stone, R. (2021). *An A to Z of Creative Teaching in Higher Education*. Sage.

Heron, T.E. and Heward, W.L. (1982). Ecological Assessment: Implications for Teachers of Learning Disabled Students. *Learning Disability Quarterly*, 5(2), 117–125. doi: 10.2307/1510572

Lave, J. and Wenger, E. (1990). *Situated Learning: Legitimate Peripheral Participation*. Cambridge: Cambridge University Press.

Lippman, P. (2015). Designing Collaborative Spaces for Schools. *The Education Digest*, 80(5), 39–44.

McGregor, J. (2007). Understanding and Managing Classroom Space. *Curriculum Briefing*, 5(2), 16–19.

Stolz, S.A. (2015). Embodied Learning. *Educational Philosophy and Theory*, 47(5), 474–487. doi: 10.1080/00131857.2013.879694

Tanner, C.K. (2008). Explaining Relationships among Student Outcomes and the School's Physical Environment. *Journal of Advanced Academics*, 19(3), 444–471. doi: 10.4219/jaa-2008-812

Inclusivity note

Physical spaces need to be first of all accessible to all. To cater for the various needs of our cohort we need to carry out a needs analysis (addressed in the next chapter) and check with students on a regular basis. Students have a variety of sensory processing needs: some may be very sensitive to light and temperature; others may need to move more often than others; others may find crowded and noisy spaces cognitively very challenging. Some students may have physical conditions which require them to sit in a particular position, for instance cross-legged on the floor; as long as it does not obstruct the view of others we should be responsive to such needs.

To support students with social anxiety, we could make videos to show students the learning spaces before they physically get there—this would prepare them for

> the type of places and interactions that are likely to happen there. However, some neurodivergent/autistic students might find it impossible to learn in a busy space. We might be able to arrange for them to join online or to be in another quiet space and only sporadically join the larger group.
>
> Even in the case of fixed furniture in rows which does not allow us to configure the space to respond to various needs and learning activity types, there are usually some elements that *are* in our control: the amount of light we let in; the air flow and temperature; student seating arrangement; access to water and being able to move in the space through the nature of students' activities. However, if a space is simply inadequate, we may need to review how much time we require students to spend in it.

This case study well illustrates how the physical learning space speaks volumes about the types of learning we hope to prompt and achieve. If you are not able to use the same room for your regular live lessons, it might be very hard to personalise the space to create a home base for the course which promotes a sense of belonging. Some teachers have resorted to the use of mobile stands or other wall-mounted displays which they can easily move to the room they are assigned for each lesson, to create a sense of identity for the module and the cohort.

From physical spaces, we now move to blended and hybrid learning spaces.

The blended learning spaces

Before the pandemic, in some parts of the world universities' 'translocality'—distributed in different places—and 'transtemporality'—transcending time—(Sheail 2018) were already a reality due to geographical context: students were in more than one campus or online and engaging with their studies in asynchronous as well as synchronous modes. But for most universities, blended learning was still a novelty because, in higher education, 'innovation diffusion, especially in pedagogy, tends to be low and slow' (Baker 2022).

Pre-pandemic, the term blended learning was used to describe the mix of synchronous on-site learning with online asynchronous activities done in between lessons. However, blended learning has acquired a broader meaning and now it is about providing flexibility to students by mixing input modes, so students have access to the course content in more than one mode. The blends can be at different levels: time blend, place blend, activity blend and media blend (Figure 1.2).

All the blends in the image are about enhancing and augmenting learning opportunities so students have more flexibility and better options regarding how, where and when to engage with their studies.

Regarding space blends, since the pandemic every university course has had to increasingly use a mix of on-site and online learning. Besides the lockdown necessity of alternatives to physical spaces, there is more and more recognition that space blends are pedagogically better—it is literally getting the best of two worlds, the physical and digital ones (AdvanceHE. n.d.). Regarding time blends, in many institutions, there is an issue of *perceived* superior value of the synchronous co-presence over all other types of

Figure 1.2 Blended learning.

learning. Asynchronous learning is often seen as less valuable, while in fact it is very beneficial for students. As teachers, we can help rebalance this view: we can use asynchronous activities to support synchronous ones and vice-versa.

With technological advances, time and space blends have multiplied the ways students can engage with a course, such as: digitally connected off site while the teachers and others are on site; on site while the teacher is online; with a time delay in the online space through a recording after the class; through pre-recorded videos before the lesson, followed by synchronous or asynchronous interactions and more.

Regarding activity and media blends, these refer to what the student will be doing—to various types of input and outputs—rather than the where and when of learning.

I prefer the term blended over hybrid because when we blend various ingredients in a literal blender, we end up with a new mixture, which has the flavour of its ingredients but is nonetheless something new and different. Likewise, in education, the possibilities of the various hybrid blends produce new ways of learning.

These varied possibilities of blends imply a major change for teachers: the potential loss of 'control' over the learning situation and the complexity of designing learning for such a variety of options. Of all the options, arguably the most demanding on teachers is the 'real' hybrid (also called hyflex, a term which combines 'hybrid' with 'flexible') where some students are on site, usually with the teacher, while some are connected, live, online *at the same time*. This effectively means designing for two modalities to happen at once.

This type of hybrid learning was forced upon teachers and students during the pandemic, in a hurry and without much learning *design*, and often resulted in a poor experience for teachers and students. Many teachers were learning about online and blended learning as they were implementing it. However, it is noteworthy that hybrid learning was successfully employed pre-covid as a pedagogical choice by various organisations and institutions around the world. Beatty (2019) writes that there are 'four fundamental values in Hybrid-Flexible Design: Learner Choice; Equivalency; Reusability; Accessibility'. He was writing in the pre-pandemic educational landscape, and yet those values are more relevant than ever, especially the choice aspect: students expect to be able to interact with the course in a variety of ways. Students with caring responsibilities, first in family, neurodivergent students and those whose first language is not the language of instruction all benefit from being able to choose various pathways of engagements with the learning material. Blended learning offers the possibility of more tailored access, supports and services.

The following case study challenges the negative perception teachers have acquired regarding hybrid teaching and learning. It discusses why such hybrid learning can be an intentional pedagogic *choice* and why it is valuable. It also provides some useful pointers about how to set it up so that all students, both on site and online, can benefit.

Collaboration in the hybrid classroom

By Stanimira Velikova (UK/Bulgaria)

We should be preparing our students now to learn how to navigate our post-pandemic virtual/physical learning world successfully. For instance, students need to prepare for the new online world of work as it is our new reality. Students (and educators) need to skill up for the world of work where online interaction and collaboration will be critical skills.

Today's classroom should encourage learners and educators to virtually and physically interact seamlessly in what is called hybrid learning: a type of blended learning where some students are physically co-present with a teacher while others follow the lessons online, synchronously. This hybrid classroom creates an opportunity for more tailored education and learning 'with some element of student control over path, pace, time, and place' (O'Byrne and Pytash 2015).

Figure 1.3 illustrates blended learning, in terms of where learning happens. Hybrid is towards the 'fully online' side.

Hybrid learning is the opposite of a one-size-fits-all approach but rather enables various pathways which can increase student engagement and performance (Nobre

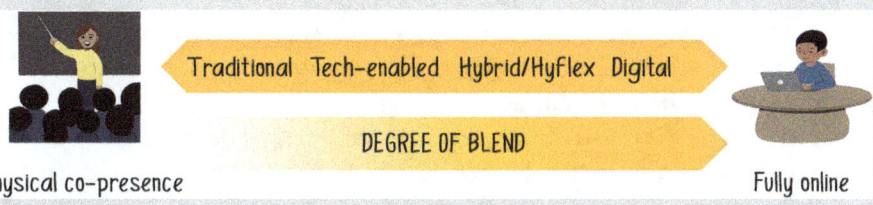

Figure 1.3 Blends from physical co-presence to fully online.

et al. n.d.). Some critical and interrelated components of hybrid learning are inclusion, access and collaboration. Integrating virtual interaction with what is happening with the class in the physical space requires extra attention to ensure that everyone on the course feels included and a part of the ongoing dialogue and learning.

In a hybrid class, students who are co-present with teachers can be unfairly advantaged over their online peers. Therefore, both educators and students on site will need devices to log into the video conferencing platform alongside the students joining digitally. Ensuring peers online can see and interact with those on site is essential to creating an inclusive learning environment. It is useful to consider the *online* space as the shared space, rather than the on-site space.

For all students to engage equitably, the ones who are physically co-present should learn to work with each other and with their peers online. The first step to achieving this interaction model is to foster collaborative learning in the hybrid classroom. To enable both physically present and online students to work with one another, educators must consider how the class might be organised differently pedagogically, technologically and spatially.

The hybrid classroom requires learning environments which are hyper-flexible and tech-enabled to provide enough choice for educators and learners who are physically co-present to personalise the way they will work with their online peers. In this regard, it is important to acknowledge the practical, technical and digital challenges of a successful hybrid lesson.

Learning from the hybrid workplace, we can now apply these lessons to educational environments too:

Any information that would help the students with the lesson needs to be shared prior to the lesson, which includes the structure/agenda of the lesson so everyone starts on the same page and can follow the progression of the lesson.

Testing technology prior to the start of the lesson. All participants should test that their devices and headsets work sometime before the start of the lesson. That will make the beginning of the lesson smoother and will save time for everyone.

Providing for all participants headsets or high-quality microphones that will pick up audio from across the entire classroom. Certain meeting software and headsets allow for a smoother experience when multiple people have their microphones on and talk while in the same room.

A large screen to allow participants online to have 'live size' within the room and allow for equal presence and as a reminder to include the students at home.

Smart Cameras that automatically zoom in on one speaker or zoom out to the group.

Think about what the remote students/teachers will perceive—what would make them engage the most—seeing a presentation, the room of students, the teacher explaining or all of this at once?

Acoustics—poor acoustics can be very distracting. Making sure the sound flows correctly and is not bouncing off hard surfaces like floors, walls and hard non-absorbent furniture is key to any classroom design, especially the hybrid classroom.

The interior design and surfaces should be considered for better acoustics and sound experience.

If possible, there should be a helper (this could be a student) to monitor the chat and the online interactions. And of course, technical support or IT staff should be at hand to troubleshoot, particularly for the first run of such lessons.

In terms of the learning activities to be carried out during the hybrid lesson, each task or learning assignment should be challenging enough to require multiple voices and answers and equal responsibility from each student to solve the problem. To achieve this, the educator should allow students to express their diverse talents and skills. How can they as individuals use their skills to contribute to the learning at hand while also learning from each other? Students will feel appreciated if their voice is heard and valued, and that will inspire them to contribute to the conversation no matter where they are located or what skills they have.

Another equally important part of collaboration is peer-to-peer sharing of ideas and feedback. Getting students to present to the rest of the class is critical. Students online and in class should regularly share what they have accomplished and their understanding and interpretation. Sharing should be done in a 'safe' environment, without fear of one's ideas being rejected. As part of the process, students should learn how to deliver and receive constructive feedback and use it to their benefit.

Group assignments actively engage students with the learning material at hand. To make them successful, the educators should help facilitate group conversations within each group, both during live lessons and asynchronously. At times, mixed on-site and online learners form hybrid groups; at other times on-site and online groups work separately, before presenting to each other. Where possible, teachers can join online forums and contribute to the conversation. In this way, students accessing learning only online will feel equally supported.

Teachers and students together can select the best platforms and digital tools for the synchronous learning activities.

Helping students understand that no matter where they are, all voices are equally important and valued will build their self-confidence and prepare them for the world of work, where working from home while being online is likely to be normalised. Virtual collaboration will likely continue to prevail alongside in-person interaction. Hence, as educators, we should make it a priority to support our students develop the needed skills and abilities to succeed by providing hybrid learning experiences which mirror these new work dynamics.

Bibliography

Nobre, P., Cubbison, E. and Bulgart, A. (n.d.) Designing for All Learners: 5 Myths Debunked. [Blog] *Dialogue blog*, Available at: https://www.gensler.com/blog/designing-for-all-learners-5-myths-debunked

O'Byrne, W. and Pytash, K. (2015). Hybrid and Blended Learning. *Journal of Adolescent & Adult Literacy*, 59, 137–140. doi: 10.1002/jaal.463

> **Inclusivity note**
>
> Hybrid lessons are more flexible but they do not eliminate the need for other types of academic support for students.
>
> Once ground rules and clear expectations are set (including the use of microphones and cameras on/off), in order not to disadvantage the online participants, teachers need to see the two groups as one, build a sense of community and use the chat or other backchannels to receive ongoing feedback about the lesson.
>
> The biggest challenge is the cognitive load for teachers. Besides rethinking how the lesson develops, a key issue is getting the technology to work for the types of planned learning activities. Having the right technology and appropriate support is vital.
>
> The use of hybrid lessons supports in particular students who are not able to join live on-site lessons, such as poorer students (it saves on expensive commuting) and those with caring responsibilities. Where hybrid/hyflex is not possible, but as teachers we'd like to provide similar benefits, we could run on-site lessons and shorter, online 'catch up' lessons.

As the case study illustrated, once we have the right technology and support in place, the key is in intentionally designing suitable activities that blend the on-site and online participants and make them feel equally valued during the live lesson.

Besides planned live synchronous lessons, another example of such integrated use of hybrid learning is to organise an **e-trip**: a field or other educational trip where some students are able to physically travel to the destination and engage with on-site activities and experiences, while others who are not able to join in person can do so digitally—they can watch their peers, interact with them synchronously, ask questions, follow the development of the trip. If we plan both experiences in parallel, everyone will have a meaningful share whether they are physically present or digitally connected.

As we settle in new post-pandemic hybrid learning blends, we may want to intentionally pilot *some* synchronous hybrid sessions. Interestingly, due to the required integration of technology, the design of blended learning is increasingly the result of collaboration between learning technologists and discipline specialists, crossing boundaries and blending roles.

From hybrid spaces, we now move to fully online learning.

The digital learning spaces

The digital world is fast-moving, and the novel technological tools released at a fast pace create new possibilities that deeply affect the way we teach and learn such as the experimental 'metaversities' or immersive virtual reality campuses. Teaching, learning, research and technology are so deeply entangled that it does not make sense (anymore) to separate them—they form an overall pedagogical ecosystem.

Digital learning spaces are populated by more and more fully online courses, which present their own distinct challenges in terms of inclusive learning design. Taking a critical pedagogy stance, Morris and Stommel (2018) state that 'teaching online, designing online learning, is in fact an act of learning online ... both learning in an online environment and learning what "online" even means'. This is a good way to look at it, because, arguably, learning to teach online is a challenging threshold for individual academics and institutions: one of the biggest challenges for traditional education providers wanting to develop digital learning is being able to design education experiences that are not very time and place *dependent*. It is also recognising that there is unpredictability in the way students engage with educational technology: 'there is only a loose connection between how you intend or expect your students to engage with particular technologies, and what they will actually do (or even which technologies they will actually use)' (Fawns et al. 2020).

The **design of the virtual learning environment** (VLE) used by a course, even if it is run mostly on site, should receive at least the same attention as the physical space design as it constitutes the digital home base of the course, not a simple content repository. The materials on the VLE should be an evolving, curated collection with signposts and interactive elements, integrated with on-site lessons.

Nearly all teachers in higher education are expected to use and contribute to the recommended VLE and while two decades ago very few of us needed to *produce* online multimedia materials, now very few of us can escape doing so. However, not all institutions are fully aware of or compliant with the government guidelines for digital accessibility of public digital spaces. Yet, this is an essential first step towards inclusivity. You can check the latest guidance and regulations at www.gov.uk/government/digital-accessibility.

Before embarking on learning design at course level, it is imperative that in our role as teachers, we carry out a thorough, critical **technology audit**. First, we need to determine the digital access and accessibility needs of our students. Second, we need to get the big picture of what we have access to: what is the recommended VLE? What other software and tools are available through the university? Then we need to analyse the affordances of each tool, and particularly of the VLE we are going to use. What does it allow us to do? How easily? What accessibility does it require? What are its limitations? What additional tools does it easily integrate with? At this point we can determine what mix of tools suits us and our students and this allows us to facilitate engagement with the curriculum according to our educational values, bearing in mind that there is no neutral technology: every educational software stems from particular philosophies of teaching and learning whether these have been acknowledged or not.

Many digital platforms tend to give control almost exclusively to the teacher, for instance student-to-student interaction is not possible unless it is in response to a *teacher-initiated* post or communication. Students and teachers should be more fully involved 'in design decisions related to the adoption and use of technologies in their institutions, and in the selection of technologies that promote student self-determination rather than external control' (Bali and Zamorra 2022).

Our digital space needs to be welcoming, well organised, easy to navigate and inclusive. We should either co-create it with students or at the very least consult them as soon as the space is ready and goes live to check what enhancements we can make for it to be more accessible to all.

For live online lessons, to create a principled learning space, it is vital to establish appropriate, shared ground rules such as background space, use of the chat, raising hands and cameras on/off during live lessons as well as general *netiquette*. It is important to 'humanise' our online course by incorporating 'kindness cues of social inclusion'

(Estrada et al. 2018) especially into the 'high opportunity zone' of a course, which is 'the week prior to the start of instruction and the first week of a class' (Pacansky-Brock 2020).

A useful model for teachers and teacher educators to build more inclusive online spaces is Gilly Salmon's five-stage model, which promotes 'digital empathy' (Salmon 2021). The following case study discusses how teacher educators can use Salmon's model and UDL principles to set up and *model* a more inclusive online learning space, in particular for teacher-students.

Socialisation and engagement online using Gilly Salmon's Carpe Diem and five-stage model: A case study from the University of Stirling

By Ros Walker (Scotland)

Learning institutions have not always provided the best online environment for supporting students (Wheeler 2015). Online resources can consist of a collection of files, with little signposting, varying amounts of interaction, and resources, lacking in context and narrative, often leaving students bewildered.

The challenge facing us as teacher educators was to develop a framework to make our modules more accessible and to improve the student experience. We did this in four steps:

Choose and adapt a learning framework:

We wanted to use a simple approach to curriculum planning that could be readily understood by academic staff whatever their level of teaching experience, applicable to both online and face-to-face courses. It was also essential to make sure that modules built in accessibility. We wanted to use 'Universal Design for Learning (UDL) principles' to ensure that content is 'born accessible' and flexible enough for any adjustments to be made (Rose 2007).

After examining several models for online learning, we chose to base our new approach around Gilly Salmon's 'five-stage model' and her 'Carpe Diem' model—'a team-based approach to learning design'.

The five-stage model shows how learning (particularly online) moves through five stages.

1. **Access and motivation**: How to access the system and feel welcome
2. **Online socialisation**: Getting to know others on the course and your tutor
3. **Information exchange**: Begin learning, but also using discussion with peers
4. **Knowledge construction**: Students begin to take charge of their own learning and build their learning

5   **Development**: A much more 'free flow' stage in which the tutor steps back and allows the students to take full control (with support still available) but students support each other and learn together.

This model can be built into the Carpe Diem model where these stages take place over a number of weeks or months. They form the 'foundation' layer, onto which the tutor maps the learning objectives and how these can be attained through content, activity and interaction.

We chose this approach because it was simple to understand, provided an ideal basis for a training course for staff and could be readily adapted to the needs of different disciplines across the University.

Demonstrating to staff how it works:

We wanted staff to 'buy into' the model, because they had experienced it themselves and could see that it worked. We offered a course which would allow them to learn in the new environment. The course would *model* inclusive approaches and accessible design and would stress the 'human' interactions that take place in learning. As part of the course all staff learn about accessible design and consider how they approach the 'protected characteristics' mentioned in the UK Equality Act. Staff are encouraged to look objectively at any bias or prejudice in their course or towards their students (AdvanceHE 2015).

A new VLE template

Hand-in-hand with the experiential course, we designed a new template for the VLE which is designed to be fully user-friendly and accessible. It walks students through their course, with each week or topic mapped and embedded into a narrative. It is no longer possible for tutors to upload a document, file or image without some commentary and an 'active learning' task for students.

A 'planner' for inclusion

Once familiar with the approaches and template, staff are encouraged to use the Microsoft Office365 Planner to develop their own module(s). There is a focus on inclusion embedded into every step from disability to protected characteristics. Staff begin with overall Development Details and then work collaboratively online to complete a detailed plan before they move to develop content on the VLE itself—see Figure 1.4.

The outcome of this approach has been an institution-wide change to module design with all modules being remodelled for the 2020–2021 academic year.

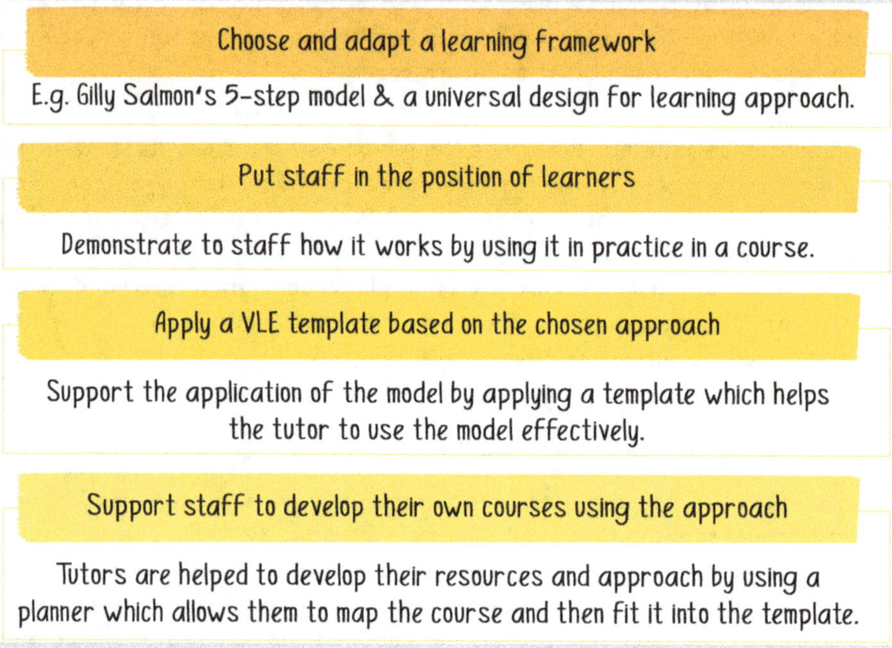

Choose and adapt a learning framework
E.g. Gilly Salmon's 5-step model & a universal design for learning approach.

Put staff in the position of learners
Demonstrate to staff how it works by using it in practice in a course.

Apply a VLE template based on the chosen approach
Support the application of the model by applying a template which helps the tutor to use the model effectively.

Support staff to develop their own courses using the approach
Tutors are helped to develop their resources and approach by using a planner which allows them to map the course and then fit it into the template.

Figure 1.4 Four steps to model a more inclusive online learning design framework.

Bibliography

AdvanceHE (2015). Embedding Equality and Diversity in the Curriculum Discipline-Specific Guides | Advance HE. [online] Available at: https://www.advance-he.ac.uk/knowledge-hub/embedding-equality-and-diversity-curriculum-discipline-specific-guides

Rose, D. (2007). Universal Design For Learning. [video] Available at: https://www.youtube.com/watch?v=DDCNZ9cN3SM&t=2s

Salmon, G. (n.d.). Carpe Diem Learning Design. [online] Gilly Salmon. Available at: https://www.gillysalmon.com/carpe-diem.html

Wheeler, S. (2015). *Learning with 'E's*. Carmarthen, Wales: Crown House Publishing.

Inclusivity note

Besides the way the VLE is structured, to support neurodivergent and non-native speakers, all digital teaching materials should be available on the virtual learning environment in such a way that students can access them when they are needed, before or after formal teaching.

We should also aim at improving the accessibility of all digital materials we provide on the VLE by doing the following *at a minimum*, by default:

- signposting (for instance using pins and subheadings)
- appropriate use of font and colours
- checking compatibility of tools with screen readers and screen magnifiers
- using 'alternative text' (alt text) for all digital images
- using captions for videos

Online learning is often regarded as more user-friendly for students with disabilities. However, we need to check with each student who has declared a disability what their specific learning and support needs are in terms of tools, technology and other supports.

This example demonstrates the importance for teacher educators to *model* the approaches they promote by selecting an approach or framework and then building their teacher education course around it, so student-teachers can 'live' the model, because it can be hard to fully grasp the affordances and limitations of a learning design model or approach unless they *experience* it.

The ideas and principles discussed in this case study are not just for teacher educators—Gilly Salmon's five stages is a very useful framework for *all* teachers, irrespective of field of study, who are designing online courses. The ideas I discuss in this section very much relate to the first two stages of the five-stage model: (1) access and motivation and (2) online socialisation. By taking the time to design the online learning space in a welcoming and supporting way, we remove barriers and pave the way for students' success.

We have come to the last aspect of learning spaces I address in this chapter. It is a special type of digital learning space: the mobile one.

The mobile learning spaces

Nearly all our students join our courses with an existing, evolving digital identity. We live in a 'distributed technology–human environment' where, as professionals, we need to develop 'capabilities to work with different kinds of knowledge and embrace diverse ways of knowing that are distributed across humans with different expertise and machines' (Trede et al. 2019). Besides personal use, digital skills and capabilities have become indispensable for professional use: digital communication, creation and collaboration are needed in most jobs our students might do in their future lives. For this reason, using digital and mobile tools to further students' learning is both an opportunity and a duty.

The full integration of mobile technologies in our lives, with everything being one click away in the palm of our hands, has changed students' expectations when it comes to their university course: mobile, flexible learning is gradually becoming an expectation, although not all the universities and academics are prepared for it. We should view mobile devices as a type of digital learning space. Indeed, the ubiquitous presence of mobile devices, even in poor or remote areas, makes it an ideal platform for learning. The VLE spills into the mobile environment through apps and other tools. There is even the possibility of creating a 'Mobile Virtual Campus' (Tan et al. 2010). As academics we should look for opportunities to more fully integrate the possibilities offered by mobile digital tools and platforms into the digitally enhanced or fully digital learning experiences and environments we design. In designing digital, mobile friendly learning, open educational resources (OER) can help in terms of affordable access to resources, especially in disciplines requiring very expensive textbooks, although there might still be issues of resources accessibility.

Contentiously, Boehm (2021) writes: 'We cannot "own" knowledge anymore, we do not need to "curate" knowledge anymore. We should focus our efforts on the design of learning environments, where knowledge is brought in by learners from all directions, and where academics are empowered to facilitate the act of learning by flexibly shaping this environment'. One of the directions from which students bring knowledge into the learning space is through their mobile devices, viewed as a tool for learning enhancement rather than a source of distraction. I advocate designing learning experiences to bring learning into the students' daily spaces via mobile devices.

The following case study discusses the affordances of using mobile technology for teaching and learning in the classroom. It is more provocative in nature than strictly practical and it offers a critical perspective on mobile technology.

Understanding the bridge that divides us: Can mobile technologies be the missing link in e-learning?

By Ashiya Abdool Satar (South Africa)

Digital innovation in education gives us the opportunity to create pedagogically dynamic, innovative and interactive learning spaces irrespective of geographical and spatial boundaries. However, despite the rapid advances in technology, the digital divide poses a challenge for promulgating equitable educational opportunities (Jantjies 2020, Soomro et al. 2020). South Africa's educational system, as in most developing countries, is a case in point that showcases historical inequalities, exacerbated by the digital divide. Nonetheless, statistics reveal a positive trend towards digital access through the use of mobile devices that suggests that mobile learning can help bridge the digital divide in education as it provides a solution to the issue of digital access, accessibility and literacy in developing regions. However, while the widescale penetration of mobile devices in developing countries provides immense opportunities for mobile learning, these merits should not overshadow the drawbacks associated with digital repression in developing countries (Feldstein 2021). The argument is that while instructors have a remarkable opportunity to traverse the digital divide through the affordances of mobile learning, the path is laden with the obstacles of digital colonialism that need to be dismantled along the journey of digital innovation (Abdool Satar 2022).

The image (Figure 1.5) refers to the affordances of the mobile learning environment in developing regions that facilitate the three elements of digital inclusion:

- digital access (the procurement of technologies that permits individuals to enter the digital realm),
- digital accessibility (adaptable applications for persons with disabilities and particular learning needs), and
- digital literacy (the knowledge and skills required to manoeuvre the different technologies and applications required for different tasks and environments)

The digital divide centres on issues of access and accessibility. Accessibility, in the form of assistive technologies and applications that make digital tools and online platforms more fit for use, is useful to persons with disabilities and individuals with varying learning needs. Access, on the other hand, refers to the ability to fully participate in the digital society, which includes access to digital apparatuses, such as the Internet and computers; and the proficiencies we need to use these technologies (Moyo 2019).

We refer to the ability to access, manage, understand, integrate, communicate, evaluate and create information safely and appropriately through digital devices

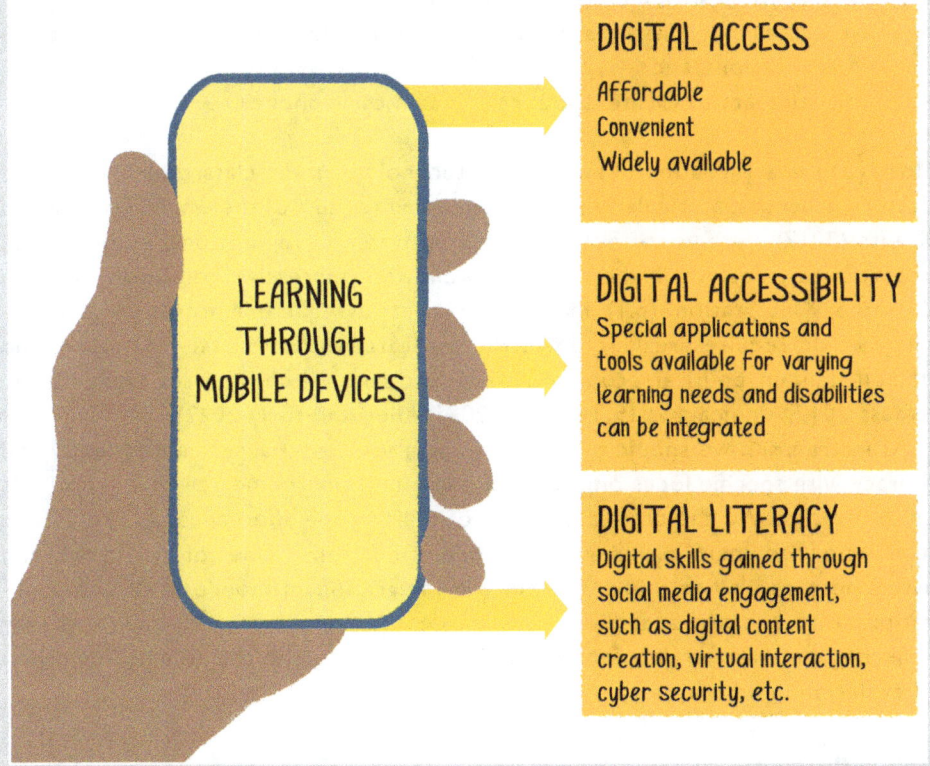

Figure 1.5 Affordances of the mobile learning environment in developing regions.

and networked technologies for e-learning as digital literacy. Digital literacy includes competencies that are variously referred to as: computer literacy, ICT literacy, information literacy and media literacy. Although there is a lack of comprehensive statistics on digital literacy in each country, the Digital Literacy Review (UNESCO 2018) reveals that a lack of digital competence is a barrier to participation in digital and networked communications.

Mobile learning provides a solution to the issue of digital access, accessibility, and literacy in developing regions. The penetration of mobile internet usage in southern Africa, Latin America and the Middle East and North African (MENA) regions provides a pedagogically, technologically and economically sustainable solution to the challenges of the digital divide (Clement 2020). Not only are mobile devices and mobile Internet connections more affordable to students in these regions, but through engaging on social networks on mobile devices students gain valuable digital competency skills. We can capitalise on these digital proficiencies if we structure our courses around a mobile learning environment (Dyson 2016, Jantjies 2020). For instance, we can design instructional resources that:

- are compatible with mobile technologies,
- have accessibility features embedded therein through various mobile tools and applications, and
- allow students to create digital content on their phones.

However, the assimilation of educational technology in the classroom is not without its challenges, particularly in the developing regions of the world. Tshuma and Krauss (2017) alert us to the 'dichotomy between its [educational technology's] potential to transform higher education and the oppressive politics inherent in technology integration' (p.1). In other words, truly equitable access and accessibility would require breaking down the intricate web of digital colonialism and its concomitant political, economic, social and cultural consociates (Tshuma and Krauss 2017, Alhumaid 2019, Feldstein 2021, Allen and Kelly 2022).

As instructors, we should envision and plan for digital access, accessibility and literacy with specific focus on the mobile learning environment, *with a critical lens on our practice*. We can do this in terms of utilising the affordances of the mobile learning environment, planning for the use of different modes of instruction and assessment, as well as thinking about the integration of mobile tools and applications that enhance accessibility for students with disabilities, while critically reflecting on ways to decolonise the digital sphere along this journey of digital (r)evolution in education.

Self-reflection

Would you say that the digital divide is only applicable to the Global South? Think about the rural and remote areas as well as the poorer neighbourhoods in different parts of the world that are digitally redlined. Also, reflect on the privileged areas in the Global South that usually have good infrastructure. What would your analysis be on the digital divide now, as this phenomenon usually hides a spectrum of digital access within both North and South?

Is mobile learning viable within your context? Why do you say so? Where do your students feature on the continuum of digital literacy?

What factors do you need to consider in decolonising the digital sphere in education in terms of access and accessibility in the political, economic, cultural and social milieus?

Would the design and structure of a mobile learning course differ from a conventional online course? **What are some affordances of mobile learning that you might benefit from to enhance or transform the learning experience?**

Taking all these points into consideration, how does this change the way in which you would design learning?

Bibliography

Abdool Satar, A. (2022). Digitally (Dis)Connected: Digitally (De)Colonized. In Fovet, F. (Ed.) *Implementing Transformative Student-Centered Pedagogies in the Neoliberal Academy: Constraints and Opportunities.* India: CSMFL Publications (Still in Print).

Alhumaid, K. (2019). Four Ways Technology Has Negatively Changed Education. *Journal of Educational and Social Research,* 9(4), 10–20. Available at: https://www.mcser.org/journal/index.php/jesr/article/view/10526/10155

Allen, N. and Kelly, C.L. (2022). Deluge of Digital Repression Threatens African Security. Africa Center for Strategic Studies, [online]. Available at: https://africacenter.org/spotlight/deluge-digital-repression-threatens-african-security/

Clement, J. (2020). Global Digital Population as of April 2020. Statista [online]. Available at: https://www.statista.com/statistics/617136/digital-population-worldwide/

Dyson, L. (2016). Achieving Sustainable Mobile Learning through Student-owned Devices and Student-generated Multimedia Content. In Ng, W. and Cumming, T. (Ed.) *Sustaining Mobile Learning Theory: Research and Practice* (1st ed., pp. 212–227) [online]. London: Routledge. Available at:https://www.routledge.com/Sustaining-Mobile-Learning-Theory-research-and-practice/Ng-Cumming/p/book/9781138787384?utm_source=shared_link&utm_medium=post&utm_campaign=B190504862

Feldstein, S. (2021). Digital Technology's Evolving Role in Politics, Protest and Repression: The Cycle of Technological Innovation Will Continue to Power a Global Cat-and-Mouse Struggle between Autocrats and Those Who Oppose Them. Available at: https://www.usip.org/publications/2021/07/digital-technologys-evolving-role-politics-protest-and-repression

Jantjies, M. (2020). How South Africa Can Address Digital Inequalities in e-learning. The Conversation [online] Available at: https://theconversation.com/how-south-africa-can-address-digital-inequalities-in-e-learning-137086

Moyo, R. (2019). Adoption of Information and Communication Technologies in Teaching and Learning at a University. *South African Journal of Higher Education,* 33(5), 42–60. doi: 10.20853/33-5-3592

Soomro, K., Kale, U., Curtis, R., Akcaoglu, M. and Bernstein, M. (2020). Digital divide among higher education faculty. *International Journal of Educational Technology in Higher Education*, 17(1). doi: 10.1186/s41239-020-00191-5

Tshuma, N. and Krauss, K.E.M. (2017). Towards Using Critical Reflection to Interrogate the Oppressive Effects of Educational Technology Use in South African Higher Education. Available at: https://www.researchgate.net/publication/316999364_Towards_using_critical_reflection_to_interrogate_the_oppressive_effects_of_educational_technology_use_in_South_African_higher_education

UNESCO (2018). *Global Education Monitoring Report, 2019: Migration, Displacement and Education: Building Bridges, Not Walls* (2nd ed.). Paris: UNESCO. Available at: https://unesdoc.unesco.org/ark:/48223/pf0000265866

Inclusivity note

With new trends such as influencer educators who have millions of followers on social media platforms, mobile learning is more and more interwoven with students' daily lives. However, the main inclusivity challenge with students using mobile platforms for learning is *multi-layered digital inequality* in terms of differences in access to equipment and bandwidth, and also differences in technological ability and competence (accessibility), which in turn affect motivation.

How many of our students access learning mostly through their mobile, on the go? Once we find out, we can acknowledge this by prefacing an activity or lesson with:

- ways of preparing for efficient mobile learning (suggest students download apps such as voice-to-text to take notes on the go and revisit later on)
- ways of maximising mobile learning time (suggest to dedicate 20 or 30 minutes of focused time at a time to understand the key points of the lesson, rather than very long study sessions)
- empathy (suggest to students that if their learning space gets too crowded and noisy, due to life's duties such as caring responsibilities, they may have to postpone the planned mobile learning session to a quieter moment when they can concentrate)
- screen well-being tips (such as avoiding straining the eyes, taking regular breaks from screens, minding posture and more)

For international cohorts, it is also useful to understand what mobile tools and apps are popular in the students' home country and use those alongside the one(s) we are familiar with.

Head to the companion website (under Section 2) for an additional case study by Zachary Walker (UK) entitled 'Why embracing mobile learning is key for inclusivity and the future'.

Both these narratives show that mobile 'back pocket' learning (Middleton 2015) can unlock more accessible and inclusive education, but it must be managed well and not taken uncritically. The pandemic has at once shown what can be done remotely and it has also magnified the problems for those struggling with digital connectivity (students who relied on campus devices and connectivity were greatly disadvantaged). And there is much work needed to empower students to become digitally competent. Hence, whatever mobile technology or tool we intend to use to enhance teaching and learning we need to have a critical eye towards it, and always consider access, accessibility and digital poverty issues.

Asynchronous digital learning has its own challenges. To help students navigate such challenges, based on the 'intentionally equitable' and 'nurturing' principles discussed in Section 1, it is useful to engage them in regular learning awareness reflection exercises (Gopal 2022). We could propose questions such as:

- What digital devices and tools did you use to engage with the learning? What are their affordances and limitations?
- What physical space were you in when you accessed the lesson? What helped/hindered your learning there?
- What mental and emotional space were you in? How can you create suitable conditions for cognitive engagement while you study?

These questions communicate to students that we are aware and empathise with the challenges of asynchronous, digital learning (Gopal 2022) and that we are their learning *ally*, assisting them so they can succeed.

Having read about the pedagogically sound reasons to make use of mobile technologies in class, you may be eager to integrate them on your own courses. In this book you will find a number of practice case studies that showcase innovative ways of using mobile technologies: Chapter 3 has a case study about using WhatsApp to support students at assessment time; Chapter 7 has a case study about 'photovoice' and how students can create very meaningful assessment outputs straight from their mobile phones. Other case studies demonstrate approaches that work particularly well with mobile technologies such as online reading lists (Chapter 6) and using podcasts (Chapter 7).

Besides these mobile learning examples, every new or existing app or tool has the potential to be used for educational purposes. For example, some social media platforms such as Twitter can be used live, even during lessons, to reach out to very large external audiences for more authentic learning. We could also combine mobile learning with physical movement: with walking classrooms students walk and post or walk and chat (with peers through a suitable mobile platform) while engaging with some learning prompts or questions. The possibilities are truly endless.

Conclusion

In this chapter I reviewed the affordances of physical, blended, digital and mobile learning spaces. Although I addressed the various types of spaces separately, this was to highlight how we can leverage their affordances to design more inclusive learning. It is important to note that the physical, blended, digital and mobile learning spaces that we use on our courses overlap and form a *learning ecosystem* that is deeply interconnected.

Peter Bryant (2022) has written a series of blog posts about connected learning, where he states: 'Our definition of *connected learning* recognises the powerful affordances that come from designing a teaching and learning experience that supports students to engage, create, critique, reflect and learn in social settings across a complex ecosystem of networks and engagements'. One key way of making connected learning a reality is by 'making learning through media truly synchronously asynchronous, where time, space and location don't limit the capacity to connect and engage with information and each other' (Bryant 2022). Designing learning in a way that supports students to create meaningful connections both with concepts and people supports the academic and social growth of our students in the short and long term.

Of course, the effectiveness of all the learning spaces we have access to needs to be checked continually, not just at initial learning design stage. Perhaps it can also be specifically addressed in mid-term or mid-course evaluations where students can have a say in more formal ways about the impact of the learning environment on their learning experience.

At the start of this chapter, I proposed these reflection prompts:

> **Activate your inner dialogue. ... How would you answer?**
>
> What impact do physical and digital spaces and places have on learning?
> How can you design the physical and digital spaces more inclusively?

My attempted answers, which sum up this chapter are:

Digital and physical spaces greatly affect the creation of a learning *place*, from a cognitive, social and emotional perspective. Our use of spaces matters not only for the academic growth of students, but also to support them develop their social presence, in both physical and digital learning spaces. Most learning experiences today are a blend of various spaces and this has created a plethora of learning possibilities, at scale, that would have been hard to imagine just a few years ago. By carrying out an audit of the affordances of the physical and digital spaces at our disposal we will have a clearer picture of their affordances and limitations. This will enhance our empathy for our students' access and accessibility needs and will allow us to make the best use of the spaces where we prompt learning to create inclusive leaning *places*.

The design of the space goes hand in hand with the needs analysis of the space *users*. In the next chapter I discuss these further as well as related contextual factors: the initial needs analysis and the orientation we set up for our courses.

Bibliography

Adams Becker, S., Cummins, M., Davis, A., Freeman, A., Hall Giesinger, C. and Ananthanarayanan, V. (2017). NMC Horizon Report: 2017 Higher Education Edition. Austin, TX: The New Media Consortium.

AdvanceHE. (n.d.) Blended Learning. [online] Available at: https://www.advance-he.ac.uk/knowledge-hub/blended-learning-0

Baker, N. (2022). Hyflex Pedagogies: From Pandemic Panacea to a Permanent Fixture on the Higher Education Landscape. *Educational Developments*, 23(1) (ISSN 1469 - 326).

Bali, M. and Zamora, M. (2022). The Equity-Care Matrix: Theory and Practice. *Italian Journal of Educational Technology*, 30(1), 92–115.. doi: 10.17471/2499-4324/1241

Beatty, B.J. (2019). *Hybrid-Flexible Course Design* (1st ed.). EdTech Books. https://edtechbooks.org/hyflex

Boehm, C. (2021). A Letter to Those Leading Universities for the Future. [Blog] WonkHE. Available at: https://wonkhe.com/blogs/a-letter-to-those-leading-universities-for-the-future/

Bryant, P. (2021). Making the Most of the Spaces We Have: Design Principles for Successful Hybrid and Hyflex Learning. [Blog] The University of Sydney Co-design Research Group Blog, Available at: https://cdrg.blog/2021/10/08/making-the-most-of-the-spaces-we-have-design-principles-for-successful-hybrid-and-hyflex-learning/

Bryant, P. (2022). Transforming Business Education Through Connected Learning—Part 3. [Blog] The University of Sydney Co-design Research Group Blog. Available at: https://cdrg.blog/2022/03/03/transforming-business-education-through-connected-learning-part-3/

Building the Anti-Racist Classroom (BARC) (n.d.). *Principled Space*. [online] Available at: https://barcworkshop.org/resources/principled-space/

Doorley, S., Witthoft, S. and Kelley, D. (2012). *Make Space*. Hoboken, NJ: John Wiley & Sons.

Elkington, S. and Bligh, B. (2019). *The Physical University—Contours of Space and Place in Higher Education*. [online] York: AdvanceHE. Available at: https://research.tees.ac.uk/ws/portalfiles/portal/6770557/Future_Learning_Spaces.pdf

Estrada, M., Eroy-Reveles, A. and Matsui, J. (2018). The Influence of Affirming Kindness and Community on Broadening Participation in STEM Career Pathways: Kindness, Community, & STEM. *Social Issues and Policy Review*, 12, 258–297. doi: 10.1111/sipr.12046

Fawns, T. (2022). An Entangled Pedagogy: Looking Beyond the Pedagogy—Technology Dichotomy. *Postdigital Science and Education*. doi: 10.1007/s42438-022-00302-7

Fawns, T., Aitken, G. and Jones, D. (2020). Explaining and Applying a Postdigital Perspective on Curriculum Design and Teaching. In *UoE Learning and Teaching Conference 2020*. [online] Edinburgh. Available at: https://media.ed.ac.uk/media/1_bp8346zs

Gopal, N. (2022). The Peculiar Case of Space and Its Relationship with Equity in Asynchronous Online Learning. [online] facultyfocus.com. Available at: https://www.facultyfocus.com/articles/online-education/online-course-delivery-and-instruction/the-peculiar-case-of-space-and-its-relationship-with-equity-in-asynchronous-online-learning/

Gunawardena, C.N., Frechette, C. and Layne, L. (2018). *Culturally Inclusive Instructional Design: A Framework and Guide for Building Online Wisdom Communities* (1st ed.). Routledge. doi: 10.4324/9781315439204

Hattie, J. (2015). *What Doesn't Work in Education: The Politics of Distraction*. London: Pearson.

Hillman, T. (2022). [Twitter] 1 April. Available at: https://twitter.com/thomhillman/status/1509773871901196289?s=27

Krajewski, S. and Khoury, M. (2018). Daring Spaces: The Rise and Demise of an Alternative Space for International Student Groups in a University Setting. *Learning Environments Research*, 89–113.

Krajewski, S. and Khoury, M. (2021). Daring Spaces: Creating Multi-sensory Learning Environments. *Learning and Teaching*, 14(1), 89–113. doi: 10.3167/latiss.2021.140105

Lave, J. and Wenger, E. (1990). *Situated Learning: Legitimate Peripheral Participation*. Cambridge: Cambridge University Press.

Leijon, M. and Lundgren, B. (2019). Connecting Physical and Virtual Spaces in a HyFlex Pedagogic Model with a Focus on Teacher Interaction. *Journal of Learning Spaces*, 8(1). Available at: http://libjournal.uncg.edu/jls/article/view/1640

McArthur, J. (2008). Instructional Proxemics: Creating a Place for Space in Instructional Communication Discourse. All Dissertations. 197. Available at: https://tigerprints.clemson.edu/all_dissertations/197

Middleton, A. (Ed.). (2015). Smart Learning: Teaching and Learning with Smartphones and Tablets in Post-compulsory Education. Sheffield Hallam University, MELSIG.

Morris, S.M. and Stommel, J. (2018). *An Urgency of Teachers: The Work of Critical Digital Pedagogy*. Hybrid Pedagogy Inc.

Pacansky-Brock, M. (2020). How to Humanize Your Online Class, version 2.0 [Infographic]. https://brocansky.com/humanizing/infographic2

Salmon, G. (2021). *Digital Empathy Using the 5 Stage Model*. Available at: https://www.youtube.com/watch?app=desktop&v=S2pBAl_6fbg

Sheail, P. (2018). The Digital University and the Shifting Time–Space of the Campus. *Learning, Media and Technology*, 43(1), 56–69. doi: 10.1080/17439884.2017.1387139

Tan, Q., Yu-Lin Jeng, K. and Huang, Y. (2010). A Collaborative Mobile Virtual Campus System Based on Location-Based Dynamic Grouping. In *Proceedings of the 2010 10th IEEE International Conference on Advanced Learning Technologies (ICALT '10)*. IEEE Computer Society, 16–18. doi: 10.1109/ICALT.2010.11

Temple, P. (2014). *The Physical University – Contours of Space and Place in Higher Education*. Oxon: Routledge.

Trede, F., Markauskaite, L., McEwen, C. and Macfarlane, S. (2019). Epistemic Fluency and Mobile Technology: A Professional-Plus Perspective. In *Education for Practice in a Hybrid Space*. Understanding Teaching-Learning Practice. Singapore: Springer. doi: 10.1007/978-981-13-7410-4_12

UNESCO (2012). *A Place to Learn: Lessons from Research on Learning Environments*. [online] Montreal: UNESCO. Available at: https://unesdoc.unesco.org/ark:/48223/pf0000215468

Chapter 2

Steady? Needs analysis and orientation

> To teach in a manner that respects and cares for the souls of our students is essential if we are to provide the necessary conditions where learning can mostly deeply and intimately begin
>
> bell hooks

This chapter is about two related pedagogical actions we should take at the start of a course: needs analysis and orientation. Needs analysis is about the crucial steps we take to get to know and understand who our students are; what their academic, social, cultural and emotional capital is; and what their needs are in each area. The needs analysis is part of a wider process of contextual analysis and orientation to the course. Orientation here refers to something besides and beyond the overall, generic 'induction' students usually experience when they join a university. It refers to a course orientation *phase* which supports the various transitions students experience while at university.

> **Activate your inner dialogue. ... How would you answer?**
>
> How can you find out the needs of the students in your cohorts before and at the start of the course?
> How can you set up inclusive orientation activities to support transition into your course?

When designing a course, the first and main things we need to define are: its purpose; its audience and the relationship between the two. Even if you run courses that have been formally set up by others through internal quality systems, you are likely aware of the *raison d'être* of your course and where it fits in the wider programmes and institutional offer. In the early stages of course design, and again just before the course starts, in order to design its inclusive implementation, it is very useful to think once more about the purpose of the course and then relate this to the students it is for. Before any other learning design activity you may engage with, you may want to jot down a few lines about: what is this course about, what is it for and who is it for? Once you have articulated that, you can start making links with prospective students through a needs analysis.

I will first discuss the needs analysis and then the orientation to the course.

Needs analysis

Getting to know your students and ascertaining their needs is a multi-step, recursive process. In most cases, we can identify three key stages in the life of a course when students' needs analysis is *particularly* useful: at initial design stage, shortly before the course is due to start and at the start of the course.

The first opportunity to carry out needs analysis is during the initial stages of learning design, when we can come up with likely student *personas*: expected profiles of students, based on the type of course, demographics and context of the institution. The use of personas comes with a warning: these models representing potential students can reinforce stereotypes, hence it is important to add or bear in mind students who may be very different from expected or *typical* personas. The main point of creating these personas is to proceed to a 'systematic analysis of what matters to the individual for whom we are designing learning' (Shackleton-Jones 2019). In this way we can ensure that our offer is relevant to and suitable for the intended audience.

Once students start enrolling on a course, we have a second opportunity for students' needs analysis: a *literal* reality check. At enrolment and admission stage the institution is likely to gather some basic data about the students formally joining the course. Although the timing, quantity and quality of information you are given about your cohort varies greatly from institution to institution, in most cases, it's *not* enough for us as academics to further our learning design by tailoring the course to the needs of the 'students *who turned up*' (Fawns et al. 2021), because it is unlikely that we get enough information *of the type that we need* on our students from the admission process. Hence, our biggest chance to find out more about who they are, what they are interested in and what learning needs they have, is by putting in place our own needs analysis when the course starts and we meet the students.

In this chapter I make the case for teachers to have an active role in setting up appropriate initial needs analysis, perhaps as part of the wider course induction/orientation process. Of course, this needs to complement (not replace) admission processes and must be done in full respect of privacy laws and internal policies. The reason it is a good idea for teachers to carry out a needs analysis is because students are more likely to disclose additional learning requirements to their teacher than through initial enrolment forms, both because as teachers we can explain our rationale behind the types of questions we ask, perhaps in the context of our first lesson, and because this needs analysis happens within the course space, which quickly becomes a student's *family space* within the institution.

It may mean a little extra work on our part to decide how and when to carry out such needs analysis, as well as to analyse the responses and create a classroom profile, but it pays off: this information is invaluable for us to be able to cater for our students' learning needs and to make the course relevant because the 'who' we are teaching should directly impact 'how' we aspire to teach. According to cohort size, needs analysis can take the form of short surveys or questionnaires, talking to students individually or in groups, or even following a few learners around for half a day or a day—this 'job shadowing' can be very revealing and provide us with a much richer context picture as well as better understanding of the daily realities of our students.

As learners' profiles are as 'individual as DNA or fingerprints' (Rose and Strangman 2007), every classroom profile will be spiky in more than one dimension. Learners may have sensory disabilities, neurodiversity, socio-cultural needs, linguistic (dis)abilities and more differences (Gronseth et al. 2020). Through needs analysis we get a sense of the types of diversities we need to design for and gain a better picture of who we need to cater for at curriculum enactment stage, where the designed curriculum is offered to the cohort. Of course, students may decide not to declare a learning need or might not be aware of a particular need they have until they start tackling the assessment on the course, while other needs emerge *during* the course. For this reason, besides an initial learning needs analysis, teachers need to have systems in place to address emergent needs *as they arise* (Cowan 2012).

How should we carry out the needs analysis for it to be as inclusive as we can? How can it be culturally responsive, so as to inform our inclusive learning design at course implementation stage? These questions are addressed in three international case studies to follow: undertaking a needs analysis before the course starts; doing a needs analysis right at the start of a course; and doing a needs analysis before placements using a tool co-created with students.

Head to the companion website inclusivelearningdesign.com (under Section 2) to read a case study by Maida Ali (Pakistan) about 'E-persona cards to get to know your students *before* the course starts'. The narrative demonstrates the value of designing a 'getting to know you' questionnaire in order to create a group profile. Besides a basic skills audit, the questionnaire provides a more holistic picture about students' backgrounds and social contexts (Dirksen 2015). Maida was able to do this *before* her course started, in spite of having a very large cohort.

Unfortunately, many academics operate in systems where it is not possible to communicate with students *before* the course starts. In this case, it is still possible to create a group profile right at the *start* of the course. The next case study, from Eswatini, is about challenging the 'single story' through a students' cultural awareness survey done in lesson 1. Notice the cultural wealth approach taken by the author to become a more culturally responsive teacher.

Challenging the 'single story'

By Nokuthula Vilakati (Eswatini)

The resource selected for this narrative is motivated by an idea encapsulated in a TED Talk on *The Danger of a Single Story*, delivered by Nigerian writer, Chimamanda Ngozi Adichie (2009). The talk warned against the risks of deficit thinking about other cultures as definitive without reservation, by not questioning our biases or prejudices. I used Adichie's talk as an inclusive learning design danger of a single story 'metaphor' during an academic staff development workshop. An overarching aim was to redesign courses by being responsive to the learning needs of diverse groups of students new to distance and blended learning. The workshop was for academic staff working on redesigning blended courses in the University of Eswatini, for a nursing sciences completion programme. The academic staff shared their reflections on how they were challenged to confront preconceived ideas that they had held about non-traditional students' re-entry into higher education study. This case study fits in with currency of knowledge in higher education curriculum studies that tend to lay more emphasis on cultural sensitivity, equity, diversity and inclusion by being cautious about the dangers of the 'single story' (Adichie 2009, Behari-Leak and Mokou 2019, Kieran and Anderson 2019).

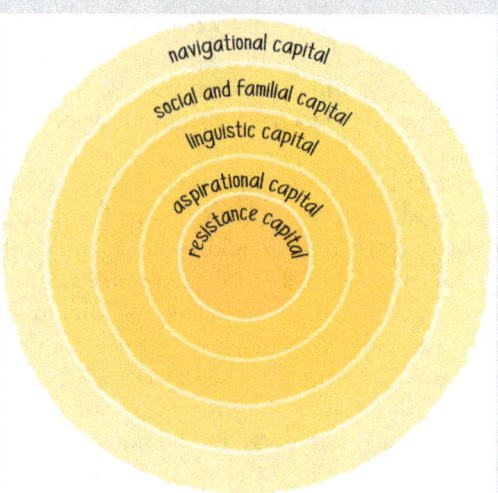

Figure 2.1 Cultural wealth model by Yosso (Adapted from Gurley 2019).

For reflective practice, a cultural wealth conceptual framework (Gurley 2019) provided tools to guide practices on implementing a non-deficit approach to the redesign of distance and blended courses (illustrated in Figure 2.1).

Such a cultural wealth perspective offers course teams alternative ways of valuing various forms of cultural capital that diverse, including non-traditional, students bring to bear as they transition into higher education. Course teams are motivated to adapt a cultural awareness survey to collect microdata on student cultural capital for cultural competence and critical consciousness. In response, lecturers can adapt their pedagogies accordingly by acknowledging cultural and linguistic differences and their effect on non-traditional students' learning as an essential prerequisite to culturally responsive teaching (CRT).

The survey consisted of seven questions, ranging from 'What would you like me to call you?' and 'What is your cultural identity or background?' to 'How can I support you learn?'. Teachers used the digital questionnaire during the first live lesson as part of community building, highlighting that students were free to give as much or as little information as they wished and that responses were going to be kept strictly confidential.

Potential benefits of administering such a cultural awareness survey include habits of mind teachers develop through cultural mindfulness which can include recognition of students' strengths and abilities, backgrounds, skills, cultures, and preferences. Such thinking can enable academic staff to positively regard the benefits of their students' diversity, rather than viewing student difference through a deficit lens. In turn, the students are likely to better navigate their distance and blended learning pathways by assuming more self-directed learning roles alongside the targeted support of lecturers and peers. For example, based on the survey microdata lecturers would be more supportive to high opportunity students who would benefit from more individualised, high-touch communication (Pacansky-Brock et al. 2020). As a result, they would differentiate their input on how to sequence study sessions (what order/progression), pacing (how much time/credit), and student evaluation (what counts for assessment, by opting for a wide array of authentic tasks with varied digital outputs such as infographics and e-portfolios).

Early feedback from some of the academic staff is that many of their diverse—including non-traditional—students have been successful in most of the courses offered in the completion programme. The improved student learning outcomes can be attributed to, among other factors, intentionally designing-in culturally responsive teaching through an equity framework. Such practice is likely to influence course teams towards non-deficit thinking through validation of the cultural capital of differently positioned students learning various courses. Pacansky-Brock et al. (2020) contrast student learning experiences in courses taught by faculty with a growth versus a fixed growth mindset about student ability, mainly influenced by cultural stereotypes. Similarly, Carey et al. (2015) favour varied academic practices that support students' interactions with disciplinary knowledge, through examples of students' own engagement with other forms of knowledge. For example, the design of course learning outcomes and course level assessments can tap into the various forms of capital that the students draw from, including from work-based experiences, in nursing professional practice and community health engagements.

Bibliography

Adichie, C.A. (2009). The Danger of a Single Story. TED: Ideas Worth Spreading. Available at: https://bit.ly/1kMOnud

Behari-Leak, K. and Mokou, G. (2019). Disrupting Metaphors of Coloniality to Mediate Social Inclusion in the Global South. *International Journal for Academic Development*, 24(2), 135–147. doi: 10.1080/1360144X.2019.1594236

Carey, T., Davis, A., Ferreras, S. and Porter, D. (2015). Using Open Educational Practices to Support Institutional Strategic Excellence in Teaching. *Learning & Scholarship. Open Praxis*, 7(2), 161–171. doi: 10.5944/openpraxis.7.2.201

Gurley, A. (2019). Cueltural Wealth Wheel. University of North Texas Libraries, UNT Digital Library. Available at: https://digital.library.unt.edu/ark:/67531/metadc1464202/

Kieran, L. and Anderson, C. (2019). Connecting Universal Design for Learning with Culturally Responsive Teaching. *Education and Urban Society*, 51(9), 1202–1216. doi: 10.1177/0013124518785012

Pacansky-Brock, M., Smedshammer, M. and Vincent-Layton, K. (2020). Humanizing Online Teaching to Equitize Higher Education. *Current Issues in Education*, 21(2). Available at: http://cie.asu.edu/ojs/index.php/cieatasu/article/view/1905

Yosso, T.J. (2005). Whose Culture Has Capital? A Critical Race Theory Discussion of Community Cultural Wealth. *Race, Ethnicity and Education*, 8, 69–91.

> **Inclusivity note**
>
> Setting up an initial students' needs analysis with a focus on cultural capital changes the whole dynamic of a class: teachers see students as carriers of a rich socio-cultural capital that they can tap into for all aspects of learning, including assessment.
>
> To be more inclusive, there are ways in which we can make the initial needs analysis a two-way process: we could answer the questions ourselves (by disclosing something about ourselves we help students see we are also human, with our own fragilities) and we could finish off with something like: I asked you lots of questions, what question(s) would you like to ask me?
>
> One challenge could be that students may share some very sensitive information, perhaps something we are not (professionally) prepared to deal with. For example, due to past trauma or other lived experiences a student may need counselling. In this case, we would reach out to the student(s) in question to let them know about university services and supports they can access to receive help, if they wish.
>
> Students may also share personal views which conflict with our own beliefs or values—here we need to exercise professional judgement and allow the students free speech, as long as it does not endanger others.

The case study you have just read sheds light on the importance of viewing each student as having a rich cultural wealth. By setting up a culturally sensitive initial students' needs analysis, we will be in a much better position to provide culturally responsive learning environments and experiences. Why this matters is well encapsulated in this quote from P. David Pearson (n.d.): 'If you are a kid who believes that your cultural capital doesn't matter in school—you don't have anything to hang your hat on'.

The last case study regarding the initial needs analysis is from Australia and discusses a collaborative activity where students co-created a readiness for learning tool for placements.

> **Co-creating an assessment tool for 'readiness for learning'**
>
> *By Belinda Judd and Jennie Brentnall (Australia)*
>
> Students who are 'ready for learning' are, by definition, positioned to optimise their opportunities, maximising the positives and minimising undue stressors and failures. But readiness to learn can be difficult to quantify. It is rarely explicitly defined and has often been judged from the perspective of the experienced educator. This case study explores an example of co-creating an assessment tool with higher education students, measuring readiness to learn on placements. The tool was originally developed with health sciences students but is broadly applicable across higher education.

Work integrated learning placements with industry partners are crucial experiential learning opportunities for higher education students developing employability skills. Placements are, however, stressful for students (Delany et al. 2015) given that they are highly authentic and therefore consequential, and that learning activities are typically structured around industry activities rather than student learning. Placements are also high stakes and entail reputational, emotional, physical and material risks to students, industry hosts, and stakeholders such as consumers and universities. To minimise the risks of poor performance and optimise learning, it is imperative that students are 'ready for learning' on placements. Therefore, we recognised the need to develop and assess their readiness *before placements commence*.

Most university students are of collaborative and social generations who focus on understanding and building their knowledge in a variety of ways, compelling educators to create environments for engagement and discovery (Monaco and Martin 2007). Seeking to influence students' readiness behaviours, including the ability to manage their own learning, it was critical for us to include the student perspective and voice in our work.

Firstly, we mentored current students to facilitate three focus groups with peers who had been on placement already. These focus groups sought insights from students about what they felt it meant to be ready for placement and what skills and competencies they required. The student-researchers adopted innovative and tailored recruitment strategies to engage their peers, such as a hybrid animated recruitment video presented by students, which participants accessed from QR codes on posters across the campus and peer network sharing. Peer-led conversation also enabled frank discussion. Key findings include that willingness to learn and having a positive attitude and good communication skills were foundational to being ready to begin placements. Cues from the language used by students were also invaluable to making assessment, feedback and learning strategies accessible.

Secondly, students who had already completed both preparation and placements also participated alongside educators in a more traditional, researcher-led, online survey method to determine what critical behaviours and skills they perceive can be assessed in on-campus preparation programs, the relative importance of these, and the thresholds that indicate for them 'readiness' to embark on placement. There was generally agreement between students and staff, generating consensus on what was least feasible and important to develop and assess (professional dress and skills to document patient interactions). There was also evidence that students have more difficulty than educators in prioritising relative importance and might therefore (erroneously) focus on trying to achieve everything in a scattered approach.

With these strategies, we have developed, tested and revised a multidisciplinary assessment of students' readiness for healthcare placements. In practice, the tool consists of a 20-item assessment, covering domains of learner and professional behaviour, information gathering, communication and reasoning. The tool is typically completed by educators after several observations of student performance and can also be used to facilitate self and peer assessment and feedback. Educators use the data gathered to engage students in feedback conversations about their performance and to direct students to tailored support and remediation activities prior to the start of placements. Figure 2.2 sums up the elements we have discussed.

This assessment is well-accepted across institutions and disciplines. It is accompanied by other tools and approaches that continue to incorporate student perspectives to also successfully engage students in self-reflection. We have also utilised interactive technologies to further personalise student engagement with feedback and strategies for ongoing development.

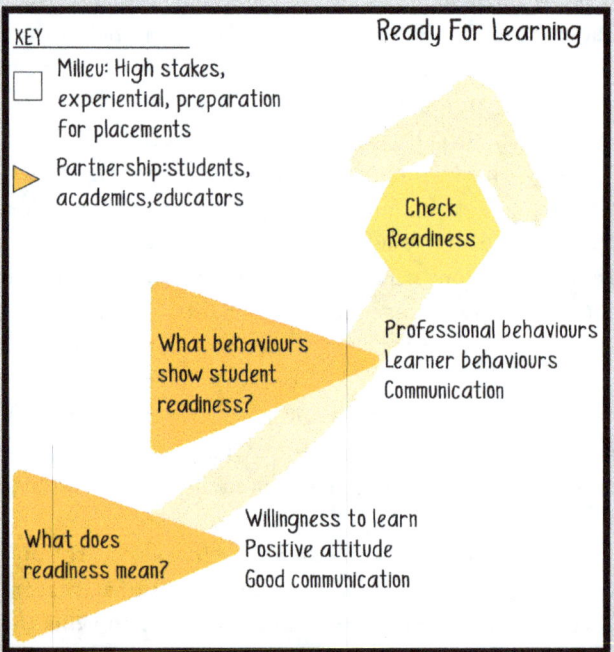

Figure 2.2 The 'readiness for learning on placements' journey.

Bibliography

Delany, C., Miller, K., El-Ansary, D., Remedios, L., Hosseini, A. and McLeod, S. (2015). Replacing Stressful Challenges with Positive Coping Strategies: A Resilience Program for Clinical Placement Learning. *Advances in Health Sciences Education*, 20(5), 1303–1324.

Monaco, M. and Martin, M. (2007). The Millennial Student: A New Generation of Learners. *Athletic Training Education Journal*, 2(2), 42–46.

> **Inclusivity note**
>
> The readiness tool is a valuable safety net to ensure students are better prepared for their placement; however, realistically, its use might highlight some gaps that are very hard to fill before the placement, hence it will not prevent all students who are not ready for the placement to join one.
>
> With every use and iteration, the tool needs to be reviewed and enhanced as cohorts and circumstances change.

This case study is inclusive in many respects as it combines a number of the values discussed in Section 1, particularly 'Nurturing' and 'Co-created'. Students themselves (including recent alumni) helped co-create a tool to support future students before placements, a key learning experience. This has resulted in students' readiness for learning being checked and potential gaps being filled *before* the placement takes place, so students are in a better position to succeed.

Readiness for learning matters not only for placements, but in all fields of study. As students have various levels of academic and professional readiness at the start of a course, you may want to design (or co-create with students) a readiness for learning tool for your course.

Through the discussion and the three case studies in this first part of the chapter, it is clear that carrying out a needs analysis is key to informing more inclusive learning design and practices. However, teachers should be aware that needs analysis is only one element of a broader, initial phase of learning that is often termed orientation, the subject of the second part of this chapter.

Orientation

Think back to the time when you started your university studies—How did you feel? How were you welcomed in the institution? What helped you 'settle in'? What has your own experience taught you about the value of supported transition (via orientation) at the start of a course?

Starting university is like visiting a foreign land for the first time. Everything is new: there are new faces and places, there is a different language, a new currency, new rules, a new culture and so on. If you read a guidebook before travelling there, you have a local map and you are welcomed by a local guide with a welcome pack, who gives you a tour of the new surroundings and makes sure you have all you need, the impact of all the novelty will not be overwhelming and you will soon feel at ease. If none of those things happen, you will probably still get by, if you are resourceful, but your experience, especially at the start of your visit, might be less positive. I will discuss the equivalent to those welcoming elements to help your students settle into their university studies more easily: orientation at the start of a course.

As shown in Figure 2.3, orientation is a complex transition concept, spanning the social, emotional and academic dimensions of learning. Transition is the big idea behind all the other elements. In the previously used analogy, each transition can be likened to a border crossing.

Transitions are a critical time and often a make-or-break point for student success. Some students struggle to make the leap between their previous educational setting and

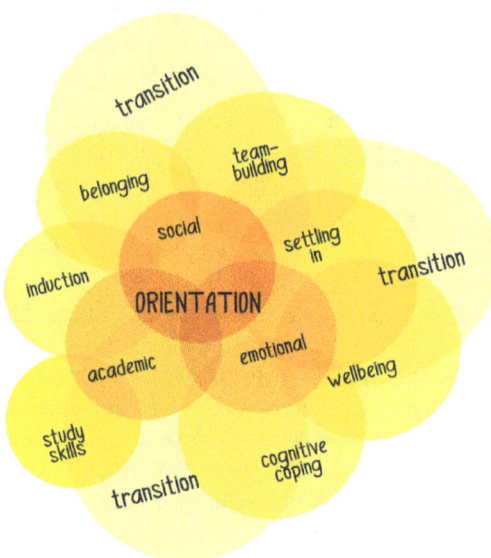

Figure 2.3 The many facets of orientation.

the new one. A supported transition programme, which I will call here orientation, works like the 'welcome pack' I mentioned earlier and can make all the difference between successful university life and ongoing struggles.

Universities usually have a standardised cohort *induction* programme which is the start of the student learning journey with the institution. However, these processes rarely cater for the diversity of our cohorts, hence they are not usually very inclusive. Orientation is a longer process and tends to be more personalised than induction. I make the case for creating more inclusive and personalised *orientation programmes* on the course(s) you teach. They do not need to be very extensive, but they should be part of 'transition pedagogies' (Kift 2009) to support the move from earlier learning experiences and contexts into new ones.

The most crucial time to welcome and orient students is in the **first weeks** (particularly of the first year) at university. All students need time to settle in, but international students and students from underserved minority groups may experience a variety of additional 'shocks' to those experienced by home students: cultural, academic, linguistic. It can take months for students to feel at ease in the new university environment, especially if they are first generation as they do not have a shared family higher education understanding to refer back to. For this reason, more and more institutions are setting up peer-mentoring schemes and buddy systems in addition to the traditional support provided by tutors and other centralised support services. Having this type of support from peers with 'insider knowledge' can be invaluable and make all the difference to new students.

It is useful to pause and reflect on the way you currently orient students who start your course. At the start of this chapter, I invited you to reflect on the question:

How can you set up inclusive orientation activities to support transition into your course?

The following two case studies discuss practical ways to set up more inclusive inductions *and* transition programmes. As you read them, make notes of how the ideas presented could help you enhance the induction and orientation programmes on your course.

The first case study highlights a belonging-based practice for *inductions*. Notice the structure of such induction and the use of questions to foster peer learning and dialogue to build community.

Student-generated induction: A belonging-based practice

By Nicholas Bowskill (UK)

Student induction is an important part of arrival into university. It influences retention and supports student success. Until recently, induction has traditionally been delivered in a series of talks to new arrivals. This risks information overload and alienation in a top-down approach. It fails to socialise students into university.

In the 'student-generated' design presented here, mental health, well-being and inclusion are all addressed in a way which also integrates the institutional agenda. This process is primarily designed to invoke a sense of social group membership and belonging through discussion, collaboration and the visualisation of shared views made public to all involved.

This student-led model of induction is based on a group-level theory derived from social psychology known as a 'social identity approach' (Tajfel and Turner 1979). In this model, student induction is designed to invoke a sense of group membership and inclusion by leveraging diverse views and making them visible using technology. Students see they are not alone in having those concerns and realise they do belong. The class then have their situated concerns addressed in a socially contingent manner. The session is 'about' them. Additional input from staff is then added after having addressed those concerns.

Basic structure

In contrast to Mazur's 'Peer Instruction' (Crouch and Mazur 2001) and conventional uses of classroom technology, a novel alternative was designed inverting the standard use of clickers. The aim is not to achieve consensus but to show the common concerns held within the group. This new model (Shared Thinking) is applied to student-generated induction as follows:

1 A focus question is posed to the class without any pre-set options for the poll that follows
2 Individuals begin by noting their personal concerns
3 Students move into small groups and share their views
4 Each group identifies one concern which is then recorded on the main screen
5 The resulting set of group-inputs become the polling options
6 Individuals vote for their preferred option using clickers or related technologies
7 Voting generates a display on the 'public' screen
8 Tutors respond to the issues raised adding any further details afterwards

An example of a focus question is: '*What are your current concerns about arriving at University?*'. The technology scaffolds the group and carries some of the cognitive load as students build the set of options on the screen from their conversations. The same technology is then used to vote and visibly synthesise the thoughts of the group making them 'public' on the main screen.

Student-generated induction supports a participatory process of group identity formation (Figure 2.4). Using this structure and technology, students co-construct a sense of 'who we are' and 'what we think'. This dialogue and interaction creates a shared sense of group identity in keeping with a social identity approach (Tajfel and Turner 1979).

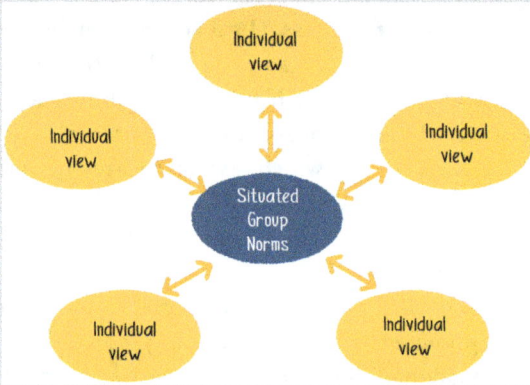

Figure 2.4 Identity formation using shared thinking as a belonging-based approach.

Evaluation

A sample of students were interviewed for the study. Following the intervention, data suggested that the activity can help to address mental health and well-being issues. This is a belonging-based practice. Seeing the way others feel can help reduce students' sense of social isolation. The small groups allowed students to talk to their peers about personal concerns in a large formal session. The technology pooled the discussion from the groups. Student-generated induction seems to help break the ice and invoke a sense of belonging.

> if you're just on your own you don't know what everyone else is thinking … whereas if it's all up on the screen you can see what everybody is thinking … and you can see if it's like a large number then it will make you feel okay. I'm not freaking out. I'm not over-reacting.
>
> [1st year student A]

> *it made you feel less of an outsider and it made you feel a bit better that you're not just on your own.*
>
> [1st year student B]

An experiential staff development workshop has since been delivered at various institutions around the UK. A simple handbook was also published to provide a script and structure enabling anyone to adapt and run the same workshop locally (Bowskill 2013).

Conclusion

A student-led model for induction and transition has been provided. A different theoretical framework for both induction and the use of classroom technologies is also presented. Shared thinking is a belonging-based practice providing a scalable and transferable model which can help address mental health, well-being and inclusion. This is an approach to learning design which can reduce anxiety and loneliness in an increasingly uncertain world.

Bibliography

Bowskill, N. (2013). *Student-Generated Induction: A Social Identity Approach: A Staff Development Guide*, CreateSpace Independent Publishing Platform.

Crouch, C.H. and Mazur, E. (2001). Peer Instruction: Ten Years of Experience and Results. *American Journal of Physics*, 69, 970–977. doi: 10.1119/1.1374249

Tajfel, H. and Turner, J.C. (1979). An Integrative Theory of Intergroup Conflict. *The Social Psychology of Intergroup Relations*, 33, 74.

Inclusivity note

First in family and non-native speakers may find it very hard to express their views on day one at university so this approach to induction provides the safety net of small group discussion and then student-led poll.

To further capture individual views and needs, a digital or physical sticky note wall can be used following the process described in the case study: students can add anonymous ideas about the questions raised. This wall can be revisited further down the line as students settle in their studies.

Through collaborative and shared thinking, the case study you just read presents a practical, zero-budget (assuming the technology is already in place), easy to implement induction where students socialise while receiving and providing peer support. This case in practice could easily be added to any existing induction you already use. It can also be scaled up (institution level) or scaled down (module or unit level).

There are many other practical ways of setting up inclusive induction/orientation to make transitions easier for students. For instance, we could reach out to them for a pre-course needs analysis and then use the qualitative data we gathered to set up appropriate support systems to scaffold their transitions. The following case study discusses several different *transition* activities you may want to try out.

Scaffolding students in their transition into higher education

By Nina Walker (UK)

Transition to higher education can be an exciting time but it can also bring with it a number of anxieties and potential obstacles to student success. A successful transition can be associated with better holistic university experiences and also improved metrics such as retention (Cook et al. 2006, Scott et al. 2008). Many institutions focus efforts on the initial induction period, however some would argue that a longer transition period is beneficial for students (Richardson and Tate 2012, Turner et al. 2017). This case study looks at initiatives I have put into place to support the transition experiences of Master of Pharmacy students at the University of Hertfordshire, where cohorts typically hold 100–120 students in each year group.

The intersectionality of my students creates cohorts with complex needs in terms of scaffolding for success in the transition to higher education study. The initiatives listed below have been created over the past few years and are implemented in addition to the traditional induction provision, in order to provide an inclusive educational experience for all students as they transition and settle from their previous learning setting into the new one, as shown in Figure 2.5.

Student feedback highlighted that the rapid delivery of material in induction was not conducive to retention of information and therefore I worked collaboratively with the students to look for ways that I could better support them in this formative period. Prior to arrival on the programme, I email students

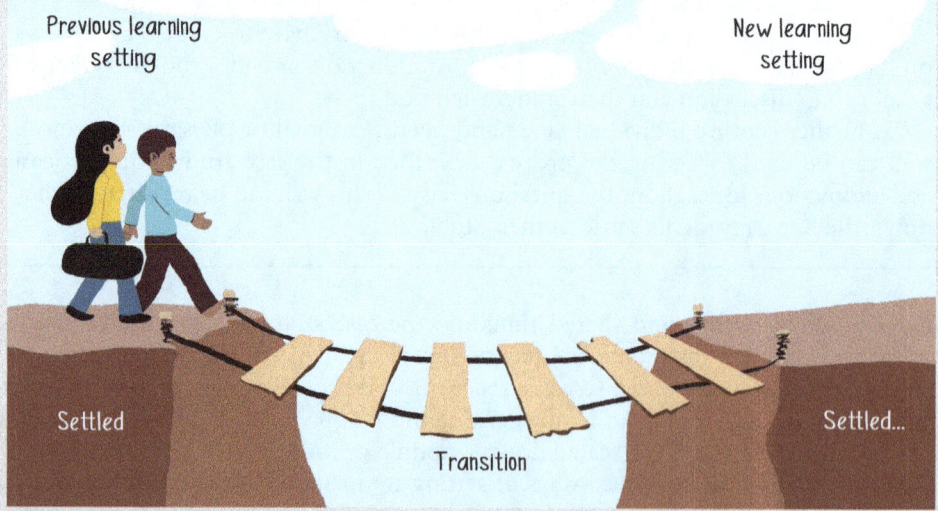

Figure 2.5 Students traverse a liminal space in between settled previous learning settings and new learning settings.

to introduce myself and welcome early questions. This is followed by an email containing an electronic 'Transition Booklet' detailing staff contact details and headshots, a digestible review of the modules that they will be undertaking, hints and tips from outgoing first year students and things to expect at university. My intention is that vicarious confidence is imparted through the use of peers to set realistic expectations for higher education and early visualisation of staff helps to encourage a sense of belonging. A personal email is intended to break down communication barriers and enhance proactive early assistance seeking. In addition to the booklet, the students also receive a motivational letter from a first-year student from the previous cohort. By doing this, new students hear directly from an existing student, creating a sense of community and belonging.

Over the past few years, I have examined the support mechanisms in place for students from discrete groups. A large proportion of my students are first-generation students, who at times exhibited hesitancies about higher education. This led to me establishing the 'First in the Family workshops'. These are open to any first-generation student to network with others who are in the same position but also importantly staff who were first generation students.

> The workshop for first people in the family attending university provided me with the support and reassurance that I needed. Afterwards I felt more confident about my studies and knew that I could approach Nina if I had any concerns or questions.
>
> (1st year student)

Impostor syndrome seems to be pervasive in higher education (Villwock et al. 2016) and this may have been compounded by the effects of the pandemic. I created an online workshop which provided a space where students could meet with other students and also staff to discuss how they experience impostor syndrome, but also mechanisms used to mitigate any negative impacts that it might have. This approach was extremely successful and the impact of staff expressing feelings of impostor syndrome was really powerful:

> Highly recommend this workshop, found it incredibly helpful and amazing to know I'm not the only one who feels this way!
>
> (3rd year student)

These initiatives are used in combination with others to scaffold the transition process. For instance, students also took part in a Jargon Busting Bingo, using playful learning to explore university terminology such as 'summative' 'referral' and 'academic integrity'. These approaches have been perceived extremely positively from a student perspective but also have the potential to positively impact metrics such as progression. They will be rolled out across the department in order to support more students. My approach to student experience is based on the important discussions that I have with my students and continually looking for ways to support them.

Bibliography

Cook, A., Rushton, B.S. and Macintosh, K.A. (Eds.). (2006). *Student Transition and Retention (STAR)*. Coleraine: University of Ulster.

Richardson, M. and Tate, S. (2012). University Is Not as Easy as A, B, C …: How an Extended Induction Can Improve the Transition to University for New Undergraduates. *Emerge*, 4, 11–25.

Scott, G., Shah, M., Grebennikov, L. and Singh, H. (2008). Improving Student Retention: A University of Western Sydney Case Study. *Journal of Institutional Research*, 14(1), 9–23.

Turner, R., Morrison, D., Cotton, D., Child, S., Stevens, S., Nash, P. and Kneale, P. (2017). Easing the Transition of First Year Undergraduates through an Immersive Induction Module. *Teaching in Higher Education*, 22(7), 805–821. doi: 10.1080/13562517.2017.1301906

Villwock, J.A., Sobin, L.B., Koester, L.A. and Harris, T.M. (2016). Impostor Syndrome and Burnout among American Medical Students: A Pilot Study. *International Journal of Medical Education*, 7, 364. doi: 10.18203/2320-6012.ijrms20184031

Inclusivity note

Transition (unsettling and resettling) and orientation activities help us academics identify students who may struggle with new environments and change. By providing a *menu* of different transition opportunities we give students choice of how and how much to engage with the orientation process.

Since the pandemic, students have reported higher levels of stress, anxiety and mental health issues. Depending on your context and the needs of your cohort, the orientation you provide could include stress management as well as cognitive coping strategies, including aspects such as emotional management, learning about learning, planning, prioritising and time management. However, above all, orientation should be about *emotional* support to cope with change. All students benefit from such orientation activities, but for first in family, those with additional caring responsibilities, those who work and study and neurodivergent students, they are vital.

To be coherent, we should design our own tailored (mini) orientation programmes where we make use of pre-course asynchronous channels, then integrate those with what we do on day one during the first online or on-site meeting, and then let this initial onboarding spill over into the rest of week one and even beyond.

This case study provides a variety of suggestions to help students cross the transition bridge and settle into their new learning context (which could be your course).

During their years with us, students experience a variety of transitions, small and big. For *each* transition, there should be an appropriate orientation period. This means that for every course a student starts, we should have a structure in place to welcome, orient and guide them both academically and in broader terms, to become more aware of relevant internal services and support systems as well as to feel part of a community. Every transition is an opportunity to further integrate the student into existing institutional systems.

Depending on your context, preferences, and cohorts, you may be able to design and set up one or more of the suggested orientation activities, alongside the more formal and institution-wide ones.

Conclusion

In this chapter I have addressed how needs analysis and orientation are key to creating a more inclusive learning environment and experience. The discussion and case studies presented embody all nine of the inclusivity roots-values discussed in Section 1 and should inspire you to enhance your inclusive practice in these areas.

Going back to the questions I proposed at the start of the chapter:

Activate your inner dialogue. ... How would you answer?

How can you find out the needs of the students in your cohorts before and at the start of the course?

How can you set up inclusive orientation activities to support transition into your course?

My attempted answers which sum up the chapter are:

You can design and implement a needs analysis to be done either before or right at the start of your course. This can be done through a questionnaire, discussion or audio-visual means which can inform more culturally responsive teaching practices. The needs analysis should be part of a wider orientation programme to the course where students are supported in their transition. Inductions can be centred on belonging and socialising, and we can create other support systems so students can settle in their new educational context, be it at the start of their studies or at subsequent, smaller transition points they experience.

Once we have configured the physical and digital learning space set up (Chapter 1) and we have designed a needs analysis and orientation (Chapter 2), we need to ensure we have further systems in place to build community and foster a support culture when the course starts—this is the subject of Chapter 3.

Bibliography

Cowan, J. (2012). To Each According to Their Needs: Thoughts on Dealing with Emergent Learning Needs. In Jackson, N. (Ed.) *Lifewide Learning, Education & Personal Development*. [online] Lifewide Education Community. Available at: http://www.lifewideebook.co.uk/uploads/1/0/8/4/10842717/chapter_a3.pdf

Dirksen, J. (2015). *Design for How People Learn*. San Francisco, CA: New Riders.

Fawns, T., Aitken, G. and Jones, D. (2021). Beyond Technology in Online Postgraduate Education. *Postdigital Science and Education*. doi: 10.1007/s42438-021-00277-x

Gronseth, S.L., Michela, E. and Ugwu, L.O. (2020). Designing for Diverse Learners. In McDonald, J.K. and West, R.E. (Eds.) *Design for Learning: Principles, Processes, and Praxis*. EdTech Books. Available at: https://edtechbooks.org/id/designing_for_diverse_learners

Higher Education Academy (2014). Induction. https://s3.eu-west-2.amazonaws.com/assets.creode.advancehe-document-manager/documents/hea/private/resources/induction_1568037224.pdf

Kift, S. (2009). Articulating a Transition Pedagogy to Scaffold and to Enhance the First Year Student Learning Experience in Australian Higher Education. Final Report for ALTC Senior Fellowship Program. Available at: http://transitionpedagogy.com/wp-content/uploads/2014/05/Kift-Sally-ALTC-Senior-Fellowship-Report-Sep-091.pdf

Kift, S. and Nelson, K. (2005). Beyond Curriculum Reform: Embedding the Transition Experience. In Brew, A. and Asmar, C. (Eds.) *HERDSA Conference 2005*. University of Sydney, Australia, New South Wales, Sydney, pp. 225–235. Available at: https://eprints.qut.edu.au/3944/1/3944.pdf

Rose, D.H. and Strangman, N. (2007). Universal Design for Learning: Meeting the Challenge of Individual Learning Differences through a Neurocognitive Perspective. *Universal Access in the Information Society*, 5(4), 381–391.

Shackleton-Jones, N. (2019). *How People Learn* (1st ed.). London and New York: Kogan Page.

Chapter 3

Go! Building community and fostering a support culture

> Classrooms are not just spaces where ideas are aired, shared, critiqued and debated; they are sites where affects emerge, circulate and enter into conflict. (And this circulation far exceeds the human). Pedagogy is at least as much a matter of affect modulation as it is a question of theories, evidence, arguments and genealogies.
>
> Nathan Snaza

This chapter is about connection before content. It addresses ways we can put into practice the pedagogy of care at the start of a course: you will read examples of support systems designed to foster students' sense of belonging and, *connected to this*, their academic progress.

Activate your inner dialogue. ... How would you answer?

How important do you think sense of belonging is for students to succeed on your course? Why?

How can you support and promote students' well-being by the way you design learning?

What support systems can you set up at the start of your course to build community?

A good way to describe a university is using the expression 'community of learners' because it is about focussing on learning within a community in a broader sense. In this chapter I discuss building community and fostering a support culture as (1) part of students' well-being and (2) something to embed when starting the course.

Students' well-being

To support students' well-being, we need to develop empathy: we need to understand their contexts, needs and potential barriers. The quality that goes beyond empathy is compassion, which moves us to action and should be embedded at every level of teaching and learning, in order to support well-being (Gilbert et al. 2017). Although at times 'signposting' to relevant institutional services and support available to students is 'the most effective student support we can provide' (Hodgson and Bretherton 2020), we also need to consider what enablers we can put in place to support them within the fabric of our course. In a nutshell, we should aim for compassion *and* signposting.

I will briefly discuss some key practices which support students' well-being: fostering a sense of belonging; using students' names; personal tutoring; peer mentoring.

Sense of belonging is key to how students experience learning. It is a complex and multi-dimensional concept which refers to 'mattering' (Flett et al. 2019) in a context, and to the alignment of identity and learning environment. It is about connectedness with others, which allows each student to bring their whole self to the learning experience. It is also closely tied with individuals' social identity within a group that they feel a sense of belonging to.

For students, sense of belonging is closely linked to well-being and mental health, though at times it is not clear whether mental health influences sense of belonging or the other way around. There is value in 'weaving mental health and well-being support and inclusive practice into every stage of the student lifecycle, especially welcome and transition, but also into courses and extra-curricular activities' (Capper and McVitty 2022). Being in 'culturally relevant and responsive campus environments' facilitates belonging which supports academic success (Museus et al. 2018).

As valuable as cultivating a sense of belonging on our courses is, we should realise that at times, due to unique circumstances, it is simply not possible for *some* students to feel they belong in *all* the learning environments and experiences we design and provide. Besides, an excessive emphasis on sense of belonging can lead to the tyranny of democracy, where we make it *compulsory* for students to belong to the group in some visible, prescribed way. Instead, we should recognise that some people are happy to be on the fringe: they still feel they belong, just not by being visibly in the centre. Inclusivity means providing a chance to everyone to find their place and support them where they are, as long as *we* are not the ones creating barriers to belonging.

How do we foster a sense of belonging? In many small and big ways, through intentional learning design. One way is by using students' names.

How do relationships start? Usually when we connect with someone new, one of the first things we ask is their **name**. Our name is very much tied to our identity, so we need it to be acknowledged and used because it affirms us. In our very cosmopolitan universities, we have students from all continents who have names that might be very unusual for us. Some students experience routine name avoidance or no effort to try and pronounce their name correctly. Using students' names and using them correctly is key to building inclusive communities because our interactions should include a sense of 'mattering' and of being valued (Prilleltensky and Prilleltensky 2021). So, it is worth designing early activities for everyone to share their name and get to know their peers by name. In large cohorts this is very challenging, but there are effective ways to learn many students' names at once—if you google it you will find a plethora of suggestions. Of course, we need to go beyond learning how to pronounce the names of our students; we need to use them respectfully and try to get to know the person behind the name. A culturally respectful icebreaker which creates community and a sense of mattering, and helps us learn students' names, is to ask students to tell the *story* of their first or family name: why they were named like that, or if they changed their name how they chose it; what it means and any other details that they want to share. It is also important that students share their pronoun (if they wish to) when they share their name.

Another important way to support students' well-being is through **personal tutoring** and advising. Considering the growing size of cohorts, having a *personal* tutor affords students the opportunity to receive some one-to-one academic and pastoral attention. Hence, personal tutoring has become key to establishing and nourishing the sense of mattering that is important to student success. As these one-to-one meetings tend to be relatively short, perhaps 20 to 30 minutes each, having the option to join digitally rather than travelling to the campus means that the students can join from anywhere, which is advantageous for working students and those with caring responsibilities. Having online tutorials results in a higher take-up and positive feedback on the part of the students who perceive it as a more informal 'chat' about their learning compared to visiting academics in their office. As it is often in the context of individual tutorials that academics find out more about who the students are and where they need support to succeed, they are key in promoting inclusion and equity.

Both due to the profound imbalance in the ratio of academics to students and to implement vertical learning where students further in their studies support those in an earlier stage, **peer mentoring** has been found to be a very effective support system. This can be an informal arrangement where there is a pool of willing mentors, including alumni, who can be contacted directly by interested students, or it can be more formally established so that each and every new student is systematically supported by a peer mentor until they are settled or even throughout the academic year. These initiatives have multiple benefits for mentors, mentees and the wider institution as found by Spiridon et al. (2020): 'peer mentoring schemes tend to be developed as retention strategies, however, they can also serve other purposes (psychosocial or career-related)'.

Even if there is no institutional policy about using students' names and pronouns, personal tutoring and peer mentoring, within our course we can be proactive and leverage these three approaches to enhance an inclusive sense of belonging for each one of our students.

Entire books have been written about students' well-being as this is a vast field. I can only scratch the surface in this chapter, by sharing three case studies which illustrate some practical ways in which teachers can show emotional intelligence as they support students' well-being: the first focuses on trauma-responsive pedagogical approaches; the second is about valuing neurodiversity; the third is about supporting students through low-tech informal social media groups.

The first case study from Botswana discusses the importance of *trauma-informed* teaching practices, particularly at the start of a course, to support students' well-being.

Students' well-being support

By Godson Gatsha (Botswana)

The advent of the covid-19 pandemic has adversely affected students' emotional and mental well-being worldwide. The effects of the pandemic on students involves painful lived experiences whose effects will continue for years to come.

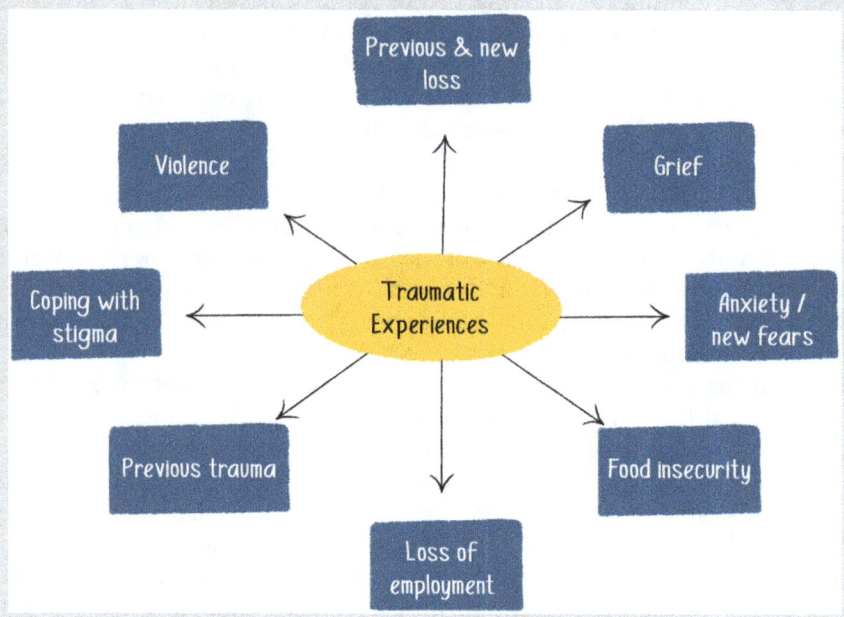

Figure 3.1 Students' traumatic experiences take many forms and can overlap.

Students have experienced loss of loved ones and other mental and emotional issues as shown in Figure 3.1.

In most cases teachers are not trained in handling these challenges. Engagement with students in such difficult times requires teachers to demonstrate warmth, empathy and genuineness so that students may feel welcomed, respected and safe. In post-trauma situations pastoral care becomes central to every teacher's role, irrespective of the discipline or course; it is not something that only one department (such as student services) deals with. An understanding of student mental and emotional needs is important for teacher readiness to help students. Information gathered about students' experiences told through dialogue, drawing, stories, songs and drama could inform teachers' practices. An analysis of students' mental and emotional needs empowers teachers to establish support structures such as pastoral teams, personal counselling rooms and opportunities for referral to clinical psychologists and psychiatrists.

Collectively teachers and educational leaders should develop a guiding policy on dealing with students affected by a variety of traumatic events. The policy should be inclusive and identify the mental and emotional needs and serve as a guide as to how these should be addressed in students as individuals and as a collective community. Context, cultural backgrounds and individual students' profiles are critical for individualised support. It is therefore critical that the policy framework underpins student-centric support systems as a point of departure. Some of the key support interventions include open and inclusive conversations and brainstorming, e-support, peer educators, peer-to-peer support, personal counselling, home visits, video calls, journaling and 'empathy interviews' (Dominguez n.d.). Open and inclusive conversations and brainstorming on new engagement rules as an institution and peer-to-peer support groups are needed in the post-pandemic 'new normal' in creating a conducive learning climate. It should embrace and foster values such as trust, tolerance, compassion, actions and perceptions that are non-judgemental and respect individual rights and dignity.

Besides having a more flexible course design to do with input/output mode and deadlines, some strategic interventions to implement trauma-informed pedagogy may include

- Engaging students on a one-on-one basis pertaining to their unique mental and emotional needs.
- Creating smaller breakaway sessions for peer-to-peer guided supportive conversations using open-ended questions.
- Affording students the opportunity to share their narratives on different experiences during the pandemic and beyond to express their lived experiences using various media such as art, games and drama, and be allowed to engage in light physical exercise. This needs to be managed empathetically and students should be able to opt-out if they so wish.
- Engaging in teacher-student or even student-to-student empathy interviews to validate students' feelings.
- Making telephone or video calls to support students who may be at home due to some mental and emotional health issues.
- If necessary, making plans for (paired) home visits as part of support (where allowed and appropriate), especially with students who have additional needs.

Teachers too need self-care so that they are strong to stand the painful stories that students may share with them so that they do not break down when they hear the stories. To build their own resilience, they should consider debriefing sessions at appropriate times with their colleagues or counsellors.

Of course, not all teachers have the training and expertise to take on the role of well-being coordinators, pastoral tutors, counsellors and more. It is up to the educational leaders in each institution to set up systems such as additional teacher education in these areas (Ghaffari 2019), or to promote more cross-fertilisation between internal departments which traditionally provide mental health support such as student support services and academics. On the other hand, teachers should strive to develop more compassionate pedagogies and consider trauma more than we did pre-pandemic.

Bibliography

Dominguez, K. (n.d.) Empathy Interviews. Available at: https://hthclassic.org/teachercenter/change-packages/empathy-interviews/

Ghaffari, N. (2019). 5 Ways Schools Can Support Student Mental Health. https://www.rehabs.com/pro-talk/5-ways-schools-support-student-mental-health/

NASP (2015). Addressing Grief. Available at: https://www.nasponline.org/resources-and-publications/resources-and-podcasts/school-safety-and-crisis/mental-health-resources/addressing-grief

---

Inclusivity note

When implementing trauma-informed pedagogies, the most difficult thing for teachers is how to respond and support students who disclose their trauma. It is imperative to maintain confidentiality, to be well aware of internal support systems and understand when the best thing is to signpost students to relevant department. However, many in the sector agree that, particularly since the start of the pandemic, there has been an exponential increase in the need for pastoral and wellbeing support and university services may struggle to keep up. At times there are small things (such as a supportive chat, peer mentoring and empathy interviews) that as teachers we can set up to show students that when it comes to the pedagogy of care, we walk the walk.

This case study highlights the need for all teachers to provide *reasonable* pastoral support to students affected by trauma. On our courses, within the home base of the classroom, we should strive to create a 'learning sanctuary' where 'the path to learning is cloaked with radical hospitality and paved with hope and moral imagination' (Imad 2020).

The pedagogy of care is particularly important for neurodivergent students. The term neurodiversity signals that all humans are unique from a neurological viewpoint, while *neurodivergence* is a relatively new term now used to include what were previously considered medical 'conditions' such as autism, dyslexia and dyscalculia. The term neurodivergence puts the emphasis on the fact that these types of intelligences are the effect of variations in the human genome. They can be construed as positive assets (strengths) or negative deficits (weaknesses) depending on the stance taken.

The following case study, from Hawai'i, discusses how we can show, in practice, that we *value* neurodiversity on our courses.

Teach to reach me: Valuing neurodiversity

By Gloria Niles (Hawai'i)

Humans have many similarities in neuroanatomical form and functional physiological processes. Yet it is the diversity of our physical characteristics, our cognition, perceptions and thoughts that make us uniquely human. Sociological and cultural values define actions and behaviors accepted as norms among societies. These norms extend to our educational environments through pedagogies where knowledge, skills and information are delivered through particular teaching methods. Pedagogies carry the expectations that learning will be ubiquitously transposed from the teacher to students. This expectation is predicated on assumptions of similarities in the neurological processes of learning. However, when learning is impeded by neurological differences, the student is marginalised and diagnosed as having a disorder or disability. Neurodiversity is a term used to signal and embrace all human cognitive variations. Within it, neurodivergence embraces neurological differences as unique learning characteristics rather than neurological, developmental or learning deficits. Through the Teach to Reach Me approach, inclusive teachers empower the learning confidence of neurodivergent students.

Valuing neurodiversity

Autism, learning disabilities and attentional deficits are labels that identify an individual as neurologically deficient or abnormal. These labels can lead teachers to preconceived notions of the learner, thereby lowering performance expectations, or anticipation of behavioral challenges. The concept of neurodiversity shifts the mindset of neurological difference from a deficit to a form of diversity. Neurodivergence is viewed as part of the unique qualities of an individual, where individualised differences in cognition, thought, expression and preferences are valued as traits similar to left-handedness, musicality, athleticism and artistic creativity (Armstrong 2020). Neurodivergent students who have been assigned deficit labels in their educational experience can develop defence mechanisms to protect their vulnerabilities (Singer 2016).

Teach to reach me approach

Learning is optimised when a student believes their teacher values who they are as a person and as a learner. The Teach to Reach Me approach is designed to dismantle barriers to learning by establishing mutually respectful teacher-student relationships. As shown in Figure 3.2, the four aspects of Teach to Reach Me include

See me
Hear me
Show me
Trust me

TEACH ME TO REACH ME
neuro diversity

SEE ME

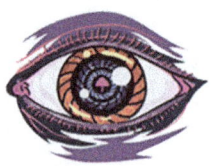

See beyond my label.
Appreciate my interests, strengths, motivations.

HEAR ME

Build rapport with me.
Learn how I communicate most effectively.

SHOW ME

Show me that you believe in my capabilities. Show me that my limitations do not define who I am.

TRUST ME

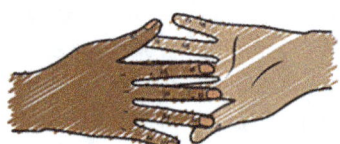

When I believe that you trust me, I will take risks, and be vulnerable. Knowing that when mistakes happen, we will be learning together.

Figure 3.2 Teach to reach me: See me, hear me, show me, trust me. Each aspect of the Teach to Reach Me approach is described herein with 'me' and 'I' representing the first-person voice of the neurodivergent learner, and 'you' representing the teacher.

When you teach to reach me, you show me that you see beyond my labels. You understand and appreciate my unique strengths, interests, thoughts and ideas. Simultaneously, you support me as I work through my fears, limitations and challenges. When you teach to reach me, you hear me because you know how I communicate most effectively. You adapt to my communication style rather than expecting me to adapt to your preferred means of communicating. When you teach to reach me you show me that I matter. I see individuals who also have neurodiverse characteristics represented in the curriculum. You highlight neurodiverse qualities of significant contributors to the discipline being studied. When you teach to reach me, you trust me, and in turn, I trust you. When I believe you trust me, I will take risks and be vulnerable. I know that if mistakes happen, through our bond of trust, together we will both learn from these mistakes.

When you teach to reach me, neurodiversity is valued, my self-identity and learner confidence is strengthened, as you and I both know my limitless potential.

Bibliography

Armstrong, T. (2020). Neurodiversity. [online] American Institute for Learning and Human Development. Available at: https://www.institute4learning.com/resources/articles/neurodiversity

Disabled-world.com. (2020). What Is Neurodiversity, Neurodivergent, Neurotypical. [online] Available at: https://www.disabled-world.com/disability/awareness/neurodiversity/

Singer, J. (2016). *Neurodiversity: The Birth of an Idea* (2nd ed.). Self-published, Judy Singer. 'Kindle'.

Inclusivity note

The first issue is getting students to disclose their neurodivergence—fear of stigmatisation and labelling are still very common. We could share ways in which we are neurodiverse ourselves or explain the advantages for teachers to know students' needs and what supports are available.

The second issue is having many divergent students to cater for within the same cohort. A universal design for learning approach can help us remove barriers *at design stage*. By providing students with voice and choice, we let them engage with the input and express their learning with outputs that better suit their learning needs. Also, personal tutoring and peer mentors can be invaluable in supporting neurodivergent students.

Neurodiversity is an asset on your courses. Although 'neurodivergent students may present in a variety of ways that are not aligned with your usual expectations' (Spaeth and Pearson 2021), many neurodivergent people have a superpower in some areas, so it is worth considering how we can value what neurodivergent students can contribute to the learning experience and environment. Each and every student can feel valued by being seen, heard, shown and trusted as the case study illustrated.

During the sudden digital switch due to the pandemic, many students reported feeling disconnected in their online learning environment, compared to the previous in-person campus learning setting. Yet, most digital tools have 'affordances to forge connection, so these feelings of disconnection may not be intrinsic to the medium, but an indication of a lack of design for pedagogy of care in online spaces' (Henriksen et al. 2022).

Head to the companion website inclusivelearningdesign.com to read a case study by Nomsa Zindela (SA) entitled 'WhatsApp as a technological affordance for supporting students from a "distance"—A case study'. The narrative illustrates the way in which WhatsApp can be used to create a support system for students at a critical assessment time to implement the 'pedagogy of care'. The case study shows that although a well-structured virtual learning environment (VLE) can provide students with the content and support they need for their studies, using more informal, low-tech spaces such as WhatsApp, an app that students (in many countries) likely use daily on their phone for their informal social exchanges, can make a big difference in the engagement of students by providing emotional support. This educational use of a low-tech social media app requires some conscious planning on the part of the teacher, but it can be very effective to provide pastoral care at a distance and to foster a peer-to-peer support culture.

Besides 'extreme' cases such as dedicated support during a pandemic, we should design appropriate and realistic backchannels for our regular classes, both for live interactions (a chat or post-it wall that you monitor during the break) or via a digital wall (such as a Padlet which allows anonymous posts) for broader support.

Having reviewed well-being and trauma-informed pedagogies, valuing neurodiversity and implementing the pedagogy of care through WhatsApp, we now move on to what is arguably the most crucial time in the life cycle of a course: its start. I am going to discuss practical ways to build community and foster a support culture in the first 'live' exchanges we have with our cohorts.

Starting the course

The first activity, the first lesson, the first week of a new course are often a make-or-break checkpoint, so it pays off for academics to dedicate enough time designing those early interactions, particularly with new cohorts. This chapter is about inclusive ways of starting a course, including support systems we can create at the start of a course, to set an inclusive tone for the entire learning experience. Think back to the nine inclusivity values discussed in Section 1:

I. Intentionally equitable
N. Nurturing
C. Co-created
L. Liberating
U. User-friendly
S. Socially responsible
I. Integrative
V. Values-based
E. Ecological

How can these values inform the start of your course? What are some key things that you could design to promote those values in your early interactions with a new cohort?

Here is a short selection of possible inclusive initial classroom activities for lesson 1 of a typical university course.

Introductions

One week before the course starts, send students a *short* video introduction of yourself and of the course. Welcome everyone, say who you are and reveal something not only about your professional background but also about your life, such as your socio-cultural background, or introduce your family or pets. This video should be easy to locate in your VLE, perhaps in a dedicated 'Welcome' section, or it could be sent to a class WhatsApp group, or shared via another social media.

For the first couple of on-site lessons, provide sticky name labels for students to wear and if the cohort is big, ask students to say their name at the start of their comment/answer so everyone can hear it and learn how to say it.

Diversity

In the first class, acknowledge everyone's presence and socio-cultural contribution to the learning situation—this is important for everyone to feel valued in the space. You could use the responses to your needs-analysis (see Chapter 2) if you have done one or tell the students how you intend to get to know them. If your cohort is multicultural, ask students to share something from their home country or from their home language.

Include a diversity statement in the syllabus or mention it during the first class—this signals your openness and that discussing inclusivity is valued in your learning space.

Invite feedback

Mention that you are keen to co-create the learning experience and environment, so you welcome students' feedback about the course and their learning experience— say in which ways they can provide you ongoing feedback.

First peer-to-peer interaction

A very effective, inclusive icebreaker activity which naturally provides opportunities for meaningful early interactions among students is to set up 'stations' for groups of students to interact with each other while simultaneously being introduced to key learning on the course. This activity takes 30–60 minutes depending on how large the cohort is, though you can choose to run it for longer.

Preparation: Identify big ideas or key learning (concepts or practices) on your course; write each one on a different A3 paper, in the form of a question. You will need enough around the room to cater for groups of four or five students, so for a cohort of 40–50 you will need 10 key questions, written on 10 sheets of A3 which will constitute 'stations'. Write a number on each station paper and stick the A3 papers all around the walls of the teaching room. When you start the activity, students may need to push the furniture in the middle of the space, if possible, to be able to more easily move around the stations.

Running the activity: Tell the students that you want them to talk to each other and discuss some key ideas of the course. Make random groups of four or five students and number each group. Ask the groups to stand around the A3 stations, according to their group number. Group 1 will go to paper 1 and so on. Tell them they have five minutes to discuss the question on the paper, propose some initial answers and, importantly, *add* their own related questions on the wall-mounted papers. At the gong (you should have one!) ask students to move to another station *and* mingle, so that they form new random groups. This is going to be a bit messy, but let students self-organise. You are aiming for them to talk to as many in the cohort as possible and to think about a few of the course key ideas. Repeat the four to five minute timing and mingling a few times, until most students have spoken to most in the class and thought about most of the key learning ideas on the course.

Plenary: Once students go back to their seats, you could ask them to comment on the activity in a plenary: what have they learnt about each other and about the course? It is also useful to link this activity to students setting their own learning goals: ask them to start journaling about their learning on your course (to enhance reflection) and to make note of a few personal learning goals they have in relation to the course learning thresholds they have just discussed. They should also add some goals in relation to their own *personal* growth. Consider the best way for students to share their individual learning goals with you and with each other, in your context.

This activity is useful beyond lesson 1, so take photos of the A3 papers with the answers and additional questions and post them on a live document or on a shared digital wall (such as a Padlet): you and the students can refer back to it throughout the course and you can add comments. Alternatively, you could post the images on your VLE. Those initial thoughts can become the subject of further discussion as you progress on the course.

This activity can be done online by using breakout rooms of four or five students and setting up a Google Jamboard or similar digital boards where each board can be numbered and added to. You will have to randomise the groups after each station.

Although this activity is very inclusive, and embodies all the nine inclusivity root-values, it can still present challenges in terms of balancing the group conversations: very shy, reserved or non-native speakers may not say anything, while conversely very chatty students may dominate the conversation. You may need to mention this risk to the students when you introduce the activity, set some basic rules and invite everyone to use empathy as they interact with each other.

In the following three case studies, you will read about other ideas to design a more inclusive course start: the first is about intercultural learning; the second about students as novices; the third is about support systems in the first week of a course.

In Section 1, I discussed how 'values-based' is an inclusivity value: understanding our own (cultural) biases and stance helps us become more culturally responsive in our practice. Linked to this there is interculturality, a key 21st-century competency, also key for transformative education (Foster and Killick 2021). The first case study narrative is about the development of intercultural competency and includes a suggested icebreaker activity.

Can we envisage 'the modern intercultural learner' in higher education?

By Pilar Teran Trueba (UK)

In this case study, I emphasise the relevance of embedding intercultural learning in the curriculum to help learners develop intercultural competence, and I draw attention to what is called the 'modern learner' (Bersin 2014) to explore what needs to be considered if we are to envisage the 'modern intercultural learner'.

There is a wealth of research from the fields of intercultural communication studies and intercultural education showing that intercultural learning promotes intercultural competence which, in turn, prepares learners for more effective and appropriate interactions across cultures. Furthermore, intercultural capabilities broaden their perspectives and their view of others and of their own disciplines, making them more globally minded and employable.

Developing intercultural competence is a gradual process of learning. A process that involves self-awareness, awareness of one's own culture/s and of others and their cultures. It also acknowledges the fact that our identity, or better still, our identities, are multiple, fluid, dynamic and changeable, which can cause tensions and contradictions. It is about complexity, open questions and reflection, which require time to consider different perspectives as well as to develop tolerance for ambiguity. And it calls for intercultural sensitivity to build long-term relationships, co-operation and inclusion (Deardorff 2006, Bennett 2008, Byram 2021).

Intercultural learning requires fostering attitudes and skills that the modern learner's profile fulfils, such as mental agility, curiosity, flexibility, openness to change and unpredictability. Simultaneously, modern learners are constantly short

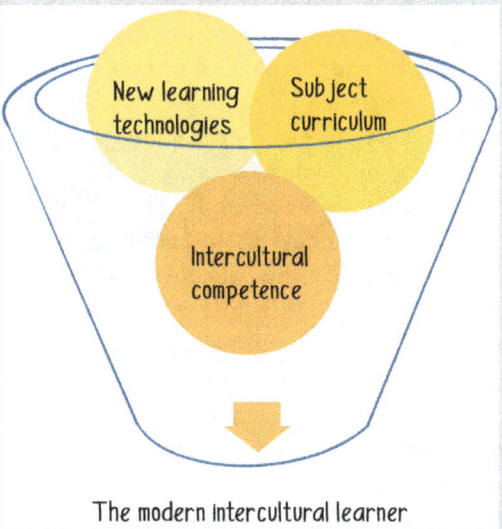

Figure 3.3 Factors which affect the development of the modern intercultural learner.

of time, distracted, overwhelmed and impatient because they operate in a fast-moving world, and this needs to be addressed for intercultural learning to occur.

There are many theoretical models for developing intercultural competence. The one I am most familiar with is the intercultural communicative competence model (Byram 2021), shown in Figure 3.3, which includes (1) new learning technologies, (2) subject curriculum and (3) intercultural competence.

There is no space here to explain in detail its application in my practice, but I include a simple activity for day one that can be adapted to any subject to illustrate how intercultural learning can be promoted.

Activity. *Day one: Introduce yourself*

Tell your students that they are about to engage in an unusual activity. Then ask them to introduce themselves by giving them the following instructions: do not mention your name or surname, place of origin/nationality or studies/profession (in some cases).

The reaction always seems to be very similar: students look confused, they struggle initially to say anything, they look uncomfortable. This is intentional. The aim is to encourage learners to move away from the familiar, the taken for granted, and towards the unfamiliar, the unknown, and to reflect upon their experience and their feelings.

Another aim is to create awareness of the risk of judging and making quick assumptions based on bias, stereotypes, prejudices associated with names, surnames, places, cultures, nationalities and professions. And to make learners rely on observation and active listening skills with an open mind.

Afterwards, a debrief is crucial, and it is important that the facilitator elicits as much information as possible. Some of the outcomes from this exercise are the ability to make sense of unfamiliar situations, to adopt new perspectives, to develop appropriateness of behaviour according to cultural context, empathy and, depending on the information they manage to obtain, opportunities to destabilise stereotypes and build relationships.

There is also an opportunity to identify common values, beliefs and norms and analyse what that says about one's culture/s.

Students who have embarked on intercultural learning report that the approach was new to them, insightful and enjoyable (especially science students). They also found it extremely interesting and highly stimulating in that it encouraged thinking about topics they had not contemplated before in great depth. It is an eye opener for many students, including the ones that considered themselves quite culturally aware.

Modern learners possess skills and attitudes conducive to intercultural learning. However, they need to be made aware by educators of what intercultural competence entails, and of its relevance in their lives: most importantly, they need to experience it within their curricula. It is only then that they will be able to expand on their existing knowledge, skills and attitudes as modern learners, and progress with their journey of intercultural development.

Bibliography

Bennett, J.M. (2008). On Becoming a Global Soul. In Savicki, V. (Ed.) *Developing Intercultural Competence and Transformation: Theory, Research and Application in International Education.* Sterling: Stylus.

Bersin, J. (2014). Leading in Learning. Deloitte. Available at: https://www.slideshare.net/jbersin/the-disruptive-nature-of-digital-learning-ten-things-weve-learned/22-Source_Meet_the_Modern_Learner

Byram, M. (2021). *Teaching and Assessing Intercultural Communicative Competence* (Revisited 2nd ed.). Clevedon: Multilingual Matters.

Deardorff, D.K. (2006). Assessing Intercultural Competence in Study Abroad Students. In Byram, M. and Fung, A. (Eds.) *Living and Studying Abroad: Research and Practice.* Clevedon: Multilingual Matters.

Inclusivity note

Having an exchange with other cultures should be a positive experience. However, due to past trauma or armed conflicts, there could be members of the group who dislike or even hate some countries or ethnic groups. If we want to use the icebreaker in the case study, in order to provide a safe and principles space, we could start by talking about trauma and painful lived experiences and providing a warning regarding the mingling and connecting with other cultures during the activity.

If you do not feel confident and competent in the area of intercultural learning but you believe that your students would benefit from some input on this topic, you may be able to find a guest speaker to help you in this, ideally for your first lesson.

The case study you just read invites you to think about ways you could bring into your course and into your classroom elements of intercultural learning, particularly at the start of the course.

Those of us academics who have an intercultural background can draw on our personal experiences to support intercultural learning. Even when that is not the case, as we all have multiple identities, we should encourage students to think of themselves as having complex identities with rich cultural capital.

Head to the companion website inclusivelearningdesign.com for the second case study by Tim Fawns, Derek Jones and Gill Aitken (UK), entitled 'Students as novices'. The authors propose an initial activity to put teacher-students in the shoes of a beginner learner. Depending on the discipline we teach, we might be able to set up a novice activity for our students at the start of the course, or at least discuss what being a novice learner entails and what metacognitive abilities can support their learning on a new course.

The third and final case study of this chapter discusses practical, inclusive systems that we can put in place to support students during the first week of a new course.

Support systems at the start of a course

By Era Savvides (UK)

In this commentary, I will reflect on the support systems I put in place for my architecture, interior architecture and urban landscape students, on the first week of a new project during their first-year course and how they promote inclusive practice. I will begin my reflection by providing an overview of some of my drivers as educator which will frame the discussion on building critical consciousness and self-reflection in my cohort.

What is important for me to evoke in my students during their first year of study, beyond the curriculum, is an emotional relationship primarily between student and tutor and, as a natural subsequence, between student and subject matter and student with self. As Quinlan (2016) writes, these are some of the key principles in supporting student development in HE. For me, these have been proven to also be key in empowering students to formulate a critical stance on design and to inspire a practice of self-reflection within the cohort—one that is not limited to academic achievements, but that is able to tap into their personal values and sensitivities as designers so that their work can start to move beyond learning outcomes, becoming more meaningful to them and propositional. This is particularly important in supporting students who have no family members or other role models in design, to engage with the course and not to feel excluded.

Engaging with some of the literature on inclusive pedagogies (Blessinger 2018), I was particularly moved to customise our traditional set-up of: deliver a lecture—allow for questions—end the lesson, into a framework where our lectures take the form of discourse. The lectures become a platform for discussion not only between tutor and students but also—and this is something I find particularly important—between tutor and tutor in front of students where we all, tutors and students, in a sense position ourselves on the same level and discuss the subject matter freely and authentically from our own perspectives and personal experiences, thus putting aside the teacher-to-student hierarchy and allowing for the organic uncovering of critical questions on the day's thematic that perhaps we as tutors might even struggle to fully answer.

These moments of authenticity and transparency are, in my experience, when we see our cohort truly come alive in engagement, not only connecting with the curriculum but also establishing a meaningful relationship between themselves and the tutors, the discipline as a whole and their own critical positioning within this. This approach also supports students to develop the 'habits of mind, hand and heart' (Shulman 2005) which are found in real studios and industry practices where the answers are openly worked out in horizontal teams.

To further support critical consciousness and self-reflection during these first important weeks, I also implement an intensive weekly support system of

Figure 3.4 Peer learning and evaluation at the end of week 1: students discuss their outputs.

workshops which finish with an afternoon review and discussion pin-up where the students are asked to stop what they are working on and anonymously pin-up or lay on the floor their often incomplete work in order to step back from it and allow for peer and tutor feedback, as shown in Figure 3.4. The tutors begin by guiding the discussion as an exchange between themselves on the successes and challenges of the day, choosing to focus this on examples from the work on show, with the students then taking over to further expand on their personal interpretations, opinions and take aways from the exercise.

In the first week of each project we also construct vertical support systems where students from year 1, 2 and 3 are 'buddied up' or placed into support groups to review and discuss each other's work privately and at their own time. Each week, one of these groups comes together to present to the course, across all years, a Pecha Kucha talk on what they have been working on during that week and ideas, inspirations and challenges with their projects. This has proven to be an invaluable opportunity for years 1 and 2 to better understand the trajectory and identity of the course and for an overall feeling of studio community to vertically emerge between the different years in the course.

Bibliography

Blessinger, P. (2018). Rethinking Higher Education in the Service of Humanity. [online] *University World News*. Available at: https://www.universityworldnews.com/post.php?story=20180711094726636

Brookfield, S. (2010). *Developing Critical Thinkers*. Baltimore, MD: Laureate Education, Inc.

Quinlan, K. (2016). How Emotion Matters in Four Key Relationships in Teaching and Learning in Higher Education. *College Teaching*, 64, 1–11. doi: 10.1080/87567555.2015.1088818

Shulman, L.S. (2005). Signature Pedagogies in the Professions. *Daedalus*, 134(3), 52–59. http://www.jstor.org/stable/20027998

> **Inclusivity note**
>
> End of week one pin-ups can be very supportive for students, provided that the peer feedback is given with tact and compassion. For a novice student, receiving a negative or overly critical *first* feedback can be crushing. So, we should prepare students by first discussing ways of providing compassionate peer feedback, perhaps proposing a simple formula such as: 'a star and a wish', or 'something I like and a question I have'. This scaffolds the feedback, makes it concise and makes it easier to give and receive.

This case study shows the importance of designing appropriate support systems at the start of a course, often a make-or-break check point. As academics, we should invest time and energy in designing appropriate support structures to respond to new students' needs, integrating those support systems into the course itself. End of week 1 check points with reflection and peer review can do much to foster a collaborative, inclusive atmosphere. Recent alumni can provide us precious evaluative comments in order to evaluate the effectiveness of existing support systems as well as suggest enhancements.

All of the approaches discussed under this subheading aim to build community and foster a support culture. They also go hand in hand with the orientation process for students to understand more about the course, get to know others on the course, establish a professional but friendly relationship with the teacher(s), and develop meta-cognition—understanding themselves better as learners. The suggestions embody the nine inclusivity values discussed in Section 1 in various ways.

Conclusion

This chapter was about designing inclusive learning environments by (1) addressing students' well-being and (2) carefully planning the start of a course.

In this chapter I have only scratched the surface of the complex area of students' well-being, in particular trauma-informed teaching and learning. Of course, this is not something we address once at the start of a course as a tick box exercise and then put it to one side. We need regular check-ins and well-being reminders. For example, I have created a well-being zone on my course VLE space so students can refer to it anytime they need to during the course. And we need to remember that the best thing we can do for students' well-being is to look after our own well-being. Tired and worn-out staff cannot create good, inclusive learning environments and experiences. This also means realising what level of emotional support we can reasonably, personally provide *and* sustain. It goes without saying that this points to the wider institutional policies and practices in place to support and sustain staff well-being.

The other aspect I addressed is inclusive ways of starting the course. I encourage you to start a shared folder or live doc within your department where you can all add your 'winning' inclusive first activities or icebreakers. This is invaluable for new staff joining the department and will help you keep your practice fresh rather than always use the same approaches. The website www.onehe.org offers a wealth of suggestions for well-being and community-building activities and is worth browsing regularly.

We started off by thinking about these questions:

> **Activate your inner dialogue. … How would you answer?**
>
> How important do you think sense of belonging is for students to succeed on your course? Why?
> How can you support and promote students' well-being by the way you design learning?
> What support systems can you set up at the start of your course to build community?

In a nutshell, my provisional and evolving answers are:

For students to thrive academically and socially, they need to feel that they matter and that they belong. Building community is something we do from before the course starts until the very end; it is ongoing. We can create a variety of support systems such as culturally respectful icebreakers, study-buddy systems, peer reviews and more. The start of the course is a critical make-or-break point for many students, hence it is worth designing and planning it carefully.

Bibliography

Capper, G. and McVitty, D. (2022). Belonging Inclusion and Mental Health Are All Connected. [blog] Wonk HE. Available at: https://wonkhe.com/blogs/belonging-inclusion-and-mental-health-are-all-connected/#comment-32921

Flett, G., Khan, A. and Su, C. (2019). Mattering and Psychological Well-being in College and University Students: Review and Recommendations for Campus-Based Initiatives. *International Journal of Mental Health and Addiction.* doi: 10.1007/s11469-019-00073-6

Foster, M. and Killick, D. (2021). *Learner Relationships in a Global Higher Education: Critical Intercultural Pedagogy for a Multicultural Globalising World.* New York: Routledge.

Gilbert, T., Doolan, M., Beka, D.S., Spencer, N., Crotta, D.M. and Davari, S. (2017). Compassion on University Degree Programmes at a UK University: The Neuroscience of Effective Group Work. *Journal of Research in Innovative Teaching and Learning.* doi: 10.1108/JRIT-09-2017-0020

Henriksen, D., Creely, E. and Gruber, N. (2022). A Conceptual Model for Pedagogies of Care in Online Learning Environments. *Italian Journal of Educational Technology.* doi: 10.17471/2499-4324/1238

Hoch, A., Stewart, D., Webb, K. and Wyandt-Hiebert, M.A. (2015). Trauma-informed Care on a College Campus. *Presentation at the annual meeting of the American College Health Association*, Orlando, FL. Available at: https://educationnorthwest.org/sites/default/files/resources/trauma-informed-practices-postsecondary-508.pdf

Hodgson, J. and Bretherton, R. (2020). Twelve Tips for Novice Academic Staff Supporting Medical Students in Distress. *Medical Teacher.* doi: 10.1080/0142159X.2020.1831464

Imad, M. (2020). Leveraging the Neuroscience of Now. [online] Available at: https://www.insidehighered.com/advice/2020/06/03/seven-recommendations-helping-students-thrive-times-trauma

Museus, S.D., Yi, V. and Saelua, N. (2018). How Culturally Engaging Campus Environments Influence Sense of Belonging in College: An Examination of Differences between White Students and Students of Color. *Journal of Diversity in Higher Education*, 11(4), 467–483. doi: 10.1037/dhe0000069

Prilleltensky, I. and Prilleltensky, O. (2021). Ways to Matter. In *How People Matter: Why it Affects Health, Happiness, Love, Work, and Society* (pp. 59–90). Cambridge: Cambridge University Press. doi: 10.1017/9781108979405.005

Snaza, N. (2020). Love and Bewilderment: On Education as Affective Encounter. In Dernikos, B., Lesko, N., McCall, S.D. and Niccolini, A. (Eds.) *Mapping the Affective Turn in Education (Theory, Research and Pedagogies)* (pp. 108–122). New York: Routledge.

Spaeth, E. and Pearson, A. (2021). A Reflective Analysis on Neurodiversity and Student Wellbeing: Conceptualising Practical Strategies for Inclusive Practice. doi: 10.31219/osf.io/cbk23

Spiridon, E., Kaye, L.K., Nicolson, R.I., Ransom, H.J., Tan, A.J.Y. and Tang, B.W.X. (2020). Integrated Learning Communities as a Peer Support Initiative for First Year University Students. *Journal of Applied Social Psychology*, 1–12. doi: 10.1111/jasp.12668

End note to Section 2

In Section 2 I have focussed on the context of learning, the set up and engagement on a course. Contextual analysis provides a holistic lens on learning design by looking at the *whole* environment where a course operates. The three chapters discussed the three areas of:

(1) the physical and digital spaces
(2) the needs analysis and orientation
(3) building community and fostering a support culture.

By intentionally addressing these three crucial contextual dimensions of learning at initial design stage, we ensure that the course has the best chances of being successful from an inclusivity viewpoint.

As suggested by the provocative chapter titles, it's like getting ready to win a race—a marathon, not a sprint: ready, steady, go …

> **Activate your inner dialogue. … How would you answer?**
>
> What have your learnt in this section about learning context?
> What are your main take aways for more inclusive practice regarding the set-up and environment of your course?

Section 3 is about the next symbolical branch of the roots-to-shoots approach: the content of the course, in other words the input and practice we design for our students.

Check the companion website to this book, inclusivelearningdesign.com for further resources about inclusive set up and engagement.

Section 3

Learning content
Input and practice

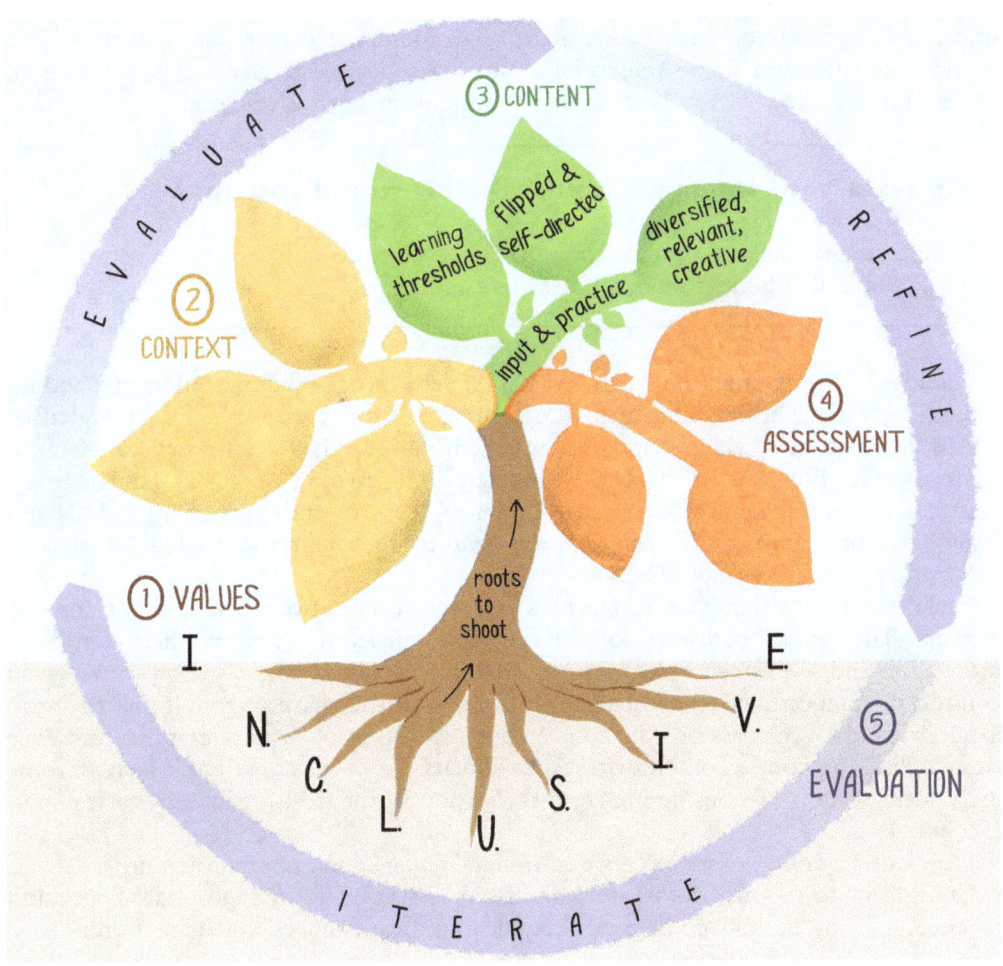

Section 1 invited you to articulate your values.
Section 2 invited you to carry out a contextual analysis and to set up support systems.
Section 3 is about the content of your course and ways to make it more inclusive.

DOI: 10.4324/9781003230144-8

This section is about *'input and practice'*: input is the content, and practice is the repeated application of knowledge. Practice does not make us perfect, but can make us masters. Cognitive science tells us that what moves something we are learning from the short-term (working) memory to the long-term memory is a process of knowing, then understanding, using and finally *mastery by practice*. When we have mastered something, it is fully integrated into our cognitive system (Furst 2022) or it is demonstrated by physical skills.

The focus of this section can be summed up by Ella Fitzgerald's song title 'Tain't What You Do (It's the Way That You Do It)': although content is perceived as core on university courses, this section is not so much about what you teach, as important as that might be, but about *how and why* you teach it, with the focus remaining firmly on learner activity.

One of the best things we can do as academics is to stop teaching content and support students as *they* develop their learning, through inquiry. However, as teachers we are expected to offer and frame the content and devise learning activities students need, so here I discuss how we can best do that, by intentional inclusive design.

> **Activate your inner dialogue. … How would you answer?**
>
> How can you offer your course content more inclusively?
> How would that benefit *all* of your students?

Content is the material, the syllabus, what students need to know, understand and do something with. The learning from the content is usually expressed in (intended or hoped for) outcomes, which shape the assessment(s) through which learners can demonstrate their learning. As in the UK we operate in a learning outcomes (LOs)–driven higher education system, in Chapter 4 I address the pros and cons of using LOs and I suggest experimenting with *learning thresholds* to determine the needed course content, rather than using only LOs.

I take the stance that: 'Good teachers are mediators between the content and the learners. They create pathways so that everyone can learn, whatever their cognition, motivation and self-esteem' (Rapanta et al. 2020). Traditionally, academics have given considerable importance to content, in the sense that they have often felt that their job is purely to teach (or pass on) the course content. This book is an attempt to rebalance this emphasis on course content with other dimensions of learning design such as: rooting values (Section 1), considering context (Section 2) and devising inclusive assessment (Section 4).

How can we design more inclusive learning *through* course content design?

Going back to the nine root-values discussed in Section 1, an appropriate 'input and practice' learning design can help us design learning experiences which are more:

I. Intentionally equitable (everything in this chapter relates to extending intentionally equitable hospitality through the input on the course)
N. Nurturing (designing a more holistic learning experience through content)
C. Co-created (most of the ideas discussed in this section are better designed in partnership with students)

L. Liberating (course content is one of the key areas that can help us liberate our learning design, for instance towards more civic responsibility and decolonisation)
U. User-friendly (we can create more accessible and user-friendly learning content and experiences)
S. Socially responsible (the content from micro to macro can promote 'wisdom' in the form of positive social impact)
I. Integrative (in this section I discuss integrating various types of course input and practices)
V. Values-based (the content that we offer students is value laden, both in terms of explicit and hidden curriculum)
E. Ecological (through both content and practice we can provide more sustainable learning experiences, in a broader sense)

Learning content has become a contested area of learning design. Some argue that, in view of the fact that nowadays practically all content on a university course can be self-taught, we should reflect on questions such as:

> Why prepare huge amounts of content when content is everywhere, and can be referenced with a URL? Why force learners into a one-size-fits-all pathway for the convenience of assessment, when each individual can be supported and encouraged to explore their own interests or be directed down individual paths that mean something to them? Why put so much effort into parading the teacher as a distant talking encyclopaedia when the technology allows the teacher to make themselves available for inspection and inquiry so that each student has the opportunity to establish a more personal relationship in class?
>
> (Johnson 2020)

However, before quickly dismissing teaching as redundant, we do well to remember that 'higher' education is not just about learners knowing more, but being able to apply and *do more* with that knowledge. In the era of huge amounts of information one click away, teachers need to go beyond the free online video tutorials that students can source themselves—teachers need to focus on the more difficult, conceptual ideas and on how ideas relate to each other.

During their university studies, students are expected to apply the content (what they know) to new contexts. And beyond that, 'there should be opportunity and prompts and support for students to consider new and interesting ways of thinking about those applications' (Moss 2021) for instance by developing critical thinking skills.

In Section 1 I discussed the question of redefining the purpose of universities, not as knowledge keepers, but to help us make sense of the 'supercomplexity' around us. As Barnett (2000) puts it:

> In such an age of supercomplexity, the university has new knowledge functions: to add to supercomplexity by offering completely new frames of understanding (so compounding supercomplexity); to help us comprehend and make sense of the resulting knowledge mayhem; and to enable us to live purposefully amid supercomplexity.

Those words penned over two decades ago are more relevant than ever today.

Content is also contested because of moves towards inclusivity and decolonising. As you read in Section 1, good questions to ask are: Whose knowledge are we teaching? What knowledge is valued in my discipline? The road to a less Eurocentric curriculum is long, but by becoming aware of the epistemological roots of your discipline, you'll be in a good position to *start* making needed changes.

How do we choose *what* content to include and what to leave out? How much content should we plan for? A good place to start is to ask: what do the students need to know (or do not know yet) in order to achieve the aims of the course? Think about where the students are now and where they need to be by the end of the course. The space in between those two points is the learning journey you design. 'For a course to have the right content, you need to identify what is the *gap*: knowledge, skills, motivation, habit, environment, communication?' (Dirksen 2016).

How do we choose *how* to teach the content? In this section there are a number of case studies that address inclusive learning approaches based on learning science, in other words they discuss approaches that are scientifically proven to support learning.

Your course content forms a **narrative**, so ask yourself: what story does my course tell? Can you visualise it? If you cannot, chances are your students cannot visualise it either. For this reason, I engage academics in my learning design workshop in a storyboard activity where they articulate the story of their course. Good stories have the right balance of big picture and close-up details—this also applies to your course design. Kirschner and Hendrick (2020) recommend starting with the big picture—setting the scene at a higher, potentially abstract level, then zooming in on a detailed aspect before coming back out to look at how it links back to that bigger picture. You should do this both at the initial learning design stage and at the implementation stage.

Once you have configured how the content should be developed, you will probably need some plans in place—make sure you do not over plan; an outline is probably best to keep space for the serendipitous, for improvisation and for dialogue with students.

We should keep in mind that students also have *their story* of the course—the story they imagine before the course (are they a hero and you, the teacher, just one of the characters?) and then the story they live through the course (the weeks or lessons are potential episodes, their classmates other characters) and the stories they will tell themselves and others about the course once it's over. Their own narrative about the course is worth hearing, especially as part of the contextual analysis and during the course of the getting-to-know-them phase addressed in Section 2.

In this section I discuss three key ways (corresponding to the three chapters) to make your course content more inclusive:

Chapter 4 'Using learning thresholds' makes a case for identifying key threshold concepts, competencies and practices as well as big ideas to formulate better LOs which drive input and practice.

Chapter 5 'Flipped and self-directed' addresses the key question: what is the best use of the precious 'live' contact lesson time? You will read a number of examples of learning design which aim to develop students' agency.

Chapter 6 'Diversified, relevant and creative' contains a plethora of practical examples of innovative and culturally responsive ways to engage students with the course content.

Bibliography

Barnett, R. (2000). University knowledge in an age of supercomplexity. *Higher Education*, 40, 409–422. doi:10.1023/A:1004159513741

Dirksen, J. (2016). *Design for how people learn*. Second edition. Indianapolis: New Riders.

Furst, E. (2022). Learning in the Brain. [online] Bridging (Neuro)Science & Education. Available at: https://sites.google.com/view/efratfurst/learning-in-the-brain?authuser=0

Johnson, M. (2020). What We Learn, We Learn about Each Other ... [Blog] Improvisation Blog, Available at: http://dailyimprovisation.blogspot.com/2020/04/what-we-learn-we-learn-about-each-other.html

Kirschner, P.A. and Hendrick, C. (2020). *How Learning Happens: Seminal Works in Educational Psychology and What They Mean in Practice*. New York: Routledge.

Moss, P. (2021). Creativity in Higher Education. [online] Paul Moss. Available at: https://paulgmoss.com/2021/08/05/creativity-in-higher-education/

Rapanta, C., Botturi, L., Goodyear, P. et al. (2020). Online University Teaching During and After the Covid-19 Crisis: Refocusing Teacher Presence and Learning Activity. *Postdigital Science and Education*, 2, 923–945. doi: 10.1007/s42438-020-00155-y

Chapter 4

Using learning thresholds

> But what is it that we agree upon that are the cornerstone pieces of the work that we're doing?
>
> Brian Schultz

The first three stages of the roots-to-shoots inclusive learning design approach I advocate through this book are:

- Articulate learning design values (Section 1)
- Carry out a contextual analysis (Section 2)
- Design input and practice (this section)

Where should we start from when designing course input (content)?

When planning a (new) course, it is useful to refer to graduate attributes, subject benchmarks and level descriptors which provide the broad view of what a course should be about and what the students *become* through the course.

A key guiding question about your course or module is: Who do you want your students to become?

I propose these other questions as well:

> **Activate your inner dialogue. ... How would you answer?**
>
> What meaningful and enduring learning does your course provoke?
> How can you (collaboratively) identify the *thresholds* you expect students to cross on your course?
> How can those thresholds inform more inclusive learning design?

The questions in the box seem simple, but actually the way you respond to them reveals the way your course content is encoded in your mind. How would you tell someone what your course content is, in a minute? The chances are that you can think of the main themes your course tackles. If you have a high level of expertise and insider knowledge you may refer to some of the official outcomes for your course, especially if they are articulated well and support learning.

DOI: 10.4324/9781003230144-9

When designing learning, whether at macro (programme), meso (course or module) or micro (lesson and activity) level, content and assessment should be linked to the learning outcomes. Occasionally, you may be designing such outcomes from scratch (especially at micro level) but more often, they will be set in the official course documentation (especially at macro level). Whatever the case, in this chapter I invite you to step back in order to consider the pros and cons of using learning outcomes and to gain both a *deeper* and a *wider* picture of the learning you intend to prompt through your course content. Like the rest of the book, my focus is on meso (course and module) level. Hence, I am going to briefly review, provide examples and contrast four things that can help teachers organise course content to prompt learning:

- learning outcomes
- threshold concepts
- learning thresholds
- big ideas.

This chapter is about experimenting with threshold concepts, learning thresholds and big ideas to see how they can support more inclusive learning design (and outcomes).

Learning outcomes

In the UK higher education sector, there is a requirement for each course to have set **learning outcomes** (LOs)—these are statements that point to what the students should be able to know or do by the end of the course. Do you remember the learning outcomes of the course (or module) you are teaching right now? You may or you may not. It may have been a long time ago or someone else may have written them in the first place. There is often a disconnect between the importance that LOs are given in official course documents and our daily practices as teachers and the immediate learning of students.

Who writes the learning outcomes? For programme or whole course level outcomes, the programme directors or course leaders, or whoever initially designs the programme or course, tend to do so. Once the programme has gone through various quality assurance loops, that is, has been validated and is ready to be offered, the individual modules (units of study) usually end up being run by academics other than those who had written the programme-level learning outcomes. Rather than letting those broader outcomes guide the development of the module, these academics usually articulate *their own* learning outcomes for the modules and lessons they teach. If teachers ignore the programme level outcomes, it follows that students will not be made aware of them. They will only be familiar with the module level outcomes but will not get the big picture and will have a fragmented, modularised experience.

Using learning outcomes has its advantages and disadvantages.

Some advantages of using learning outcomes:

- they help structure the learning process both at planning and implementation stages;
- they document learning;
- they usually highlight capabilities;
- they allow for more effective assessment and feedback;
- they are a 'quality' requirement;

- they have become a 'liability' in that institutions implicitly commit to enabling students to meet the publicised learning outcomes for a course.

Some disadvantages of using learning outcomes are:

- they limit the freedom of teachers in a lesson (because the end point is prescribed);
- they take away the 'surprise' element if shared at the outset;
- they are imposed on students (unless they are co-created);
- they might not be relevant to each student;
- they make differentiation harder (unless the outcomes themselves are differentiated, for example by ability: all students should ...; some will...);
- they 'arguably generate a codified, contractual teacher-student relationship that inhibits a dialogic one' (Cousin 2016);
- they are based on our *assumptions* about students' learning that we *might* be able to 'measure' at a given time. In fact, 'educational "outcomes" are really hard to measure. Many of them happen inside people's hearts and minds, over varying periods of time' (Schneider 2022);
- they do not necessarily measure students' understanding of a subject, they really measure the studen's understanding of the assessment process.

As long as learning outcomes are required of teachers and courses, one of the best things we teachers can do to counter many of the previously mentioned disadvantages is to apply the co-creation value discussed in Section 1. To create inclusive learning outcomes, students should work alongside teachers to formulate suitable outcomes for the course, at initial learning design stage. If that is not possible, at a minimum, we should invite students to write or articulate their own understanding of the module outcomes that we provide. Depending on their level, we could also invite them to add some of their own outcomes to our list. Although we might not be able to formally assess them, those personal, hoped for, outcomes tend to be more meaningful and relevant to the students and can be used to review and evaluate learning.

To make outcomes less prescriptive, we could call them 'indicative', 'intended' or 'desirable', to indicate that ultimately only students are in charge of what they get out of a learning experience.

Examples of (intended) learning outcomes

- *for a teacher education course*:
  By the end (of the module) you should be able to evaluate your teaching style and approaches using a variety of feedback sources, including peer observations.
  This outcome could be measured in an assessment by asking student-teachers to produce a research-informed reflection using relevant literature, students' evaluation of their teaching and lesson observation feedback reports.
- *for a photography course*
  By the end (of the module) you can critically evaluate your photographic choices, including your use of light.
  This outcome could be measured in an assessment by asking students to produce a research-informed evaluative reflection using relevant literature, peer evaluation of their photos and feedback from the teacher.

To be inclusive, learning outcomes should foremost be *achievable* by all students, hence we need to check their accessibility. For example, to allow for ability variations, we could differentiate them into: all students should ...; some should. ...

To allow for constraints due to accrediting bodies, we should ensure the course provides opportunities to discuss and become familiar with their requirements.

Some LOs might imply (cultural) understandings and experiences that might not be shared by all students—we should plan appropriate scaffolds to ensure this does not represent a barrier for some.

LOs should be written in a way which allows multiple means of representation of learning, an important universal design for learning tenet. This means that, overall, the LOs should lead to an appropriate variety of formative and summative assessment activities, providing each student the chance to demonstrate their learning in a mode that suits them, at some point. I discuss this in Chapter 7.

At design stage, how do you choose intended learning outcomes for your course? How do you check their validity? Something that can help us academics formulate meaningful and valid learning outcomes is by going both *deeper*, by identifying the learning thresholds, and *wider*, by identifying the big ideas, *before* writing the intended learning outcomes.

To explain what I mean, I will first discuss 'threshold concepts' theory, then explain and exemplify 'learning thresholds' and how these relate to 'big ideas'. Finally, I discuss how starting from thresholds and big ideas leads to creating better intended learning outcomes.

Threshold concepts

Learning outcomes codify the expectations of teachers with regards to the way that student performance will be assessed in a subject. Outcomes focus on the end result, but how about what happens *in the middle*? In 2003 Ray Land proposed a different way of articulating students' learning: **threshold concepts** (TCs). TCs can both be seen as gateways into the disciplines and help identify typical bottlenecks where students can get stuck. Because of their transformative power, they affect who the students *become*.

TCs are 'jewels' in the curriculum which, according to Meyer and Land (2003) have five characteristics:

> *transformative*—they transform the learner's perception of the field
> *irreversible*—that transformation is permanent
> *integrative*—the learner perceives interrelated ideas in the same way experts in the field might
> *troublesome* for learners
> *bounded*—mastery allows the learner to move on to other threshold concepts

Here are some examples of threshold concepts:

> 'The capturing of light' for photography
> 'Health and safety' for architecture
> 'Care' for health care studies
> 'Precedence' for law
> 'Ambiguity' for art and design

There are threshold concepts which are truly transformational as they have all five characteristics and are as rare as jewels. But there are also threshold concepts which are less rare and might lack one or more of the previously listed characteristics. For example, this happens when a threshold concept comes down to correctly defining important terms of a field of study, because that unlocks further learning and brings the students into the disciplinary community. Atherton (2013) writes: 'Easy or difficult, obvious or counter to common sense, neutral or threatening, threshold concepts are what you need to grasp to join a community—the community of people who understand a particular subject'.

Identifying threshold concepts, at different levels of granularity, is a threshold in itself but the effort pays off as students who are supported past these thresholds can potentially go much further in their learning (Atherton 2013) particularly because it means dealing with the tricky learning points (the 'troublesomeness') which might otherwise hold them back.

What threshold concepts could *relate to* the intended learning outcomes listed prior?

Examples of threshold concepts

- *for a teacher education course*:
  Teaching is not telling
  Teachers learn through feedback

In this example, the first threshold concept consists in realising that teaching is not about transmitting information. This can be transformational because previously, the teacher-students may have been taught in a didactic/transmission model themselves and likely reproduced it in their own practice. Many teacher educators would agree that this threshold concept often proves to be troublesome: it's a likely bottleneck where teacher-students can get stuck.

The second threshold concept (teachers learn through feedback) could also be transformational as previously teacher-students may have thought that to improve teaching they simply need more experience, or perhaps they need to engage with pedagogical research more. They may believe in the benefit of feedback *for their own students*, but they may not have thought about feedback as something they need *themselves* to grow professionally.

Both these threshold concepts can also be irreversible, integrative and bounded.

- *for a photography course*:
  Photography is the capturing of light (radiant energy).

In this example, the threshold concept consists in realising that photography is about light. This can be transformational because previously, the students may have held very different conceptions about what photography is about. It can also be one of the trickiest areas of learning (the troublesomeness of the threshold) to tackle. It can also be irreversible, integrative and bounded.

What differences do you notice between intended learning outcomes and threshold concepts, when put side by side (in Figure 4.1)?

I notice that threshold concepts are much deeper than learning outcomes—they point to the core of what matters in the discipline.

Course	Intended Learning Outcomes	Threshold Concepts
Teacher education course	By the end (of the module) you should be able to evaluate your teaching style and approaches using a variety of feedback sources, including peer observations	Teaching is not telling
		Teachers learn through feedback
Photography	By the end (of the module) you can critically evaluate your photographic choices, including your use of light	Photography is the capturing of light (radiant energy)

Figure 4.1 Intended learning outcomes vs related threshold concepts.

I also sense a danger: a teacher-student could meet the required learning outcome (able to evaluate their teaching style and approaches using a variety of feedback sources, including peer observations) while still missing the point of 'teaching is not telling' and 'teachers learn through feedback'. They could pass the assessment of the outcome without having undergone the transformations implied by the threshold concepts. In effect they could be missing what really matters in their learning to teach: developing the professional ways of thinking of their field of study.

This serious gap could be averted if the teacher-educator (for example someone teaching a PGCert course) had identified and used the two thresholds—'teaching is not telling' and 'teachers learn through feedback'—to design and plan their course. Perhaps identifying those threshold concepts would help the teacher-educator to reframe the learning outcomes, or to use other mechanisms such as assessment criteria to capture those transformations. In doing so, they would better support teacher-students as they grow professionally; they would likely have greater empathy when students face those tricky areas of learning; they could open up a discussion about those thresholds and ultimately ensure that the students do not miss those transformative learning concepts.

Does identifying and using TCs support more inclusive teaching and learning practices? It might do so indirectly, as Ray Land wrote to me in a personal communication (via email in 2019):

> TCs play a clarificatory role in establishing what are the modes of knowing, and the ways of thinking and practising that the students in question are being expected to achieve or perform in order to enter a particular disciplinary, professional or social community of practice.

Hence, TCs could be game changers for students to more easily integrate in the field of study, and subsequently in the field of practice. On the flip side, the inclusivity *challenge* with using threshold concepts can be due to the fact that many disciplines were born and encoded in the Global North: it could be that to make progress in a discipline, students need to give up their existing (cultural) paradigm to fit into the field, with obvious issues when we consider decolonising the curriculum.

However, threshold concepts are also a contested pedagogical theory. There are several questions that are still debated about threshold concepts: do all disciplines and all courses have them? What are threshold concepts for each discipline? Which threshold concepts are transferable and multidisciplinary? Is it always useful to point them out to students? Research is still needed to provide satisfying answers to these questions. Brown et al. (2021) have gone as far as suggesting that we need to 'close the door' on the use of threshold concepts, unless they are used as a 'reflective prompt to stimulate pedagogical discussion'.

There is also an ongoing debate about the usefulness of TCs *in practice*, for different reasons. First, because they are *not meant* to be assessed. For example, the earlier threshold concepts: 'teaching is not telling' and 'teachers learn through feedback'—for teacher-students—and 'photography is the capturing of light'—for photography students—are clearly *not* directly assessable. Second, some consider the term threshold concept problematic because it implies the primacy of theoretical knowledge over **capabilities**, understood as the range of ability, from novice to mastery, to practice in the field of study. This matters as in higher education we need an 'emphasis on developing capabilities as a learning goal so that students have the tools to handle unpredictable aspects of their future work' (Lamb et al. 2020). Students need to develop conceptual understanding and theory *as well as* practices, skills and abilities. This is particularly relevant in practice-based disciplines.

One way of making *practical* use of thresholds for learning design is to expand our use and understanding of threshold concepts to include capabilities. This leads to what I term 'learning thresholds'.

Learning thresholds

How can we make the previously listed threshold concepts—'teaching is not telling' and 'teachers learn through feedback' (for teacher-students)—and 'photography is the capturing of light' (for photography students)—more useful *in practice*? I am interested in finding out how identifying such important learning concepts can affect and inform *students' practices*, so they are not just at theoretical and conceptual level, but they are linked to developing capabilities (for students).

As a first step, I would like to rename them. In a personal communication (via email in 2021), Ray Land wrote to me that, in hindsight, 'learning threshold' would probably be a better fit than the term threshold concepts. Thus, in this book, I will use the term **learning thresholds**, to mean something slightly different than what Ray Land calls threshold concepts because they encompass both the conceptual aspect *and* the practical one.

Identifying and articulating learning thresholds for learning design means: identifying key, usually transformative, often tricky, learning building blocks; identifying threshold concepts *as well as* threshold practices or capabilities in order to create enduring understandings.

To change the prior threshold concepts into *learning* thresholds, we need to add the capabilities dimension.

Examples of learning thresholds

- *for a teacher education course*:
  Good teaching practice is more about eliciting and facilitating than telling
  Teaching practice is refined and enhanced through feedback
  In these examples, the learning thresholds go beyond realising (conceptual understanding) as implied by the threshold concepts 'teaching is not telling' and 'teachers learn through feedback'. The focus is now on how such realisations *inform* teaching capabilities (for a teacher-student). It is about how such learning transforms the teacher-student *practices*.
- *for a photography course*
  Good photos evidence the ability to capture light (radiant energy)
  In this example, the threshold is not simply in the understanding of the role of light in photography, but also in the capability of using such understanding in action, in photographic *practice*.

The emphasis is not on 'by the end' as is the case with learning outcomes, because learning thresholds, unlike outcomes, happen *during* the learning journey.

Threshold concepts and learning thresholds can help teachers go beyond the (more obvious) learning that meets intended outcomes and can be evidenced through assessment. Identifying thresholds help teachers focus their learning design on the *deeper*, most meaningful, transformational learning they expect students to experience. By doing so, they help students grow more holistically and hence they are a more inclusive way of designing learning.

In Figure 4.2 you can compare and contrast intended learning outcomes, threshold concepts and learning thresholds.

Putting the three side by side helps highlight that thresholds go to the very heart of what matters in a discipline, the core ways of thinking (threshold concepts) and doing (learning thresholds) linked to a field. Those are the things that make students 'become' and if we as teachers are aware of those thresholds, we can build a more inclusive learning design around them.

I invite you to experiment with learning thresholds to see how they can help you as you design learning. For example, I believe that identifying learning thresholds can help us formulate better learning outcomes. While LOs are useful signposts of what a student is able to do at the end, learning thresholds which involve identity shifts are dotted along

Course	Intended Learning Outcomes	Threshold Concepts	Learning Thresholds
Teacher education course	By the end (of the module) you should be able to evaluate your teaching style and approaches using a variety of feedback sources, including peer observations	Teaching is not telling	Good teaching practice is more about eliciting and facilitating than telling
		Teachers learn through feedback	Teaching practice is refined and enhanced through feedback
Photography	By the end (of the module) you can critically evaluate your photographic choices, including your use of light	Photography is the capturing of light (radiant energy)	Good photos evidence the ability to capture light (radiant energy)

Figure 4.2 Intended learning outcomes vs related threshold concepts vs related learning thresholds.

the way, in between those signposts. It is possible to link the two as those identify shifts often result in some new *capabilities* which can be expressed in the form of intended learning outcomes.

Identifying learning thresholds is a little test about how well we understand our own discipline, because they are linked to what the course and its outcomes need to be and what the students become. However, even for experienced teachers, it is not easy to identify thresholds that students are likely to experience on a course. As it is a process which requires *consultation*, you could:

- reflect on your own understanding and practice in your discipline
- identify the most meaningful learning thresholds (often linked to bottlenecks) you expect students to encounter
- share and examine the thresholds you identify *with students* (especially recent alumni)
- consult *relevant literature and colleagues* to receive constructive feedback and suggestions on how to articulate the thresholds

By their very nature, learning threshold are necessarily bound to specific contexts and cohorts and they can change with time. Yet, identifying, discussing and articulating learning thresholds develop teachers' understanding, students' understanding, the discipline's community understanding and they promote more wholistic and connected learning.

As mentioned at the start of this chapter, when designing inclusive learning it is useful to first go deeper (using thresholds), but also go *wider*, by considering the *big ideas* of the discipline that students will tackle through the course you offer.

Big ideas

Big ideas are the themes that anchor the course, providing the big picture. 'A big idea is a way of usefully seeing connections, not just another piece of knowledge' just like the *bounded* characteristic of threshold concepts. Big ideas can help students 'construct understandings that are more coherent and richly linked' (Mitchell et al. 2016). Big ideas support conceptual understanding because they help students 'generalize, summarize, and draw conclusions by looking at their learning in a holistic way' (Marschall 2022). Although threshold concepts and learning thresholds are not the same as big ideas, they overlap.

Students who tackle new concepts and practices in a new field of study need help to build the bigger picture by piecing each new bit of learning to the rest. However, if our course does *not* provide big ideas, it's like asking a student to piece a puzzle together without the picture on the box. It is possible, but much harder to achieve and definitely not an inclusive way of designing learning.

I will provide some examples of big ideas related to the previously discussed intended learning outcomes: 'By the end (of the module) you should be able to evaluate your teaching style and approaches using a variety of feedback sources, including peer observations' for teacher-students and 'By the end (of the module) you can critically evaluate your photographic choices, including your use of light' for photography students.

Examples of big ideas

- *for a teacher education course*:
  The role and purpose of feedback to develop teachers' practices
- *for a photography course*
  The role of light in photography

These big ideas are like the picture on the puzzle box which helps make sense of each puzzle piece (or new learning). Figure 4.3 shows intended learning outcomes, threshold concepts, learning thresholds and big ideas side by side.

I notice that the big ideas are not necessarily transformative and tricky areas of learning like learning thresholds are, but they are nonetheless very useful in getting the big picture of learning.

In view of this discussion of big ideas and learning thresholds, here is a provocation: What if we as educators leveraged our expertise to identify big ideas and learning thresholds and then gave students the time, space and support they needed to master them? Would that increase the chances of students engaging in deeper learning and more easily becoming part of the disciplinary community?

Course	Intended Learning Outcomes	Threshold Concepts	Learning Thresholds	Big Ideas
Teacher education course	By the end (of the module) you should be able to evaluate your teaching style and approaches using a variety of feedback sources, including peer observations	Teaching is not telling	Good teaching practice is more about eliciting and facilitating than telling	The role and purpose of feedback to develop teachers' practices
		Teachers learn through feedback	Teaching practice is refined and enhanced through feedback	
Photography	By the end (of the module) you can critically evaluate your photographic choices, including your use of light	Photography is the capturing of light (radiant energy)	Good photos evidence the ability to capture light (radiant energy)	The role of light in photography

Figure 4.3 Intended learning outcomes vs related threshold concepts vs related learning thresholds vs related big ideas.

How does a focus on big ideas and learning thresholds support inclusivity?

- It helps you as a teacher to decode the discipline you teach and identify key learning. As thresholds are often linked to tricky learning areas, identifying them can help you acquire a problem-solving perspective on learning: what is the issue to tackle so students can pass the threshold?
- It can support students who get stuck 'as you are able to identify why they are not progressing and give more useful feedback and guidance' (Ghul n.d.)
- It provides a wider-angle view which you can transmit to students: what's the bigger picture of learning? (the nurturing root-value, wholistic education)
- It helps students connect the dots (the integrative root-value)
- It helps uncover the hidden curriculum, the things that we have internalised about our discipline and do not even realise anymore (what it means to be a doctor, a lawyer, an accountant)
- You can strip away excessive content by focusing on learning what matters the most.

Putting it all together

I am now going to put this discussion and exemplification of thresholds and big ideas in the context of the 'roots to shoots' inclusive learning design approach.

The first three stages are:

- Articulate learning design values (Section 1)
- Carry out a contextual analysis (Section 2)
- Design input and practice (this section)

To design the input and practice, it is useful to

(1) think about what story your course tells
(2) start from big ideas and thresholds
(3) storyboard your course.

What's your story?

In order to design the input (course content) I invite to think about your course as a story, with a beginning (start of course), middle and end (of course), episodes (the weeks or lessons) and characters (historical characters in the field of study, as well as you, the students, the guest speakers, etc …).

Useful learning design questions are:

- What story do you want your course to tell?
- What are the big ideas and building blocks on this course? How do they relate to each other?
- What are the key transformational learning points I anticipate students will experience?
- What new concepts and practices will emerge from the transformational—and *often tricky*—points? (these are the learning thresholds)

These questions help us teachers gain more clarity about the learning that matters on the course, both if we need to design our own learning outcomes for the module we teach (perhaps derived from broader, programme-level outcomes) and if we have been provided module-level learning outcomes and want to *situate* them within big ideas and related learning thresholds. By exposing the relationship between learning outcomes and big ideas and thresholds, the whole learning journey we design will be more meaningful and logical. Besides, we will not overlook the really important, transformational learning that our course is meant to provoke.

Start from big ideas and thresholds

Rather than starting from learning outcomes, I propose that we let learning outcomes *emerge* from big ideas and likely thresholds we expect students to pass. Effectively, I suggest we reverse the order of the preceding table: going from big ideas and thresholds to learning outcomes, as shown in Figure 4.4.

Identifying big ideas and learning thresholds can help us formulate better learning outcomes.

Course	Big Ideas	Learning Thresholds	Intended Learning Outcomes
Teacher education course	The role and purpose of feedback to develop teachers' practices	Good teaching practice is more about eliciting and facilitating than telling	By the end (of the module) you should be able to evaluate your teaching style and approaches using a variety of feedback sources, including peer observations
		Teaching practice is refined and enhanced through feedback	
Photography	The role of light in photography	Good photos evidence the ability to capture light (radiant energy)	By the end (of the module) you can critically evaluate your photographic choices, including your use of light

Figure 4.4 From big ideas and learning thresholds to intended learning outcomes.

Once we have those in place, the question is: How can I design a learning journey and experience that supports the big ideas, thresholds and related outcomes?

Our planning is not a simple tick box exercise: we need to build in a *spiral* curriculum where important (core) concepts are revisited with increasing depth. In order to do this in a meaningful way and not in a rush, we should only select a few big ideas (or even just one) for each module in order to avoid crowding the course with too much content. This usually results in students spending more time with fewer concepts, which supports many types of neurodiversity and leads to deeper learning. Indeed, our rule of thumb regarding the amount of students' input should be: **less is more**. We should strive for 'content compression', which is the 'purposeful reduction of the content to be taught' (Wentzel 2021) to leave space for discussion, practice, exploration and student activity.

Once we have identified big ideas and learning thresholds, and we have formulated learning outcomes, we need to align whatever learning content (input) we have identified with our teaching practice (discussed in this section) including the assessment regime (discussed in Section 4).

Figure 4.5 shows the learning design process I advocate.

Big ideas are the big umbrella under which key learning and thresholds sit (the first circle). All of these inform intended learning outcomes with various levels of granularity (the second circle). Once you have (collaboratively) identified expected learning

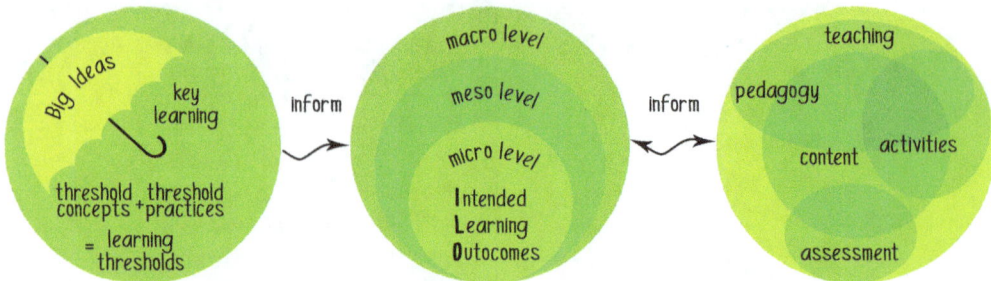

Figure 4.5 Big ideas and learning thresholds inform intended learning outcomes which inform the learning experience.

thresholds, you will find it much easier to articulate the associated LOs (if you need them) or to situate existing LOs.

These, in turn, inform the whole pedagogical approach we take in designing the learning experience, including the content (input) and assessment (outputs) on the course (the third circle).

Storyboard your course

In practice, a very effective way of visualising the design of your course input is to chart the story of your course on a simple timeline/storyboard because the various activities should form a coherent flow (or journey). You could do this with post-it notes on a wall or large paper.

Draw a timeline and use different colour/shape/size sticky notes for:

- big ideas and learning thresholds
- synchronous and asynchronous learning (or in-class and out-of-class activities)
- formative and summative assessments
- enrichment activities such as guest speakers or trips.

Within a learning design cluster with at least one colleague and one student (ideally a recent alumni), write and position the various elements of the learning design along the timeline. You will end up with a visual representation of the likely student journey on your course. These initial, broad strokes, learning design, can be your starting point for more granular planning such as more detailed schemes of learning and lesson plans.

The following four case studies illustrate a variety of approaches and pedagogical purposes in using learning thresholds to design and implement the curriculum: to explore the hidden curriculum; to support the review of a writing course; as big ideas in art; and, in combination with graphics, to explore the threshold concept of 'creativity' in care disciplines. These case studies do not use the term 'learning thresholds' as that is *my* term for an expanded view of threshold concepts which includes threshold capabilities. However, these cases in practice shed light on the benefits and challenges of using a focus on thresholds for more inclusive learning design.

In the first case, from Australia, threshold concepts are used to explore tricky areas of learning and the hidden curriculum. Notice how using cases in small group discussion assists students to unpack these sticky points of learning (thresholds).

Case-based small group learning invites exploration of the hidden curriculum and threshold concepts

By Annetta Tsang (Australia)

The case-based small group learning sessions involved second-year university students studying in the Faculty of Health and Medical Sciences. Our small group consisted of eight students (4 males, 4 females) and two facilitators. The students have 2 x 2-hour small group sessions per week to explore a case-based scenario that focuses on a broad topic. The small group sessions aim to facilitate questioning, critical thinking, reflection and discussion in a supportive learning environment. The students remain in the same small group for 12 weeks. Over time, deep trust is built.

The course was originally designed within a framework of learning goals and student outcomes. A case-based scenario is presented to the students in the first small group session of the week. As the students discuss the case and ask questions, we, the facilitators, provide clarifications and additional information and discuss points of interest. We also guide the discussion to ensure that the case is unpacked comprehensively and that learning goals are identified. For example, in one of the small group sessions, the case focused on a 16-year-old who suspected that she was pregnant. Oral contraceptives, menstruation and pregnancy were highlighted as learning goals. Many related aspects such as clinical consultation, clinician-patient-parent considerations and religious and cultural biases were discussed. During the week, core topics are further explored in other classes and through self-directed learning. In the second session of the week, key learning and insights are shared by the students and summarised in the group. Sometimes, students from all the small groups come together for further expert-led discussions.

The case-based small group learning approach combines the advantages of deep transformative learning, critical reflection, collaborative learning and self-directed learning. In the small groups, we openly explore threshold concepts through dialogues. Threshold concepts are aspects of learning that facilitate discipline-specific ways of thinking and knowing, and essential to mastery (Meyer et al. 2006). If threshold concepts are not identified and clarified by teachers and students, they may pose as barriers to student learning. Threshold concepts may be found in the formal or hidden curriculum, and include fundamental and professional concepts, integrative domains and signature thought processes, etc. that transform the learner's ways of being. (Tsang 2011, Brown et al. 2020, Ho et al. 2021).

In the small group learning sessions, the students articulate areas that are difficult to understand. When difficulties in grasping certain aspects or 'missing links' arise, we assist to unpack and identify these gaps. In the process, threshold concepts may be highlighted. However, threshold concepts are not referred to as threshold concepts in the small group. Instead, they are referred to as 'difficult aspects' or 'sticky points'. Sometimes, the threshold concepts may be basic to the profession but not yet clear to the students, for instance professional pattern of speech in case discussion. Other times, the threshold concepts may be more complex, such as clinical reasoning or critical reflection.

The students may also raise questions that pertain to the hidden curriculum, such as conflict resolution, imposter syndrome, etc. We offer insights into the ways of thinking, knowing and being a health professional. In exchange, the students offer their perspectives as evolving health professionals. The group dynamics drive the learning (Witman 2014). The supportive small group setting provides opportunities to elucidate and clarify threshold concepts including areas that are not formally taught, make the implicit tacit knowledge explicit, break down barriers that impede on deep learning and empower students to make sense of troublesome knowledge (Meyer et al. 2006, Neve et al. 2016) as shown in figure 4.6.

Before each week's sessions, the lead academic and facilitators of all the small groups meet to discuss the week's case and relevant aspects of teaching and learning. These teaching meetings aim to assist sessional facilitators in developing teaching and scholarship, consider and address feedback and promote curriculum improvement. Through the facilitators' meetings, any identified threshold concepts may be discussed in the whole-of-course context and considered for curriculum development.

Given the importance of threshold concepts in facilitating specific ways of thinking, knowing and being, future iterations of the course may benefit from educating staff and students about threshold concepts per se, and incorporating threshold concepts into its curriculum development framework as fundamental building blocks, along with learning goals, student outcomes and graduate attributes.

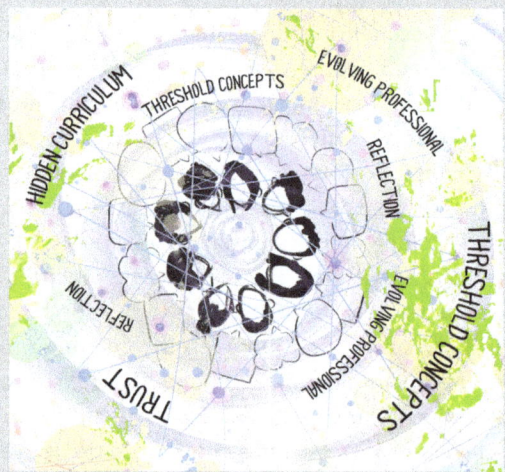

Figure 4.6 Incorporating threshold concepts and the hidden curriculum into course designs can transform deep learning to the next level. For the learner, this involves internal struggles, chaotic sense-making and integrative transformations, which occurs best within a trusting, supportive learning environment.

In sum, case-based small group learning provides opportunities to engage in in-depth inclusive discussions, to elucidate and discuss threshold concepts, including troublesome knowledge identified by the students and facilitators in a supportive setting. The process breaks down the barriers to deep transformative learning by enabling critical reflection and analyses, internalising relevant learning, clarifying assumptions and misunderstanding and enhancing students' ways of thinking, knowing and being health professionals. Threshold concepts should be incorporated into the curriculum development framework. In so doing, authentic learning and professional socialisation are embraced and integrated.

Bibliography

Brown, M., Coker, O., Heybourne, A. and Finn, G.M. (2020). Exploring the Hidden Curriculum's Impact on Medical Students: Professionalism, Identify Formation and the Need for Transparency. *Medical Science Educator*, 30, 1107–1121. doi: 10.1007/s40670-020-01021-z

Ho, C.M., Wang, J.Y., Yeh, C.C., Hu, R.H. and Lee, P.H. (2021). Experience of Applying Threshold Concepts in Medical Education. *Journal of the Formosan Medical Association*, 120(4), 1121–1126. doi: 10.1016/j.fma.2020.09.008

Meyer, J., Land, R. and Davis, P. (2006). Implications of Threshold Concepts for Course Design and Evaluation. In Meyer, J.H.F. and Land, R. (Eds.) *Overcoming Barriers to Student Learning: Threshold Concepts and Troublesome Knowledge*. London: Routledge.

Neve, H., Wearn, A. and Collett, T. (2016). What Are Threshold Concepts and How Can They Inform Medical Education? *Medical Teacher*, 38, 850–853. doi: 10.3109/0142159X.2015.1112889

Tsang, A.K.L. (2011). Students as Evolving Professionals: Turning the Hidden Curriculum around through the Threshold Concept Pedagogy. *Transformative Dialogues: Teaching and Learning Journal*, 4(3). Available at: https://twww.kpu.ca/sites/default/files/Teaching%20and%20Learning/TD.4.3.9_Tsang_Students_as_Evolving_Professionals.pdf

Witman, Y. (2014). What Do We Transfer in Case Discussions? The Hidden Curriculum in Medicine. *Perspectives on Medical Education*, 3, 113–123. doi: 10.1007/s40037-013-0101-0

Inclusivity note

A key take away for inclusivity from this case study is that an awareness of threshold concepts and practices can help teachers design better and more inclusive learning activities and experiences through tackling some aspects of the hidden curriculum.

The hidden curriculum can be a major barrier to student learning because it's as if they are playing a game whose rules they ignore. How can they win the game?

Likewise, there are often tacit rules to do with patterns of thinking and acting within departments and disciplines which can prevent students' progress and integration in the community of practice.

> International students learning in a different educational system and language than their home country, might have additional difficulties tackling threshold concepts that may be culturally bound, like in the case of communication patterns.
>
> The inclusivity challenge here is: are we indirectly expecting that students conform to a pre-set way of thinking and doing in a field, without the possibility of challenging those ways?

In the case study above, although the term threshold concept is not used directly with students, it helps academics design learning by recognising areas of difficulty which are transformative in the learning journey. This is important because unless students make sense of those pivotal learning points, they would find it hard to think, act and become a professional in the field of study.

In the second case study, from the US, threshold concepts are the starting point to redesign a first-year writing course where the LOs are dictated by the government. In this narrative, you will notice the way that threshold concepts eventually gave way to identifying learning outcomes and threshold learning *experiences* which informed curriculum design.

Threshold concepts and a first-year writing program curriculum redesign

By Heidi Estrem (USA)

In the United States, first-year college writing courses have been shown to have a direct correlation with students' retention and persistence in higher education. In a study of relationships among particular courses and students' ongoing experience in college, Nathan Garrett, Matthew Bridgewater and Bruce Feinstein report that the first-year writing course at their institution is the *single strongest predictor* of students' later success in any future major. Therefore, the curriculum of these courses is of particular importance (for further research on first-year writing and retention, see Ruecker et al. 2017).

Our first-year writing program has a long history of high instructor participation in professional development; most instructors regularly and purposefully experiment with high-impact, progressive teaching strategies while also caring deeply about students as people and as writers. Historically, when we have worked together in the past to rethink our curriculum, we have begun with revising or revisiting the course outcomes. (Also like many first-year writing programs in the US, our courses respond to the national Council of Writing Program Administrators Outcome Statements for First-Year Writing as well as our own state-mandated Written Communication Outcomes.) However, in our most recent curriculum revision project, we wanted to prioritise our shared commitment to supporting the uncertainty of student learning in process over the seemingly settled nature of outcomes. According to Jan Meyer and Ray Land, threshold concepts are 'transformative, probably irreversible, integrative, often troublesome and often disciplinarily "bounded"' (in Irvine and Carmichael 2009, 103–4). As such, their troublesomeness provided a productive entry point for intensive discussions of our curriculum.

There were several factors that led to our curriculum revision project: 1. new research on writing transfer and the content of first-year writing courses (Yancey et al. 2014, for example); 2. a new general education program on our campus, with a new vision and set of goals; 3. course outcomes that had not been revisited in nearly ten years. While a full discussion of the curriculum revision project is beyond the scope of this case study, it lasted for several years. Example activities included:

- professional development workshops that focused on prioritising writing threshold concepts (using the 35 threshold concepts for writing studies as identified in *Naming What We Know*, edited by Adler-Kassner and Wardle 2016)
- a reflective survey designed to elicit instructors' ideas on these threshold concepts, the new general education goals and their own goals
- professional reading groups around key terms that emerged from the workshops and surveys (with a discussion list-serv and notes shared regularly from each group so that there could be as much participation as possible)
- a week-long Curriculum Institute where a group of ten lead faculty designed new curricular options for each class
- co-led instructor-to-instructor workshops around identified terms of interest (this redesign process is explained in greater detail in Estrem et al. 2019: 'Threshold Concepts and Curricular Redesign in First-Year Writing')

Initiating this project with the threshold concepts of our discipline provided a cohesive yet rich starting point for considering the content and curriculum of first-year writing classes. They offered a way to integrate the messy, uneven work of student learning in context with the disciplinary content of our field. But even though threshold concepts informed our initial planning, the first workshops and the survey, they gradually faded to the background as other, more accessible language frames began to be more salient to most of our colleagues. While the threshold concepts identified and described in Adler-Kassner and Wardle's collection were illuminating and helpful for some of us, others found the language of the threshold concepts to be unnecessarily academic. However, what remained integral to this work was a shift to working together to describe student learning in process so that we could allow room for uncertainty and struggle in how we discussed our teaching with each other.

Eventually, in addition to fully developed example curricula for each class, we generated one-page framework documents for each course that include not only a list of outcomes but also a list of critically important transformative learning experiences. We all commit to engaging students with these learning experiences in each class. The learning outcomes are identified in their fairly traditional format; for example, in our first course, one learning outcome states that students will be able to 'Use flexible writing process strategies to generate, develop, revise, edit, and proofread texts'. For the same course, we identify a set of student experiences (Figure 4.7) that name what a student will *do*—likely in a new, uncomfortable, or different way—within the course. For example, students will:

Be immersed in writing as an iterative process. They can expect to write a considerable amount of informal and non-evaluated work from which their formal, evaluated work may grow.

Engage in regular peer review. As part of a community of writers, they learn to give and receive feedback.

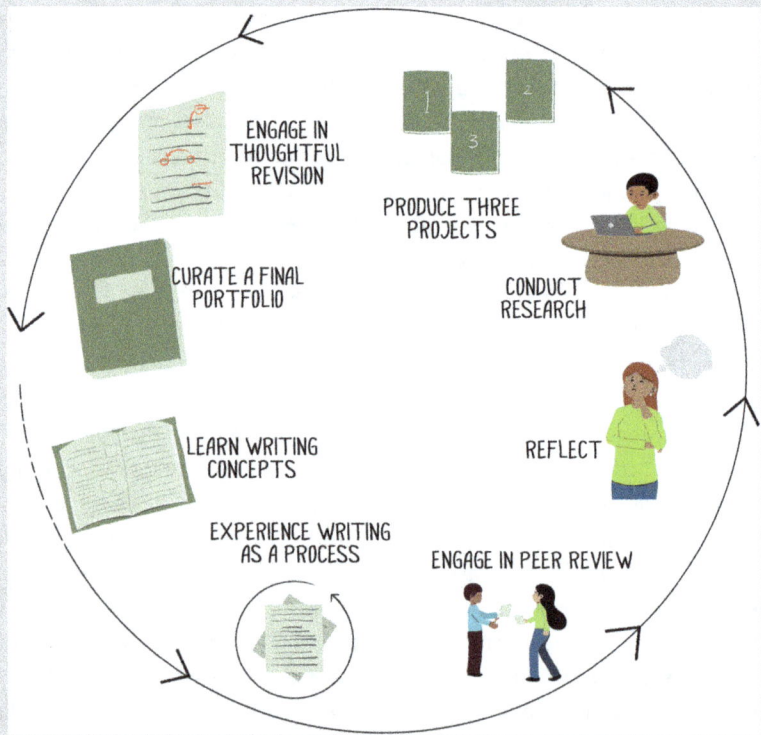

Figure 4.7 The graphic offers an example of how we have identified the student learning experiences of a course. Developing a shared set of threshold experiences for students in each of our courses enabled us to explicitly identify what students should engage with during each of our two classes.

Identifying these threshold learning experiences within our classes focusses us all on providing space for students to engage with uncomfortable, troublesome and yet potentially transformative learning. So while threshold concepts are not identified explicitly in our curricular materials, the theoretical approach behind them—one that privileges uncomfortable learning over tidy outcomes—is infused throughout our program. A focus on supporting student learning and offering particular kinds of experiences in the writing classroom helps us all move closer to deepening students' engagement with the disciplinary activities and perspectives of writing studies.

Bibliography

Adler-Kassner, L. and Wardle, E.A. (2016). *Naming What We Know: Threshold Concepts of Writing Studies*. Boulder: University Press of Colorado/Utah State University Press.

Estrem, H., Shepherd, D. and Shadle, S. (2019). Threshold Concepts and Curriculum Redesign in First-Year Writing. In L. Adler-Kassner & E. Wardle (Eds.) *(re)Considering What We Know: Learning Thresholds in Writing, Composition, Rhetoric, and Literacy*. Boulder: University Press of Colorado/Utah State University Press. http://www.jstor.org/stable/j.ctvv4189q.14

Garrett, N., Bridgewater, M. and Feinstein, B. (2017). How Student Performance in First-Year Composition Predicts Retention and Overall Student Success. In Ruecker, T., Shepherd, D., Estrem, H. and Brunk-Chavez, B. (Eds.) *Retention, Persistence, and Writing Programs*. Boulder: University Press of Colorado/Utah State University Press.

Irvine, N. and Carmichael, P. (2009). Threshold Concepts: A Point of Focus for Practitioner Researchers. *Active Learning in Higher Education*, 10(2), 103–119.

Ruecker, T., Shepherd, D., Estrem, H. and Brunk-Chavez, B. (2017). *Retention, Persistence, and Writing Programs*. Boulder: University Press of Colorado/Utah State University Press.

Yancey, K.B., Robertson, L. and Taczak, K. (2014). *Writing across Contexts: Transfer, Composition, and Sites of Writing*. Boulder: University Press of Colorado/Utah State University Press.

Inclusivity note

In a nutshell, the case study shows the learning design process from threshold concepts to learning outcomes and threshold learning experiences. Arguably, teachers who have adopted such a learning design approach have identified the most meaningful and deeper learning experiences for the students on their course. They will be able to design more impactful learning experiences, not limited to neat outcomes.

One challenge could be how to support students as they tackle the threshold learning experiences which are *meant* to unsettle them in order to produce transformative learning. Frank class conversations and peer support could help, as well as providing a space for inner dialogue such as journaling during the course.

In this case study, the teachers collaboratively engaged in a protracted dialogue about what thresholds they expected students to experience and how to articulate them. This was used as a first step in curriculum design and teachers found this exercise very useful, although the threshold concepts themselves were not ultimately explicitly used in the documentation that resulted from the design. This case study supports the argument I make in this chapter: identifying learning thresholds is a very useful, though challenging, first step in meaningful learning design, including in the articulation of more meaningful learning outcomes.

The third case study, from the UK, demonstrates the use of threshold concepts in a different way than Meyer and Land originally meant. They are used as equivalent to the *big ideas* in art to inform curriculum planning and implementation.

Threshold concepts for the art curriculum

By Chris Francis (UK)

Threshold concepts for art have become central to my teaching and learning. They have been tried, tested and established within my own department (if not indefinitely fixed); embraced by all staff as a means of exposing the 'big ideas' and 'troublesome knowledge' which we believe are—or should be—encountered within the study of a visual arts education (Francis and Nicholls n.d.).

In developing these threshold concepts, the collaborative process of identifying, agreeing-upon, writing-up and reviewing them proved to be highly rewarding professional development. To begin—initiated and inspired by a photography-based action research project led by Jon Nicholls (2015) informed by the work of Land and Meyer (2003)—we set out to define our key art and design concepts. In doing so, Jon and I identified the benefits of condensing these complex concepts into summary headlines—pithy and provocative statements that might invite reflection and curiosity from our students. These statements were to then be accompanied with more detailed elaborations and, in line with our commitment to the visual, accompanying illustrations. Here, as with the words, the possibilities and potential of each composition was discussed and debated in-depth. In fine-tuning our decisions, Jon and I drew from our collective experiences as learners, teachers and practitioners but also, via social media, invited other artists and educators to contribute to our open-source debates. As a consequence of critical discussions, wider sharing and, perhaps most significantly, trial and error in our classroom practices, we have constructed threshold concept frameworks for art and photography that, to date, have been robust and formative in theory and practice. Of course, as is the nature of (learning via) threshold concepts, we remain alert and receptive to their vulnerabilities as declarative statements, shared beliefs devised from our own particular experiences and perspectives constructed in the here and now.

Our Art & Design Threshold Concepts identify nine 'big ideas' that have provided a framework for richer art learning experiences. The project detailed here for this case study, 'Values & Measures' (available at: artpedagogy.com/couch-to-artist-task8), bridged three key concepts:

Threshold Concept #4: Artists use (and abuse) traditions;
Threshold Concept #5: Artists play—with materials, ideas and failure; and
Threshold Concept #8: Art has value, in unequal measures.

Beyond these pithy introductory statements—and with a commitment to equal and diverse representation of artists/cultures within all our activities—the key transformative knowledge here for students related to: awareness of how 'rules' and conventions within art are subject to change and challenge—and how the histories of art can be seen as stories about the friction between tradition and innovation; how—and why—artists embrace play and experimentation, often in radical and unpredictable ways; and how, over time, the value of art is contested and shaped, not always fairly or predictably.

Over a period of four weeks, via playful and challenging threshold concept thinking, students were introduced to a wide range of artworks. This was done using Neil Walton's historicist concepts of 'Traditional', 'Modern' and 'Contemporary'—a devised (and debatable) framework that both complements and contends with our own concepts. To build individual and group confidences, students were given time to reflect individually on diverse artworks and prompts and subsequently invited to share and re-form their opinions in small groups prior to wider debate. Perhaps predictably, students' initial thinking was preoccupied with common themes of portraiture, mastery, accuracy and financial value. Unsurprisingly too, when prompted to 'cite an artwork of value that comes immediately to mind', Da Vinci's *Mona Lisa* topped the list. Regardless, rather than dismiss this as predictable and too-obvious a starting point, we actively embraced its familiarity as inspiration for further threshold concept thinking and action.

Students conducted *wider* research on the *Mona Lisa*, paying particular attention to established traditions at its time of production and how, through a series of both chance and deliberate events, it has become so 'valued' in minds and histories. Initial perceptions of the work as 'traditional' and the *Mona Lisa* being mystically superior to other works became increasingly undermined as students delved deeper into Da Vinci's own experimental approaches. Descriptors for artworks that students had previously identified as 'Modern(ist)' or 'Contemporary' seemed equally appropriate for this 16th-century work. Troublesome knowledge was beginning to reveal itself via threshold concept thinking: students were being exposed to some of the problematic issues when it comes to categorising, organising and retelling art histories. Following this, students were challenged to re-interpret the *Mona Lisa* in more hands-on experimental ways, mindful of the diverse artistic approaches and ideas they had encountered within previous discussions. This exercise challenged students to think harder still with regards to relationships between artistic styles, ideas and ideologies and, significantly, the reasoning and 'values' that shape their own interests, ideas, actions and outcomes.

Consequently, the responses that students produced in conversations, notes and practical work were highly diverse, experimental, playful and, at times, profound. The practical exercise in itself—'create your own version of the *Mona Lisa*'—seems straightforward enough when put like that; an easily accessible task to offer students of all ages opportunities for creative interpretation. However, here, delivered—shaped—via a framework of threshold concepts, it was possible to provide a deeper experience for students that revealed greater disciplinary complexities whilst providing the playground for new confidences and connections to form.

The benefits of using threshold concepts in this way—frameworks for reflection, discussion, research and practice—lies in their capacity to present new doorways into unfamiliar territories (as illustrated in Figure 4.8); spaces where students can enter and explore with varying degrees of ease and (un)certainty. Consequently, the familiar and comfortable spaces that students can occupy—for example, classrooms of thematic outcome-focussed approaches—become re-positioned and

Figure 4.8 Big ideas in art are closely linked to learning thresholds.

more exposed. They might retain appeal and comfort for some, but new doorways are installed to tempt the confident and the curious.

Via threshold concepts, students are drawn to think increasingly critically about the work they encounter and make; how their perceptions and ideas are shaped, and how the words they choose can best contextualise and articulate this. On such occasions, art lessons notably shift from anticipated sequences of preconceived actions, to a sense of wider awareness, ambition and collective purpose. An increased focus on empathy and respect of others as individual creatives can also emerge—for example, with regards to side-lined, misrepresented or underappreciated artists from histories or, closer to home, for their own fellow students collectively navigating these new and previously unimagined thresholds.

Bibliography

Francis, C. and Nicholls, J. (n.d.). About Threshold Concepts. [online] Artpedagogy.com. Available at: https://www.artpedagogy.com/about-the-threshold-concepts.html

Land, R. and Meyer, J. (2003). Threshold Concepts and Troublesome Knowledge: Linkages to Ways of Thinking and Practising within the Disciplines. In ISL10 Improving Student Learning: Theory and Practice Ten Years On (pp. 412'424). Oxford Brookes University.

Nicholls, J. (2015). If I Explore Key Threshold Concepts More Explicitly with My Year 12 Photography Students Will They Develop a Stronger Sense of Themselves as Artists, Able to Reflect Critically on their Own and Others' Work? Praxis Teacher Research, [online] Available at: https://praxis-teacher-research.org/wp-content/uploads/2016/10/JN-Action-Research-Report-2015.pdf

Walton, N. (n.d.). Threshold Concepts: A Critical Point. [online] Artpedagogy.com. Available at: https://www.artpedagogy.com/threshold-concepts-a-critical-point.html

Inclusivity note

Using threshold concepts as big ideas can be very supportive for neurodivergent students and non-native speakers, because big ideas are like big umbrellas under which they can position their learning and goals, to make sense of the overall big picture.

One challenge could be the sense of loss some students can experience while in the liminal space between the old thinking and new thinking, for example in this case realising that 'modern' is a very relative term and how works of art acquire 'value'. An end of lesson debriefing and peer sharing can support this transition.

As mentioned earlier, the inclusivity challenge here is: are we indirectly expecting that students conform to a pre-set way of thinking and doing in a field (in this case art), without the possibility of challenging those ways?

In the art curriculum of the case study, the most meaningful threshold concepts have been collaboratively identified, carefully articulated and supported by accompanying audio-visual material and further details. They effectively constitute the backbone of the syllabus proposed to students and are very explicitly presented to them. The students engage with their learning through the framework of threshold concepts through various learning challenges. This approach helps teachers and students tackle the trickiest learning areas head-on.

Head to the companion website inclusivelearningdesign.com (under Section 3) for a fourth case study, by Denise Mac Giolla Rí (Ireland), entitled: 'Creativity threshold concepts—value, ownership and practice in social care education'. It discusses the innovative use of 'threshold graphics' which are not only very creative but also support students articulate and share their learning in the most troublesome areas through a variety of media.

Having offered you four case studies about using threshold concepts and big ideas, I hope you can better see their value in promoting more inclusive learning design.

Conclusion

This chapter has invited you to consider the relevance and value of learning thresholds in learning design. Through my discussion and the four very diverse case studies I made a case for experimenting with learning thresholds for a much deeper conceptualisation of a discipline, by revealing the transformative (and usually most difficult, tricky, troublesome) points around which we can build the entire curriculum. By aligning our learning design and instruction to learning thresholds, we provide students with real opportunities to engage with the deeper and more meaningful learning points and work out how to navigate the 'real terrain' of their field of study, 'and in the process to discover it anew for themselves' (Singh and Cowden 2012).

At the start of this chapter, I proposed these questions:

> **Activate your inner dialogue. ... How would you answer?**
>
> What meaningful and enduring learning does your course provoke?
> How can you collaboratively identify the thresholds you expect students to cross on your course?
> How can those thresholds inform your learning design?

Of course, I cannot answer the first question, but for the second and third, I suggest: get together (physically or digitally) with colleagues and alumni and discuss what thresholds students typically encounter on your course. Once you have articulated them, think of them as the jewels in the curriculum. Reflect on ways in which students can be supported to pass those thresholds so that they will *become* a professional in the discipline, having tackled the values, ways of thinking and doing of the field of study. However, bear in mind the danger of reinforcing disciplinary ways of thinking and doing *without* challenging them. You may be able to identify a threshold concept which disrupts the disciplinary status quo, as shown in the preceding case study.

In a nutshell, this chapter is an invitation to experiment and see whether you can articulate better and more inclusive learning outcomes *once you have* (collaboratively) identified the learning thresholds and big ideas.

In the next chapter I discuss two other ways of making the learning content more inclusive: flipped and self-directed learning.

Bibliography

Atherton, J.S. (2013). Doceo; Threshold Concepts—Another Angle [On-line] Available at: https://www.doceo.co.uk/tools/threshold_4.htm

Brown, M.E.L., Whybrow, P. and Finn, G.M. (2021). Do We Need to Close the Door on Threshold Concepts? *Teaching and Learning in Medicine*. doi: 10.1080/10401334.2021.1897598

Cousin, G. (2016). Foreword. In Land, R., Meyer, J.H.F. and Flanagan, M.T. (Eds.) *Threshold Concepts in Practice*. Rotterdam, Boston, MA & Taipei: Sense Publishers.

Ghul, R. (n.d.) Threshold Concepts and Troublesome Knowledge. [online] EDTA. Available at: https://edta.info.yorku.ca/threshold-concepts/

Lamb, P., Hsu, S-W. and Lemanski, M. (2020). A Threshold Concept and Capability Approach to the Cross-Cultural Contextualization of Western Management Education. *Journal of Management Education*, 44(1), 101–120. doi: 10.1177/1052562919851826

Land, R., Meyer, J.H.F. and Flanagan, M.T. (Eds.) (2016). *Threshold Concepts in Practice*. Rotterdam, Netherlands: Sense Publishers.

Marschall, C. (2022). 3 Ways to Boost Students' Conceptual Thinking Coaching Students to Think in Terms of Concepts Helps Them Understand How to Apply their Learning in the Future. [online] Edutopia. Available at: https://www.edutopia.org/article/3-ways-boost-students-conceptual-thinking

Meyer, J.H.F. and Land, R. (2003). Threshold Concepts and Troublesome Knowledge: Linkages to Ways of Thinking and Practising within the Disciplines. In *ISL10 Improving Student Learning: Theory and Practice Ten Years On* (pp. 412–424). Oxford Brookes University.

Mitchell, I., Keast, S., Panizzon, D. and Mitchell, J. (2016). Using 'Big Ideas' to Enhance Teaching and Student Learning. *Teachers and Teaching*, 23, 1–15. doi: 10.1080/13540602.2016.1218328

Monk, C., Cleaver, E., Hyland, C. and Brotherton, G. (2012). Nurturing the Independent-thinking Practitioner: Using Threshold Concepts to transform Undergraduate Learning. *Journal of Pedagogic Development*, 2(3). Available at: https://www.beds.ac.uk/jpd/journal-of-pedagogic-development-volume-2-issue-3/nuturing-the-independent-thinking-practitioner-using-threshold-concepts-to-transform-undergraduate-learning/

Schneider, J. (2022). [Twitter] 5 May. Available at: https://twitter.com/Edu_Historian/status/1522173991913414657?s=20&t=Jv5s0Mg3uLxQKvXg3FGS3A

Singh, G. and Cowden, S. (2012). Sat-Nav Education: A Means to an End or an End to Meaning? In *Acts of Knowing—Acts of Knowing: Critical Pedagogy in, Against and Beyond the University*. doi: 10.5040/9781472552747.CH-002

Wentzel, A. (2021). Less is More: Content Compression in CLIL. *Latin American Journal of Content & Language Integrated Learning*, 14, 9–40. doi: 10.5294/laclil.2021.14.1.1

Chapter 5

Flipped and self-directed

> A teacher is one who makes himself progressively unnecessary
>
> Thomas Carruthers

This chapter is about two related inclusive approaches: flipped learning and self-directed learning. Flipped learning can promote inclusivity, for example by supporting both neurotypical and neurodivergent learners. Self-directed learning provides students with agency—this could be from the micro level of student choice of activity within a lesson to the macro level of pathway choices.

Activate your inner dialogue. ... How would you answer?

Why and how can flipped learning promote inclusivity?
How can you design learning that supports students' agency?

Flipped

Flipped learning has become another buzz phrase in education and at times it seems that *any* independent learning done by the students outside of class is called flipped learning.

One of the official definitions of flipped learning is that it is a

> pedagogical approach in which direct instruction moves from the group learning space to the individual learning space, and the resulting group space is transformed into a dynamic, interactive learning environment where the educator guides students as they apply concepts and engage creatively in the subject matter.
>
> (FLN 2014)

The main idea of flipping the learning is to reverse or change the usual order of activities in formal education. As shown in Figure 5.1, in flipped learning students gain their first exposure to new learning *prior* to class rather than in class (Talbert 2017). Essentially, flipped learning is a type of scaffold to support learning before the synchronous class time.

Class time is a limited asset, but one which can have a very big impact on learning as it brings together teacher, students and resources in the same digital or physical environment at the same time. Each live, synchronous lesson is a special type of *gathering* and

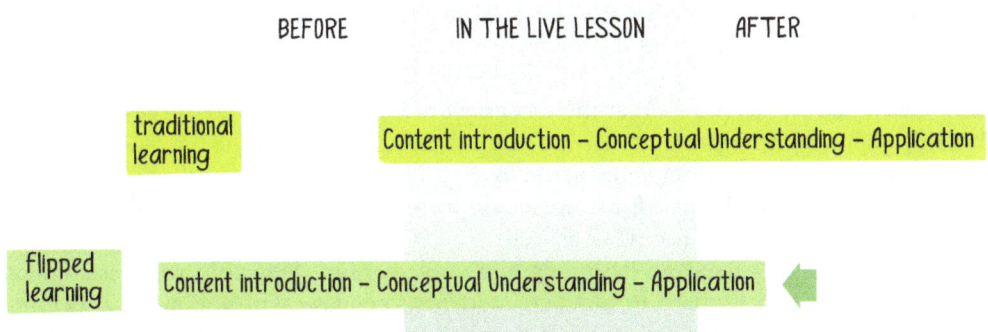

Figure 5.1 The shift from traditional learning vs flipped learning.

for it to be more meaningful we should start with its deeper purpose, beyond 'this is lesson is about X', towards 'why exactly are we gathering today?' (Parker 2018).

With flipped approaches to learning and teaching, the focus is on one of the most important questions a teacher can ask themselves regarding running a course with live, synchronous lessons: **what is the best use of in-class time (in order to advance students' learning)?**

One way to make the best use of live synchronous lessons is to focus on the kinds of activities that really *need* everyone in a room together at the same time and use the inside/outside class time to support those. Foremost, classroom time should be used for community building, peer learning, discussion and collaboration. Then also for hands-on activities that require equipment and/or the presence of an 'expert'; formative assessment presentations and peer feedback and anything where the immediacy of in-person contact is advantageous. To have time for these valuable classroom activities, you could use flipped learning to free classroom time from (passive) content 'delivery'.

Flipped learning has **many advantages**, foremost that it is a potentially much more inclusive way of engaging with the course content than having it 'delivered' by a teacher.

Bredow et al. (2021) point out that flipped learning 'allows students to incorporate foundational information into their long-term memory prior to class. This lightens the cognitive load during class, so that students can form new and deeper connections and develop more complex ideas'.

Flipped learning can be very beneficial for students who need longer processing time, neurodivergent students and those whose first language is not the language of instruction.

Other advantages of flipped learning are:

- it helps counter the tendency to provide a one-size-fits-all learning experience and environment;
- it provides natural differentiation for students working independently, for instance providing control over the pace of learning;
- if flipped learning is done via videos that provide the course content, the pause/rewind functions and the subtitles support a great variety of learning needs;
- it is more efficient, as students who have engaged with the flipped learning material enter the class prepared to contribute and more time is spent on projects and group work, or the 'apply' phase;

- it also creates more opportunities for in-class peer learning: more advanced students can teach the less advanced.

However, research has shown that there is *disciplinary* variation in the success of implementing flipped learning (Al Samarraie et al. 2019). Anecdotally, I have noticed that practice-based (applied) disciplines naturally fit a flipped learning approach. In others, where the concepts are too abstract or benefit from an in-person (dialogical) introduction, flipped learning does not work as well.

One of the biggest issues in designing and implementing flipped learning is student resistance: it can be very hard to motivate students to engage with the material beforehand as they feel that they are teaching themselves the content, when having paid for high tuition fees they expect the academics to teach them. This is especially true if flipped learning is done *properly*: it is not just about providing resources such as articles or videos ahead of lessons, but also providing appropriate 'advance organisers' (Ausubel 1960) or cognitively meaningful tasks to do while engaging with the material. So, students are not just passively watching or reading but they need to do something with the material, which requires a real commitment from their part.

One of the best counterarguments to students' resistance to flipped learning is: teaching yourself a subject is actually one of the end goals of 'higher' (read: 'meta-') education, namely education about educating oneself. This is something that employers prize: an employee who is a self-starter, being able to teach themselves the areas of work they do not know enough about yet.

Flipped learning requires several changes on the part of the teachers as well: it is front loaded and can mean a considerable amount of preparation to provide input and (some) tasks before the lesson; it assumes that students have high digital capabilities, which is not always the case, so they may need some digital literacy support to work well; it prompts the shift from 'sage on the stage' to 'meddler in the middle' and 'guide on the side' (McWilliam 2009).

Comber and Brady-Van den Bos (2018) warn that 'implementing the flipped classroom should not be undertaken lightly or be seen as a quick fix; at a minimum, it requires staff willingness and opportunities for engagement and peer learning'. Here again, you could start small and find the level of flipped learning that suits you, your students and your course (Tomas et al. 2019). Unless you work in a 'flipped institution' or 'flipped department' where flipped learning is considered the norm and is embedded from induction onwards, it is worth spending time to get buy-in from your cohort and to provide the rationale for your flipped learning approach *before* you implement it.

At the start of the course (preferably in lesson 1), you could ask students: what would you like to get out of this course?

1 To acquire information about X
2 To learn how to apply X
3 To evaluate X
4 To make X

Students may well conclude that they want to get all four out of the course.

At this point ask the students: which ones could you at least start doing by yourselves, in your own time, to have a head start, for instance through materials provided in advance? Which ones are best done in class, in collaboration with your peers and me?

They will likely conclude that number 1 is relatively easy to do independently, before the class.

After this preamble, students are usually ready to accept flipped learning as a strategy to maximise application time in class. However, even once students recognise the benefits of flipped learning, it does not mean they will like it, because it obviously requires more independent commitment and effort beforehand.

Therefore, it is vital to have a learning design strategy regarding the quantity and mode of flipped input the students need to tackle. One of the most likely avenues is to pre-record videos such as mini lectures. Other examples of flipped learning materials are: an article, two contrasting articles, a podcast, a chapter in a book, an infographic, a video presentation and more. Flipped learning activities for students to do before class, when they engage with the materials should be simple enough for students to do independently, for example a simple quiz, multiple choice questions or key points activities.

Ensure that in the live lesson you recap and use the flipped learning material so that students see the benefit. There needs to be some 'incentive' (Brame 2013) for students to engage—this could be a rewards, points or badge system. You will also need to have plan B ready for those who have not engaged with the materials before hand—they may have to watch it in class, or you may need to have one-page summaries, bearing in mind you do not want to set a precedent that could undermine flipped learning.

Realistically, flipped learning does not suit all the disciplines equally, nor all the students equally, nor all the teachers equally. But for those who want to try it, it is worth the effort as it frees class time from the traditional, didactic approach of content transmission that is ill suited for our free access information era.

One of the biggest advantages of flipped learning is that it supports students' agency and promotes self-directed learning which we should all aim for in higher education. In the following three case studies you will read about various ways of using flipped learning: in conjunction with a classroom blog; through the use of instructional videos; and within the teams-based learning approach.

The first case study, from Morocco, is about using *classroom* blogs as a shared digital space for the development of the entire course. This allows the teacher to easily post and update pre-lesson material and for students to interact with it and with each other. Notice the three key determinants of this approach and practical ways of implementing it.

Blogs for learning

By Mustapha Aabi (Morocco)

Introduction:

'No man ever steps in the same river twice, for it's not the same river and he's not the same man', says Heraclitus. Ideally, every course and every lecture should too represent a totally new experience for both students and teacher. In reality, however, our teaching is a series of repetitive learning activities we tend to present relatively in the same way in preparation for the same goals although our students are not the same and what they want is not the same.

Conceptualisation:

I teach three undergraduate groups of educational psychology, each consisting of approximately 200 students. Given their large number and the limited class time, a classroom blog was one of the natural options to consider for space, time and opportunity for the class to reflect and actively interact with the course content. A blog (a shortened version of 'weblog') is a type of online journal or informational website. It is a platform where a writer or a group of writers share their views on an individual subject. A blog can act as a central hub that contains texts, images, audios and videos, and connects individual student blogs together. For my cohorts, I used blogging as a shared online space both to engage students with the course content itself (the 'input' phase) as well as for their reflection and evaluation. While students are encouraged to create their own content and interact with each other, as a teacher, my prompts have been generally course-content related with the purpose of encouraging student ownership of knowledge and creation of change by influencing course content and delivery. I provide pre-lecture prompts, in a flipped mode, whereby students have to use both lower order thinking (discovering resources/knowledge) and higher order thinking (narrative to transfer knowledge to real life context) skills. The blog post/prompts are geared towards increasing retention as well as providing reflective feedback from the students, thus, influencing content and instruction.

Due to the large cohort size, rather than aiming at individual responses to (and feedback on) students' posts, I provided regular group feedback and encouraged peer feedback as well. Depending on your cohort size, you will need to establish appropriate netiquette rules, including response time expectations on posts.

As shown in Figure 5.2, three key determinants have been crucial for our classroom blog:

Co-select (a platform): Involving students in determining the criteria for the choice of the platform is vital to ensuring maximum engagement. It should be noted that some HE institutions may have protocols for only using certain platforms, in which case you may need to discuss with your students how to make them accessible. Generally, your platform should facilitate access for inexperienced students, allow a sufficient number of student accounts, offer privacy so only class students can access the blog content, and provide the opportunity to use RSS feed (an effective way to allow students to be automatically notified of new posts) and the possibility to manage the content of their own posts. In our case, after a week of research and experimentation, we decided to use edublogs, which is an education-designed platform widely used by teachers and students.

Facilitate: Facilitating students' self-regulation and knowledge ownership is key to their empowerment. I have tried to achieve this by providing, as much as possible, a universally designed content (Bracken and Novak 2019) of each of the course's ten themes/chapters on an individual page one week in advance of each lecture. Students are given:

Pre-lecture blog prompts
- to provide relevant links to other resources with a short description of each resource before the lecture;
- to provide a short narrative (audio, video or in writing) relating the theme of the theme/chapter to their real-life story by illustrating with authentic examples from their or their family and friends' daily experiences.

Post-lecture blog prompts
- to add their comments, questions or reviews about the lecture and tag other students to discuss any of them;
- I regularly monitor student productions and when necessary, which is kept to a minimal degree, provide guidance in the classroom to maintain course direction and engagement.

Empower: It is about students becoming creators of knowledge and change. They take a leading role in the ownership and the management of the knowledge created as a result of the lecture-prompts. They are equally engaged in the creation of processes which determine the planning, implementation and evaluation of the course through their posts. However, to formalise their voice, I have encouraged them to actively participate in the processes of continuous change and adaptation of our course by providing feedback through the link of a shared Google form on the blog. We collectively discuss and evaluate the opinions voiced in the form (i) at the beginning of the course and act upon them, and (ii) at the end of the course and the results are also shared with the next year group to be acted upon accordingly.

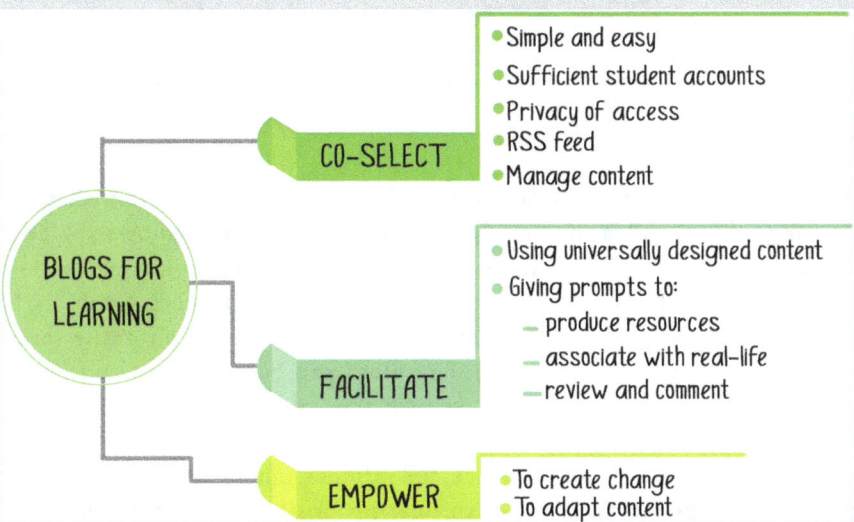

Figure 5.2 Advantages of classroom blogs for learning.

Conclusion:

Blogging has transformed my students into enthusiastic creators of new knowledge, which started at first with questions such as 'can I blog this, sir?' to fully autonomous bloggers. Providing short video narratives about course concepts helped them make sense of their authentic experiences and increased their engagement with the course, leading them to take pride in their knowledge and inviting other students to share it with. I also think that assessing (and marking) blogs may increase engagement among some students, especially those who tend to be more performance-oriented students, and is worth considering if your class size and time allow it. Blogs can be part of formative or summative assessment and they can even be published, becoming very authentic outputs.

Using blogs in the previously mentioned ways supports inclusive education because blogs are accessible, dialogic, iterative, personalised and developmental.

Bibliography

Bracken, S. and Novak, K. (Eds.) (2019). *Transforming Higher Education through Universal Design for Learning*. Oxen: Routledge.

Gibbs, L. (2020). Be There with Blogging: A Guide for Teachers. [Blog] OU Digital Teaching. Available at: https://oudigitools.blogspot.com/2020/03/be-there-with-blogging-guide-for.html

Parisi, L. and Crosby, B. (2012). *Making Connections with Blogging: Authentic Learning for Today's Classrooms*. Eugene, OR: Society for Integration of Technology in Education.

Inclusivity note

Blogging is a dialogic genre which invites responses and reflection. Classroom blogs support flipped learning really well as the blog format allows the course to be presented as a developing narrative, where student voice matters—this is very supportive for neurodivergent and non-native speakers. Students have their own individual space within the classroom blog and can easily interact with each other and the teacher(s). The blogs can be populated and progressively shared to avoid cognitive overload; they are user-friendly, with easily embedded live links.

Challenges can be: blog maintenance; for instance once the blog becomes very long it needs the be managed well, with clear signposting, subheading and chunked content; students' response expectations (from you and from peers) and use of non-written content. Hence, it is vital to agree and enforce a reasonable netiquette, to safeguard all users from misuse or even abuse.

This case study highlights the advantages of using classroom blogs, rather than individual blogs which are more widely used in HE. The classroom blog becomes a shared digital (home)space where all the main asynchronous (flipped) learning is prompted and discussed. Irrespective of the virtual learning environment you use, classroom blogs can be an innovative and supportive space to develop your flipped course.

Videos are undoubtedly the most popular form of flipped learning materials teachers provide to their students before the synchronous classes. The second case study, from Australia, is about various ways of using instructional videos to support learning, and it highlights different types of 'flips' that they make possible.

Instructional Video for inclusion

By Steven Kolber (Australia)

The benefits of being able to differentiate for, and include, all students may already be self-evident to you if you're reading this book, so I will focus on the effect upon the teacher and the pedagogies made possible by this shift. For me, instructional video has dramatically transformed my professional life, allowing me the freedom to never deliver the same lesson twice. The process of planning, filming and editing my teaching content has caused me to reflect on and improve my delivery, clarity of explanations and examples. It has, as a side effect, made my work visible to the students and teachers of the world, which in turn has improved my connections with others.

It has allowed me to become more of a 'facilitator' or designer of learning whereas previously I was primarily a deliverer of content at the front of the room, the 'sage on the stage'. Importantly, this is not a linear, binary, dichotomy, but rather a progressive process. As more instructional video artefacts are produced, the potential for this shift increases exponentially—all without abandoning the possibility and utility of direct instruction, but rather a choice and a flexibility is granted that empowers the teacher, where a range of creative choices abound.

It is easy to become overwhelmed with inclusive learning design, but it is enough to note that a significant element of inclusive practices is located within the beliefs and actions of the instructor. Applying instructional video is my means of allowing more time for reflection, planning and differentiation for specific students, whilst also the practice itself being inherently more inclusive than a text-centric classroom. Research into human cognition notes as a core element the benefits of the 'multimedia principle' which allows students to engage with content through different inputs and allows captioning and playback speed to be altered among other affordances. This also resonates with Universal Design for Learning principles aimed at improving outcomes for all students.

Using instructional video has two primary components for teachers: the manner in which the video content is leveraged; and the pedagogy or learning activities that are applied in the 'live' time made available. Whilst the 'regular' flipped learning approach is relatively common and well understood (Sams and Bergmann 2013, Bergmann and Sams 2014a, 2014b), there are actually many approaches possible for leveraging the learning tool of instructional video. The application of these videos can be understood by the following six options (visually represented in Figure 5.3), which can be used flexibly depending on the needs of students and the content being discovered:

1 Direct classroom instruction, lecture: the standard class is delivered, except that the instructor records their lesson via video, making it available after the fact, on demand, for their students
2 Shared viewing of instructional content: a class group watching a video together
3 A partial flip: some content completed in class, some viewed at home
4 In-class station rotation: students move through multiple stations with screens covering different topics in a sequential or non-sequential manner
5 Blended, flexible model: a mixture of the above models, typically shaped by the content and the student cohort
6 Full flip: all content is covered at home, via video or text, and the learning within class becomes active, group- and student-centric

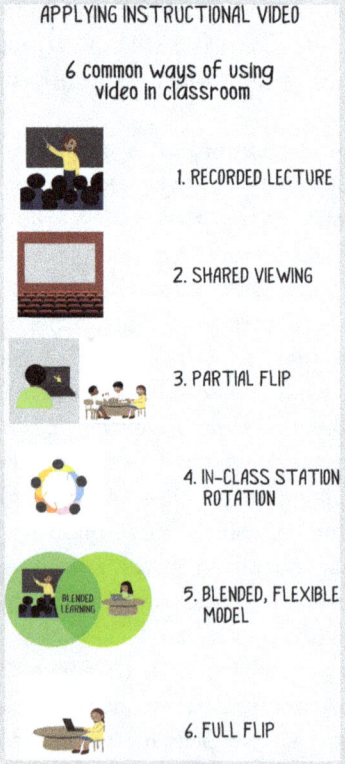

Figure 5.3 Six ways of using videos in teaching and learning.

Each of these six styles of delivery of video has concomitant impacts on the amount of time available for different pedagogies, with the first option allowing very little and the sixth allowing the most. The principles that should guide the use of the 'full flip' in-class time are that students should be applying the information delivered via video and performing higher order tasks, as well as testing for understanding to ensure the videos have been watched. The higher order thinking, application tasks and assessment options are, as ever, open to the practitioner to decide. A full coverage of available options isn't possible here, but I will mention the strategies that I've found to be most fruitful in my own practice: student-led discussions, Socratic circles, student-led mini-lessons, video feedback and approaches that put the learner at the centre of the classroom. Finding what you most value in the space made available by instructional video (full flip) will be a personal, exciting journey.

In practice, I use this approach every day to support all students, allowing asynchronous access of content, which has proven especially accessible for those in low internet settings. I have seen my students with additional needs flourish in their work through this medium and this has led many teachers to follow these techniques to do the same. I encourage all teachers to consider using these approaches.

Bibliography

Bergmann, J. and Sams, A. (2014a). *Flipped Learning: Gateway to Student Engagement*. Washington, DC: International Society for Technology in Education.

Bergmann, J. and Sams, A. (2014b). *Flipped Learning for Science Instruction* (Vol. 1). Washington, DC: International Society for Technology in Education.

Sams, A. and Bergmann, J. (2013). Flip Your Students' Learning. *Educational leadership*, 70(6), 16–20. Available at: https://www.ascd.org/el/articles/flip-your-students-learning

Inclusivity note

Flipped learning is often implemented through the use of pre-lesson videos. One way to clear misconceptions and set reasonable ground rules for flipped learning through videos is by providing students with an overview one-page introduction to your approach, explaining how much time you expect students to spend in flipped 'watching' mode and what types of activities will typically accompany them, and how the flipped learning will be used in class.

One challenge is the negative perception from students, due to increased cognitive demands during self-study. Discuss practical ways of doing the flipped learning, show students the benefits and discuss the learning gain in class.

> Another important inclusivity aspect is video accessibility: students (especially non-native speakers and dyslexics) might struggle with various accents, speed of delivery or poor enunciation. We need to anticipate such needs and build them into the design of videos—for instance providing subtitles and/or transcripts and the option of speed control. Keep videos short (around 5 minutes if possible) and propose before/during/after watching quizzes or activities (Costa 2020).
>
> To make the production of instructional videos more sustainable for teachers, it is important to consider the durability of the video content. Ask yourself: what would make this video content suitable for the next few iterations of this course?

Instructional videos are invaluable to a flipped practitioner. This case study has shown that besides the 'usual' full flip, there are other ways in which videos can be used to enhance students' learning both synchronously and asynchronously. As you think about additional ways of making your learning design more inclusive, you may want to explore the possibilities offered by more unusual approaches such as partial flip or in-class station rotation. These innovative uses of video can better support all neurodiversities in our courses.

Indeed, besides the six mentioned ways that teachers can use instructional videos, *students* themselves are creating new ways of engaging with them. For instance, some students have 'watch parties' (Macneill 2021): they watch recorded lectures or other instructional videos, before or after class, in study groups (not necessarily in co-presence) and then discuss the content together. It is worth checking with your students how, in practice, they interact with the flipped learning you provide through videos. This will help you decide on best ways of designing and using those videos.

The third case study, from the Spain/UK, is about teams-based learning, a highly structured approach that puts students' collaboration—within the same groups for the whole duration of the course—at the heart of learning, relying on pre-class (flipped) and peer learning to advance on the course.

Team-based learning

By Daniel Beneroso (Spain/UK)

In a nutshell, team-based learning (TBL) is a methodology that uses a systematic sequence of individual work and team decision-making application exercises, whereby students receive immediate feedback on their performance—both from their peers and the educator—based on the social-constructivist learning theory (Haidet et al. 2014). Drawing on my experience, TBL can be regarded as an inclusive teaching model in the sense that educators can—and should—create diverse, long-term teams of up to five to seven students ideally blending genders, ethnicities, nationalities and cognitive abilities, and where the learning experience allows to reduce the attainment gap commonly observed between White students and

Black, Asian, Minority Ethnics (BAME) and other underserved communities of students. These features make TBL completely different from one-off group activities since the teams stay together, grow and develop over the duration of the module.

Figure 5.4 visually represents the teams-based learning cycle.

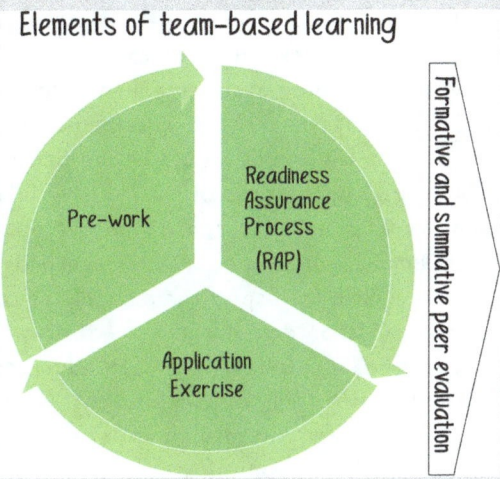

Figure 5.4 Team-based learning cycle.

A module based on the TBL model starts with individual students studying the subject-specific material at home through a pre-reading document or watching an instructional video designed to introduce the underpinning theoretical concepts that they need to be familiar with in order to effectively participate later in class within their teams. This first stage makes effective use of flipped learning. If I were to recommend the means of designing this first TBL stage, TEDEd (https://ed.ted.com) would be an extraordinary platform that may help educators to easily integrate conceptual videos along with multichoice questions with formative feedback that takes the student back to the specific part of the video where the question is explained. Moreover, the platform includes a section that allows embedding of additional resources to be explored and a final section for guided discussion.

The second stage of the TBL methodology is based on an in-class readiness assurance process by means of which students complete an individual summary multichoice test that supports them in identifying whether they have achieved the learning outcomes covered in the first stage, followed by a summative team test where all the peers within the team work along to complete the same test. The questions are usually focused on assessing lower levels of cognitive skills—for example, recalling and understanding—and immediate feedback is given by means of, for instance, scratch cards that reveal the right answers (http://www.epsteineducation.com/). This is probably the TBL stage where I observed the students to be more enthused and motivated to get the right answers; what is taking place behind the scenes is a process of peer support and feedback, where students can perceive their own competence and identify the areas of improvement by themselves (Jeno et al. 2017). Educators provide a brief explanation or a mini-lecture on topics that may need further insight following the teams' answers.

The final phase of a TBL module represents the bulk of class time and consists of a collection of team application exercises or case studies where peers work together by applying, analysing and/or evaluating higher cognitive level concepts based on the acquired knowledge earlier on. The quality design of these team exercises ultimately underpins the effectiveness of the peers' interaction and is the engine behind maximising the chances of an inclusive learning environment. The so-called 4S framework is usually used: *significant* problems, *same* problem, *specific* choice and *simultaneous* report. Teams are provided with a set of potential solutions and they have to display their choice at the same time —for example, by using colour cards or digital clickers—after which a feedback on the quality of their decision-making follows between educator and all the teams to address potential shortcomings (Michaelsen and Sweet 2008). What is great about TBL is that it is suitable for any discipline where decision-making processes are involved.

Applying the TBL model on my engineering modules has posed both benefits and challenges to my learning communities. Whilst TBL prompted fruitful discussions during the summative team tests, and the great majority of my students enjoyed the idea of group working to achieve a substantial mark towards the overall module mark, a few of them recognised that those struggling with the subject found it hard to become better at it, as they would not feel able to answer some of the questions and would rather avoid asking team members for help. Over the years, I have realised that introducing additional support through more direct instruction–based resources, and creating a confident, safe and inclusive group environment—for instance, by having a teaching buddy and spending more time with groups that don't seem to interact—is a way forward to support everyone, but especially the weakest students.

Bibliography

Haidet, P., Kubitz, K. and McCormack, W.T. (2014). Analysis of the Team-Based Learning Literature: TBL Comes of Age. *Journal on Excellence in College Teaching*, 25(3–4), 303–333. Available at: https://www.ncbi.nlm.nih.gov/pmc/articles/PMC4643940/

Jeno, L.M., Raaheim, A., Kristensen, S.M., Kristensen, K.D., Hole, T.N., Haugland, M.J. and Mæland, S. (2017). The Relative Effect of Team-based Learning on Motivation and Learning: A Self-determination Theory Perspective. *CBE—Life Sciences Education*, 16(4), ar59. doi: 10.1187/cbe.17-03-0055

Michaelsen, L.K. and Sweet, M. (2008). The Essential Elements of Team-based Learning. *New directions for teaching and learning*, 2008(116), 7–27. doi: 10.1002/tl.330

> **Inclusivity note**
>
> The case study already mentions some specific inclusivity pros and cons of team-based learning.
>
> Firstly, conflicts can arise if groups are not well balanced and if there are free riders. To balance teams, we need to know our students, perhaps even doing a personality test to ensure that we have a good balance of types and intellectual abilities in each group. In this case, inclusivity is *not* in letting students choose who to work with, but, mirroring real life where we do not usually choose colleagues to work with, they need to learn to work in diverse groups. Free riders soon get peer pressure because besides individual readiness tests, each student affects the group performance.
>
> Secondly, team-based learning assignments must promote both learning *and* team development. The activities should not rely on individual but on team outputs. This means that for some students who prefer lurking in group situations, there will be no possibility of hiding.

Team-based learning strategies provide a framework that fits well with flipped learning as it requires pre-lesson preparation followed by collaboration (Lanier 2021), which mean that the same potential challenges mentioned earlier regarding students actually doing the learning beforehand apply to teams-based learning. Teams-based learning effectively bridges the two aspects of this chapter: it is both about flipped learning and about self-directed learning (within groups).

Self-directed

Many academics likely associate self-directed learning with the provision of independent study hours typical on most university courses. However, the self-directed learning I discuss in this chapter is about allowing students the freedom to direct their learning both in class and out of class, both in synchronous and asynchronous course spaces. It really means increasing students' agency to the highest level we can, allowing students to take the driver's seat by choosing their pathway, choosing their end goals, negotiating outputs and timing, and even generating the success criteria.

In this chapter I discuss ideas to do with (1) negotiated learning, (2) self-directed learning, and (3) enquiry-based learning—these overlap and the case studies address them all (with thanks to Tunde Varga-Atkins for suggesting I use these terms). This can take many forms from macro to micro level: non-linear micro-credential courses; MOOCs; self-mapped learning pathways; choose your own adventure (one of the case studies); genius hour (when students pursue their own learning passion in a set weekly slot); and more.

Guided instruction is a hot topic, with some advocating for its disappearance from universities altogether and others claiming that cognitive science shows it is a superior form of learning.

Irrespective of the quantity of direct instruction you choose to provide on your course, the ultimate goal of student autonomy does not change, as 'people are motivated by autonomy' (Weinschenk 2011). An 'extreme' example of autonomy is 'rhizomatic learning', an approach where there is little structure to guide learning as community and networking make learning happen. There is no pre-packaged learning, but students negotiate the curriculum, create and share outputs (Bali et al. 2016). This loose structure will appeal to many social science disciplines, especially creative courses. But even then, it is not always the best approach. Gaining autonomy is a *process* and we can support it by increasingly letting go of 'control', scaffolds and direct instruction.

The reality on the ground is that most university teachers operate in a system that is modularised and prescriptive, with expected classroom contact time, a syllabus and very little leeway on the timescale of running and completing a course. However, in most cases, it is in the *enactment* of the learning design, when we 'deliver' the course, that as academics we usually have a considerable amount of freedom to encourage students' autonomy. This is where the 'artistry of teaching' comes to the fore, when we are orchestrating, live, the learning event (Hassard 2013). Ask yourself: where can I let go and allow students to decide the *what* and *how* of learning? Is there a module—or part of it—where I can allow students freedom to choose for themselves how to direct their learning?

The answer to these questions depends on many factors, foremost: the students' personal learning environment and the stage they are at in their studies.

The students' personal learning environment refers to the *combination* of personal academic tools, services and communities available to the students and that assists them in taking control of and managing their own learning.

Regarding the importance of the stage students are at, this determines how much direct instruction and support they need. Obviously, the first term of the first year at university is a time to get settled and build community, hence at this time students particularly benefit from the presence of the teacher and to have more (direct) guidance. Later in their studies, once students have tackled the foundation of the course and they 'have sufficiently high prior knowledge to provide "internal" guidance', teacher guidance is not needed as much and can indeed hinder academic growth towards autonomy (Kirschner et al. 2006). However, even when students are at a more advanced level, they benefit from the right *balance* of teacher guidance and instruction, and academic freedom, while students with additional needs crave and genuinely need more direct guidance throughout. Ultimately how much structure and guidance to provide depends on the outcomes of the contextual analysis suggested in Section 2.

New technologies, including machine learning, help academics to create or curate personalised learning experiences and environments in which students study at their own pace. The customised curriculum is inclusive, but the *customisable* curriculum is superior as it allows students to make choices and take ownership of their learning, usually in the form of a personal inquiry whereby students are able to 'tell their own story of what they have learned, how and why' (Watkins 2006). This often happens at post-graduate level, but in the spirit of cross-pollination we could borrow this approach for undergraduate learning too.

Interestingly, for strategic learners trying to cut corners and complete the course without too much commitment, an inquiry-based module 'appears to be the worst of all possible worlds: "basically, they don't teach you anything, and you have to find your own way". Since even inquiry-based modules will have learning outcomes, a strategic approach may work, but result in very dissatisfactory learning experiences ("I didn't learn anything!")' (Johnson 2018). On the other hand, self-directed learning is welcomed by students who crave autonomy and want to pursue their own academic interests. For all types of students, metacognition has a key role in supporting self-regulated learning, hence enough time and resources need to be dedicated to support students plan, monitor and evaluate their learning.

In the following case studies, you will read about a variety of self-directed pedagogical ideas and approaches: first about personalised learning and advocacy; second about 'choose your own adventure'; and third about students designing their own course.

The first contribution, from the US, is about personalised learning and advocacy. Notice how the teacher sets up negotiated learning enriched by a call to action.

Personalised learning and advocacy

By Erin C. King (USA)

As an educator, my norm for a lesson in the classroom typically is designed for students to show me what they know using their interests or passions. Writing can be a difficult skill for most students, even if it is just in growing or polishing their academic writing skills. So, I allow my students to personalise their learning by co-designing a lesson plan that incorporates research, argumentative writing and speaking standards using their topic of choice.

I want students to have a platform to take a stand or express an opinion about a topic that means something to them. The younger generation have a strong want or need for advocacy and even activism. As shown in Figure 5.5, I divide the lesson into three sections: Research—students research a topic to develop an educated argument for a paper; Present—students present a TED Talk–like presentation to their peers; and Advocate—a call to action is required so that students can influence outside of their classroom.

Most students are not accustomed to this kind of personalised experience when it comes to their learning. However, I am guided by the saying: 'Tell me and I forget. Teach me and I remember. Involve me and I learn'.

In an inclusive lesson plan, ideally we should try not to set major expectations on the *order* of completion nor establish a direct plan on what the students should be working on day to day. A teacher still creates a plan but they allow for flexibility so the students can own it. Students should own their schedule and their work. Do not panic. This does not mean that I don't suggest a timeline or set dates. The key to just-in-time instruction is to provide support. You will prepare your students as the lesson plan builds and a learning team will be established amongst the teacher and students. I always plan on some ways to facilitate the student's learning and gain informal assessments of their process through weekly student reflections, stations and teacher conferencing.

Figure 5.5 Students are engaged and informed in student-led approaches when they have time to research, present and advocate.

Another component to this personalised learning is varied strategies. Although guidelines and measures will be put in place, the students discover new platforms and ideas to present their research and argument. I am always excited when a student creates their own path to learning. Students have even invited field experts to come speak to our class to learn hands-on information about their topic. One of my students did research on the importance of recycling. I pushed him out of his comfort zone, a little, and created an opportunity for him to present his findings to our community-based programme which was made of special education students who collected our school's recycling.

I like asking my students for a call to action, and in most cases, it typically shows in the form of advocacy. Build their pride! Remember, the students pick their topic, so they are passionate about it. My favourite thing is when a student picks a topic and as they get deeper into their research, their opinions evolve and change. Once they have spent time researching, collaborating and writing, the students present to their peers in a TED Talk–like format. This gives the students a chance to share their work with their peers and discuss why we should care about their topic.

Here is where the real magic happens. I am always pleasantly surprised to see all students shining because they were co-planning their learning. I am thinking of one student in particular who was very shy and overly anxious when any sort of attention was put on her. This was a high-achieving student, but she struggled when it came to any speaking assignment. Her chosen topic was on the stigma towards depression in the Black community. I knew this was a subject that she felt connected to personally. So on the day of her presentation, I was outwardly cheering her on to present in front of her peers because I knew that this was something her peers never really thought about or maybe even talked about. I was so inspired to hear her talk about a possible taboo subject that turned into a deep and vulnerable conversation amongst her peers of different races and ethnicities.

Get ready for your students to go above and beyond any expectations. At the end of the student's research and final draft of a paper, the presentation and call-to-action must be done; thus, we are encouraging critical thinking skills and influential citizens. As a teacher, I end up learning so much about my students and the teacher-student relationship grows based on that two-way interaction and vulnerability. Furthermore, students truly shine, especially the ones who usually seem unengaged. Why? We involved the student to be a part of their learning process.

Bibliography

Borup, J. and Archambault, L. (2019). Designing for Young Learners. *Library Technology Reports*, 55(4), 17–21. Available at: https://journals.ala.org/index.php/ltr/article/view/7001/9490

Novak, G.M. (2011). Just-in-time Teaching. *New Directions for Teaching & Learning*, 2011(128), 63–73. doi: 10.1002/tl.469

Inclusivity note

This approach is very inclusive on many levels: students choose their topic, with some social impact aspect; they self-regulate their research and they develop public speaking and advocacy skills, likely supporting some underserved group or important cause.

If we want to direct students towards worthwhile causes for their project, we could encourage them to choose one of the 17 SDGs discussed under the root-value 'ecological' in Section 1.

The challenges of using this approach could come from sensitive issues that students may choose which could be triggers or be religiously offensive for some. To deal with this challenge we could: have an initial free speech discussion, where we highlight its value, while acknowledging the difficulties it can pose; provide trigger warnings, for example ensuring everyone is aware of *all* the topics that will be presented; and ask students who choose a particularly sensitive topic to present a balanced argument where they acknowledge various positions rather than simply a one-sided presentation (which will also develop their empathy).

The approach discussed in the preceding case study can lead to meaningful community projects and interdisciplinary collaboration. Perhaps you will find a way to introduce an element of negotiated learning within your course(s). This will be highly motivational, empowering and inclusive for all your students.

The second narrative, from Canada, shows the rationale behind the redesign of a 'Choose your own adventure' course. The course itself initially aimed at providing maximum choice to students, but this proved challenging and had to be scaled down. Within this self-directed learning course, notice how the authors made use of UDL principles and how they included a readiness for learning check.

Choose your own adventure

By Seanna Takacs and Arley Cruthers (Canada)

This case study is from a 'Communications 3000' course in the School of Business at Kwantlen Polytechnic University, taken by students of diverse backgrounds and disciplines. The course was designed to support the development of business communications skills for students with widely varying educational and career goals. By maximising learner choice and voice, the intervention at course design level supports meaningful learning.

Arley Cruthers, an applied communications instructor, and Seanna Takacs, a UDL specialist worked together to turn a tangled 'Choose Your Own Adventure' project into one with clear paths. There were three key values that formed the basis of the design:

- The course was co-created with students; by giving students voice and choice it supported their engagement, collective agency (Giroux 2018) and enjoyment of the material.
- Working collaboratively in the online format meant that they could tailor the course to their own writing goals which was key, given that it was a final course in many students' programme.
- The course established learning goals and activities that were community oriented to support online learning.

Step 1   Instructor concerns, UDL support
In Arley's advanced professional communications course, students come to the course with different majors, levels of writing confidence, and prior knowledge. Arley created a 'Choose Your Own Adventure' (CYOA) framework for the course: a comprehensive menu of assignment choices and modules which are sorted by learning outcome and type with flexible due dates. She was concerned that the course components were overwhelming and students in fact, had *too much* choice. She approached Seanna to ask for help in streamlining the project.

Seanna agreed that the very process of coordinating so many course elements would likely obscure the content by creating working memory barriers—students had to navigate assignment choice, content and due dates on a continuous and contingent basis. She suggested a Group Campaign (GC) instead: The class as a whole could negotiate a narrower set of assignments derived from the broad CYOA menu. Arley wondered which option would be best for the students and Seanna suggested allowing the class to decide for themselves: a) co-design the course as a group or b) take the highly individualised self-design path (CYOA). Arley did a survey before the class started and the vast majority selected the group course with consistent consolidated course elements; a few students preferred CYOA for the flexibility and choice that other students in the class found overwhelming. Arley was able to address learner variability and learning preferences, and support emotional energy and investment (Posey 2019) using this design tweak. Since both the group course and CYOA met course learning outcomes in different ways, it underscored the value of UDL in addressing meaningful learning through decision-making and in addressing diversity in prior knowledge, experience and goal-setting.

Step 2   Readiness for learning check
To start the course, Arley designed a formative engagement assessment to help students reflect on the breadth and depth of their knowledge from the introductory class. Topics covered in the intro class were written on sheets of paper around the room with a continuum graphic below. Students placed stickers along each continuum to rate their recall from 'didn't remember/not confident' to 'remember/very confident' (Figure 5.6). This enabled students to activate knowledge they had previously learned and what they would like to review. It enabled Arley to have a sense of what students were coming to the class with instead of guessing at students' starting point and setting the bar too low or high.

Step 3   Meaningful learning
In the name of true pedagogy oriented towards navigating the student's mind (Morris and Stommel 2018), students in both the group class and CYOA drove the organisation of course content in a top-down manner, making constitutive choices regarding content and pathway. Student feedback from the survey coupled with the co-design meant that Arley acted as a consultant and coordinator, working with students to incorporate the most engaging types of assignments. This approach translated to more meaningful content tied to past learning experiences and future learning goals. Given a menu of choices, students planned the syllabus, chose how to meet the learning outcomes and negotiated how they wished to demonstrate their learning either with other learners (group course) or independently (CYOA). Of note is that Arley filled in some additional activities for the course including guest speakers and was only ever a week ahead of students given that design decisions were made to serve the expressed needs of the students (not as an afterthought or convenient fun activity).

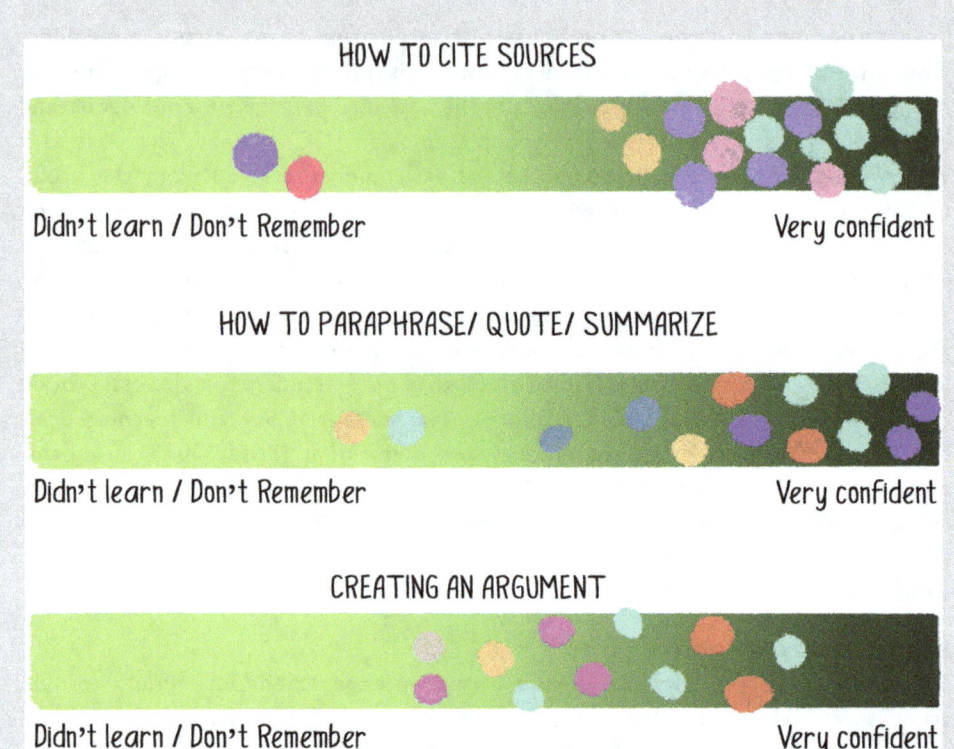

Figure 5.6 A piece of paper with three topics covered in the introductory class with a continuum below that goes from 'didn't learn/ don't remember' to 'very confident'. Learners place stickers on the continuum to mark their level of confidence with the topic.

Step 4   Reflective blogs

Sadly, covid-19 struck halfway through the semester, and students were unable to complete their original plan. Instead, the class decided to create archives of their lives during social distancing. Many produced moving blogs and video blogs and said that the activity helped them process a difficult time. (Example: https://youtu.be/MuIPXYIqUyo)

Bibliography

Giroux, H. (2018). Educated Hope in Dark Times: The Challenge of the Educator/Artist as a Public Intellectual. *Education & Democracy* [online]. truthout.org. Available at: https://truthout.org/articles/educated-hope-in-dark-times-the-challenge-of-the-educator-artist-as-a-public-intellectual/

Morris, S.M. and Stommel, J. (2018). *An Urgency of Teachers: The Work of Critical Digital Pedagogy*. Hybrid Pedagogy Inc. https://hybridpedagogy.org/books/

Posey, A. (2019). *Engage the Brain: How to Design for Learning That Taps into the Power of Emotion*. ACSD: Alexandria.

> **Inclusivity note**
>
> This case study highlights students' agency in more than one way: it not only shows ways to make good use of a choose-your-own-adventure approach for a module, but when a sudden change occurred (in this case when covid struck) the teachers were able to use that same mindset to repurpose the module, because flexibility was already built in the course and it made changing the direction of learning easier.
>
> Challenges: neurodivergent and non-native speakers might find it difficult to handle too much choice, so it is vital to provide a small range of choices and provide enough scaffolding and support for each option.

In this case study, the authors modified a 'choose your own adventure' course to provide enough choice and agency without overwhelming students. They used UDL principles to provide multiple means of expression and they carried out a readiness for learning check, which is very supportive and useful for teachers to inform their learning design.

Head to the companion website inclusivelearningdesign.com for the third case study, by David and Carole Baume (UK), entitled 'Students, each designing their own course', a provocative narrative about enquiry-based learning, challenging us academics to create at least *some* opportunities for students to step out of the directed and siloed modularised learning they often experience at university.

Conclusion

This chapter has invited you to consider flipped and self-directed learning as more 'democratic' and inclusive ways of providing course input and practice to your students.

Clearly, the capacity of our students to self-direct is not to be assumed, and it is not fixed. Rather, students are on a journey, a continuum towards learning autonomy. Teachers can support them on that journey, especially by tuning in, becoming aware of the readiness of their students to tackle the learning at hand at the required level.

At the start of this chapter, I proposed these questions:

> **Activate your inner dialogue. ... How would you answer?**
>
> Why and how can flipped learning promote inclusivity?
> How can you design learning that supports students' agency?

In a nutshell, my provisional and evolving answers, based on the ideas in this chapter are:
Flipped learning supports more inclusive practices by allowing students to take their time, at their pace, before the lesson, to familiarise themselves with new content, rather than provide new input in class *and* expect students to use it straight away. Flipped learning also changes classroom dynamics and teacher-student relationships by making the

live lesson time about collaboration and practice. Practice-based disciplines and contexts are often better suited to flipped learning.

To enhance students' agency, we should strive to provide as many opportunities as possible for them to negotiate, personalise and direct their learning. This can be done at a small scale of lesson level, all the way to module and course level. However, when it comes to choice and letting go, teachers can overdo it and students can feel overwhelmed.

The recurring idea in this chapter has been that teachers need to carefully consider how much instruction and guidance students need, according to their make-up and to the stage they are at. If flipped and self-directed learning are carefully designed and implemented according to context, they will support more inclusive learning.

In the next chapter I discuss how the input phase of our courses can be: diversified, relevant and creative.

Bibliography

Flipped

Al Samarraie, H., Shamsuddin, A. and Alzahrani, A.I. (2019). A Flipped Classroom Model in Higher Education: A Review of the Evidence across Disciplines. *Educational Technology Research and Development*, 68, 1017–1051. doi: 10.1007/s11423-019-09718-8

Ausubel, D.P. (1960). The Use of Advance Organizers in the Learning and Retention of Meaningful Verbal Material. *Journal of Educational Psychology*, 51, 267–272. doi: 10.1037/h0046669

Brame, C. (2013). *Flipping the Classroom*. Vanderbilt University Center for Teaching. Available from http://cft.vanderbilt.edu/guides-sub-pages/flipping-the-classroom/

Bredow, C.A., Roehling, P.V., Knorp, A.J. and Sweet, A.M. (2021). To Flip or Not to Flip? A Meta-Analysis of the Efficacy of Flipped Learning in Higher Education. *Review of Educational Research*, 91(6), 878–918. doi: 10.3102/00346543211019122

Cheng, L., Ritzhaupt, A.D. and Antonenko, P. (2018). Effects of the Flipped Classroom Instructional Strategy on Students' Learning Outcomes: A Meta-analysis, *Education Technology Research and Development*, 67, 793–824. doi: 10.1007/s11423-018-9633-7

Costa, K. (2020). *99 Tips for Creating Simple and Sustainable Educational Videos: A Guide for Online Teachers and Flipped Classes*. Sterling, Virginia: Stylus Publishing.

Comber, D.P.M. and Brady-Van den Bos, M. (2018). Too Much, Too Soon? A Critical Investigation into Factors That Make Flipped Classrooms Effective. *Higher Education Research & Development*, 37(4), 683–697, doi: 10.1080/07294360.2018.1455642

Educational Development Unit - Greenwich University (2016). *Don't Flop when You Flip: Simon Thomson*. [video] Available at: https://vimeo.com/158489454

Educause (2012). 7 Things You Should Know about the Flipped Classroom. [ebook]. Available at: https://library.educause.edu/-/media/files/library/2012/2/eli7081-pdf.pdf

Flipped Learning Network (FLN) (2014). The Four Pillars of F-L-I-P™. Available at: https://flippedlearning.org/definition-of-flipped-learning/

Hew, K.F., Jia, C., Gonda, D.E. and Bai, S. (2020). Transitioning to the "New Normal" of Learning in Unpredictable Times: Pedagogical Practices and Learning Performance in Fully Online Flipped Classrooms. *International Journal of Educational Technology in Higher Education*, 17, 1–22. doi: 10.1186/s41239-020-00234-x

Lanier, K. (2021). Flipped Team Based Learning Introduction. [video] Available at: https://www.youtube.com/watch?v=dcUQfKLb2FA

Macneill, F. (2021). Watch Parties—What, Why, Who, Where, How. Elearning Team. Available at: https://blogs.brighton.ac.uk/elearningteam/2021/03/03/watch-parties-what-whywho-where-how/

McWilliam, E. (2009). Teaching for Creativity: From Sage to Guide to Meddler. *Asia Pacific Journal of Education*, 29(3), 281–293. doi: 10.1080/02188790903092787

Parker, P. (2018). *The Art of Gathering: How We Meet and Why It Matters*. New York: Riverhead Books.

Talbert, R. (2017). *Flipped Learning: A Guide for Higher Education Faculty; Foreword by Jon Bergmann*. Sterling, VA: Stylus Publishing, LLC.

Tomas, L., Evans, N.S., Doyle, T. and Skamp, K. (2019). Are First Year Students Ready for a Flipped Classroom? A Case for a Flipped Learning Continuum. *International Journal of Educational Technology in Higher Education*, 16(5), 1–22. doi: 10.1186/s41239-019-0135-4

Self-directed

Bali, M., Honeychurch, S., Hamon, K., Hogue, R.J., Koutropoulos, A., Johnson, S., Leunissen, R. and Singh, L. (2016). What Is It Like to Learn and Participate in Rhizomatic MOOCs? A Collaborative Autoethnography of #RHIZO14. *Current Issues in Emerging eLearning*, 3(1), Article 4. Available at: https://scholarworks.umb.edu/ciee/vol3/iss1/4

Hassard, J. (2013). The Artistry of Teaching. [Blog] The Art of Teaching Science. Available at: https://jackhassard.org/artistry-teaching/

Johnson, M. (2018). Seven Problems of Pointing to the Future of Education (with our hands tied behind our back) and Seven Suggestions for Addressing It. [Blog] Improvisation. Available at: https://dailyimprovisation.blogspot.com/search?q=seven+problems

Kirschner, P., Sweller, J. and Clark, R. (2006). Why Minimal Guidance During Instruction Does Not Work: An Analysis of the Failure of Constructivist, Discovery, Problem-Based, Experiential, and Inquiry-Based Teaching. *Educational Psychologist*, 41(2), 75–86. doi: 10.1207/s15326985ep4102_1

Watkins, C. (2006). *Personalised Classroom Learning*. London: Institute of Education—International Network for School Improvement (Research Matters series No 29).

Weinschenk, S. (2011). *100 Things Every Designer Needs to Know About People*. Berkley, CA: New Riders—Voices that matter.

Chapter 6

Diversified, relevant and creative

> If something is fun, or messy, or beautiful, you remember it
>
> Mary Lea Harris

After discussing learning thresholds in Chapter 4 and flipped and self-directed learning in Chapter 5, in this chapter I discuss three characteristics that make our input more inclusive and memorable: it needs to be diversified, relevant and creative.

> **Activate your inner dialogue. ... How would you answer?**
>
> How can you design learning input that is (more) diversified?
> How can the learning you design be more relevant to students? Why does this matter?
> What's the role of creativity in making learning input more inclusive?

Diversified input refers to more than one thing. It applies to the mode in which the information is presented or accessed (for instance providing written material as well as audio-visual resources) to the variety of activity types we design; it also refers to the need of culturally diversified input, which links back to the root-value 'liberating' and to decolonisation discussed in Section 1 (Gabriel 2020). Making many ways available to students allows them to choose the best way for them to learn.

Relevant refers to learning that creates a real connection with the lives and interests of the students; it's learning that supports their holistic growth and also helps them integrate in the world beyond academia more easily. Why this matters is obvious by considering what the opposite of relevant is: irrelevant. If we do not make our learning relevant, it risks being irrelevant, unimportant, trivial.

Creative refers to ways of making the input innovative, for instance through playful approaches to teaching and learning and kinaesthetic activities. Some disciplines use creative approaches by default, for instance art courses, but in the spirit of cross-pollination I advocate that we can provide creative input and activities in *all* disciplines.

I illustrate the praxis of inclusive learning input through many different case studies: how these three qualities can support us design more inclusive learning environments, experiences and activities.

DOI: 10.4324/9781003230144-11

Diversified

You may have heard the expression 'different strokes for different folks', of African-American origin, meaning that different ways of doing something are appropriate for different people. Going back to the definition of inclusive learning design offered at the start of the book, it is easy to see that catering for diversity is the core business of any inclusive pedagogy:

> Inclusive learning design is design that considers the full range of human diversity with its complexity. It is designing learning environments, experiences, activities, tasks, assessment and feedback with students' voice and choice at its heart, so that students can grow academically, culturally and socially.

I will briefly discuss the role that (1) diverse materials types, (2) diverse learning activity types and (3) culturally diverse resources play to cater for our students' diversity.

To diversify our input means first of all analysing the **types of materials** we use on our courses. We should aim at providing multiple means of engagement with the learning materials we provide, which is one of the main UDL tenets. UDL is not the same as differentiated instruction: 'UDL is like preparing a buffet where there is ample choice, help yourself and choice of what/when you'll eat. Differentiated instruction is like providing individual meals for each student, bearing in mind their eating habits, preferences and needs' (Gronseth et al. 2020). Although both meals require time to prepare, we can easily see which is easier to do.

When it comes to preparing a buffet of learning materials for the input phase of our courses, one of the first issues we face is the hegemony of written educational materials (for most disciplines), which has typically penalised any student who does not process text-dense resources well. Dyslexic and neurodivergent students usually find long printed text very difficult to process. In a study, Roberts (2021) found that 'dyslexic learners' engagement across the spectrum is greater when exposed to multimedia methods than monomedia'. We may also have students with vision impairment or attention deficits who need materials which they can access and engage with.

Consider the course(s) you teach: how do students access the content? Is your course input based on monomedia? It is worth auditing the types of materials we provide to students and ask ourselves: is there a variety and balance between written, visual, audio?

The following case study, from Northern Ireland, is about how applying UDL principles to content design has meant producing content in multiple formats to cater for various learning needs. Notice the effect of this diversification on the users.

Universal Design for Learning: Using multiple formats of representation to engage and support staff in understanding accessibility

By Tracy Galvin and Jen McParland (Northern Ireland)

It is widely understood that not all learners engage with content in the same way. In fact, some are disadvantaged when trying to access the same information and content, if it follows a one-size-fits-all approach. Recently, there has been a shift away from teaching to the average learner and more of a focus on learner variability delivered through Universal Design for Learning (UDL). UDL is gaining significant traction across all education sectors globally where learner variability, flexibility, choice and representation are key (Novak and Tucker 2021). By integrating UDL when planning and developing content, activities and assessment, individual adaptation and retrofit accommodations can significantly be reduced. The Centre for Applied Special Technology (CAST) offers a detailed description of the guidelines and three UDL principles:

1 Multiple means of Engagement (Why of learning)
2 Multiple means of Action and Expression (How of learning)
3 Multiple means of Representation (What of learning)

The focus of this case study is to showcase that if content is represented using multiple formats, learners would engage with the content and materials at a deeper level, would be more motivated and have an invested interest in the learning process (Meyer et al. 2014). When developing digital content, we often over-rely on text as the only medium when designing, developing and presenting learning materials and assessments. This can often lead to barriers for learning, in particular for neurodivergent learners and those who are blind or visually impaired. Another common way to teach is with content-rich presentations using PowerPoint slides. As presentations are very text heavy, one way to make them more inclusive, accessible and effective is by combining text, video and visual or schematic representations. As part of the development of an Accessibility Series, to support staff as content developers, we identified four areas of focus (Text Documents, Videos, Presentations and Visuals) as the most common methods of content delivery and design.

Underpinned by UDL, we provided learner autonomy so that, for each topic, staff could either read a blog post (~10 minutes), listen and watch a video (~2 minutes), or review a poster (~1 minute) that also included an audio version for accessibility purposes (Figure 6.1). It is more effective to provide multiple ways of representing the content by offering choice (Lowrey et al. 2016). The intention was to model good practices and to increase staff awareness and understanding around learning design, inclusion and accessibility, regardless of their preferred format. We also significantly increased engagement with the content with this approach (Smith 2012). With the evolving trend for more learner-generated content, especially through presentations, the series formed part of a self-study Accessibility Toolkit hosted on the institutional VLE Canvas, which was underpinned by UDL and co-designed with the Student Union and key stakeholders across the institution to broaden the impact of UDL and accessibility.

The feedback from staff regarding the series has been overwhelmingly positive in terms of simplicity of the guidance, understanding UDL and Accessibility and how their practice and content design will change moving forward. Some comments were:

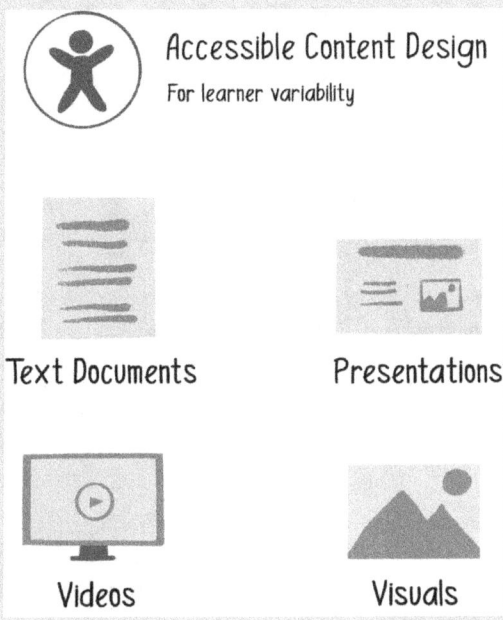

Figure 6.1 Four types of accessible content design for learner variability: text documents, presentations, videos and visuals.

'I feel that I'd be able to make a far superior and more accessible presentation using the information from the series' (PhD graduate, 1st year teaching).

'Sometimes it can be too easy to make font smaller to fit everything in one page or slide without considering that you might be making it a lot harder for someone to access the content' (new staff member, 1 year teaching experience).

'After reviewing the series, I fell down on Alt text and captions for images and charts, it's not something I have ever done before but will do now going forward. I also need to get into the habit of using 1.5 spacing in documents, so it's reader friendly'. (Lecturer with 2 years' experience).

Finally, a lecturer with 8 years' experience after getting one-to-one support commented on the series:

'I made a number of small changes to my practice based on UDL principles and the accessibility series around uploading PowerPoint presentations at least 24 hours in advance and reviewing all its content, chunking pre-recorded lectures into bite-size pieces, co-creating the assessment rubric, changing my module handbook to be more accessible that resulted in increased participation and engagement from learners as stated in the module evaluation'.

This accessibility series is a free and open resource on the Digital Learning at Queen's blog page under the category Accessibility.

Bibliography

Lowrey, K.A., Smith, S.J. and Khoo, J. (2016). Multiple Means of Representation in Distance Education. In Scott, L.A. and Thoma, C.A. (Eds.) *Universal Design for Distance Education: A Guide for Online Course Development* (pp. 29–43). Acton, MA: XanEdu.

Meyer, A., Rose, D. and Gordon, D. (2014). *Universal Design for Learning: Theory and Practice.* Wakefield, MA: CAST Professional Publishing.

Novak, K. and Tucker, C.R. (2021). *UDL and Blended Learning: Thriving in Flexible. Learning Landscapes.* Impress.

Smith, F. (2012). Analyzing a College Course that Adheres to the Universal Design for Learning (UDL) Framework. *Journal of the Scholarship of Teaching and Learning*, 12(3), 31–61.

Inclusivity note

A UDL approach can help us provide much better accessibility to the learning materials. Some learning disabilities are not declared or are hidden, but by providing a menu of options we automatically cater for most needs and preferences, for a better learning experience.

No matter what discipline we teach, we probably already have a body of research or content that supports the course 'delivery', probably in one mode, such as in the form of written text(s). It is not realistic to change the whole course content that we have at once, in order to provide more variety of input mode. We could select the trickiest areas (linked to the learning thresholds on the course) and provide dual code input (materials in two modes, such as written and audio) for *those* areas, initially. Then, we can gradually add to the menu of choices for the users of our course to interact with the content by adding additional modes.

To make the process of resources diversification sustainable, we academics need to find a balance between *creating* and *curating* resources and find ways to *crowd-source* materials, within our department, on social media (such as Twitter) and with our students.

This case study will strike a chord with educational developers: it is very important to model the practices we advocate so teachers can *experience* the approach we promote. In this case, UDL was the guiding principle, and it was demonstrated in the way the material is presented, in multiple formats.

As an example of how to vary input mode, in recent years podcasts have made a significant come-back, particularly since the pandemic. In Section 4 I will discuss podcasts in more detail and there is a case study on using them for assessment. For now, it suffices to say that podcasts are very accessible and flexible media (except for hearing impaired students who would need a transcript). Can we crowdsource a list of suitable podcasts with our students? Can future cohorts add to the list so that it is living and cumulative? Or even, can students create course materials such as podcasts for peer teaching and learning? Of course, this needs to be managed carefully so that students do not feel that we have abdicated our teacher role.

Another example is using reading circles where a range of formats are available, including audio, unbound/unrolled horizontal scrolls, as well as traditional printed texts. This would allow users of screen readers and those who feel alienated by traditional academic reading modes to relate to the text in new and emancipatory ways.

If you add a variety of (crowdsourced) resources in every course iteration, within a few years you will have a very wide variety of material types.

How much material should we provide the students? Assuming that we are trying to teach less so that students can learn more, our input should be as 'compressed' as possible (Wentzel 2021). This is because students nowadays have multiple demands on their time and attention and are cognitively stretched most of the time, hence 'their brains are engaging in a continuous process of triaging for the allocation of finite neural resources' (Friedlander et al. 2011 in Wentzel 2021). It is better to assume that most students on our courses have depleted cognitive capacity for learning. So, we need to decide what is 'core' for students to know or master and that will help them tackle the learning thresholds discussed in Chapter 4; we need to highlight it to them, provide it in small chunks and gauge an approximate time it should take to engage with it. Everything else should be 'further' resources or learning, for those who have the time to go beyond the core learning.

Besides the quality and quantity of input we also need to differentiate in the amount of support (such as scaffolding) that students require. Differentiated input and scaffolding are examples of **cognitive science**—the study of the mind and its processes—applied to learning and teaching. In the following three case studies, you will read about various aspects of cognitive science applied to classroom learning which show other nuances of 'diversified' learning input: first *scaffolding* by varying the pace and amount of new content; second using *chunking and checking*; and third *making learning visible*.

In the first case study, from Hong Kong, read about the importance of reducing cognitive load and effectively using scaffolding to allow for deeper learning at a pace the students can handle. Notice the things that can cause cognitive overload and practical ways in which scaffolding can help avoid it.

Scaffolding to reduce cognitive overload

By Lisa Low, Alexandra Sanderson and Helen Handley (HK)

Brief introduction to cognitive load

Cognitive load is the amount of information that working memory can hold at one time. Working memory is best described as a mental workspace where we store information while we conduct mental processes. It is like a post-it note which holds information for a short period of time. However, when the post-it note is full, there is no more room or capacity for additional information to be held. Learning is active and fluid, so in order to learn we need to make connections between what we already know, such as information in our long-term memory, and what we are learning and vice versa.

What is cognitive overload?

Cognitive overload can arise when the amount of information in our working memory exceeds the capacity of the individual processing it. As educators, our role is to support our learners by managing the cognitive load and task demands in order to reduce the risk of cognitive overload.

As inclusive educators, we must be encouraged to look for common signs of cognitive overload:

- **Incomplete recall**
- **Difficulties following instructions**
- **Place-keeping errors**
- **Confusion and/or frustration**
- **Task abandonment**

One approach to supporting our learners is to follow the 3 As. Our research guided us to the work of Braaten and Willoughby (2014), in 'Bright Kids Who Can't Keep Up' and her inclusive model, the 3 As: Accept, Accommodate, Advocate. Using Braaten and Willoughby's (2014) framework, we interpreted it in this way:

1 Accept
It is through understanding and compassion that we are able to show acceptance of one's learning differences. Understanding how working memory impacts learning can help to find ways to reduce cognitive overload.

2 Accommodate
Once an individual's cognitive load is reached, learning can no longer take place with efficiency. Therefore, it is essential that educators are aware of ways to ensure that learners focus on the important information that must be retained and/or manipulated.

3 Advocate
With increased understanding, awareness and knowledge of the impact of working memory on cognitive load, educators and individuals alike can advocate for the need for scaffolding in order to reduce cognitive overload. Scaffolding takes time, but it enhances the quality of the learning experience for all involved.

For the purpose of this case study, we will focus on the practical examples of accommodations in the classroom through scaffolding (Figure 6.2).

How to accommodate?

A. Scaffolding by design (in planning)
Accommodation occurs when teachers make reasonable adjustments to their instructional practices. This can be done at the planning stage by making the

learning explicit. Explicit instruction can be seen as comprising four elements: explaining, modelling, scaffolding and practising. By planning for each learning opportunity using these elements, students will be able to focus on the salient features of the lesson, 'overlearn' and embed new learning more deeply. In their planning, teachers should anticipate the problems their learners may have and look for points of overload. They should provide concrete and visual prompts to allow students to externalise their thinking rather than having to manipulate information in the abstract. Breaking the learning down into explicit and manageable chunks, or 'chaptering' the lesson, allows for additional processing and thinking time. Providing clear instructions, limited in number, with models to support where the learning is going will support task completion. Scaffolding the learning by providing graphic organisers will help to reduce an overload of information. Teachers should ask themselves, for example: do the learning outcomes need to be presented in written form? Could cognitive load be reduced by the use of assistive technology?

B. **Scaffolding by Interaction (in spontaneous interaction e.g. in the moment)**
Accommodation occurs not only at the planning stage, but also in the teaching moment. It is important that inclusive educators practise 'noticing'. This means they actively look for signs of cognitive overload before it is too late and intervene by scaffolding the task, for instance provide additional time, reduce the information, repeat only the salient information and check understanding regularly. Support the students to break down complex processes using visuals. Identify the key skill to work on and give regular and specific feedback. Consider the pace and clarity of instructions when presenting new information and limit the distractions, tangentials or additional requirements.

Figure 6.2 Scaffolding to reach the learning goal.

Next steps

Help students to create paths for the future. Inclusive education means embedding the 3 As into your practice making it your default position. These no-cost strategies can benefit everyone. The complexities of life contribute to our cognitive loads, far beyond the classroom. Scaffold to reduce cognitive load because it can make all the difference in learning.

Bibliography

Alloway, T.P., Gathercole, S.E., Kirkwood, H. and Elliott, J. (2009). The Cognitive and Behavioral Characteristics of Children with Low Working Memory. *Child Development, 80*(2), 606–621. doi: 10.1111/j.1467-8624.2009.01282.x

Braaten, E. and Willoughby, B. (2014). *Bright Kids Who Can't Keep Up: Help Your Child Overcome Slow Processing Speed and Succeed in a Fast-paced World*. New York: Guilford Publications.

Gibbons, P. (2002). *Scaffolding Language, Scaffolding Learning*. Portsmouth, NH: Heinemann.

Sweller, J. (1994). Cognitive Load Theory, Learning Difficulty, and Instructional Design. *Learning and Instruction, 4*(4), 295–312. doi: 10.1016/0959-4752(94)90003-5

Inclusivity note

Scaffolding is a very inclusive approach to learning design because it makes us anticipate and implement needed supports for different types of students, which reduces frustration and builds confidence for all students, but particularly for neurodivergent ones.

Designing and planning relevant scaffolds can be challenging because it needs more preparation and usually more time to implement. We can manage these challenges by designing scaffolds according to the contextual needs analysis discussed in Section 2, and then having an ongoing evaluation mechanism in place so students can let us know when their scaffolding needs change (increase or decrease).

This case study well illustrates that 'less is more' when it comes to content, although this seems counter-intuitive in a system that seeks to cram as much information and knowledge into students' heads in the shortest amount of time. Scaffolding by design and in the moment can be highly beneficial for students to reach their learning goal.

The authors highlighted the benefits of using graphic or visual representations of what the students need to do (learning activities), and of providing regular feedback to progress the learning. There are other ways of scaffolding learning, but the main tenet remains: providing the needed support (scaffold) to progress learning and gradually fading it away as students increase in their understanding. Taking account of the wide variety of potential support needs in our classes, we should 'scaffold for complexity' (Moore 2019), anticipating as many different needs as possible, for example providing, by default, different levels of supports for an activity or project: fast track as well as more supported learning pathways so students can self-select the level of support they require. In practice this means aiming for a customisable learning journey.

Other important cognitive aids to support more dialogical and inclusive learning and teaching are *chunking and checking*, discussed in a case study by Vicki Dale (Scotland), on the companion website inclusivelearningdesign.com under Section 3. Starting from a medical communication model, the author applies it more broadly to explain how chunking the content into smaller units and ongoing checking for understanding can support more inclusive input design.

Once we have provided the input, we need to ensure students have 'got it', that they have understood it and are able to use it. The next case study, from Mexico, discusses one way of checking learning: allowing students to show it to us, in a *visible* way. Notice three ways of making learning visible.

Making thinking and learning visible in our classes

By Margarita del Pilar Silva Rojas (Mexico)

Why make thinking visible? Is it even possible? To educate is not the same as to transfer and load content into the students' brains. We are at a time in which the covid-19 pandemic has helped us realise that teaching should be primarily focused not on the curriculum to be 'covered', but on the students' skills and processes as stated in the OECD report (Reimers and Schleicher 2020). Get their brains actively engaged in deeper thinking, to foster deeper learning and understanding, which in turn enables even deeper thinking, creating a virtuous thinking–learning cycle.

Making thinking visible supports inclusive teaching and learning because it draws students out, it supports their cognitive processes by using more than one sense, and it enhances meta-learning and self-reflection (Ritchhart et al. 2011).

If we are to foster deeper thinking, understanding and learning, we have to know what's going on in each of the students' minds. But those processes, being electrochemical, are invisible to the bare eye. So, how can we make thinking and learning visible in our classes? As shown in Figure 6.3, I will briefly address three possible ways to make thinking visible: questions, pictures and thinking routines.

The power of questions

Thinking processes need to be scaffolded and explicitly taught, and that can be done from the earliest stages of life. Especially in academic contexts, by the correct use of language, but also through open questions. Every question holds the power of a thousand possible answers and their different inquiry paths, which in turn can spark even more questions as a virtuous thinking–learning cycle through which you go deeper in understanding.

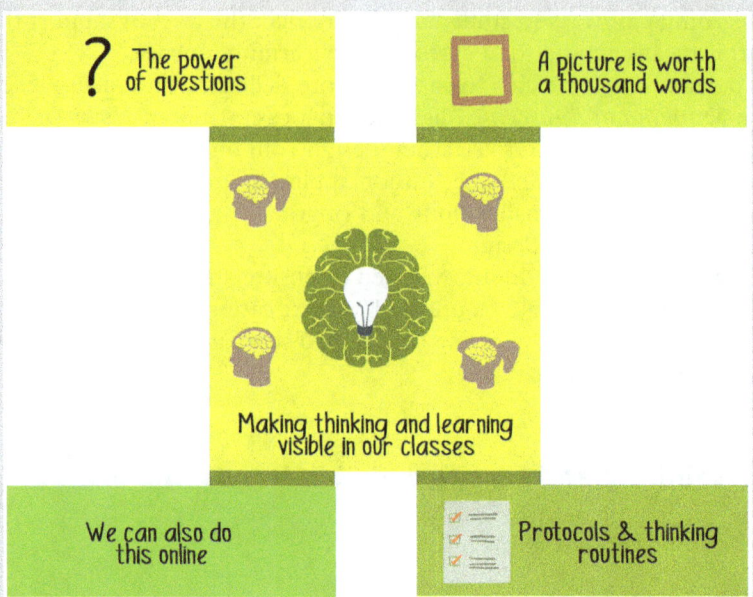

Figure 6.3 Making thinking visible can be done with the support of powerful questions, pictures, protocols and thinking routines, both in person and online.

The more you learn and think about something to answer a big question, the more questions you get, and so on. That's why the kinds of questions that are asked in a class are so important, not just the ones the teacher/professor poses, but especially the ones the students come up with since they can measure (like a thermometer) and provoke (like a detonator) their understanding and learning. It is interesting to note that The Harvard Graduate School of Education and the Right Question Institute offers a course entitled: 'Teaching Students to Ask Their Own Questions: Best Practices in the Question Formulation Technique' (link to course: https://www.gse.harvard.edu/ppe/program/teaching-students-ask-their-own-questions-best-practices-question-formulation-technique).

A picture is worth a thousand words

Each brain processes differently, so words are not always the only, nor the best option; like Loris Malaguzzi has acknowledged in the Reggio Emilia approach (Giudici et al. 2001), drawings, icons, symbols and graphic organizers are great both as an input and as a form of expression of a student's thinking and learning path. This also supports Universal Design for Learning principles.

Protocols and thinking routines

Thinking takes time: to process something, to think about a topic or subject, and even more to think with that knowledge. It's not the same to think like a student about geography and to think like a geographer, with the key thinking skills and perspectives to analyse and come up with solutions for a given problem or situation. And it's not just that; the brain needs time to build neural connections and store information in the long-term memory.

Protocols and thinking routines are strategies to scaffold our individual reflections and also to share and co-construct deeper learning and thinking. For example, the technique of See-Think-Wonder in which individual learners are given a stimulus and asked to describe what's there, by answering the question 'What do you see?' then, they reflect on 'What do you think about that?' to finally come up with some questions about it. 'What does it make you wonder?'

We can also do this online

We should also bear in mind that regardless of the topic or subject that we're working on with our students, there are ways to make those learning experiences possible both in person or in remote scenarios through technology.

In conclusion, using these three techniques can help all teachers, irrespective of their 'discipline' to better support their students; and all students, no matter what age and or ability, to learn better.

Bibliography

Giudici, C., Rinaldi, C., Krechevsky, M. and Barchi, P. (2001). *Making Learning Visible: Children as Individual and Group Learners*. Cambridge (MA) and Reggio Emilia (Italy): Project Zero and Reggio Childre.

Reimers, F., and Schleicher, A. (2020). *Schooling Disrupted, Schooling Rethought. How the Covid-19 Pandemic is Changing Education*. OECD. Available at: https://read.oecd-ilibrary.org/view/?ref=133_133390-1rtuknc0hi&title=Schooling-disrupted-schooling-rethought-How-the-Covid-19-pandemic-is-changing-education

Ritchhart, R., Church, M. and Morrison, K. (2011). *Making Thinking Visible. How to Promote Engagement, Understanding, and Independence for All Learners*. San Francisco: Josey-Bass.

Inclusivity note

Making thinking visible can help draw out shy students who might not say much in live lessons. It also provides options to evidence learning to neurodivergent students.

Here's a brief overview of the inclusivity opportunities and challenges for each method mentioned in the case study.

1. How many (thought provoking, intriguing or controversial) questions do I ask students in my classes? How many do they ask me or each other? We should design questions that tap into students' lived experiences and support students as they pass through various learning thresholds. To be inclusive,

> we need to think about how students will *answer*—besides speaking up, we could for instance provide digital or physical walls for students to share their thoughts through sticky notes.
> 2. How many images or visual aids do I use in each class? What is their purpose? How many opportunities do my students have to express their learning visually? With students creating artistic representations of their learning such as drawing, a challenge is students' feeling of inadequacy in that medium. One solution is getting students to choose the medium they feel comfortable with. We could also scaffold the visual method we ask students to use. For example, if we ask students to use mapping (mind-maps or concept maps), we could provide a template of a partially filled map, especially for the first attempt, rather than students creating one from scratch.
> 3. Have I built in thinking routines that scaffold and support learning? Have I tried 'see, think, wonder' or 'think, pair, share'? We need to observe how students use each type and see which ones generate richer learning (conversations).

This case study invites us to reflect on how we can make learning visible, providing means for students to access and express learning in a visible way. This makes thought processes which would otherwise remain hidden and unexamined, visible and shareable. This outward manifestation of the inner learning process can help the student, their peers and we teachers gauge where the student is at and where they may need support to extend their learning.

Diverse activity materials matter as much as the diversification of *activity types*.

Students need to experience quiet, individual activities as well as lively, group collaborative ones. We also need to think about the right balance of activity purposes, in order to achieve the desired outcomes or to support learning thresholds. Diana Laurillard (2012) classified learning activities into six types: acquisition, inquiry, discussion, practice, collaboration and production. Every lesson and every course should have an appropriate balance of these six types.

In recent years **active learning** has been linked to more inclusive practices in teaching and learning because it is about providing a learning environment and experiences which position learners as active seekers, users and makers of knowledge and meaning, rather than passive recipients. Active learning rebalances the responsibility for learning by highlighting the student's role in it. Active learning is based on a constructivist view of learning, where students are empowered to 'develop more responsibility, participate in the construction of knowledge, and challenge mainstream thinking and opinions. And this is an essential step in the development of informed, socially responsible, and creative individuals' (Misseyanni et al. 2018). Metacognition is key for active learning: students need to go beyond 'doing' by reflecting on *how* they are learning. Active learning is not easy to manage unless well designed, planned and understood, particularly for large classes with an excess of 100 students.

An example of active peer learning is the **jigsaw** approach: a lively, collaborative activity which de-centres the teacher as the source of knowledge as the students first interact with the activity materials and with each other in their safe groups, then engage in peer teaching and learning in new groups. This is how to set up a jigsaw class:

Assign students to two to five small groups (named A, B, C ...) where each group has a different chunk of content or a section/task/prompt of the learning at hand. First, they individually interact with their own task/content, then they collaboratively complete the related task in their groups, becoming 'experts' in that chunk of content. In the second phase, members of each 'expert' group reconfigure themselves so that new groups are formed of at least one A, one B, and one C etc. representative. They then share what they learned/produced in their initial groupings. In the end, all students will have learnt all parts of the content from each other, not just their chunk.

The jigsaw approach is a type of 'interleaved' learning, where students engage with related concepts around one central idea, in contrast with the traditional blocked learning which requires students to stay on one concept until they have mastered it. As noted by Nguyen (2021): 'Massed practice remains an important component of initial learning, but interleaving can be especially valuable when used at strategic intervals to solidify deeper learning'.

As with many interactive classroom activities, jigsaw requires careful advance preparation and planning, especially regarding the make-up of groups. Jigsaw maximises peer learning and provides natural differentiation (students go at their speed, ask for and provide peer support, clarify the learning input in small groups) particularly supportive for non-native speakers and neurodivergent students.

In the following case study read about active, collaborative and above all *kinaesthetic* learning: hands-on activities which literally *move* students to learn. Notice the benefits of using such activities and some practical ideas for implementation.

Kinaesthetic and active learning

By Joanne Tippett (UK)

To learn is to move, to move from one idea to another, to make connections between areas of knowledge, even to shift from one way of understanding the world to another. Physical movement can help in this process. Kinaesthetic learning is learning through movement, and is one of the four components of the VARK model of learning styles (Visual, Aural, Reading/writing, Kinaesthetic) and a key component of Gardner's (2000) multiple intelligences.

Kinaesthetic learning is often encouraged through movement of objects, for instance matching images, or through making models with clay or LEGO and discussing the ideas sparked by this process. My own practice has led to the development of a hands-on tool for the co-creation of knowledge, Ketso (Figure 6.4). This combines visual communication and the written and spoken word, along with movement of ideas to create clusters and develop connections (Tippett and How 2020).

Whilst there has been critique of the idea of encouraging students to focus on their 'preferred learning style' possibly to the exclusion of other styles, teaching

Figure 6.4 Undergraduate students collaboratively use Ketso to develop ideas for an upcoming assignment.

that embeds a *diverse range* of learning strategies and approaches is more likely to work for a higher proportion of students. Multi-sensory learning increases inclusivity, as it gives more opportunities to engage with concepts for people who experience dyslexia-type challenges, or who are not learning in their first language. At the same time, engaging more of the senses can lead to more profound comprehension, enhanced critical thinking and better retention for all learners. Such an approach builds on the work of the educationalist John Dewey (1938), who recognised that learning emerges from the complex interactions of an organism with its environment.

Kinaesthetic learning tends to become less common after primary school, where we are well aware that we need to allow children to move around, and encourage learning through moving and matching up images and words. Indeed, I have had disparaging comments made about my own teaching by both students and colleagues, that it is a bit 'primary school'. I have learned to show a few slides of business people and high-level public sector officials using hands-on tools to develop new approaches to policy and projects, to help overcome this initial dismissive reaction.

In designing learning experiences, you can create opportunities to move images, objects, words and even people, in various combinations. For instance, in flat classroom spaces, you can include stages when people move around a room to look at the work of another group (which could itself have been developed using hands-on tools) or to swap groups and discuss ideas with a different set of people. I find this very movement can often help break up difficult dynamics or motivate a group who is not taking the tasks very seriously—especially when they realise that someone else is going to review their work.

In a lecture hall, online or hybrid learning, you can include short bursts of activities where learners engage with hands-on tools and discuss their ideas in small groups or digital breakout rooms (possibly sharing pictures of their work in progress via digital tools such as Padlet). It is even more important to consider how to engage all of the senses in online learning, which can be very focused on the written word, and/or passive intake of audio-visual imagery. Such on-screen resources can be inspiring and evocative, but they do not require as much effort on behalf of the learner to be constructed and interrogated, thus they are less likely to fully sink in.

Learning design questions:

> What are the key learning goals and how might debate and deeper learning be encouraged through hands-on and kinaesthetic engagement?
>
> What hands-on tools might be used, so that learners move and manipulate images and objects? These can be images, printed materials designed to be arranged in different ways, LEGO, clay, kits such as Ketso designed for creative communication, or purpose designed tools, such as the RoundView learning games (with a range of formats from large wooden puzzles to laminated images, to downloadable resources where the learners cut the images out to paste on to worksheets).

Bibliography

Dewey, J. (1938). *Experience and Education*. New York: MacMillan.

Gardner, H. (2000). *Intelligence Reframed: Multiple Intelligences for the 21st Century*. New York: Basic Books.

Tippett, J., and How, F. (2020). Where to Lean the Ladder of Participation: A Normative Heuristic for Effective Coproduction Processes. *Town Planning Review*, 91(2), 109–132. doi: 10.3828/tpr.2020.7

Inclusivity note

Kinaesthetic activities are inclusive because they engage learners in different ways than the typical spoken, written or even visual activities. Moving and placing objects or cards stimulates a different part of the brain than simply reading or watching (which can be much more passive activities), literally making learning memorable.

We need to check with students with physical or motor skills impairments regarding the types of hands-on activities that they would feel comfortable with. If they cannot manipulate materials, they might be able to produce a digital representation or use drawing instead.

This activity is an example of making thinking and learning visible by using hands-on activities in class. Kinaesthetic tools and activities (such as Ketso) are underused in higher education, especially because many academics and students see them as childish. On the contrary, physically moving and using hands-on activities for learning is highly inclusive because it caters for *adult* students who are more tactile.

In Section 5, when discussing Evaluation, I present another case study which also makes use of Ketso. Other examples of easy kinaesthetic classroom activities that you may want to design into your course are:

Students in a group use (various sizes) post-its to write down ideas during a discussion or brainstorm, and then move them to group or rank them.

On an A4 paper, print or write key words for the lesson or discipline in a column on the left, with their corresponding definition in a column on the right. Cut them up and give them to the students mixed up, for them to correctly match. This is useful to introduce important jargon or to create a glossary for the course.

Students make a collage for key themes (you can provide old magazines to cut words and images from), which can be combined into a 'meta' class collage revealing shared or contrasting views.

Make simple cards with images, prompts or key words and have students find the connections, creating mind-maps or concept maps.

The last diversity dimension for course input I am going to address is that it needs to be **culturally responsive** (Hammond 2017). Providing culturally diversified content is an ongoing challenge and part of the efforts to decolonise learning as discussed in Section 1. Bearing in mind the complex intersectionality that each student contributes to the learning experience, we can adopt a transformative approach to education: 'a culturally relevant education recognizes the culture, attributes, and knowledge that ethnically diverse students bring to their learning experiences and uses those resources to maximize their learning' (Howard 2012 in Gronseth et al. 2020).

At times, the nature of the course itself is inclusive, so teachers may think that they do not need to make extra efforts in terms of diversity—for example: 'I teach Intercultural Communication'. At other times the field or discipline seems unrelated to cultural diversity—for example: 'I teach Statistics, there's no culture in that'. However, no matter the field or discipline, when it comes to course content, whose knowledge counts and is portrayed is a question that each academic needs to address. The cultural diversity needs to be obvious in the different perspectives and viewpoints included in the course content and resources.

To provide culturally responsive content, we need to use the data gathered during our context analysis discussed in Section 2. For instance, we can ask ourselves: how can I make the most of the unique (socio-cultural) experiences and strengths that each student brings to my classrooms? How can I draw on my own experiences of both learning and diversity to help students learn?

It is hard to know where to start from when attempting to culturally diversify one's course. Academics usually point to the reading list as an important place where we can start decolonising the curriculum. Of course, the sources, what body of literature frames a discipline and is the students' main entry point into the discipline has a very big impact. So, it is worth making the effort to review and enhance the reading lists we use, starting from diversifying it with authors from the Global South. But there are several issues with that process. For instance, it is not easy to decide who is from the Global South. Is someone from the Global South because they were born or live there? Or because their parents are from the Global South, even though they themselves were educated in the Global North? Issues of (cultural) identity are complicated so it might be hard to answer that question. But it is fair to state that the academic world has traditionally been dominated by white male professors, so anything which comes from non-white, non-male is a step towards more balanced and diversified resources and learning.

Head to the companion website inclusivelearningdesign.com (under Section 3) for a case study from Edward Windus (UK), entitled 'Inclusive Reading Lists' which discusses the role of a culturally responsive, digital and live reading list. The case study points to the crucial role of the reading list (I prefer the term 'resource list') as an important gateway into understanding the discipline. It also shows the key role of libraries in supporting diversification and decolonisation by building 'multi-stories' (Darby and Dowling 2021).

Efforts towards decolonisation also mean moving away from the typical privileged ways of doing, publishing and ranking research in the Global North and which inform reading lists which in turn inform the understanding of a discipline. There are some very valid, 'alternative' types of resources which we could promote, such as multimedia, podcasts and blogs. Without compromising on the quality and validity of the ideas, these shift the emphasis from formal written pieces in typical Global North outlets to less formal, conversational modes often perceived as less prestigious. This is another way of liberating learning, one of the values-roots of the inclusive learning design tree.

Decolonising the curriculum goes beyond adding diversity (e.g. through making reading lists more diverse) as it is an 'interrogation of our ways of knowing and to consider what has been validated by commission but also what has become marginalised and hidden by omission' (Arshad and Bagchi 2021).

In the next case study, the authors have created a learning environment and experience where students are provided with a critical lens on the 'standard' curriculum. As you read it, notice how the authors went from their own interrogation of the hidden curriculum in film studies to applying critical pedagogy in their practice to challenge the traditional film canon taught in UK universities.

Applying critical race theory to teaching film in higher education

By Kolton Lee and Rosemary Stott (UK)

There is a standard approach to designing film curricula and delivering practical and theoretical learning in the UK and that is one in which the white experience is privileged. The fact that we are teaching film in universities in London with student cohorts which comprise predominantly students of colour and other minority groups makes the need to transform the pedagogy particularly acute. Having said that, even with cohorts that have no students of colour, we would argue that accepted norms in this context need to be challenged.

Our objective is to teach film in a global context, to bring representations and experiences of people from the global majority (normally marginalised in film) to the centre, rather than leave them at the periphery of the curriculum.

Firstly, we critically engaged with the canon of films taught in universities, deliberately broadening out to include filmmakers of colour, filmmakers of different genders, as well as filmmakers from different parts of the world with multiple perspectives. When it came to the secondary literature, again we took an inclusive position and broadened it to scaffold our more inclusive canon of work.

Secondly, we shifted the emphasis away from the film text towards the reception of films, engaging with the students' own knowledge and culture and encouraging them to express their own voice and perspectives in the films that they make.

A concrete example is a class focused on directing actors. The class explores a scene in which power dynamics between two characters are played out in the film *Pressure* (1976 by Horace Ové). The scene is set in West London between a young, Black British man of 16 and a white middle-aged man, who is the managing director of a finance company. The scenario is that the young man is there for a job interview and the session explores who has the power in the scene and how the audience is made aware of this, through the performance of the actors.

The fact that the film was made during a time of political and racial turbulence in British society is reflected in the narrative in the film; the discussion with students about *how* this is reflected is designed to spark reflection on our own, contemporary times and therefore to deepen the practice of the students when producing their own films. What is the relationship between Black people and white people in Britain at this time? Has this relationship changed or evolved since the 70s? Why are there Black (and Asian) people in Britain? And how does the question of race permeate our reading of the scene we have just watched?

The final part of the class concludes with students taking it in turns to direct professional actors or other students themselves, in such a way as to express a power dynamic between two characters that they themselves create. After each performance, students are encouraged to share with the class their decision-making process when directing the characters that they have created.

Over the duration of the course, this approach empowers all students, enabling them to speak with confidence about the intentionality behind their decision making. This ability to articulate their thoughts comes from a place of confidence where they recognise that their voice is one amongst many and there is a democracy of voices—with no one voice, or one narrative dominating, whilst others are pushed to the periphery (Figure 6.5).

More generally, feedback we have received from this approach to film education is that a number of students—white students and students of colour—have

Figure 6.5 Whose story is it?

expressed both surprise and delight at the opening up of an area of investigation of which they were unaware, particularly when this area of investigation is in a British context. What this then does for students of colour is allow them to move forward with their own practice, working within a context and a history that should enrich and empower.

Bibliography

Mountford-Zimdars, A. (Ed.) (2015). *Teaching in the Context of Diversity: Reflections and Tips from Educators at King's College London.* Higher Education Research Network Journal: King's CollegeLondon. Available at: https://www.kcl.ac.uk/study/learningteaching/kli/research/hern/hernjvol9.pdf

Richardson, J.T.E. (2015). The Under-attainment of Ethnic Minority Students in UK Higher Education: What We Know and What We Don't Know. *Journal of Further & Higher Education*, 39(2), 278–291.

Runnymede Trust (2015). *Aiming Higher: Race, Inequality and Diversity in the Academy.* London: Runnymede Trust. Available at: http://www.runnymedetrust.org/uploads/Aiming%20Higher.pdf

Universities UK and NUS (2019). Black, Asian and Minority Ethnic Student Attainment at UK Universities: #closingthegap. [online] Available at: https://www.universitiesuk.ac.uk/sites/default/files/field/downloads/2021-07/bame-student-attainment.pdf

Inclusivity note

Although in this case the nature of the subject lends itself to enactment, role play scenarios are valuable inclusive learning activities that can help us diversify the learning we offer, support students' learning through experiencing a simulation of reality in a safe space, and promote empathy and perspective taking. For these reasons role plays are useful to progress students' learning in cognitive, behavioural and social domains.

In our efforts to provide liberated, inclusive learning environments, role plays can help us tackle sensitive ethnic and ethical issues, such as in this case exploration of racial power dynamics. However, this case study is also an example of learning which 'requires courage' (Mintz 2022) because it can be emotionally unsettling and even painful.

When discussing emotionally charged subjects such as racism, rape or armed conflict, we should bear in mind students' previous trauma, as discussed in Chapter 3. Although activities such as the one in the cases study are very valuable to enhance the inclusivity message of the course, they could also trigger a strong emotional response. Hence, we should have trigger warnings, and we should allow vulnerable students to opt out from directly participating in the role play—they could have an alternative role, such as audience and reviewers of others' role plays.

In this case study, through dialogue and enactment, the students become more aware of power dynamics, especially in the context of multi-ethnic situations.

But why does it matter to design culturally diversified learning? Because we want our learning design and enactment to provide both 'mirrors and windows' for each student:

> All students deserve a curriculum which mirrors their own experience back to them, upon occasion—thus validating it in the public world of the school. But curriculum must also insist upon the fresh air of windows into the experience of others—who also need and deserve the public validation of the school curriculum.
>
> (Style 1988)

Diversifying the course input includes at once portraying students' own cultural diversity (mirrors) and opening up towards others' perspectives (windows).

No matter what field or discipline we teach, we can all move away from typical higher education Eurocentric views and ways towards a more decolonised learning design. We can achieve more inclusive learning design if we apply the term 'diversified' both to the content itself and to the ways in which we provide such content on our course.

Relevant

Relevance is about ways of connecting the course content to your students' lives and to the wider world. This means that the learning thresholds discussed in Chapter 4 need to be, as much as possible, *relatable* and *applicable* to real-life situations and problems. The students should be able to see the significance of what they are learning in the wider context of their lives, future goals and the world at large. In a nutshell, the course should be personally relevant, culturally relevant and community relevant.

If we take the community of learning approach, rather than thinking about how the learning on the course is relevant to life outside, it should be the other way round: how does life (the broader, wider learning in it) fit into the university course? This excerpt explains this well:

> the school is not the privileged locus of learning. ... The class is not the primary learning event. It is life itself that is the main learning event. Schools, classrooms, and training sessions still have a role to play in this vision, but they have to be in the service of the learning that happens in the world.
>
> (Wenger-Trayner and Wenger-Trayner 2015)

Students should be encouraged to draw upon and reflect on their own life experiences and then relate those to the course they are studying both at local and global level. The root-value 'integrate' discussed in Section 1 takes centre stage here, as Maringe (2021) states: 'Integration of local and global knowledge must always be a priority at all stages of teaching and learning and of curriculum construction and instruction'.

There is also a cognitive imperative for this: 'what matters to an individual governs cognitive processes, including attention, association and memory' (Shackleton-Jones 2019)—in other words for us to meaningfully learn and retain *anything*, it needs to matter to us. To know what matters to students, we need to have in place a thorough contextual analysis as discussed in Section 2. Of course, curiosity is also a big driver for learning, and it can sustain effortful learning in apparently 'useless' areas. This type of learning 'for fun' has its own place too. But here I am concerned with making a case for designing learning that matters to the students because *they* view it relevant, even if it is only because it triggers their curiosity.

The following two case studies (learning within context and 'real world' learning) well illustrate the importance of providing relevant learning experiences. The first is from Australia and discusses 'learning within context', which supports the transition between studies and the post-university world of work, while making students better citizens. Notice the way *questions* are used to prompt and promote learning.

Learning within context

By Camille Dickson-Deane (Australia)

The learning process has evolved from being philosophical to industrialised and now, personalised. At the higher education level, achieving learning outcomes is a tangible value with the esoteric hope of lifelong learning. Assuring that learning is achieved is in part any higher education's mission. But, how does a student assure their own learning?

As a student pursues a course, their learning must have relevance to their everyday life. Without this, the value of what is being taught will be undermined if a student finds it difficult to see how the course content can be used in their day-to-day life. In turn, how can they convince others not only that they know, but that they know how to explain, apply, share and elaborate on the core principles of their own learning. Achieving this desire from a student perspective requires an instructor to step back and think critically of how the disciplinary knowledge can be conveyed, whilst engaging in designing meaning-making for the student. The following can be used as a way to help design learning tasks and assessments so that the meaning is situated firmly in the students' context.

Identify the key learning outcome you would like the student to achieve. This is simple as it is a task that outlines the benefit of learning a subject.

In a direct dialogue, make students use situations through descriptions of context which are passionate/familiar to them. Whatever your subject/topic, students have more attachments to activities that they easily recall and that, in turn, are tied to an emotion (Honebein et al. 1993). The passion is activated whether the emotion felt is positive or negative. For example:

the desire to fix a problem,
the feeling that a solution can be enhanced,
sharing a lesson learned with someone of a different age group.

These are all examples of what can be seen as both positive and negative with core emotional feelings. The situation must be explicitly stated by the student so as to immediately activate that value proposition for the student.

Build a system for the student to organise the knowledge they seek. Begin building a bridge between the students' described context (i.e. 'real world') and the discipline-focussed learning outcome(s), as shown in Figure 6.6. As you build your bridge, you will create a system of questions, some of which:

> you answer in your design of the task [Instructor Knowledge]
> they can immediately answer to complete the task [Student Knowledge]
> are left blank as a form of scaffolding to encourage enquiry, towards building knowledge [Germane Knowledge]

This uses the Socratic method (questioning) embedded in 'A Simple Knowledge' (ASK) system, to create a knowledge management system around your topic (Thompson and Thompson 1983, Yang et al. 2005) which they can draw from as they close the gap between what they know and what they seek to know.

Figure 6.6 Designing a bridge between students' formal learning and the 'real-world'.

As you create this system, some questions that can help this learning design progress are:

1. How would a student achieve the learning outcome in the 'real world'?
2. Where will the student use this skill/knowledge/ability?
3. What in their everyday context is easily accessible to the student to create a synaptic bridge between the discipline and the 'real-world'?

In practice, this process has been used to teach students how to create a Work Breakdown Structure (WBS) for a project. A WBS is a tool used in project management and I teach this topic in various disciplines (i.e., business management, information technology, education, science, etc.). The analogy of painting walls in a house is best suited to explain how a WBS is used as all students can relate to this activity in some way or the other. This key approach is to help students understand how the WBS is used as a task analysis method to break big project goals into smaller actionable tasks. So, to walk you through the process above:

1. Identify the key learning outcome you would like the student to achieve.
   Complete a WBS for an assigned project.
2. In a direct dialogue, make students use situations through descriptions of context which are passionate/familiar to them.
   We will use the painting of the walls in your bedroom as the project. You can think of that colour you've always wanted or a pattern that you always wanted to try out.
3. Build a system for the student to organise the knowledge they seek.

'A Simple Knowledge' (ASK) System for using a WBS to paint **my (the student's)** bedroom walls:

> [Instructor Knowledge prompt] How many walls are there?
> Instructor Response: Let's say four walls.
> [Germane Knowledge prompt] How big is the bedroom?
> Instructor Response: Why does the size matter?

WBS Lesson Note: The larger the room the more paint they will need.

> [Germane Knowledge prompt] What if I have posters on my walls?
> Instructor Response: Well, what if you do?

WBS Lesson Note: All of the work will be accommodated into the activity so if they ignore the posters, it will affect quality of the project; if they remove the posters, they have to include it in the WBS as an actionable subtask.

- [Student Knowledge] Am I painting the room by myself?
- Instructor Response: Well, who else will do it?
  WBS Lesson Note: Students typically opt for doing it themselves
- [Student Knowledge] Can I use absolutely any colour?
- Instructor Response: Whatever you want.

WBS Lesson Note: Of course, this also matters for cost, quality and time of the project to complete, but they don't realise this until later on in the exercise.

This process can go on and on as the WBS slowly takes shape using a project they can easily relate to and most importantly, it is a project they all are actively participating in as individuals and collaborators. Whether they have the explicit experience of painting a wall or not, it still allows them to individually complete the activity, using questions to guide their next steps by critically thinking through the process with a system of situated question prompts.

Bibliography

Honebein, P.C., Duffy, T.M. and Fishman, B.J. (1993). Constructivism and the Design of Learning Environments: Context and Authentic Activities for Learning. In *Designing Environments for Constructive Learning* (pp. 87–108). Berlin, Heidelberg: Springer.

Thompson, B.H. and Thompson, F.B. (1983). Introducing ASK A Simple Knowledgeable System. In Proceedings of the 1st Conference on Applied Natural Language Processing, pages 17–24. Santa Monica, California. California Institute of Technology.

Yang, Y.T.C., Newby, T.J. and Bill, R.L. (2005). Using Socratic Questioning to a Skills through Asynchronous Discussion Forums in Distance Learning Environments. *The American Journal of Distance Education*, 19(3), 163–181. doi: 10.1207/s15389286ajde1903_4

Inclusivity note

Relevant and dialogical learning and assessment are important for all, but they are vital for first-in-family and working-class students who may otherwise disengage from academic learning.

It is important to bear in mind our and students' cultural assumptions about the balance between instructor and student knowledge. In some cultures, rote learning and being factual are seen as the route to academic success, while in other cultures questioning and student inquiry are (now) considered a better route. In our culturally diverse cohorts, we should beware of making assumptions and we should provide the rationale of our approach to get buy-in from students.

In this case study, after identifying a learning threshold or key outcome for the course, the teacher builds a *bridge* between that and the wider world, using questions to engage students in a work breakdown structure. Students work things out themselves with the help of the teacher and the whole process becomes very dialogical and collaborative. Relevant learning matters *to the students*, so wherever possible we could ask them to apply the learning or concepts to a scenario of *their* choice.

Another term often used to mean relevant is 'authentic'. I discuss the term 'authentic' in more detail in Section 4, in connection with assessment, which is relevant to the students *and* to the wider world. In this chapter, I use authentic in relation to work integrated learning, learning which connects students *with the world of work*.

For disciplines with a direct line to specific industries, working with industry is 'authentic' if there's mutual recognition between the employer and the student, bearing in mind that students could be 'caught between two worlds' (Jan McArthur 2021)—they are students but are being treated as employees. Besides benefitting employers and the institution, students benefit because work integrated learning 'connects higher education activities to *current* workplace practices' (Bayerlein et al. 2021). However, it is better to talk about developing graduate *attributes and competencies*, which refer to broad academic, professional and personal qualities that a student acquires during the course of their studies than to focus narrowly on 'being employable'.

The following case study illustrates ways in which we can provide more relevant learning experiences by making connections with industry and community engagement. Note how to create such links directly through the course content as well as through extra-curricular activities.

Facilitating 'real-world' learning through community and industry engagement

By Aranee Manoharan (UK)

This case study discusses how to design inclusive curricula by engaging with community organisations, employers and/or industry professionals to facilitate 'real-world' learning.

Considering the diverse student demographics across higher education, it is important to empower *all* students to cultivate their social and cultural capital (Tomlinson 2017) so that students not only have the knowledge, but also the skills, experiences and confidence to be able to successfully navigate life in the 21st century (Bakhshi et al. 2017). The experiences required are often gained outside of the curriculum, for instance through internships and placements, but for students from disadvantaged contexts these opportunities may not be accessible, which is why designing real-world learning *into* the curriculum, throughout the student journey, is so important. How best to do this?

The ideal curriculum enables all students to develop the required knowledge, skills and experiences by utilising a range of pedagogical approaches and assessment methods. Vital to this are high-impact approaches (e.g. enquiry-based learning) that encourage and enable students to transfer their theoretical learning into practice/performance, that is, academic praxis (Druckman and Bjork 1994). This learning experience is enhanced further when it is designed through engagement with community/industry partners. By involving external stakeholders from the outset of the course design process, educators can create and deliver significant experiences in the curriculum that allow all students to practice their theoretical learning in an authentic real-world context. These can be designed and scaffolded for all levels of study and across all disciplines.

Questions to consider

What are the local or global challenges relevant to your discipline and student cohort? It is important to identify problems/topics that are inclusive and culturally responsive (Hammond 2014) enabling all students to access, engage and contribute to the learning process.

How can this be integrated into your curriculum? A common way of doing this is by identifying partners who can contribute to the curriculum by:

- Posing a real problem (i.e. a live brief) that students have to research/design solutions for and present back
- Delivering a guest lecture on the problem/topic to make it come alive for students
- Contributing to the development, design and delivery of the curriculum through Industrial Advisory Boards (IABs) to ensure it is up to date and future fit.

Who in your local area is working on this problem/topic and would they be interested in being involved with your class? The benefit of finding local partners is that students can work with them directly in person, potentially liaising with the relevant service users/clients/customers as well. However, with the increase in digitally enabled learning, the potential to source and secure national and international partners for students to work with has increased and can bring a global dynamic to your teaching.

Potential solutions

Developing external relationships can be daunting, especially if you are not already connected to relevant networks. However, there are a few ways to embark upon this approach of teaching and learning:

> **Existing Support:** There may be teams within your organisation dedicated to developing external relationships, who can support you in identifying potential partners such as Alumni, Careers & Employability, or Business Development teams.
> **Sustainable Partnerships:** Try to arrange it so that one external partner can contribute to an IAB or provide a live brief/guest lecture that caters for all students in a cohort, so that you only need a small group of sustainable partnerships to facilitate ongoing community/industry-engaged learning.
> **Leverage Existing Networks:** Most cities/regions have charity/business networks that you can tap into. Local charities/Small and Medium size Enterprises are keen to engage with students to leverage their energy, expertise and

skills. It could be as simple as putting an advert in local networks' newsletters to generate relevant partners.

Partnership Agreements: Develop and maintain a partnership agreement that is signed by both you and the partner. This provides clarity and accountability from the outset, increasing the likelihood of a successful outcome for all involved.

Further considerations

Implementing guest lectures and advisory boards are much simpler aspects of the community and industry-engaged learning approach compared to live briefs, which can be challenging for staff and students, as it is a less common way of teaching and learning that both parties may not be familiar with. However, it is this learning activity that creates a significant experience in the curriculum that is so valuable for students.

Having worked with academic teams across a broad range of subjects to implement live briefs, I have found that it works best when the teaching team is committed to the approach and frames the activity with clear and consistent guidance for the students and the external partner, for example, explicitly stating the expectations of student, partner and teacher so that there is clarity of each role in the learning process.

The live brief activity is usually achieved through the vehicle of group work, which students can often dislike. Therefore, it may also be useful to deliver a teamworking skills workshop at the start of the project to prepare students with tools and strategies for effective group work. Often the Careers & Employability Service is able to support in designing and delivering such skills workshops to support assessment success.

Scaffolding is critical for this learning activity to be as effective as it can be, especially with multi-ability cohorts. Therefore, the key to success is to introduce such high-impact learning approaches in the first year of the degree programme, with greater support, and build upon this in each year of study, providing students greater independence to achieve more meaningful outputs as they grow in confidence and capability. Figure 6.7 shows an example of how key in-curricular and extra-curricular activities can be designed and integrated to support students' professional development throughout their university journey.

This teaching approach benefits from a 'meddler-in-the-middle' pedagogical stance (McWilliam 2009), where the educator is 'mutually involved with students in assembling and/or dis-assembling knowledge and cultural products. Meddling is a re-positioning of teacher and student as co-directors and co-editors of their social world' (McWilliam 2009:287). This means that whilst students take the lead in their own learning, educators take an active interventionist position to support students in this process.

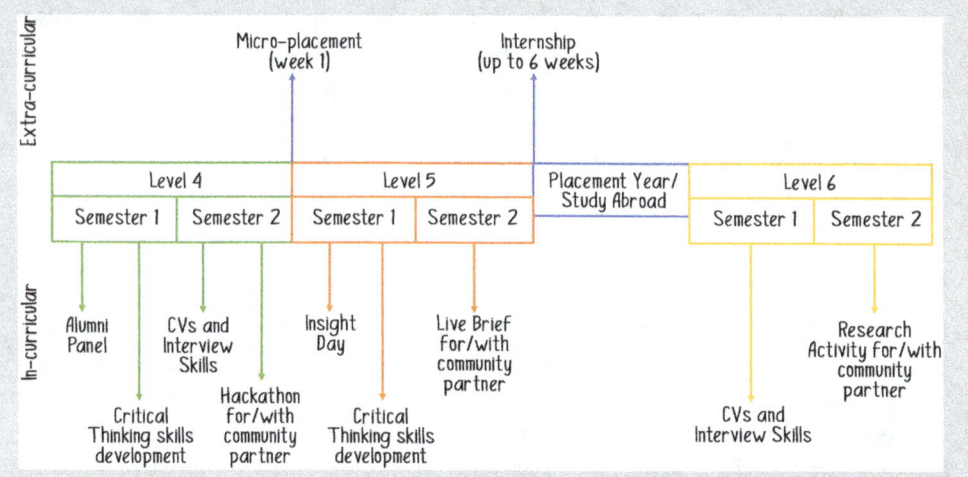

Figure 6.7 An example of a student development journey that incorporates community/industry-engaged pedagogical approaches and assessment methods.

Bibliography

Bakhshi, H., Downing, J.M., Osborne, M.A. and Schneider, P. (2017). *The Future of Skills: Employment in 2030*. London: Pearson.

Druckman, D.E. and Bjork, R.A. (1994). *Learning, Remembering, Believing: Enhancing Human Performance*. Washington, DC: National Academy Press.

Hammond, Z. (2014). *Culturally Responsive Teaching and The Brain: Promoting Authentic Engagement and Rigor among Culturally and Linguistically Diverse Students*. Thousand Oaks, CA: Corwin.

McArthur, J. (2021). The Inclusive University: A Critical Theory Perspective Using a Recognition-Based Approach. *Social Inclusion*, 9(3), 6–15. doi: 10.17645/si.v9i3.4122

McWilliam, E.L. (2009). Teaching for Creativity: From Sage to Guide to Meddler. *Asia Pacific Journal of Education*, 29(3), 281–293. doi: 10.1080/02188790903092787

Tomlinson, M. (2017). Forms of Graduate Capital and their Relationship to Graduate Employability. *Education + Training*, 59(4), 338–352. doi: 10.1108/ET-05-2016-0090

Inclusivity note

Although for some students such as first in family—who may lack the social capital to easily enter the job market upon graduation—a professional skills plan well integrated in the curriculum is very valuable, working closely with industry has its challenges.

> Scaffolding which is gradually removed as shown in the case study is important, as well as a focus on teamwork for industry.
>
> Industry practices need to be discussed and questioned in a safe space, so students know what to expect.
>
> To avoid reinforcing stereotypes, it is important to use the hidden curriculum to our advantage: for instance, we could choose industry partners who are inclusivity champions and can offer diverse guest speakers or live projects where students can see diverse role-models.

This case study clearly shows how in both small and big ways, career-readiness education should be (more) integrated into the academic curriculum. This should not just be the remit of the 'careers team' or the like: to develop suitable professional abilities, part of graduate attributes, we need to create a strong intra- and extra-curricular engagement, within each course, with the community and industry.

You may not have agency over a whole academic degree programme to influence the way professional attributes are developed over a typical three-year degree course, but there are a number of things you can do within your sphere (your course) to embed entrepreneurship education principles.

First, in the spirit of co-creation, there is nothing better than involving the employers in the learning design process, not so that they impose on us academics their employment needs, but for us to better understand the types of skills and abilities they are looking for in graduates. And also, to clarify to them that university education is more than employability.

Second, you could ask yourself: how can I progress my students' professionalism on *my* course? Can I involve relevant guest speakers to inspire my students on their post-studies journey? What role could alumni play in the development and support of my current students?

Once you have designed the broad students' journey on your course (as discussed in Chapter 4), you should ensure there are opportunities at various points for students' professional development.

Besides being diversified and relevant, inclusive education needs to make full use of creativity—the subject of the last section of this chapter.

Creative

What is creativity? Although some define creativity as creating something new from strictly original ideas, for this chapter, I will adopt a broader definition to include *innovative* learning and teaching approaches which *add* value to the learning environment and experiences. Matraeva et al. (2020) state that:

> creativity is considered as an integrative property, the key characteristics of which are the ability to produce original ideas, result-orientation, solution of practical problems, originality and speed of thinking, openness to new experience, and tolerance for uncertainty.

Creative teaching is very much about innovating not for the sake of it, but to find novel ways to motivate, involve and support our students:

> As a teacher you're committed to enabling your students to learn, but that might mean coming at the subject in a whole new way, trying out a number of approaches, listening to what the learners have to say or simply pausing and asking: 'How can we do this differently?
>
> (Ashton and Stone 2021)

My discussion will particularly focus on two creative approaches: (1) the use of play and (2) art integration in all disciplines.

Playful approaches

When is the last time you played? Did you play a game? What type of game was it? How did it make you feel? We would probably instinctively agree in saying that play is an important part of learning … for kids. However, after the teenage years, once young people enter higher education, it seems that academia is all but playful. Some institutions and academics send the message that education is a 'serious' business with no place for being playful or playing games, unless 'Games' is the subject of study. This unfortunately means that, in most universities, learning and playing are divorced.

There is most definitely a cultural background perspective with regards to how play is regarded in an educational space and specifically in HE. There is the overlap of (macro) sector and disciplinary culture and (micro) cultural background of individuals within the institution(s). Students'—and teachers'—view of play is greatly impacted by the presence or absence of play in previous learning experiences. Overseas students who come from very prescriptive educational settings might feel very uncomfortable with the idea of playing to learn, while others may view it as childish and irrelevant.

How do playful approaches support inclusivity?

- Through play students can experience real scenarios and authentic situations in a non-threatening way, creating safer learning spaces
- Playful approaches 'invite a different mind-set and environment, providing a formative space in which failure is not only encouraged, but a necessary part of the learning paradigm' (Toft Nørgård et al. 2017)—this 'nurtures' students' growth
- the participatory, social and collaborative nature of playing touches the affective domain of adults' learning experiences

There are different levels of play integration in teaching and learning, from light-touch playful approaches to full gamification of learning, which is applying game mechanisms for educational purposes. It is useful to clarify the difference between play and games. Play is entertaining and does not need to have a competitive element. Games do *not* need to be entertaining but they have rules and are usually competitive (Headleand 2021).

However, questions that require further study are: what is the long-term impact of playful approaches on learning? Do they result in better learning outcomes? In the case of games, do they foster intrinsic motivation? Games have reward structures such as badges, which are motivational. But what happens when the reward goes? Does the motivation stay? How about losers of the game?

The four case studies presented in this section discuss different ways of using playful approaches and art integration to support more inclusive learning in higher education: the first is about using digital games; the second is about art integrated learning; the third is about making use of artistic imagery to teach non-art subjects and the fourth is about LEGO© Serious Play.

What **games** can we use? There is a plethora of freely available digital games, video games, card games and board games to name just a few. There are team games, strategy games, escape room games and many other games genres. There are also 'serious games' such as role plays and simulation of real-world features. In recent years, it has become increasingly easier to *create* games online and make them freely available.

Games can be used to design more inclusive learning, for instance to:

- introduce or practice new or difficult concepts—games based on course content (Mayo 2007)
- create or enhance team spirit—games not necessarily related to course content
- prepare for assessment or as an assessment mode—games to revise, consolidate and evidence learning
- connect with students for pastoral support—students and staff play games while they 'chat' about academic or other needs (Headland 2021)
- enhance social responsibility and ecological learning—ethical games

In the following case study, from the US, read about using game boards to teach mathematics. Notice how both playing and *creating* games help students learn.

Game On: Cultivating educational discourse through digital game boards

By Adrienne Baytops Paul (USA)

Employing online presentation programs (such as Power Point or Google Slides) to instruct is no longer a novel idea. Using the slides effectively, however, is key to cultivating deep learning and engaging learners on multiple levels. This is a teaching and learning methodology which fosters inclusion of learners of all levels due to its natural appeal and accessibility.

I was exposed to the pedagogical dynamism of digital games (using Google Slides) during my time as a mathematics leadership graduate student at George Mason University. Having experienced their effectiveness as a student, digital games became a feature of my own teaching practice. Designing game slides is a popular means of igniting mathematical discourse among students just like playing games was often the preliminary activity of the class for a number of my graduate courses.

There are innumerable ways to design a digital game board, for example on a Google Slide or on a PowerPoint slide. The myriad of free online tools such as spinners, dice and timers, for example, make game boards on online presentation platforms an inexhaustible possibility for including various levels of learning to take place in an intriguing way.

As an example, I redesigned a probability game for my students to play virtually on a Google slide. During this game, students discussed the likelihood of their chances of winning, recorded their data and even made predictions on their play during and after the game. Conducting the game in this way encouraged all students to pay attention to the decisions and results of one another, ensuring each player's voice was included and valued in the play.

Another powerful extension of this technique is to allow learners to create their own digital games. Graduating students, for example, could make digital games, share them with one another, receive and provide feedback, revamp and immediately integrate the games into their peer-teaching experiences. Because the slide decks are so accessible, the games could easily be shared with other cohorts and year groups and even with other institutions. This could also provide students with a sense of agency and independence when it comes to their learning.

In *Limitless Mind*, Jo Boaler asserts: 'when you connect with someone else's idea in mathematics [and other subjects], it both requires and creates a deeper level of understanding' (Boaler 2019). Requiring learners to create—or co-create in small groups—and share their own games makes them the proprietors of their own learning and imposes upon them the responsibility of teaching others. Because it is such an inclusive project, it is grounded in differentiation and provides a space for all voices to be significant during the brainstorming and development of the game. Furthermore, designing a game requires a mastery of the focus or goal of play, so students would have to have a deep conceptual understanding of their mathematical content to effectively create and produce a fair, logical game. I have always required that students work in groups to complete such a project for that very reason: diverse minds are likely to produce diverse ideas and reinforce the significance of including ideas and influences from students with various perspectives and backgrounds.

Figure 6.8 illustrates the stages of a framework to facilitate mathematics game design.

Game design has proven to be a popular activity among students, so making collaboration a prerequisite improves the overall project. While working towards the creation of a mathematics game, students help one another master the concept at hand. Students were especially eager to share their games with students in lower year groups; an element of leadership was also borne from this activity for my students. The lasting effects of students creating games was palpable—students were excited to make a game with their peers and work on it rigorously each day, and results on assessments were particularly remarkable after students shared such a rich experience.

Inventing these games for an external audience would authenticate the process of learning for students, since students would have to create infallible rules, appealing extensions and reasonable boundaries.

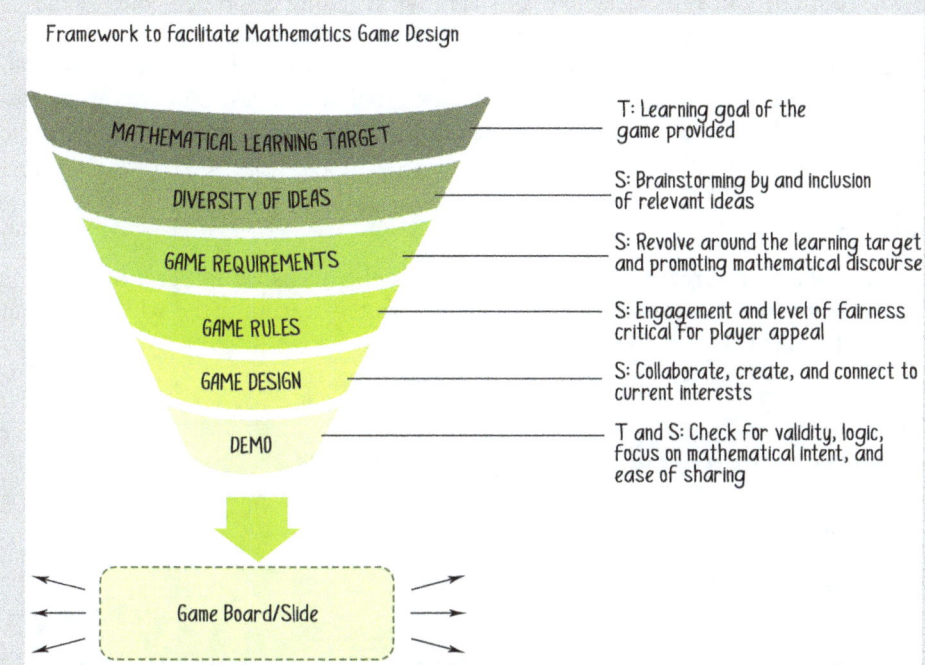

Figure 6.8 Teacher (T) and students (S) roles within a framework to facilitate mathematics game design.

Designing games on suitable digital platforms such as Google Slides or PowerPoint will allow educators and students alike to share their game boards with other students and educators almost anywhere. This method of purposeful, engaging game-based learning knows no bounds.

Bibliography

Boaler, J. (2019). *Limitless Mind: Learn, Lead, and Live Without Barriers*. New York: Harper One.

Inclusivity note

We should recognise that the fact that students like playing games with their peers in their spare time does not automatically mean they will want to play games on their university courses. Also, games tastes vary, and some features such as points can be off-putting for some students. For these reasons, games should be used judiciously, and it is advisable that they mostly have a pedagogical focus (playing to learn, not just playing for fun). For variety, if games/quizzes become a weekly feature, consider having quiz-free weeks.

There are benefits in playing/designing educational games *in groups*, however this can be very challenging for students on the autism spectrum, so we should allow them to design games individually if that suits them better.

Playing (digital) games is an active and creative teaching approach, but as the case study shows, asking students to *create* games themselves brings the activity to a whole new, higher level of conceptual understanding, collaboration and negotiation as well as being a very authentic output, potentially for external audiences. Students in all disciplines could create digital or physical games, such as card or board games, as part of peer-teaching or as an output of the course.

Art integration

Another dimension of creative course input of this chapter is art integration. The next case study, from India, shows the value of art integrated learning (the why), but it also provides four practical steps to implement it (the how).

Art integrated learning

By Divya Kapoor (India)

> '*Change is the end result of all true learning*'
>
> —Leo Buscaglia

The changes and complexities of today's world present new challenges to our education system. Teachers today work as facilitators to support student learning and expression. All students are unique and so are their needs. Inclusive instructional strategies thus form an imperative component of a happy and involved classroom. Experimenting and manoeuvring through different methodologies, I explored a very effective one—art integrated learning (AIL).

AIL is an inclusive, cross-curricular approach to teaching and learning based on the amalgamation of teaching subjects with the teaching of art (both visual and performing), where art is taken as the primary medium to learn and comprehend the subject. This integration makes the learning process joyful and promotes deeper understanding of concepts along with a greater appreciation for the art form being integrated.

AIL provides wings to student thoughts. It brings forward the passion into learning. My students utterly enjoy the classroom experience as they engage in deep learning of concepts with their chosen art as a medium to learn. I often share the feeling of Eureka with my students when we establish the conceptual learning we desire and simultaneously create an artistic composition. It may not be a masterpiece, but it empowers the learning journey.

Figure 6.9 points to some of the ways in which art integrated learning benefits students:

- Passion—Develops amongst students a zeal to learn about various local and international art forms.
- Deep Learning—Students apply the concepts using art as a medium which promotes deeper learning of concepts.

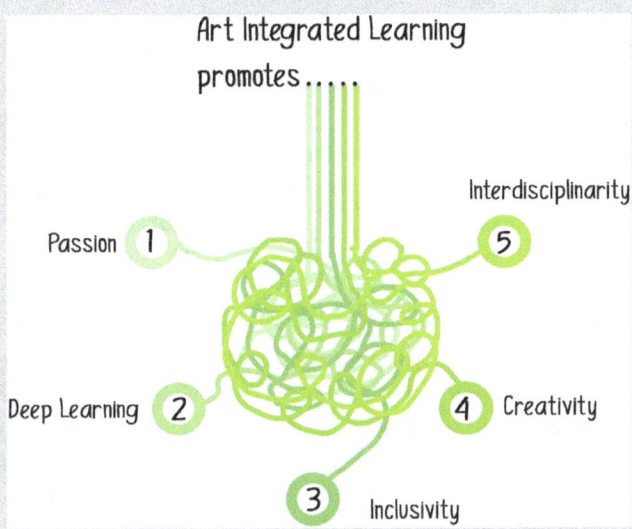

Figure 6.9 How art integrated learning benefits students.

Inclusivity—Free will to choose from a variety of art forms both visual and performing expands the scope for the learners.

Creativity—Students get an opportunity to explore and express the content ideas creatively.

Interdisciplinarity—Students use art as a medium to understand and connect various subjects.

We as facilitators can help in inculcating art-based enquiry by providing many opportunities in our classes. To incorporate AIL, our classroom transactions may include activities like plays, song composition, graphic creation, clay modelling, puppetry, dance, sketching, culinary art, jewellery designing, poetry, creative writing, collage etc.

For AIL to bring about the desired outcome, it is important for us to have an unambiguous thought process, that is, clarity on the topic and the process that we want to take up and a well laid out plan for its classroom implementation. These are some steps that may be referred to while planning an art interaction in classes:

Step 1   Choice of Topic

The selection of the topic/theme is essential for providing learners with a fulfilling art integrated experience. We should ensure that the topic draws upon the previous learning experiences of the students. A class discussion can be initiated to extract information about the past learning experiences based upon which a suitable theme for the activity/project can be selected.

Step 2   Artistic enquiry
Once an appropriate theme is selected, we should provide opportunities for artistic enquiry. Students should be motivated to explore and come up with their choice of artistic means to represent the chosen theme. One may provide real life instances to help evoke critical thinking amongst the students. We should provide abundant opportunities for learning through collaboration. As teachers, we can help students explore the topic as a part of group work and come up with their own findings.

Step 3   Expression of the knowledge using an appropriate art from
Arts integration creates equity because the arts are naturally differentiated. Students can learn in a manner that best meets their needs. This is where we need to work as a team with our students. Together we may select one particular art form (visual or performing) to display the findings. We may also offer flexibility by allowing students to choose the art form they are most fond of to reflect upon their learning. This will bring forward a blend of various forms of art and help project the creativity of the learners in their own unique way. The art experience can be used as a mode of introduction to the concept, which we can build upon by adding details about the chosen topic/theme.

Step 4   Assessment for learning (both subject and art)
We should also prepare an appropriate *rubric* to assess the student's learning. Rubrics could include constructs such as: Comprehension of key ideas and details; Development of the idea; Organisation/presentation; Application of artistic conventions/creativity; Use of art to enhance or complement meaning; or Quality of final product. Self-assessment and peer-assessment can be used as effective tools. These provide students with opportunities to understand their own learning outputs as well as the work of their peers as a part of the deeper learning experience.

We are often afraid of what a new approach might do to us instead of what it will do for us. But we should not hesitate in trying out new things and exploring new techniques. Each attempt we make may open an innovative window of opportunities for our students. AIL is one such unique and effective instructional strategy that has changed the face of many classrooms.

Bibliography

Bowkett, S. (1997). *Imagine That… A Handbook for Creative Learning Activities for the Classroom*. Trowbridge: Redwood Books.
Craft, A., Dugal, J., Dyer, G., Jeffrey, B. and Lyons, T. (1997). *Can You Teach Creativity?* Nottingham: Education Now Publishing Co-operative Ltd.
Fryer, M. (1996). *Creative Teaching and Learning*. London: Chapman.
Wallas, G. (1926). *The Art of Thought*. London: Jonathan Cape.

> **Inclusivity note**
>
> Art integrated learning promotes the development of many transversal skills (useful in many workplace situations) such as: research, comparison, artistic expression, sharing, aesthetic appreciation. This happens in a creative, non-judgemental and naturally differentiated environment.
>
> Although art is often linked to 'free expression', this does not mean that art integrated learning is chaotic: for classroom use it is better to have a structure where, within current learning, art provides a different outlet which promotes productive reflection.
>
> Challenges such as teachers' knowledge and skills in various artistic expressions and students' reticence in using a different medium for their formal learning can be overcome by careful design and planning, perhaps including guest speakers with expertise in innovative art integrated learning, such as dance for math or drawing for literature.

Any discipline can be taught through and can benefit from art integration, because art is an expression of human thought (and emotion) in all fields. If you would like to try out art integration, I suggest you go back to the learning thresholds of your course and ask yourself which one of those you could address through art. The case study of Threshold Graphics, in Chapter 4, on the companion website, is a perfect example of art integration in what would normally be considered a non-artistic field (Care). Another example, in the next section, is photovoice: using photography to advocate for a social cause as learning output.

In the next case study, discover how anatomical art supports the learning of research methods.

Online teaching using medical and anatomical imagery to explore research methods

By Ourania Varsou (UK)

Introduction

The incorporation of art and humanities in anatomy teaching has included creative writing and personal narratives (Canby and Bush 2010), body painting (Finn 2018), and dramatic performances (Canby and Bush 2010, Hammer et al. 2010). The pedagogical value of art in anatomy has been discussed in the context of clinical examination and professional attributes such as communication skills (Finn 2018). It has also been proposed as a means of promoting humanistic values (Canby and Bush 2010), understanding emotions (Hammer et al. 2010) and encouraging reflection (Canby and Bush 2010), which are all holistic and inclusive ways to design learning.

In this case study, I will discuss the online delivery of interactive and collaborative workshops utilising medical and anatomical imagery in the form of virtual illustrations (Figure 6.10), coupled with storytelling as an accompanying verbal narrative, for the exploration of research methods (study design, data collection methods). Online delivery enables participation of learners from any part of the world, irrespective of their stage of academic studies/clinical training (open to students and qualified professionals) and background (open to healthcare and humanities professionals), promoting inclusivity while also resulting in rich multi-disciplinary discussions.

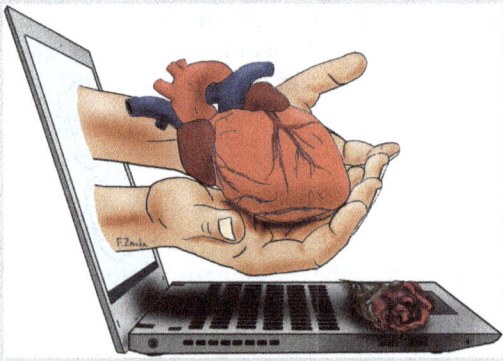

Figure 6.10 Online teaching utilising medical and anatomical imagery to explore research methods (Illustration: Filip Zmuda).

Case study

Pre-sessional information, such as intended learning outcomes (ILOs) and a biography, have played an important role in highlighting the purpose of and acting as a catalyst for learning. For a 45-minute online workshop, I used two to three ILOs with one targeting functioning knowledge (adapting and applying existing knowledge to new learning). A five-minute personal biography seized the learners' attention and emphasised my academic practice. Pre- and post-sessional activities promoted further engagement during the workshop and information consolidation respectively; these included critical appraisal of a pre-selected peer-reviewed scientific publication or *critique with reflection of a virtual anatomical/medical image*. Online interactive walls (open source digital tools, with settings ensuring anonymity, where learners can post their thoughts) were ideal media for these activities.

For the online workshop, I used between seven and nine medical or anatomical images, coupled with storytelling, which were discussed via video communication software with screen sharing capabilities. The selection of these was of paramount importance, acting as a springboard for interactive discussion of research methods. The cases have included eminent historical and contemporary anatomists/

physicians/surgeons, digital anatomical art, a personal anatomical/medical art piece, a recent news article linked with anatomical/medical art and/or research methods, and one to two relevant peer-reviewed scientific publications. I used online interactive walls and real-time audience response systems with open-ended questions to promote discussion of pertinent topics; the latter technology allowed for co-creation of powerful visual outputs (word clouds). All the questions used in the session were linked to the medical/anatomical images and the accompanying narrative. I concluded the workshop by summarising key messages.

My advice for colleagues is to have a disclaimer when human cadaveric images are used and to tailor such content accordingly depending on local anatomy legislation and the audience's professional background.

Final remarks

Although access to digital communication platforms/reliable Internet connection could be an issue, depending on the location/facilities of the participants, remote active exploration of medical and anatomical imagery coupled with storytelling, in the context of research methods, is an excellent way to stimulate rich multidisciplinary discussions. This approach also promotes better insight into challenging scientific topics and threshold concepts (research reliability vs validity), inclusivity and reflection.

Bibliography

Canby, C.A. and Bush, T.A. (2010). Humanities in Gross Anatomy Project: A Novel Humanistic Learning Tool at Des Moines University. *Anatomical Sciences Education*, 3(2), 94–96. doi: 10.1002/ase.129

Finn, G.M. (2018). Current Perspectives on the Role of Body Painting in Medical Education. *Advances in Medical Education and Practice*, 9, 701–706. doi: 10.2147/AMEP.S142212

Hammer, R.R., Jones, T.W., Hussain, F.T.N., Bringe, K., Harvey, R.E., Person-Rennell, N.H. and Newman, J.S. (2010). Students as Resurrectionists—A Multimodal Humanities Project in Anatomy Putting Ethics and Professionalism in Historical Context. *Anatomical Sciences Education*, 3(5), 244–248. doi: 10.1002/ase.174

Inclusivity note

Using images to teach abstract concepts such as research methods is a very powerful and engaging approach to provide more varied input for our diverse students' cohorts. The choice of images is paramount and this entails the responsibility of providing trigger warnings where needed. For visually impaired students, we will need a very accurate alt-text and narration.

The case study shows how artistic imagery can be used to support learning thresholds acquisition in research methods. It demonstrates that art integrated learning is possible on any course of study. Other examples of art integrated learning possibilities for various disciplines are:

Origami (maths and geometry used to make an artistic 3D shape)
Poems (example: responding to a text being studied with a poem)
Collage (example: to represent study skills)
Performing art (example: to study medicine or medical conditions)
Painting or photography (example: to show how law and lawyers are perceived by people)
Dancing (example: to demonstrate chemical reactions)
Fractal music (using a maths concept to create music)
Architecture inspired fashion (using images, paintings or photos of buildings to inspire new fashion design)

Head to the companion website inclusivelearningdesign.com (under Section 3) for the fourth case study, by Elaine Fisher (UK), about the use of LEGO© Serious Play on a teacher education course. You will notice how using a kinaesthetic tool such as LEGO© helped teacher-students represent and articulate some of the tricky thresholds they encountered on the course.

In summary, creative input (playful approaches, including using games, and art integration) is more inclusive because it strikes a chord with our more imaginative side, is linked to pleasure and fun and can be very effective in involving all different types of students, providing them with multiple means of engagement.

Conclusion

This chapter has invited you to consider three related and overlapping characteristics of more inclusive input and practice: diversified, relevant and creative.

At the start of this chapter, I proposed these questions:

> **Activate your inner dialogue. ... How would you answer?**
>
> How can you design learning input that is (more) diversified?
> How can the learning you design be more relevant to students? Why does this matter?
> What's the role of creativity in making learning input more inclusive?

In a nutshell, summing up the ideas of this chapter, we can design input that is more:
Diversified—using diverse materials types, diverse learning activity types and culturally diverse resources
Relevant—connecting the course content to the students' lives and to the wider world (so that it *matters* to them)
Creative—designing playful approaches, using games and integrating art

End note to Section 3

While in Section 1 I addressed the values at the roots of the tree and in Section 2 I discussed the context, environment and set-up, in this Section (3) I addressed the course content, the design of input and practice activities.

In Chapter 4 I made a case for using **learning thresholds** as a starting point for more inclusive learning design rather than learning outcomes; in Chapter 5 I discussed opportunities and challenges of **flipped and self-directed** learning; and finally, in Chapter 6, I highlighted three characteristics of inclusive learning content: it needs to be **diversified, relevant and creative**.

> **Activate your inner dialogue. ... How would you answer?**
>
> What have your learnt in this section about learning content?
> What are your main take aways for more inclusive 'input and practice' on your course?

As you try out some of the approaches discussed in this section to make your input more inclusive, one way to understand what works best in terms of facilitated interactions is to observe your students as they interact: what types of learning activities produce a buzz and a flow and how can you have more of those?

The next step to design more inclusive learning is to design inclusive assessment: what outputs will the students produce? What is the role of assessment feedback in promoting inclusivity? I address these questions in the next section, about learning assessment.

Check the companion website to this book, inclusivelearningdesign.com for further resources about inclusive input and practice.

Bibliography

Gabriel, D. (2020). *Teaching to Transgress through 3D Pedagogy: Decolonising, Democratising and Diversifying the Higher Education Curriculum in Transforming the Ivory Tower: Models for Gender Equality and Social Justice*. Gabriel, D. (Ed.). London: UCL Press.

Style, E. (1988) *'Curriculum as Windows and Mirrors'. In Listening for all Voices: Gender Balancing the School Curriculum* (pp 6–12). Summit, NJ: Oak Knoll.

Diversified

Arshad, R. and Bagchi, P. (2021). From Inclusion to Transformation to Decolonisation. [blog] Teaching Matters Blog. Available at: https://www.teaching-matters-blog.ed.ac.uk/from-inclusion-to-transformation-to-decolonisation/

Darby, F. and Dowling, L. (2021). Building MultiStories: Embedding the Library Services for Inclusive Teaching and Learning in a Diverse Curriculum. *Irish Journal of Academic Practice*, 9(2), Article 8. doi: 10.21427/25XM-X994 Available at: https://arrow.tudublin.ie/ijap/vol9/iss2/8

Gronseth, S.L., Michela, E. and Ugwu, L.O. (2020). Designing for Diverse Learners. In McDonald, J.K. and West, R.E. (Eds.) *Design for Learning: Principles, Processes, and Praxis*. EdTech Books. Available at: https://edtechbooks.org/id/designing_for_diverse_learners

Hammond, Z. (2017). Start with Responsive. [podcast] Culturally Responsive Teaching and the Brain. Available at: https://crtandthebrain.com/start-with-responsive/

Laurillard, D. (2012). *Teaching as a Design Science: Building Pedagogical Patterns for Learning and Technology* (1st ed.). Routledge. doi: 10.4324/9780203125083

Mintz, S. (2022). Leveraging Cognitive Dissonance to Enhance Student Learning. [blog]. Inside Higher Ed. [online] Available at https://www.insidehighered.com/blogs/higher-ed-gamma/leveraging-cognitive-dissonance-enhance-student-learning

Misseyanni, A., Lytras, M., Papadopoulou, P. and Marouli, C. (2018). *Active Learning Strategies in Higher Education: Teaching for Leadership, Innovation, and Creativity*. Bingley: Emerald Publishing.

Moore, S. (2019). Dr. Baked Potato: How Can We Scaffold Complexity?. [video] YouTube. Available at: https://www.youtube.com/watch?v=7j0oL1CNXAs

Nguyen, H. (2021). How to Use Interleaving to Foster Deeper Learning. [online] Edutopia. Available at: https://www.edutopia.org/article/how-use-interleaving-foster-deeper-learning

Roberts, D. (2021). Multimedia Learning Methods and Affective, Behavioural and Cognitive Engagement: A Universal Approach to Dyslexia? *Journal of Further and Higher Education*. doi: 10.1080/0309877X.2021.1879746

Wenger-Trayner, E. and Wenger-Trayner, B. (2015). An introduction to communities of practice: a brief overview of the concept and its uses. Available from authors at https://www.wenger-trayner.com/introduction-to-communities-of-practice

Wentzel, A. (2021). Less is More: Content Compression in CLIL. *Latin American Journal of Content & Language Integrated Learning*, 14(1), 9–40. doi: 10.5294/laclil.2021.14.1.1

Relevant

Akilli, G. K. (2011a). Games and Simulations: A New Approach in Education? In I. Management Association (Ed.), *Gaming and Simulations: Concepts, Methodologies, Tools and Applications* (pp. 150–167). IGI Global. doi: 10.4018/978-1-60960-195-9.ch109

Bayerlein, L., Hora, M.T., Dean, B.A. and Perkiss, S. (2021). Developing Skills in Higher Education for Post-pandemic Work. *Labour and Industry*, 31(4), 418–429. doi: 10.1080/10301763.2021.1966292

Maringe, F. (Ed.) (2021). Higher Education in the Melting Pot: Emerging Discourses of the Fourth Industrial Revolution and Decolonisation. In *Disruptions in Higher Education: Impact and Implication* (Vol. 1, pp. i–210). Cape Town: AOSIS.

Shackleton-Jones, N. (2019). *How People Learn*. (1st ed.). Kogan Page. Available at: https://www.perlego.com/book/1589713/how-people-learn-pdf

Creative

Akilli, G.K. (2011b). Games and Simulations: A New Approach in Education? In *Gaming and Simulations: Concepts, Methodologies, Tools and Applications* (pp. 150–167). IGI Global. doi: 10.4018/978-1-60960-195-9.ch109

Ashton, S. and Stone, R. (2021). *An A–Z of Creative Teaching in Higher Education* (2nd ed.). London: Sage.

Conole, G. (2008). The Role of Mediating Artefacts in Learning Design. In *Handbook of Research on Learning Design and Learning Objects: Issues, Applications and Technologies.* doi: 10.4018/9781599048611.ch008

Giorza, T. (2016). Playing with Learning: Childhood Pedagogies for Higher Education. doi: 10.1057/9781137538697_16

Headleand, C. (2021). Using Games in Higher Education. [Blog] Pedagogy and Pancakes. Available at: https://chrisheadleand.com/2021/03/07/using-games-in-higher-education/

Hughes, J., Morrison, L. and Petrarca, D. (2022). Fostering Creativity and Critical Thinking Online. In Kay, R. and Hunter, W. (ed.) *Thriving Online: A Guide for Busy Educators.* [online] PressBooks. Available at: https://ecampusontario.pressbooks.pub/aguideforbusyeducators/chapter/fostering-creativity-and-critical-thinking-online/

Matraeva, A.D., Rybakova, M.V., Vinichenko, M.V., Oseev, A.A. and Ljapunova, N.V. (2020). Development of Creativity of Students in Higher Educational Institutions: Assessment of Students and Experts. *Universal Journal of Educational Research*, 8(1), 8–16. doi: 10.13189/ujer.2020.080102

Mayo, M.J. (2007). Games for Science and Engineering Education. *Communications of the ACM*, 50(7), 31–35.

Swanton, D. (2016). Learning with Lego. [Blog] Teaching Matters Blog, Available at: https://www.teaching-matters-blog.ed.ac.uk/learning-with-lego/

Toft Nørgård, R., Toft-Nielsen, C. and Whitton, N. (2017). Playful Learning in Higher Education: Developing a Signature Pedagogy. *International Journal of Play*, 6(3), 272–282. doi: 10.1080/21594937.2017.1382997

Section 4

Learning assessment
Output and feedback

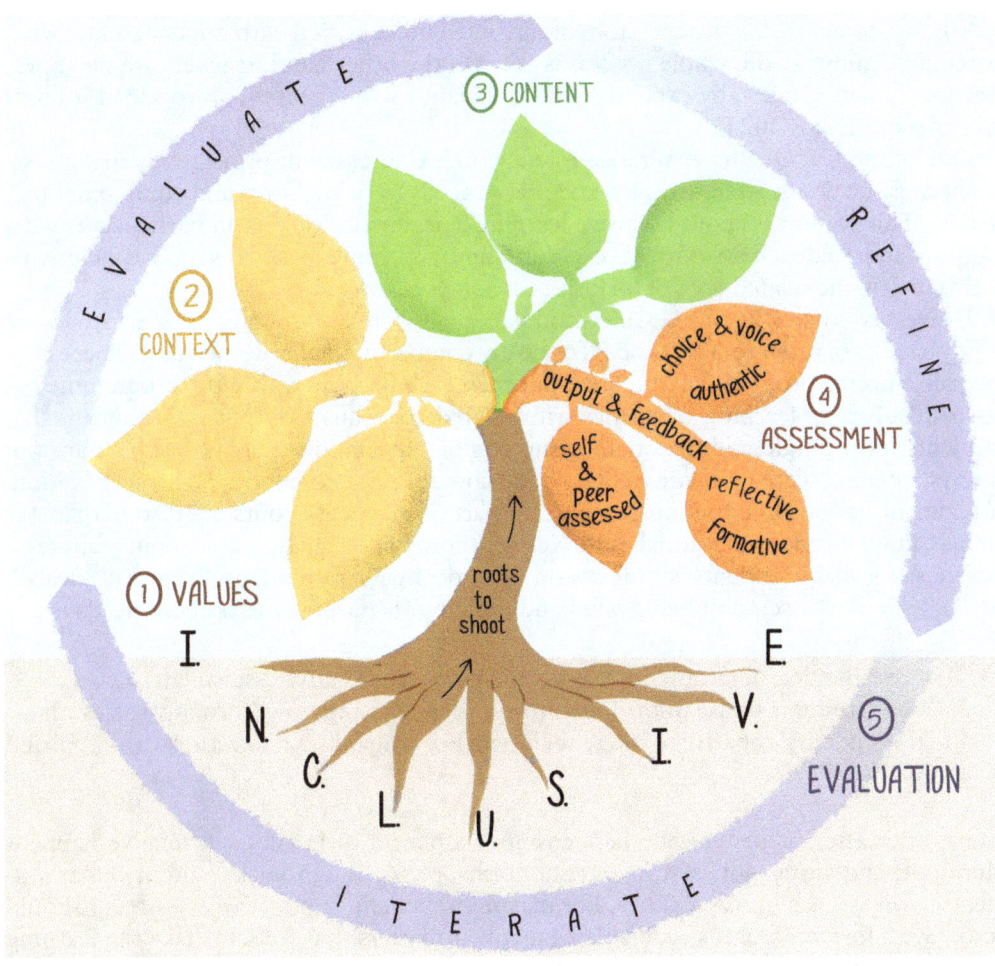

Now that you have articulated your **values** (Section 1); carried out a **contextual analysis** of the environment and of your students (Section 2); and considered how to make your course **content** more inclusive (Section 3), I invite you to address one of the most critical areas of teaching and learning: **assessment**. My view of assessment is that of a supportive phase of learning, done with the students (not to them), reclaiming the

Latin meaning of the term 'assess'—namely a 'form of the Latin verb assidere, meaning "to sit with"' (Green 1998).

> **Activate your inner dialogue. ... How would you answer?**
>
> What would (more) inclusive assessment on your course look like?
> How would it benefit all students?
> What assessment feedback practices can support inclusivity?

When it comes to assessment, students are most preoccupied with understanding what is required and that the whole process is fair. On the other hand, teachers are most preoccupied by its validity, by expected standards and by the (excessive) workload it tends to generate (Evans 2021).

One of the UK Quality Assurance Agency (QAA) assessment principles is that assessment must be designed holistically, and that it needs to be inclusive and equitable (QAA 2018). This section is about inclusive learning assessment, looking in particular at what outputs and feedback systems we can configure and implement to support inclusivity. I also review the related area of inclusive assessment *feedback*.

University studies in the UK are modularised: to obtain a degree, students need to study a series of often totally 'siloed' (or neatly compartmentalised) modules. There is an overall expected programme outcome, but then each module within the programme has its own subset of learning outcomes with related assessment outputs. This means that students must juggle and negotiate many sets of expectations (at once) which are not always interconnected or coherent. As passing the assessment leads to certification, assessment has become the most important part of university courses. It's one that students cannot escape, and it touches the very purpose of universities. The coping/strategic response for many students is to focus on 'how do I pass' rather than 'what will I learn'.

To work, in the sense of being valid and fulfilling its purpose, assessment needs to:

'Assure—that learning outcomes have been met (summative assessment)
Enable—students to use information to aid their learning now (formative assessment)
Build—students' capacity to judge their own learning (sustainable assessment)' (Boud 2022).

Summative assessment typically happens after a period of learning; formative happens during it; and sustainable assessment should happen throughout because it builds students' own assessment capabilities. For maximum benefit, summative assessment should also have a formative and sustainable element. It matters that students take the learning and feedback of assessment forward into the next thing they do (academic or professional) because 'students are equipped for future not primarily through knowledge and skills *but* their capacity to make informed decisions through their own practice' (Boud 2022).

However, some common critiques (by academics and students) to current university assessment are:

- it's divorced from learning and rarely useful beyond the course remit
- it's too focused on summative 'tests', giving the message that grades matter more than learning
- there's too much of it and often too much at once
- it's stressful (to the point of harming both staff and students)
- it highlights some skills (usually writing) and neglects others (such as spoken communication)
- it's not inclusive—lack of flexibility and choice, and one-size-fits-all 'standard' assessment practices (such as essays) advantage some students and disadvantage others.

Despite these issues, at this time, 'there is no evidence of systematic implementation of inclusive assessment' *yet*. This is 'unsurprising given literature highlighting that assessment practice is resistant to change' (Tai et al. 2021). Many high-ranking academic leaders do not see any problem with the existing assessment regime as it has often served *them* well. The reality on the ground is very different: academics and students often complain that assessment does not work.

Nieminen (2022) makes a case for 'assessment for inclusion' and states that 'if mass higher education truly wishes to include students from increasingly diverse backgrounds, assessment needs to be rethought from the viewpoint of inclusion'. Inclusive assessment means considering all aspects of assessment—from the development of assessment criteria and rubrics to method and mode of assessment feedback—to ensure that barriers are removed as much as possible and appropriate support systems are in place for all to succeed.

This is important for the well-being of everyone involved in assessment. Many university teachers find themselves trapped in a continuous cycle of assessment accommodations due to—at times obvious—gaps in the way assessment has been designed. Rather than relying on 'reactive modifications', assessment should be inclusive at *design stage* (QAA 2018). Through intentional, inclusive assessment design, we can solve the assessment issues mentioned earlier and offer interesting, satisfying assessment that fulfils its main purpose: to support learning. Brown and Sambell (2021) state: 'assessment can be designed to promote, support and extend future learning, not just measure it'.

How can we design more inclusive learning *through* assessment?

Going back to the nine root-values discussed in Section 1, inclusive 'output and feedback' learning design is:

I. Intentionally equitable (assessment is a key way in which we can promote equity, for instance using inclusive language and diverse examples; through a menu of flexible outputs, providing students with voice and choice)
N. Nurturing (assessment design can support a more holistic learning experience)
C. Co-created (most of the ideas discussed in this section are better designed in partnership with students)
L. Liberating (assessment can be used as a tool to liberate our learning design, for instance towards more civic responsibility and decolonisation)
U. User-friendly (we can create more accessible and user-friendly learning assessment where we provide assessment guidelines and supports in a variety of modes, including visually, and students have multiple means of expressing and evidencing learning)

- S. Socially responsible (assessment should have an orientation to society, with the goal of benefiting the wider world)
- I. Integrative (assessment is a powerful 'integrative' tool, with the power to integrate the students' lived experiences, research and practice, academic and social skills, interdisciplinary understanding and more)
- V. Values-based (the outputs we ask our students to produce evidence the values that drive us)
- E. Ecological (through the assessment regime, we can draw attention to sustainability, in a broader sense)

Through inclusive assessment, we aim at enabling all students to demonstrate to their full potential what they know, understand and can do as well as provide them with the means to have real impact on the world.

One of the best things we can do to improve assessment is to have a *programmatic* approach to its design and implementation. As academics, we tend to be concerned with the here and now of assessment on the (part of the) course we teach. However, getting the big picture of assessment, at programme level, is very helpful both for us academics and for our students. Jessop and Tomas (2016) discuss the 'implications of programme assessment patterns for student learning' and advocate a 'programmatic and evidence-led approach to' assessment design. And O'Neill (2009) points to the importance of holistic, integrated and programmatic assessment,

> ensuring that over the duration of a full programme students will: have adequate opportunity to be assessed in different ways; receive on-going feedback on their progress; be ensured of a valid and reliable final outcome; and be assessed in both simple and complex tasks.

If you teach one module only, become familiar with the bigger picture documents which outline the programme level outcomes and outputs, so you can better situate the module within the whole student journey. Once you better understand how different parts of your course fit together, invite your students to discuss *their* understanding of the course assessment. A useful way to do so is by mapping what is required. This can be done in person, for instance with post-it notes, or digitally with interactive walls or software such as Padlet. Mapping the assessment journey with the students can be an eye opener for you (it reveals what is not clear or even not known to students) and for the students (it makes them situate assessment in the bigger picture and can lessen anxiety if they better understand what is required).

In this section, I consider some key aspects of inclusive assessment design and implementation by addressing three interrelated approaches:

Chapter 7 'Choice, voice and authentic' is about the way we promote students' agency through the design of outputs useful beyond the course.

Chapter 8 'Reflective and formative' is about developing the key capabilities of self-reflection and self-regulation through formative tasks for students to gauge the quality of their own progress.

Chapter 9 'Self and peer assessment and feedback' is about developing students' metacognition, inner feedback voice and peer learning throughout the course, not simply at the end of it.

Bibliography

Boud, D. (2022). *Reimagining the Student Experience—A New Focus for Assessment (Online Presentation)*. SEDA Spring Event [online].

Brown, S. and Sambell, K. (2021). Changing Assessment for Good: Building on the Emergency Switch to Promote Future-oriented Assessment and Feedback Designs. In Baughan, P. (Ed.) *Assessment and Feedback in a Post-Pandemic Era: A Time for Learning and Inclusion*. AdvanceHE.

Evans, C. (2021). Equity, Agency and Transparency: Making Assessment Work Better for Students and Academics. [online] THE. Available at: https://www.timeshighereducation.com/campus/equity-agency-and-transparency-making-assessment-work-better-students-and-academics

Green, J. M. (1998). Constructing the Way Forward for All Students: What Are the Essential Determinants of a Useful Assessment System Which Can Contribute to Improve Teaching and Learning? *Education Canada*, 38(3), 8–12.

Jessop, T. and Tomas, C. (2016). The Implications of Programme Assessment Patterns for Student Learning. *Assessment & Evaluation in Higher Education*, 1–10. doi: 10.1080/02602938.2016.1217501

Nieminen, J.H. (2022). Assessment for Inclusion: Rethinking Inclusive Assessment in Higher Education. *Teaching in Higher Education*, 1–19. doi: 10.1080/13562517.2021.2021395

O'Neill, G. (2009). A Programme-Wide Approach to Assessment: A Reflection On Some Curriculum Mapping Tools. In: *AISHE International Conference—Valuing Complexity*. [online] Available at: http://ocs.aishe.org/index.php/international/2009/schedConf/presentations

Tai, J., Ajjawi, R. and Umarova, A. (2021). How Do Students Experience Inclusive Assessment? A Critical Review of Contemporary Literature. *International Journal of Inclusive Education*, 1–18. doi: 10.1080/13603116.2021.2011441

QAA (2018). UK Quality Code, Advice and Guidance: Assessment. Available at: https://www.qaa.ac.uk/quality-code/advice-and-guidance/assessment#:~:text=Guiding%20Principles,-Assessment%20methods%20and&text=Assessment%20is%20reliable%2C%20consistent%2C%20fair,Assessment%20is%20explicit%20and%20transparent

Chapter 7

Choice, voice and authentic

> Student agency boils down to students having a voice in the classroom
> Laurie Manville & Alva Lefevre

In a highly provocative book, entitled *Freedom to Learn: The threat to student academic freedom and why it needs to be reclaimed*, Macfarlane (2016) shows that there is a paradox unfolding in front of our eyes: students are being deprived of freedom to learn by policies and practices such as compulsory attendance and grading class contribution, while universities claim to promote student-centred pedagogies. Clearly, students are being deprived of freedom of choice in many aspects of their learning journey due to inflexible university systems and what comes down to the tyranny of democracy.

I make a case for providing students with voice and choice, in all aspects of their learning and particularly in the area of assessment. One of the best ways to promote students' agency in assessment is to co-create it with students, so that they own the process. Bearman et al. (2014) propose an assessment design decisions framework made up of six categories:

1. Purposes of assessment
2. Context of assessment
3. Learner outcomes
4. Tasks
5. Feedback processes
6. Interaction

If we cannot co-create all of these with students, could we at least involve them in partnership and consultation over categories 3 to 6? This would allow us to build in flexibility and choice as needed by the direct assessment users.

> **Activate your inner dialogue. … How would you answer?**
>
> How does assessment choice promote inclusivity?
> How can students' voice inform assessment design?
> What barriers do you currently experience in designing more flexible and authentic assessment? How can you overcome them?

In this chapter I will discuss, and 'show rather than tell' through relevant case studies, three interrelated approaches to assessment design that support more inclusive practices:

- providing assessment choice
- lifting students' voice and
- designing authentic outputs.

Choice

Having choice is a right that adults fight for, in all aspects of life. As teachers we prize the choices we can make in our practice (Juliani 2015). As adult learners, university students have the *right* to choose (Macfarlane 2016), unless we take it away from them by the way we design and present learning. Providing choice is about shifting the 'locus of control' from the teacher to the student (Jopp and Cohen 2020). Of course, choice can apply to all aspects of teaching and learning: the pace at which students learn, the place they learn from and the pathways that are available to them as part of optimally flexible design (Hack et al. 2022).

The main purpose of providing assessment choice is for students to *self-differentiate* according to needs and preference. In typical one-size-fits-all assessment approaches, the students who shine are those whose academic level, abilities and preferences match the required assessment mode. What about everyone else? Susan Cain (author of the book *Quiet*) has said: 'Everyone shines, given the right lighting'. By providing *some* flexibility and choice we support more students to find a suitable fit to demonstrate their learning.

Choice in assessment doesn't mean that standard assessment types such as essays are eliminated—what it means is that students go from *every* assignment being an essay to having variety and options which allow teachers to measure and reward different learning skills (Hack et al. 2022).

It seems intuitive that providing assessment choice to students in terms of types of outputs and other aspects must support inclusivity. However, in practice, it is not as straightforward as that. Just as noted for flipped and self-directed learning in Chapter 5, all approaches which provide considerable academic freedom to students must be carefully considered and designed to see whether they will benefit students in a particular context and what related support systems might be needed. Once more, the contextual analysis discussed in Section 2 will provide the qualitative data to decide what choices to provide.

The following two case studies explore first, ways of providing assessment choice and second, how this naturally happens within project-based learning.

The first case study discusses the pros and cons of providing assessment choice. Notice some suggested alternatives to 'standard' assessment and how to handle challenges linked to providing choice.

Choice of output

By Gustavo Espinoza Ramos (Peru/UK)

Definition

Assessment choice uses the principles of Universal Design for Learning (UDL) to offer alternative assessment methods per each component of module assessment

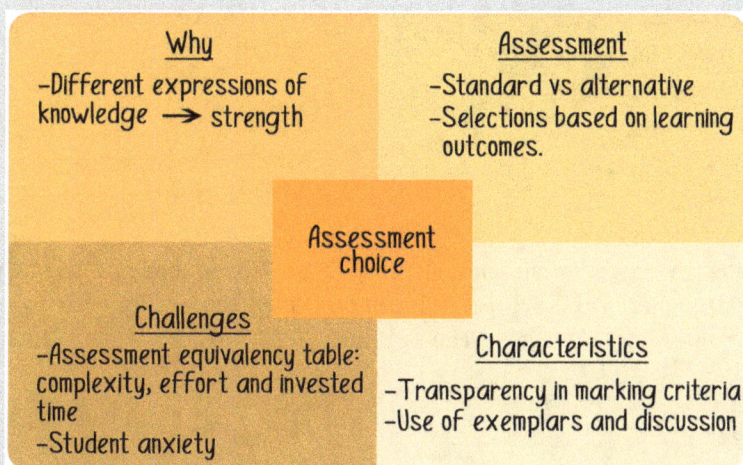

Figure 7.1 Four dimensions of assessment choice.

that allows students to demonstrate the accomplishment of learning outcomes. Its main characteristics can be seen in the above image (Figure 7.1).

Benefits

Assessment choice offers benefits to students and teachers. For students, they can demonstrate creativity, knowledge and skills based on their learning preferences and time constraints, and they can feel more empowered in the selection of their own learning output (DeWitt 2017). For teachers, it represents an opportunity to be more creative in the development of assessment, it can be more interesting when marking different types of assessment and it can reduce costly arrangements such as additional exam rooms and invigilators.

Assessment methods

Educational institutions traditionally tend to focus more on written assessment and should explore other alternatives to demonstrate student learning.

When developing summative assessment choices, the teacher should select between standard and alternative assessment types that meet the learning outcomes, whether they will be individual or group activities, and consider the authenticity of the activities that simulate real-life contexts as it will improve student engagement (University of Plymouth 2014).

For instance, where standard assessment outputs are written or oral exams, reports or essays, we could offer alternatives such as:

- Portfolio
- Presentations: poster
- Project/Product development

- Podcasts
- Simulation and online games
- Blogs/Vlogs/Journals
- Wikis/Web pages
- Experiments
- Role plays

Additionally, the assessment choices should be *limited* options to avoid overwhelming students with too many options (O'Neill 2010); for that reason it is advisable to keep only two or three options.

Challenges

The main challenge in providing assessment choice is the development of an equivalency table that determines the workload per assessment method as the different types should have a similar level of complexity, effort and invested time (McConlogue 2020) to complete the activity. Many academics deem this important for students to understand the different types and size of assessment methods. But this can also increase students' anxiety as they need to become familiar with many different types of assessment. It is important to remember that student workload is most usefully measured by notional learning hours rather than word count (Fielding 2008), especially when using alternative assessments such as simulation games. Hence, instead of an assessment equivalency table, it is recommended to provide more clarity on what the assessment method is intended to do in alignment with the intended learning outcomes.

Regardless of the type of assessment method used, it is advisable to use exemplars and rubrics when discussing with students the differences between the given assessment choices and to show transparency in the standards descriptors for each assessment criterion. Finally, tutors can use formative assessment so that the student becomes an assessor of their own performance and can exercise peer evaluation that will help them to improve.

Conclusion

Assessment choice offers opportunities to students and teachers to improve student engagement and empower students in their own learning based on their preferences. Despite the challenge of determining the equivalence of workload, providing assessment choice while focusing on the purpose of the assessment methods and how each meets the intended learning outcomes positively contributes to inclusive learning design in higher education.

Bibliography

DeWitt, P. (2017). Student-Driven Differentiation: Putting Student Voice behind the Wheel. *Education Week*, June 08. Available at: http://blogs.edweek.org/edweek/finding_common_ground/2017/06/student-driven_differentiation_putting_student_voice_behind_the_wheel.html

Fielding, A. (2008). Student Assessment Workloads: A Review. Manchester Metropolitan University. Autumn 2008. Available from http://www.celt.mmu.ac.uk/ltia/issue17/fielding.php

McConlogue, T. (2020). *Assessment and Feedback in Higher Education: A Guide for Teachers.* UCL Press. Available at: https://www.uclpress.co.uk/products/111601

O'Neill, G. (2010). Choice of Assessment Methods within a Module: Students' Experiences and Staff Recommendations for Practice. Interim Report. UCD. Available at: https://www.ucd.ie/t4cms/Interim%20Inclusive%20Assessment%20Report,%20June%202010%20.pdf

University of Plymouth (2014). 7 Steps to: Inclusive Assessment. Available at: https://www.plymouth.ac.uk/uploads/production/document/path/2/2401/7_Steps_to_Inclusive_Assessment.pdf

Inclusivity note

Benefits for students:

Creativity, knowledge and skills based on their learning preferences and time constraints
Empowerment in the selection of their own learning output

Challenges for students:

Higher student anxiety if there are too many choices or if they are not well supported

Benefits for teachers:

Creativity in the development of assessment
Reduction of (costly) arrangements for students with particular learning needs

Challenges for teachers:

Providing enough clarity on what each assessment method is intended to do in alignment with the intended learning outcomes
The development of an equivalency table that determines the workload per assessment method
The level of expertise in the various assessment modes, to provide enough support and guidance for each choice
Potential institutional objections, for instance to do with quality systems for resits.

This case study provides a balanced view of assessment choice: it has many benefits, *but*, to be meaningful, it is better to provide a *limited* amount of choices, especially as they each need supporting materials, exemplars and guidance.

For some students, or some cohorts, providing great flexibility and choice might be counterproductive because it depends on their readiness for learning as well as on their previous assessment experiences.

Choice also depends on the nature of the course. If the course is based on a specific skill, such as public speaking, it follows that the assessment should be a public speaking task. The choice could be in other aspects such as the content, length, delivery mode and more. Once the learning thresholds are clarified and appropriate learning outcomes are in place, *how* to achieve them can be a matter of negotiation.

Assessment rubrics are invaluable in making assessment more inclusive, because the criteria can be co-created with the students (What does 'quality' look like in X type of output? What competencies should be evident?) and because they can be aligned to the intended learning outcomes, the criteria can be generic enough to fit *any* output. Criteria might be around discipline understanding and practices, language used, clarity of communication or argument, critical analysis, collaboration, etc. where the method or output chosen to provide evidence is in many respects irrelevant.

If, on the course you teach, you have little power to alter the final, summative assessment mode, you may have the flexibility to provide various formative assessment points which scaffold learning towards the summative one(s). Formative assessment could afford students more choice of outputs in a developmental lens. However, this requires balance, because to become proficient in one assessment mode, students need practice. So, if the final assessment is a 5000-word essay, the formative tasks should help them towards that goal.

This book is about inclusive learning design *for teachers*, but through assessment outputs we can help *our students* develop *their own* 'inclusivity practices' as a life-wide competency. For example, irrespective of the specific output students choose (or what audience the output is meant for), students should make their outputs accessible to all. Video, audio or written outputs all have accessibility issues, so asking students to add captions or transcripts or making the text reader-friendly is one way of enhancing their understanding of inclusivity as a life-long ethos as well as enhancing their digital literacy.

The next case study is about a type of assessment which affords choice and differentiation by its very nature: using projects. Notice how project-based learning encompasses the three aspects of this chapter: choice, voice and authentic.

Project-based learning and assessment

By Stephan Hughes (Trinidad/Brazil)

To provide an overview of how project-based learning (PBL) can be applied in the most diverse learning contexts, my suggestions and recommendations to use PBL are grounded on the results obtained by applying projects as a requirement for Jerome Bruner's notion that epistemic (intrinsic) motivation acts as an internal force driving people to better understand the world and for John Dewey's principle of autonomous learning and emphasis on learning in answer to—and in interaction with—real-life events. This case study is about using project-based learning and assessment with those taking my teacher education programme. Attendees are majors in humanities, language studies, and social sciences, the majority being either pre- or in-service teachers. The proposed framework can be applied at other educational levels and as a short course for professional purposes.

The term *inclusive* here is used to mean a wide-reaching learning experience for participants with varied academic backgrounds and consequent varied 'gaps' in theoretical knowledge. The use of a project-based approach as the final output in a postgraduate program levels the field for teachers who come from such diverse teaching contexts and academic backgrounds, proving to be a very inclusive way of prompting learning. This inclusivity is couched in cognitive research results that show meta-cognition and social factors have a strong influence on learning (Gijselaers 1996).

Roughly two-thirds of the teachers under my tutoring have had random practice with the skills needed to draft a short 'scientific' article, such as hypothesizing, defining variables, setting main and secondary aims, reviewing specialized literature, applying varied research methods, and collecting and analyzing quantitative and qualitative data. These skills are directly related to PBL, considering the principle defended by Barrows (1996) that educational formats should foster students' teamwork with authentic or simulated real-life problems. This 'irreducible core of PBL' sets it apart from other active, co-operative, student-centered, process-centered or case-based educational approaches.

Providing a student-centered, process-based, learning-oriented framework in which student-teachers need to perform tasks that simulate professionally related practice exposes them indirectly to these skills that are rooted in theoretical study.

Student-teachers on my program are required to design an educational product or service that meets a need they have identified in their area of work or that is aimed at a specific target group, such as providing consulting services for private schools or offering language learning platforms for professionals, commonly referred to as English for Specific Purposes. A recent example of this was a teacher-student who created a training program for hotel staff and an adaptive learning application for Brazilian taxi drivers to achieve working knowledge of English.

Using a hands-on, start-up project-based approach for the summative assessment in the postgraduate program means including participant voice and choice—they have the autonomy to decide on the 'what', the 'how' and the 'why' of their project and are given support and guidance as necessary. This reflects that project-based learning is grounded in what I refer to as the three As—Amiability, Agency and Accountability: students should take pleasure in carrying out the project, take charge of the process and be responsible for the results. The flip side to giving learners this amount of freedom to design and develop a project of their choice is the risk for students feeling ill-equipped to carry out the tasks included in the process such as mastering new or unfamiliar digital resources and making management-like decisions. This means that I need to be involved, resourceful and supportive to help them fill those gaps in order to produce a suitable project output.

I also promote ongoing self-assessment, which caters for personalization and individualization and generates real input for qualitative narrative-based research. Designing your classes on a project-based approach fosters the repetition of tasks to generate a desired result (iteration); the documentation of learners' impressions and analysis of the process (reflection); the fusion of diverse skills sets and social capital that is unique to each team member (collaboration) and the evaluation of classmates based on clear and academically sound criteria (peer assessment).

As shown in Figure 7.2, this approach to teaching and assessing hinges on four main areas:

Student—the learner must have voice and choice in the ideation, design and execution
Feedback—constant evaluation on the process and progress is key
Product—the project should culminate in something of real use, as evidence of learning
Process—making the learning process more formative and informative allows for a blend of teacher, peer and self-assessment

By using projects, students can choose from a myriad of possibilities to expose their learning: a vlog, a digital portfolio, a podcast, a slide show or an infographic. Prensky (2010) is credited with saying that if we teachers must learn new ways to do old stuff, we *must* learn to change our expectations of what learning is or should be.

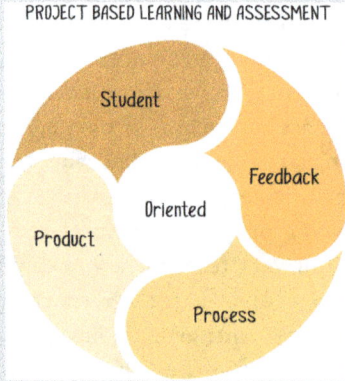

Figure 7.2 The four dimensions of project based learning.

Bibliography

Barrows, H.S. (1996). Problem-based Learning in Medicine and Beyond: A Brief Overview. In Wilkerson, L. and Gijselaers, W.H. (Eds.) *Bringing Problem-based Learning to Higher Education: Theory and Practice* (pp. 3–12). San Francisco, CA: Jossey-Bass.

Gijselaers, W.H. (1996). Connecting Problem-based Practices with Educational Theory. In Wilkerson, L. and Gijselaers, W.H. (Eds.) *Bringing Problem-based Learning to Higher Education: Theory and Practice* (pp. 13–21). San Francisco, CA: Jossey-Bass.

Prensky, M. (2010). *Teaching Digital Natives—Partnering for Real Learning*. Thousand Oaks, CA: Corwin.

Schmidt, H.G. (1993). Foundations of Problem-based Learning: Some Explanatory Notes. *Medical Education*, 27, 422–432. doi: 10.1111/j.1365-2923.1993.tb00296.x

Inclusivity note

Projects provide natural differentiation and multiple ways for students to evidence their learning. They can result in authentic, genuinely useful outputs where students have real impact on wider audiences.

'Open' projects where students have total freedom to choose their outputs and processes require agility from the part of the teacher: providing the necessary support and guidance will require flexibility and resourcefulness. It might be better to ask students to work in small groups (or even to set up collaborative projects) so that they can provide and receive ongoing peer support and feedback and to share the workload.

This case study highlights the multiple benefits of project-based learning, often considered a high impact educational practice (Kuh 2008, WIP 2019). There are entire fields (such as art and design) where projects are the default way for students to engage with and evidence their learning (part of their signature pedagogy). However, projects can be used in *all* fields of study—they can culminate in very interesting outputs with potential benefits to wider audiences beyond the university walls. This is one example in which disciplinary cross-pollination can enrich us: the hallmark pedagogical practices of one field can inspire us to create innovative assessment outputs in our field.

I invite you to think about ways in which you could introduce projects into your course, perhaps on a small scale to start off. Projects are a step in the right direction to apply most of the points I raised in the previous section, to make course *content* more inclusive, as well as to apply most of the points in this section, to make course *assessment* more inclusive.

Student choice matters in assessment, especially when it is accompanied by students' *voice*.

Voice

Voice is about communicating, vocalising views and opinions. Student voice has become another educational buzz word in the past 20 years. Student voice initiatives have mushroomed in all universities, but not all result in the desired change. Young and Jerome (2020) see student voice as a 'feedback loop' that universities are constantly trying to close by responding to it in meaningful ways. In fact, Cook-Sather (2006) points that some particular words are associated with the term student voice: 'rights', 'respect' and 'listening'.

In this discussion, the concept of student voice refers to what students say, their expression of values, opinions, beliefs and perspectives, as individuals and as groups. It also refers to pedagogical approaches based on student choices, interests, passions and ambitions.

Giving students voice is part of intentionally equitable hospitality, the first root-value discussed in Section 1, where Maha Bali discussed the importance of welcoming and providing a space for each and every learner under our care. As discussed in the 'Co-creation' chapter in Section 1, one of the best ways in which students' voice can inform assessment design is by co-creating the why, what, how and when of formative and summative assessment with the students themselves.

Student voice has another dimension: it is also about allowing students agency to advocate for a particular cause they care about. In Chapter 5, you read a case study about 'Personalised Learning and Advocacy' where students are provided a space to research and advocate for a cause they want to support. On a similar vein, the following case study offers an innovative assessment output which integrates many of the root-values discussed in Section 1: photovoice, a combination of students' produced photographic images which give *voice* to a social issue they want to advocate for.

Why did you click? The use of Photovoice (PV) methods in assessment to advance student agency

By Fionnuala Darby (Ireland)

Visual representation as an inclusive learning design has the ability to transmit messages on issues students see as relevant and important from their perspectives (Dunne et al. 2018). Photovoice (PV) offers alternative ways of knowing by allowing students to document their reality through images along with supporting text (Wang and Burris 1994) and provides an alternative and underused method of assessment in education. In practical terms, PV consists of images and explanatory text, selected by the student for an assignment.

The epistemological roots or knowledge beliefs of photovoice are located in empowerment education, feminist theory and documentary photography (Ciolan and Manasia 2017). Each of these theoretical frameworks ignites individual agency and provides a site for learning through the eyes of the students' lived experiences.

By validating the lived experience of students on campus, PV allows them to name and see their own world and to hear from voices that may have been overlooked (Sutton-Brown 2014). A unique adventure for me and I was curious about how it might work, PV offered alternative ways of finding out about places and spaces on campus that included and excluded students, by allowing the students to document their reality through images (Darby 2018). In addition, the students provided accompanying text to contextualise the images that they had taken, in order to provide meaning and interpretation. PV also proved enticing to the students as a form of assessment that was an alternative to an 'another' essay, report or presentation. PV can be applied to all disciplines and requires minimum digital skills.

I adapted Luttrell's (2010) lens for viewing the students' images and text (Figure 7.3):

- The centre of the *lens* represents the students' voice and agency in completing the assignment.
- The *picture taking* and the *picture content* is the student's representation of what they have chosen to make visible about inclusion and exclusion on campus through images and text.
- The *picture viewing* promotes dialogue and discussion during class time through a photo showcase of the collective efforts of the students' images and explanatory text.
- Coding the emerging *themes* identified through the images and the accompanying text allows for an analytical approach to the content in the assignments.

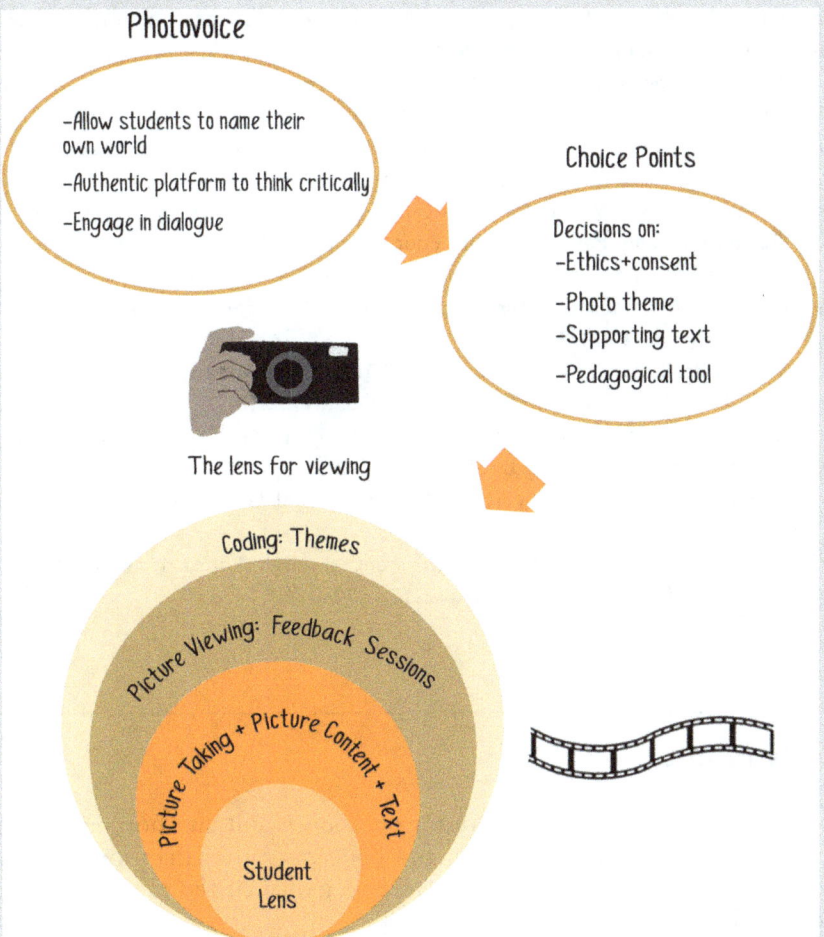

Figure 7.3 Lens for viewing meaning and interpretation through photovoice methodology of inclusion and exclusion on campus (adapted from Luttrell 2010).

If the images find the appropriate audiences, this can influence policymakers to improve a situation and promote critical dialogue for social change, reflecting the commitment of participatory action research to social change. While the photos aim to capture and reflect on personal experience, they will also shed light on what has been overlooked or ignored from the students' perspectives. Photovoice has liberatory potential as it helps to centralise marginalised voices within dominant knowledge claims (Malherbe et al. 2017).

Students are motivated to learn when an activity captures attention, is relevant to them and sparks curiosity. Try PV as an assessment method and allow the students to become your eyesight on a topic. Enjoy what they decide to reveal.

Bibliography

Ciolan, L., and Manasia, L. (2017). Reframing Photovoice to Boost Its Potential for Learning Research. *International Journal of Qualitative Method*, 16(1), 1–15.

Darby, F. (2018). *Belonging at ITB—The Use of Photovoice Methodology to Investigate Inclusion and Belonging at ITB Based on Ethnicity and Nationality from a Student Perspective.* E-book Library [online] Transforming our World through Design, Diversity and Education. Available at: http://ebooks.iospress.nl/volumearticle/50613

Dunne, L., Hallett, F., Kay, V., and Woolhouse, C. (2018). Spaces of Inclusion: Investigating Place, Positioning and Perspective in Educational Settings through Photo-elicitation. *International Journal of Inclusive Education*, 22(1), 21–37.

Luttrell, W. (2010). A Camera Is a Big Responsibility: A Lens for Analysing Children's Visual Voices. *Visual Studies*, 25(3), 224–237.

Malherbe, N., Suffla, S., Seedat, M. and Bawa, U. (2017). Photovoice as Liberatory Enactment: The Case of Youth as Epistemic Agents. In Seedat, M., Suffla, S. and Christie, D. (Eds.) *Emancipatory and Participatory Methodologies in Peace, Critical, and Community Psychology* (pp. 165–178). Peace Psychology Book Series. Springer Publishing.

Sutton-Brown, C.A. (2014). Photovoice: A Methodological Guide. *Photography and Culture*, 7(2), 169–185.

Wang, C., and Burris, M. (1994). Empowerment through Photo Novella: Portraits of Participation. *Health Education Quarterly*, 21(2), 171–186.

Inclusivity note

Photovoice is particularly supportive for neurodivergent and non-native speaker students as it relies more on images and concepts rather than long writing or speaking tasks. It can help all students develop global citizen capabilities, such as advocacy skills.

The tools needed are simple as most mobile phones have good, embedded cameras, although some classroom discussion (or providing a support sheet) about 'framing' and image, the use of light, editing and caption writing can be helpful.

> The challenges can be if a student chooses to advocate for a cause that is controversial and might even be offensive for some in the cohort. In this case, following the PV presentation, we could propose a classroom debate where students respectfully discuss the difficult topic.

Photovoice assignments can be an eyeopener for all involved. As the case study illustrates, students choosing a theme and then taking photos to represent the ideas, forming a narrative which includes text, can be a very interesting assignment; it involves real audiences beyond the course, and the advocacy side of it can provoke small and big changes.

This type of assignment provides choice, voice *and* is authentic.

Authentic

Far too often, assessment outputs remain only within the teacher-student relationship, within the course, and are not designed for broad or lasting impact (Clifton and Hoffman 2021). An antidote to this is authentic assessment.

Authentic is another buzz word in education and it has become a popular way to describe work-related assessment which develops and evaluates professional competencies. But not everyone likes this understanding, because it implies that we seek to provide assessment that simply supports employers' agendas. As noted in Chapter 6, relevant learning is highly motivational for students, and this equally applies to assessment, hence employability should not be the only purpose for more authentic learning and assessment but also because it makes learning and assessment more personally relevant to students and supports them to *become* their authentic future self.

What is considered authentic is a matter of subjective judgement; however, as shown in Figure 7.4, in this chapter I will adopt a broad—'thick' according to Shaffer and Resnick (1999)—understanding of the term authentic assessment to mean the types of outputs which are:

- genuinely *relevant* to the students within their context
- aligned with industry practices and challenges (*realistic*)
- useful beyond the course and often *impactful* on the wider world

Ideally, learning and assessment should not simply be personally relevant and useful for disciplinary practices, but it should also have an orientation to the wider world with students able to situate their outputs within a *social value* context.

Work-related assignments are one option to provide authentic assessment. Irrespective of the field of study, all degrees lead to one or more practices (jobs), so a useful guiding question to design more inclusive, authentic assessment task is: What do practitioners in this field do in their 'job'? It would be useful for students to have at least some of their assessments during their studies reflect practitioners' practices. However, an important factor is whether students are at the stage where they can cope with *real* industry practices or whether simulations are a better option (Gulikers et al. 2004). As academics, we

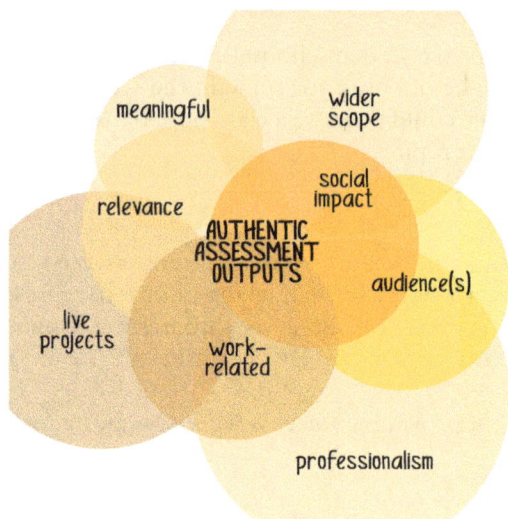

Figure 7.4 Common, overlapping elements of authentic assessment outputs.

can move towards more authentic outputs if we provide assessment tasks which better *reflect* what a practitioner might do in their professional practice(s).

Here are some examples of authentic assessment outputs which are also 'renewable' (Clifton and Hoffman 2021) as their usefulness extends in time and scope, becoming a 'legacy' (Gilson 2017) for future cohorts:

- book review on a public website or other outlet for general or specialist audiences
- annotated bibliography in collaboration with librarians to make recommendations on enhancing the library collections
- museum collaboration: create augmented reality options for visitors to interact with the exhibits
- write and publish a journal article about a specific theme or topic
- a public blog or vlog to share learning ideas or outputs, inviting responses from the public (many students do this anyway, blurring the lines between learning, teaching, research and technology and showing us teachers that it is possible to make assessment more authentically useful)

For more specific work-related outputs, students can design and make:

- Infographic reports for companies/employers
- Leaflets or one-pagers that a company/employer can use
- An app that a company/employer can use
- A poster to advertise a product, event or service

Once students have made such authentic outputs, they can also build on them by organising a (digital?) conference themselves with external audiences to display and discuss their outputs. Or the output could be the first phase of a larger research project which can lead to publication.

Notice that all the preceding examples imply that assessment outputs connect students to diverse, often 'real' audiences—this makes assessment much more authentic.

What are the benefits of authentic assessment outputs? Besides increasing students' motivation and engagement, they usually promote academic integrity because they are hard to plagiarise, hence they equip students with 'essential skills for their future professional life, such as communication skills, collaboration skills, critical-thinking and problem-solving skills, self-awareness, and self-confidence' (Sokhanvara et al. 2021). Hence, the emphasis in authentic assessment is on learning transfer, to be world-ready.

Authentic assessment tasks can be very exciting for academics, but it is very important to be realistic about what they require. Students need support in the form of exemplars, guidance, scaffolding, drafting, peer-review and specific technical skills that the task may require. To be authentic ourselves and not ask students to do something we would not do ourselves, we should *try the assessment ourselves*, so we get a sense of the workload involved and we can identify tricky areas. This will help us put in place appropriate assessment support systems.

The following two case studies address two examples of authentic assessment outputs: using podcasts and using Wikipedia.

The first case study discusses the use of podcasts. Notice how the author used podcasts as input *and output* of the learning experience and the effect on students.

Listen to what I produced: Student produced podcasts for learning and assessment

By Nellie El Enany (Egypt)

The use of student produced podcasts for learning and assessment can encourage students' creative learning, a crucial factor in the drive towards aligning education with employer needs, and innovative curriculum design and delivery. It was also an ideal experience of learning and assessment for online instruction.

The podcast assessment was part of a course which was fully online in Spring 2021, Entrepreneurial Leadership and Critical Global Issues, part of the Core Curriculum Program at The American University in Cairo, Egypt. The students enrolled in this course were first- and second-year students from a range of different degree majors. The class was made up of 20 students and there were five students in each group. The groups can also be made up of four students; more than five can cause issues in terms of the work assigned to each one.

At the beginning of the module, the different assessments were explained to the students including the one on student produced podcasts. Central to this explanation was the relevance of podcasts to higher education, why it was being used as an assessment compared to conventional assessments such as exams or presentations, and the expected value students may gain from the task including skills such as enhanced communication, research and critical judgement. The end product of a podcast was also highlighted as being meaningful for their future careers, where they could share the podcast with their potential employers highlighting their diverse skillset.

I also explained to them that over the course of the module they would be listening to several podcasts based on research and practice to prepare for class, and at times short ones during class, to help prepare them for their own student produced podcast assessment—an authentic assignment for wider audiences, as show in Figure 7.5.

Figure 7.5 Students become producers and consumers of podcasts.

The timing of the assessment was carefully planned out to ensure that the students had been given enough time to understand about podcasts through listening to ones in their own time as part of pre-class preparation. The assessment brief was shared halfway through the 16-week term. They were then given two weeks to develop a script outline where feedback was then provided, and then given three more weeks until the submission of the podcast script and recording. They were instructed that they had to include rigorous research, a guest speaker, evidence of critical reflection and focus on any critical global issue of their choice while relating it to different cultural and country contexts and to the Sustainable Development Goals.

As part of the assessment, which made up 25% of the total course assessment weight, and in addition to the group podcast recording of up to 15 minutes and script, to enhance reflective thought and deep learning (Moon 2004) the students were asked to write an individual reflection of one or two pages of their experiences of the assessment one week after they completed the assessment. The students were told they could write reflectively about any aspect of the learning and assessment and were given examples of what they could think about in writing their reflection, including how the podcast impacted their skill development, and subject knowledge and learning, in particular around the critical global issues they chose and whether they enjoyed the assessment and found it fun.

In the reflections students highlighted that although the experience was challenging, it was also fun, which was important for their learning, and interviewing the guest speaker(s) increased their awareness and appreciation of the topic.

By conducting the podcast, my engagement and motivation for the subject of entrepreneurship and the topic of health care grew due to many factors. One of these factors is the interview that was conducted with Dr. Hany Omar who had helped enrich the podcast with a lot of medical information. Having a guest speaker helped me understand both the strengths and the weaknesses of the MENA region in terms of health. I found that the most enjoyable part of the podcast was the back-and-forth conversations we had with each other that were backed up by genuine statistics and not personal opinions. In order to make an assessment engaging for any student, I think that projects need to be somewhat enjoyable so that nobody feels burnt out, like this one. (Freshman Year)

There was also clear learning in terms of subject knowledge through the research they had to undertake and skill development around speaking, listening, confidence building and research.

This assessment was very insightful to me as I learned a lot of new information about clean and sustainable energy. Prior to this assessment, I knew some basic things about clean energy, however, after completing the assessment I feel like my knowledge of the topic has greatly increased. I was interested to make a podcast about this topic as I felt that there are a lot of things to talk about and learn, and that was exactly what happened. While working on the podcast and researching the topic I learned many new things, especially about Egypt and how the Egyptian government is working hard to develop the country's infrastructure and integrate renewable energy into it. (Sophomore Year, Business Administration)

By enabling students to be knowledge creators (McGarr 2009), the process helped them to develop key competencies including collaborative and teamwork knowledge–building skills (Lee et al. 2008) and critical thinking skills (Frydenberg 2008). There were further advantages in terms of knowledge acquisition, improving depth of understanding of the subject (Schwartz and Digiovanni 2009), the development of reflective learning and positive collaborative behaviour (Lazzari 2009). Podcasts are an interesting and reflective tool for learning and assessment and useful for synchronous and asynchronous learning and for all ability groups.

Bibliography

Frydenberg, M. (2008). Principles and Pedagogy: The Two Ps of Podcasting in the Information Technology Classroom. *Information Systems Education Journal*, 6(6), 3–11. Available at: http://isedj.org/6/6/

Lazzari, M. (2009). Creative Use of Podcasting in Higher Education and its Effect on Competitive Agency. *Computers and Education*, 52, 27–34. doi: 10.1016/j.compedu.2008.06.002

Lee, M.J.W., McLoughlin, C. and Chan, A. (2008). Talk the Talk: Learner-generated Podcasts as Catalysts for Knowledge Creation. *British Journal of Educational Technology*, 39(3), 501–521. doi: 10.1111/j.1467-8535.2007.00746.x

McGarr, O. (2009). A Review of Podcasting in Higher Education: Its Influence on the Traditional Lecture. *Australasian Journal of Educational Technology*, 25(3), 309–321. doi: 10.14742/ajet.1136

Moon, J.A. (2004). *Reflection in Learning and Professional Development*. New York: Routledge Falmer.

Schwartz, S. and Digiovanni, L. (2009). About, for, and with Students: Connecting Teaching and Teacher Education through Digital Literacy. In Siemens, G. and Fulford, C. (Eds.) *Proceedings of World Conference on Educational Multimedia, Hypermedia and Telecommunications 2009* (pp. 2047–2050). Chesapeake, VA: AACE.

Inclusivity note

Podcasts do not necessarily require fully equipped studios; they can be made with very simple, low technology such as mobile phone audio-recording apps, which can support learning on the go for busy students such as those with caring responsibilities.

Some challenges are:

Sourcing enough suitable podcasts for students to listen to in order to better understand the genre. As Honeycutt (2021) suggests: 'find podcasts that are already out there that integrate with your course learning outcomes, course goals, and course topics and leverage those'. Also, could students put together a podcast playlist, after having set some quality criteria?

The need to work as a team—this can be a barrier for students with caring responsibilities issues. Can students identify the key times they need to be physically co-present, and do the rest of the meetings/prep asynchronously and online?

Hearing-impaired students or non-natives who might struggle with accents and absence of visual cues. Could those students have different roles, such as script writer? And the student-produced podcasts could have a transcript.

Data shows that since the wider spread of mobile apps, and especially since the pandemic, podcasts have grown in popularity. A study found that podcast listeners display traits such as 'openness to experience, interest-based curiosity, and need for cognition' (Tobin and Guadagno 2022). By using podcasts as both input and output on our courses we support the development of these positive traits both in our students and in wider audiences. Another study found that podcasts (used as input and output) enhanced learning outcomes by promoting deeper learning (Pegrum et al. 2014). Academically, podcasts support learning because they force students to 'teach' a topic in a very succinct way, with the added awareness of a real audience.

As explained in the preceding case study, podcasts as learning outputs are better achieved as a collective effort, hence a group assessment regime suits it best. This can be a very effective large class assessment for all disciplines: reading 100 short essays (of 1000 words each) takes about six hours (and can be very tedious!); dividing the cohort into groups of five, who produce 20 podcasts of five minutes each, it would take 1 hour and 40 minutes to listen to them all (and it can be interesting and fun).

The next case study discusses Wikipedia assessment outputs where students *contribute* to Wikipedia, a platform which has gone from foe to friend for teaching and learning.

A Quickie Wiki, that's not tricky in the classroom

By Abd Alsattar Ardati (Scotland)

Mossab Banat (Jordan)

Wiki-Wiki:

A wiki is a web-based software named after a Hawaiian free wiki-wiki shuttle bus, with wiki-wiki meaning 'quick-quick' in Hawaiian. Wiki technology permits any person with access to its web pages to alter its content using a browser. Wiki, which powers Wikipedia and its sister projects such as Wikidata, Wikiversity and Wikibooks, has already been adopted by many individuals and educators as a web-based solution to asynchronously harnessing, managing and interconnecting the collaborative input of its users.

Setting up a stand-alone Wiki in your institution requires investing time and technical know-how. In this chapter, we will focus on an easier way of getting the benefits of this technology through engaging students with Wikipedia, the free online encyclopaedia that anyone is permitted to edit.

Wikipedia is one of the most notable, widely visited, voluntarily crowdsourced websites of our era. Traditionally Wikipedia has been considered an unreliable academic resource; however, more recently, academics have been exploiting the potential of Wikis for educational purposes. According to the WikiEdu organisation, since 2010, more than 73,000 students in the United States have taken assignments using Wikipedia. Wikipedia's status has gone from foe to friend!

Wikipedia group work assignments:

Research by the Wikimedia UK charity shows that training the students on how to make the best use of Wikipedia has various benefits, such as improving their computer and internet literacy, data and information literacy, content creation skills, collaboration skills and advanced IT skills, which would aid future employment. Above all, students value the opportunity of engaging with authentic outputs which can potentially reach and benefit millions of users. Figure 7.6 shows some

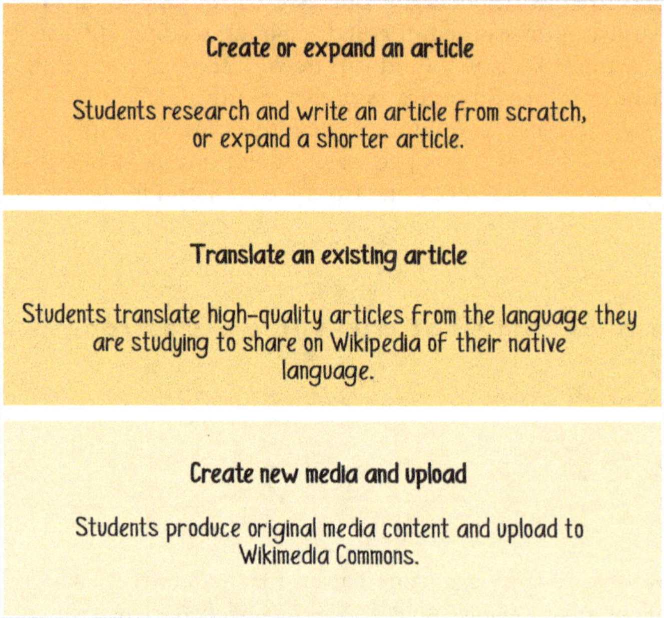

Create or expand an article

Students research and write an article from scratch, or expand a shorter article.

Translate an existing article

Students translate high-quality articles from the language they are studying to share on Wikipedia of their native language.

Create new media and upload

Students produce original media content and upload to Wikimedia Commons.

Figure 7.6 Overview of possible Wikipedia assignments.

possible Wikipedia assignments: create or expand an article; translate an existing article; and create new media and upload.

In his article 'Translating Wikipedia Articles', Szymczak (2013) highlights the promising benefit of assigning Wikipedia translation tasks to improve his students' translation skills and engagement level. According to Szymczak, the assignments were embraced 'enthusiastically' by the students who had the chance to pick their topics and knew that their translated text would be used outside the classroom environment. The researcher describes the results of students' learning as 'overwhelmingly superior' to traditional classroom tasks (Szymczak 2013).

The University of Edinburgh has a long history of engaging its students with Wikipedia in education projects. For example, the Reproductive Biology BSc course leaders have successfully organised the creation of eight new Wikipedia articles to enhance their students' collaborative group research capabilities. By working collaboratively, students improve their critical thinking, grow their knowledge effectively and benefit positively from the 'competitive' environment and peer pressure, which, in turn, contributes to developing their understanding of collaborative work (Dooly 2008 cited by Al-Shehari 2017).

Utilising Wikipedia could produce significant improvements over the conventional classroom assignments. However, planning is an essential component of successful implementation and outcome. It is important to equip students with easy to access, well-organised, reliable sources of knowledge about Wikipedia technology and social norms to avoid any potential challenges in dealing with Wikipedia interfaces and rules.

Before incorporating a Wikipedia assignment into your course, you can start small by reaching out to your local Wikimedia chapter to plan a Wikipedia training event or an edit-a-thon or even an education programme.

The Hashemite University case in running a Wikipedia education programme

In the Spring of 2017, the Wikipedia Club, which is hosted by Hashemite University in Jordan and founded by me, Mossab Banat, coordinated with the lecturers to add Wikipedia editing components to 12 University level courses. Over 500 students participated in modules, such as Advanced Cell Biology, Skin Pharmacological Preparations, Food Sciences, and Nursing Communication Skills. Of the 163 new articles created, two were selected as featured articles by the Arabic Wikipedia community.

The impact on the student body

Through leading the Hashemite University Wikipedia education programme, I have noticed that the Wikipedia education program significantly impacts students' reading, writing, translating and citing articles abilities. It ensures making the best of their academic journey on your module. Students get to share their knowledge with others as well as utilise the computers and the Internet in a beneficial way that supports interdisciplinary learning and improves their research skills. Lastly, it positively affects teachers by saving their time by minimizing paperwork and making them more digitized and web friendly. It also affects the academic reputation of the university in that students contribute to add academically authenticated knowledge to the web, which serves a vast number of readers worldwide. It also could be considered part of the university's role towards serving their local community along with the broader global one.

Examples of featured Wikipedia articles that were developed by the Digital Arabic Content Club in Hashemite University are: Skin Whitening, Chagas Disease, Hydrochloric Acid and Nuclear Reactor.

You can find out more about setting up Wikipedia assignments by searching: Wikipedia Education Programme and Wikimedia Foundation Outreach Programme.

Bibliography

Al-Shehari, K. (2017). Collaborative learning: trainee translators tasked to translate Wikipedia entries from English into Arabic. *The Interpreter and Translator Trainer*, 11(4), 357–372.

Dooly, M. (2008). *Telecollaborative Language Learning: A Guidebook to Moderating Intercultural Collaboration Online*. Bern: Peter Lang.

Szymczak, P. (2013). Translating Wikipedia Articles: A Preliminary Report on Authentic Translation Projects in Formal Translator Training. Wydział Neofilologii, Uniwersytet Warszawski. Available at: https://depot.ceon.pl/handle/123456789/6762

> **Inclusivity note**
>
> Using Wikipedia as an assessment platform opens up a myriad of possible uses, with assignments that suit all fields of study and work very well with large cohorts where groups can tackle different Wikipedia entries or the same entry from different perspectives.
>
> The choice of potential controversial entries to work on means that students need to understand the concepts of integrity and positionality so they can produce inclusive and objective Wikipedia outputs.

This case study constitutes a provocative challenge to shift teachers' thinking about Wikipedia and its related sites: from foe to friend, from source of (unreliable?) learning input to potential, varied learning *outputs*. What is your relationship with this platform? Is there scope within your assessment regime to design a Wikipedia assignment with one of the suggested outputs?

Both podcasts and Wikipedia assignments usually require a *collaborative* submission which help develop transferrable skills expected of the modern graduate. However, when designing assessment, *before* requiring collaborative summative outputs, teachers should leverage smaller, formative (preferably pass/fail rather than graded) assessment opportunities as 'practice' for bigger collaborative submissions. To prevent individuals being penalised or unfairly advantaged by the group dynamics, they can also require an individual reflection/submission *alongside* the final collaborative submission.

Conclusion

This chapter has invited you to consider three related assessment dimensions: outputs should provide students with (1) choice, (2) voice, and they should be (3) authentic.

At the start of this chapter, I proposed these questions:

> **Activate your inner dialogue. ... How would you answer?**
>
> How does assessment choice promote inclusivity?
> How can students' voice inform assessment design?
> What barriers do you currently experience in designing more flexible and authentic assessment? How can you overcome them?

My provisional and evolving answers, based on the ideas in this chapter are:

Assessment choice is about having an optimally flexible assessment design that allows students to choose types of outputs, within boundaries. Project-based learning is particularly inclusive in allowing students to direct their own learning and it *naturally* affords choice.

Students' voice means allowing students to express themselves and to 'voice' their interests. This can be linked to assessment by using learning outputs to provide students with a platform to advocate for a cause, such as one of the 17 Sustainable Development Goals. Photovoice is an excellent example of such outputs.

Authentic assessment is relevant, has social value and supports students' future working lives. Podcasts and Wikipedia are two possible authentic outputs that can provide very meaningful, integrated learning (for instance enhanced digital literacy) with the added advantage of world-wide real audiences.

If we design more authentic assessment with students' voice and choice at its heart, we will provide a much more meaningful form of assessment which both we and the students might actually enjoy. Bingo!

In the next chapter I discuss the importance of developing students' self-regulation through assessment: their outputs need to be reflective and formative.

Bibliography

Bearman, M., Dawson, P., Boud, D., Hall, M., Bennett, S., Molloy, E. and Joughin, G. (2014). Guide to the Assessment Design Decisions Framework. Available at: http://www.assessmentdecisions.org/guide

Macfarlane, B. (2016). *Freedom to LEARN: The Threat to Student Academic Freedom and Why it Needs to Be Reclaimed* (1st ed.). Routledge. doi: 10.4324/9781315529455

Choice

Hack, K., Seagreaves, E., Pettifer, S. and Knight, S. (2022). Flexible by Design Podcast. [podcast] The Advance HE Podcast. Available at: https://advancehe.podbean.com/

Jopp, R. and Cohen, J. (2020). Choose Your Own Assessment—Assessment Choice for Students in Online Higher Education, *Teaching in Higher Education*. doi: 10.1080/13562517.2020.1742680

Juliani, A.J. (2015). *Learning by Choice: 10 Ways Choice and Differentiation Create an Engaged Learning Experience for Every Student.* Amazon: CreateSpace.

Kuh, G.D. (2008). *High-impact Educational Practices: What They are, Who Has Access to Them, and Why They Matter.* Washington, DC: AAC&U.

WIP (2019). Project-Based Learning (PBL) as a Vehicle for High-Impact Practices: Reinventing Courses. [webinar] Available at: https://www.youtube.com/watch?v=vc0S5fdwng0

Voice

Cook-Sather, A. (2006). Sound, Presence, and Power: "Student Voice" in Educational Research and Reform. *Curriculum Inquiry*, 36(4), 359–390. doi: 10.1111/j.1467-873X.2006.00363.x

Young, H. and Jerome, L. (2020). Student Voice in Higher Education: Opening the Loop. *British Educational Research Journal*, 46. doi: 10.1002/berj.3603

Authentic

Clifton, A. and Hoffman, K.D. (2021). Open Pedagogy Approaches—Faculty, Library, and Student Collaborations—Milney Publishing. Available at: https://milnepublishing.geneseo.edu/openpedagogyapproaches/

Gilson, J. (2017). 'Leaving a Legacy': Documentary Work in a Learning Environment. *European Political Science*, 16, 135–147. doi: 10.1057/eps.2016.19

Gulikers, J., Bastiaens, T. and Kirschner, P. (2004). The Five-Dimensional Framework for Authentic Assessment. *Educational Technology Research and Development*, 52, 67–86. doi: 10.1007/BF02504676

Honeycutt, B. (2021). How to Use Podcasts in Teaching [podcast]. Teaching in HigherEd podcast Episode 381. Available at: https://teachinginhighered.com/podcast/how-to-use-podcasts-in-teaching/

Kuh, G.D. (2008). *High-impact Educational Practices: What They Are, Who Has Access to Them, and Why They Matter*. Washington, DC: AAC&U.

Pegrum, M., Bartle, E. and Longnecker, N. (2014). Can Creative Podcasting Promote Deep Learning? The Use of Podcasting for Learning Content in an Undergraduate Science Unit. *British Journal of Educational Technology*, 46(1). doi: 10.1111/BJET.12133

Shaffer, D. and Resnick, M. (1999). "Thick" Authenticity: New Media and Authentic Learning. *Journal of Interactive Learning Research*, 70, 101030, ISSN 0191-491X.

Sokhanvara, Z., Salehib, K. and Sokhanvar, F. (2021). Advantages of Authentic Assessment for Improving the Learning Experience and Employability Skills of Higher Education Students: A Systematic Literature Review. *Studies in Educational Evaluation*. doi: 10.1016/j.stueduc.2021.101030

Tobin, S.J. and Guadagno, R.E. (2022). Why people listen: Motivations and outcomes of podcast listening. *PLoS One*, 17(4), e0265806. doi: 10.1371/journal.pone.0265806

Vu, T. and Dall'Alba, G. (2014). Authentic Assessment for Student Learning: An Ontological Conceptualisation. *Educational Philosophy and Theory*, 46(7), 778–791. doi: 10.1080/00131857.2013.795110

Chapter 8

Reflective and formative

> If you study but don't reflect you'll be lost. If you reflect but don't study you'll get into trouble.
>
> Confucius' Analects, Book 2 part 15

Although assessment and feedback literacies are situated—in other words they are context-dependant—globally, in recent years, there has been much more emphasis on students engaging and learning from assessment feedback, rather than simply about teachers giving 'good' feedback.

This is part of a shift towards much greater students' *self-regulation*. As Evans (2021) puts it:

> Self-regulation is multifaceted. It encompasses the strategies learners use when they go about learning, including how they identify the demands of a task, set goals and manage their progress towards achieving such goals, evaluate and reflect on their performance.

A good way to enhance students' assessment self-regulation is to increase the quantity and quality of reflective, formative, self and peer assessment and feedback opportunities because these will improve feedback literacy, provide multiple sources of feedback and support students make sense of and apply feedback.

> **Activate your inner dialogue. ... How would you answer?**
>
> How can you design and implement a reflective and formative assessment and feedback regime on your course? How will this support more inclusive learning practices?

In this chapter I address assessment and feedback *mode* (reflective and formative), while in Chapter 9 I discuss assessment and feedback *source* (self and peer assessment).

This chapter is about the crucial developmental role that reflective and formative assessment and feedback play in the learning journey. Although not all reflective assessment is also formative and vice versa, I make the case that the two aspects (reflective and formative) are often two sides of the same medal and *should* be designed as such.

DOI: 10.4324/9781003230144-14

Many typical, standard assessment and feedback modes do not promote students' deep thinking and reflection. They do not prompt students' *evaluation* of their learning journey and how far they have travelled academically and otherwise. Most are an end point, at the end of the course and represent assessment and feedback *of* learning, not *for* learning. Formative assessment and feedback are about refocusing on how assessment *supports* learning, rather than simply testing it. Key to this is students not simply learning and evidencing learning, but also having the opportunity to deeply think (reflect) on their learning and express evaluative judgements on their own progress in relation to the learning goals and 'their identification with disciplinary practices' (Shepard et al. 2018).

An example of an assessment regime that has formative and reflective features is:

1. Towards the start of the course, once the assessment has been introduced, students in groups and as a class discuss exemplars and determine 'quality' criteria for the required outputs.
2. Students have multiple opportunities for smaller, scaffolded, low stake, formative assessment tasks which build towards the final summative one.
3. Students have multiple opportunities for self and peer review of their work in progress at formative stage. Ideally, they use their own set quality criteria to make evaluative judgements regarding their outputs.
4. At final submission, students attach their own self and peer feedback to the submission.
5. Teachers review the self and peer feedback and provide further feedback comments to refine (calibrate) the students' understanding of quality in relation to their outputs.
6. Students respond to the feedback with an action plan saying how they will implement it in future outputs. This is also used at the start of the next learning experience (module).

Points 1 and 2 could be swapped, depending on context, because at times it is better for students to have a go and *then* see exemplars. Clearly, this type of assessment and feedback regime only works if we take a wider, integrated and programmatic view of learning and assessment.

Core to the success of such regime is formative and reflective learning facilitated by the use and discussion of exemplars, rubrics, formative and/or draft assignments.

I will discuss and illustrate with case studies:

(1) reflective and formative assessment and
(2) reflective and formative feedback.

Reflective and formative assessment

In their literature review about 'reflection literacy', Chan and Lee (2021) highlight five main strategies as guidelines which can be useful for teachers seeking to make fuller use of reflection for assessment:

- Articulate the purpose and expectations of the task clearly to students
- Provide structure and scaffolding for student reflection

- Give an option for students to choose whether to share their reflections with peers
- Allow ample time for students to engage in the process
- Provide constructive, sensitive feedback (Chan and Lee 2021)

Whatever level of reflection we expect from students, we should be clear about *why* we are asking students to reflect and *how* this will benefit them. However, it is not easy to strike the right balance between prompting reflection through (formative) assessment and imposing assessment which makes students 'confess' their learning journey and which results in 'emotional performativity' (Macfarlane 2016).

Formative assessment is about development, for students and teachers to gain qualitative insights about student experience and thinking, including their progressive assimilation of disciplinary practices—are students developing the needed ways of thinking and doing associated with the field of study?

Besides, formative assessment helps clarify, understand and share the learning intentions (Dylan 2011). A very useful and inclusive formative task is to ask students to submit at least one *draft* of the final submission, as work in progress, to undergo self, peer and tutor assessment. This is an important safety net for the teacher as it provides a preview of where the students are at, what the gaps are at cohort level and indirectly provides feedback on the teaching. By asking students, by default, to do some self-evaluation first, it also clearly helps students develop their inner dialogue (self-feedback) which is a key element of meta-cognition (Nicol 2019).

One inclusive approach to design reflective and formative assessment is by adopting an **assessment as learning** stance because it encompasses both formative and summative features and positions learners as active and reflective agents in the assessment process.

Yan and Yang (2022) propose that 'assessment as learning is a learning strategy enacted in the form of assessment' and:

> If assessment for learning is a big step in terms of conceptualising assessment as an integral part of learning, rather than just a summary of learning, then assessment as learning takes a further step in advocating the role of the assessment activity in maximising learning opportunities and student responsibility in the assessment process.

Assessment as learning supports assessment literacy in another important way: by providing multiple opportunities to interact with the success criteria, standards and evidence, and by receiving ongoing feedback from multiple sources, it lets 'students into the secret' that assessment judgements are subjective and fragile (Bloxham 2007). It develops a much deeper understanding of the intricacies of making assessment judgements.

In the following three case studies you are going to read about various types of reflective, formative assessment which support a more inclusive learning assessment design: first about assessment as learning; second about e-portfolios; and third about team charters.

The first case study is from Italy and discusses the outcomes of a research project where a teacher education course used an assessment as learning regime. Notice the pros and cons of the approach and practical considerations for those who would like to implement it.

Focus on metacognitive processes with Assessment as Learning

By Alessia Bevilacqua and Claudio Girelli (Italy)

Assessment as learning (AaL) includes assessment strategies aimed at *'generating learning opportunities for students through their active engagement in seeking, interrelating, and using evidence'* (Yan and Boud 2022:13). Through AaL students may gain awareness of the information they receive through feedback, give meaning to their learning and build new understandings, the keystone lies in the activation of reflective processes. AaL can be considered an inclusive approach as students' activation of metacognitive processes facilitates the self-regulation of learning: the frequent use of self and peer-assessment tools throughout the course helps students on one side to evaluate each step of their learning journey and on the other side to see the big picture, that is to say gain an overview of the whole learning framework (Bevilacqua 2019).

We are going to briefly discuss how we implemented AaL on our teacher education programme. Students attending the degree course in primary teacher education at the University of Verona (Italy) have been asked to engage with an authentic task to facilitate the acquisition of research and assessment skills as they are considered essential to the continuous development of the professionalism of future teachers. They were asked to take part in a simulated grant application for the financing of educational research projects. To support each student in elaborating this complex task, we implemented two specific scaffolding actions, which come under the umbrella of sustainable assessment framework (Boud and Soler 2016): AaL and feedback literacy (Winstone and Carless 2019).

AaL required that, for each phase of the project students:

1. submit the draft of each phase of the project with self-assessment and a double-blind peer review
2. review their draft for the final submission in light of the feedback received from peers; carry out a second self-assessment, and
3. fill in an individual reflective form to acquire an awareness of the cognitive and learning processes implemented.

To support students in taking on the role of reviewers effectively, and consequently to meet the requirements of AaL, we also put in place feedback literacy interventions aimed at improving the understanding, capacities and dispositions needed to make sense of comments on 'performance' and use them for enhancement purposes (Carless and Boud 2018). This helped students provide effective evaluative judgments (to themselves and to others).

We evaluated the teaching innovation based on the AaL framework through a mixed-method research, aimed at collecting and understanding the students' perceptions regarding the teaching approach. The results highlighted the pros and cons of the experience. The AaL experience was positively perceived because it led students to acquire greater awareness of the subject through the reflection stimulated by the assessment practices and to improve their assignment through the self and peer assessments. Students enhanced their assessment skills and were able to make sense of the placement school's assessment regime, which supported their personal professional development. The critical issues that we have identified, namely the significant requirement for time and the commitment for planning, implementing and evaluating reflective activities, point to the reasons why AaL has not been universally adopted.

Drawing on our experience, these are our 'how-to' suggestions for others to consider before implementing AaL:

- to make the assessment formative, design a multifocal (considering multiple points of view) and multiphase (which allows monitoring each phase of the process) assessment framework (as shown in Figure 8.1);
- to support students learning from experience, introduce a specific tool that helps students activate and make explicit their inner reflexive processes (Mortari 2003);
- to balance formative and summative assessment, do not plan too many assessment points and find techniques to make assessment practices fast and simple (educational technologies are very helpful in this regard);

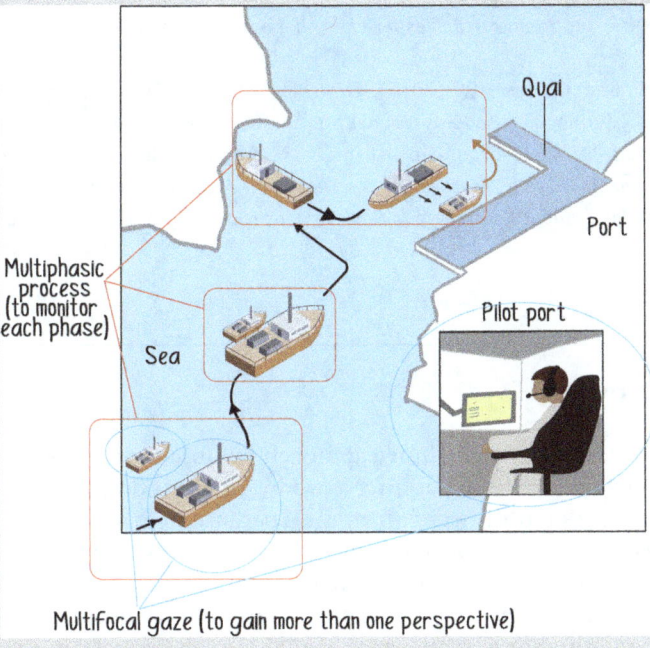

Figure 8.1 An assessment as learning regime affords us and the students a multiphasic process and a multifocal gaze.

- to understand the impact of the educational approach, pick up the students' voices during the course. It is useful to use student feedback collected through face-to-face dialogue or through online consultation tools such as Mentimeter or Microsoft Forms to modulate the course during its development.

The research results highlight how the AaL regime has supported students to better cope with authentic assessment tasks. The activation of meta-cognitive processes proved to be useful both for passing the final exam but also for strengthening those transversal skills—learning to learn, in particular—essential for their personal and professional future, in a lifelong learning perspective.

Bibliography

Bevilacqua, A. (2019). Un'esperienza di valutazione formante in ambito universitario. Il contributo delle tecnologie educative per la promozione della didattica attiva nelle classi numerose. *Giornale Italiano della Ricerca Educativa*. Special Issue, 291–298. doi: 10.7346/SIRD-1S2019-P291

Boud, D. and Soler, R. (2016). Sustainable Assessment Revisited. *Assessment and Evaluation in Higher Education*, 41(3), 400–413. doi: 10.1080/02602938.2015.1018133

Carless, D. and Boud, D. (2018). The Development of Student Feedback Literacy: Enabling Uptake of Feedback. *Assessment and Evaluation in Higher Education*, 43(8), 1315–1325. doi: 10.1080/02602938.2018.1463354

Mortari, L. (2003). *Apprendere dall'esperienza: Il pensare riflessivo nella formazione*. Roma: Carocci.

Winstone, N.E. and Carless, D. (2019). *Designing Effective Feedback Processes in Higher Education – A Learning-Focused Approach*. London: Routledge.

Yan, Z. and Boud, D. (2022). Conceptualising Assessment as learning. In Yan, Z. and Yang, L. (Eds.), *Conceptualising Assessment as learning. Assessment as Learning: Maximising Opportunities for Student Learning and Achievement* (pp. 11–24). London: Routledge.

Inclusivity note

Assessment as learning is an inclusive approach because it develops students holistically, especially their self-regulation. Neurodivergent students or those who need additional learning support benefit from AaL because they have multiple opportunities and plenty of peer support as they develop their assessment outputs.

The biggest challenge is the fact that it requires much front-loaded activities design from the part of the teacher, responsive students (who may otherwise delay others) and commitment from the part of all. One way to make it easier is to have only one or two formative assessment points (in a module) to ease the workload of teachers and students.

The preceding case study shows that there are clear benefits of implementing assessment as learning. I particularly like the idea of a multifocal (with various perspectives) and multiphase (supporting each phase of the process) assessment framework.

In theory assessment as learning should ease the heavy assessment and feedback load for staff and students. In practice, assessment as learning is demanding because many support systems and iterations need to be put in place and monitored by teachers beforehand. However, by experience, I believe the extra work is worth it because ultimately, assessment as learning is about self-regulation.

The next case study, from Ireland, discusses ways in which portfolio assessment better supports developmental and inclusive learning. Notice the many ways in which eportfolios, often considered a high impact practice (Kuh 2008), promote holistic learning and assessment.

Building on your strengths: Bringing it all together with an eportfolio

By Laura Costelloe (Ireland)

There is increasing evidence of the growing use of eportfolios as an assessment tool across the further and higher education landscapes. Defined by Corley and Zubizarreta (2012) as 'a vehicle for bringing together judiciously selected samples of students' work and achievements inside and outside the classroom for authentic assessment over time', they are typically composed of a collection of artefacts (text, audio, visual) which are created and curated in evidence of the achievement of modular learning outcomes. Although the structure, approach and purpose of eportfolio assessment varies greatly, it is a mode of assessment which has enormous potential to support inclusive, formative and reflective academic practice and to enact the principles of Universal Design for Learning (UDL) (Burgstahler and Cory 2010).

In the first instance, eportfolios move away from an emphasis on the written word and instead encourage learners to use audio-visual approaches to demonstrate their understanding and application of concepts and ideas. In an academic system which tends to privilege the written word, eportfolios offer learners a variety of media through which to represent their learning and therefore encourage a creative approach to engaging critically with concepts. Nerantzi (2012) promotes the idea of 'patchwork eportfolios' as they encourage students to 'build on their strengths, boost self-confidence and belief in their abilities and embrace diversity and individuality'. Most eportfolio platforms enable the inclusion of audio, visual and written artefacts and students are therefore encouraged to represent their learning in modes which are best aligned to their preferences. Learners can thus be facilitated to express their learning using a diversity of approaches, which is beneficial for future employability and broadens their literacy in a range of modes.

Furthermore, typically a portfolio-based assessment promotes a semester-long formative approach to assessment, rather than focusing on an end-of-semester summative task. Frequently, eportfolios encourage learners to critically engage with and reflect on module concepts and ideas and to gather evidence of such engagement throughout the duration of the module. Portfolios thus encourage learners to consider the learning opportunities throughout the semester and can act as a tool to motivate and engage students and consequently avoid the 'assessment spike' and associated pressures at the end of the semester.

Finally, while many institutions support and promote particular eportfolio platforms (e.g. Mahara, Pebble Pad, OneNote etc.), there are numerous open source platforms freely available to students. Learners can therefore choose to create portfolios which can be shared with peers, colleagues and prospective employers, and consequently the use of eportfolios encourages learners to consider the relevance of their assessment tasks to 'real world' contexts. Where institutions adopt a programmatic approach to assessment which embeds portfolio practice across a range of modules, learners are afforded the opportunity to develop a rich and lively archive of their learning journey throughout their academic career. Such an approach enables learners to connect concepts across modules through an integrated programmatic assessment and can boost employability as learners are provided with a rich set of artifacts to assist the recruitment process.

It is important to note, however, that students require considerable support in the development of eportfolios; this support should extend to pedagogical support to promote reflective practice, as well as technological support to overcome any learning curve with regard to mastery of the particular eportfolio platform. As with any unfamiliar mode of assessment, the development of students' literacy is crucial to ensure that they know what 'good' looks like; opportunities for self and peer assessment, as well as the analysis of exemplars and use of rubrics, can help to develop students' evaluative judgment, competence and confidence in developing their own eportfolio (Carless et al. 2018).

Figure 8.2 visually represents a summary of current key emergent themes and recommendations for implementing eportfolios in HE.

From experience, it is unquestionable that eportfolios offer considerable opportunities as a flexible and innovative assessment approach and tool for documenting and evidencing various forms of learning (Costelloe et al. 2019). However, it is important to recognise the learning curve that is associated with this, and indeed any other, new form of assessment for both HE teachers and students. Still, with careful scaffolding and ongoing support, it can offer a hugely beneficial learning opportunity for students which extends beyond the module and programme of study.

Figure 8.2 A summary of key emergent themes and recommendations for implementing eportfolios in HE, based on a National Survey of Irish Eportfolio Practice, undertaken by EPortfolio Ireland, 2020 (reproduced with permission).

Bibliography

Burgstahler, S.E. and Cory, R.C. (2010). *Universal Design in Higher Education: from Principles to Practice*. Cambridge, MA: Harvard Education Press.

Carless, D., Chan, K.K.H., To, J., Lo, M. and Barrett, E. (2018). Developing Students' Capacities for Evaluative Judgement through Analysing Exemplars. In Boud, D., Ajjawi, R., Dawson, P. and Tai, J. (Eds.) *Developing Evaluative Judgement in Higher Education: Assessment for Knowing and Producing Quality Work*. London: Routledge.

Corley, C.R. and Zubizarreta, J. (2012). The Power and Utility of Reflective Learning Portfolios in Honors. *Journal of the National Collegiate Honours Council—Online Archive*, 334. Available at: https://core.ac.uk/download/pdf/188084426.pdf

Costelloe, L., Gormley, C. and O'Riordan, F. (2019). Walking the Talk: Academic Developers Reflect on the Use of Digital Learning Portfolios to Support Professional Development. *Educational Developments*, 20(4), 11–13. doi: 10.22554/ijtel.v6i1.72

Kuh, G.D. (2008). High-impact educational practices: What they are, who has access to them, and why they matter. Report from the Association of American Colleges and Universities. Washington, DC.

Nerantzi, C. (2012). Patchwork e-portfolio on the PGCAP Programme with a Focus on How it is Used on the LTHE Module. Chrissi Nerantzi: my development space. Available at: https://chrissinerantzi.wordpress.com/2012/09/01/patchwork-e-portfolio-on-the-pgcap-programme-with-a-focus-on-how-it-is-used-on-the-lthe-module-pgcap

> **Inclusivity note**
>
> As the case study shows, eportfolios offer a wide variety of learning opportunities in content, digital and assessment literacy, and especially as a formative and reflective assessment mode. This is very supportive for students with various learning disabilities and needs as they have a variety of output choices within the eportfolio.
>
> However, we need to be realistic about the often considerable (hidden) labour involved in assembling an eportfolio, especially when students work on multiple eportfolio elements at once. Co-selecting with students a suitable digital platform is key for the success of the eportfolio, as well as setting up suitable support systems such as exemplars and technical support and guidance.
>
> As having a totally open format where students can add anything to the eportfolio can be counterproductive, it is better to provide a template or structure with *some* (well-supported) required elements and others which are free choice.

I have been using eportfolio assessment for many years in teacher education and I have invariably noticed that the eportfolio building process is at least as valuable as the end product. In particular, eportoflios are useful to get buy-in for reflective tasks which otherwise students often deem irrelevant to future practice. Indeed, the benefits of eportfolios can stretch much further than the course and its assessment: they can become a life-long and even life-wide platform for students to build, document and reflect on their learning, which can be used for academic as well as work-related purposes.

The next case study, from Australia, discusses a tricky aspect of formative assessment: group assessment. You will learn about a practical way of making such formative team assessment fairer.

Team charters for more inclusive team assessments

By Joanne L. Hall and Asha Rao (Australia)

Working in a team led by a manager or working freelance with clients and suppliers forms an important aspect of work. Teamwork skills are a requirement in many professionally accredited degrees, including engineering and nursing. Furthermore, with teamwork skills listed in many job advertisements across many fields, educators are incorporating teamwork into their curriculum. Employee contracts and codes of behaviour are common across most workplaces; a team charter mimics such industry practices, is a useful reflective learning tool and reduces the risks of dissatisfied students.

Assigning team-based tasks is often used to develop teamwork skills in university students. In courses with team-based assessments, every student needs to be included in a team. Teams vary in size, being small (2–3 students), or larger (5–6 students) depending on the nature of the tasks. Unfortunately, team-based assessments are often cause for angst among students; high performing students fear impact on grades from team members not sharing their academic skills, motivation, availability or behavioural norms (Riebe et al. 2017).

Team-based assessments carry the potential of negatively impacting the learning experience of diverse groups. Even prior knowledge of team members doesn't reduce variation in expectations. Discussing, writing and submitting a team charter and project plan at the beginning of a team project provides students the opportunity to reflect on their own approach to teamwork and project management. Giving students ownership of their contribution and behaviour helps reduce the incidence of dissatisfied teams.

Team charters require both teachers and students to take actions, as shown in Figure 8.3.

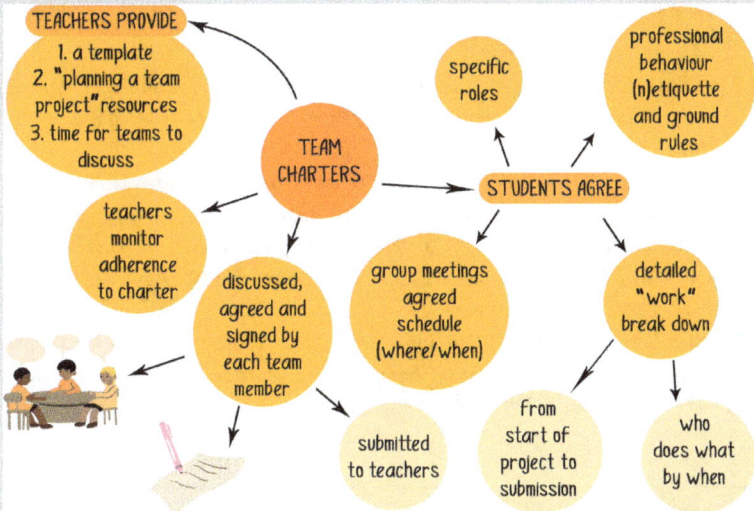

Figure 8.3 Clockwise, from the top left corner, teachers' and students' roles in team charters.

Teamwork skills can be learned (Dweck 2008) and team-based assessments could be the ideal setting. As educators we need to plan experiences that reinforce successful teamwork skills, providing opportunities to reflect on learning experiences. A team charter framework enables the team to understand each other's skills and motivations at the beginning of a project. By providing a pathway to a more productive and inclusive environment, it provides a reflective and formative assessment opportunity to students. A team charter promotes shared understanding of expectations within a team. By including a statement about respectful behaviour, a good team charter ensures each student is cognisant of the behaviours expected of them (Sverdrup and Schei 2015). Providing an interim opportunity for students to update (and submit) their team charter and project plan enables each team to reflect and report on their progress. This allows problems with team dynamics as well as the project to be addressed, either by the team, or in collaboration with teaching staff, before the assessment due date.

Teams benefit from explicit initial discussions about project tasks, behavioural norms, time commitment and work quality (Hughston 2013). While students, initially, often do not see the point of a formal team charter, those that experience even minor obstacles within their team report the value they see in the formally documented team charter as a tool for conflict resolution.

In conclusion, teamwork is a key employability skill for all disciplines. Having a team charter is one way of creating an inclusive environment, supporting critical self and peer reflection on teamwork skills and supporting the success of team-based assessments.

Bibliography

Dweck, C.S. (2008). Can Personality Be Changed? The Role of Beliefs in Personality and Change. *Current Directions in Psychological Science*, 17(6), 391–394. doi: 10.1111/j.1467-8721.2008.00612.x

Hughston, V.C. (2013). An Empirical Study: Team Charters and Viability in Freshmen Engineering Design. In *2013 IEEE Frontiers in Education Conference (FIE)* (pp. 629–631). IEEE.

Riebe, L., Girardi, A. and Whitsed, C. (2017). Teaching Teamwork in Australian University Business Disciplines: Evidence from a Systematic Literature Review. *Issues in Educational Research*, 27(1), 134. Available at: http://www.iier.org.au/iier27/riebe.pdf

Sverdrup, T.E. and Schei, V. (2015). "Cut Me Some Slack" The Psychological Contracts as a Foundation for Understanding Team Charters. *The Journal of Applied Behavioral Science*, 51(4), 451–478. doi: 10.1177/0021886314566075

Inclusivity note

Learning within a team for extended periods helps students develop resilience and mediation strategies to solve disagreements and even conflicts. However, assigning specific roles within a team and helping students agree team rules and etiquette is a big help in all these scenarios as it provides an important safety net for the success of the teamwork activity. For some students such as neurodivergent, very shy or non-native speakers from other cultural backgrounds, working in teams can be overwhelming and even ineffective. The reasons are multiple: having to mask one's neurodivergence, needing to go at another person's learning speed, having to articulate in speaking deep ideas in a social group, lack of clear expectations and roles. Team charters can help.

Besides, for working students and those with caring responsibilities, attending in-person group meetings can be challenging. Groups should agree a reasonable number of meetings, online if possible, and with asynchronous elements which provide enough flexibility.

This case study is about a simple yet powerful self-regulation mechanism we can design to support teamwork: student-generated team charters where students agree on academic and professional behaviour. Charters are very useful in case of group conflict, but even when the group dynamic is good, it is a very useful exercise to set ground rules and clarify expectations. Such charters can themselves be a formative and reflective assessment task for students, best done towards the beginning of a course.

Having discussed reflective and formative assessment, I will now address reflective and formative feedback.

Reflective and formative feedback

Feedback is very much about establishing a dialogue about learning, an exchange. It is also about power and locus of control in teaching, learning and assessment. In this section, I will discuss mostly assessment feedback, but feedback should be peppered *throughout* the learning journey, definitely not just at assessment stage or at the end of the learning journey.

There are currently three main views about what feedback is: it's information provided by teachers to learner; it's a process in which students have to make sense of the information provided by teachers or peers; it's something that people generate themselves through comparison (against resources, peers and experts—Nicol 2019). My view is a mix of the three: feedback refers to the information a learner gets regarding their learning from multiple sources, including their own inner dialogue and how they process such information.

Strictly speaking, feed-back should mean feed-forward because it is about helping students reach their future learning goals. To be formative, feedback for learning should not be simply a number or letter grade, but rather it should be information, opinions and comments on student learning and outputs. To be inclusive, the feedback process needs to include and involve the learners rather being perceived as the sole responsibility of the teacher and it needs to be given in the modality that suits the student.

The term *students' feedback literacy* is used to refer to how well students understand and make use of feedback processes to advance their learning. However, we also need to talk about 'teacher feedback literacy' (Boud and Dawson 2021)—how much *teachers* understand feedback systems and approaches and how to use them effectively. Feedback needs to be part of a wider assessment design strategy, to facilitate its 'translation' and transfer into better future learning, practices and assessment outputs. Instead, often feedback is not properly, intentionally designed and planned, but it happens as a tailpiece.

In your institution, it is possible that the department responsible for quality sets feedback rules and policies regarding the quality and quantity of assessment feedback students should receive from teachers which are quite clear to staff but are rarely communicated to students. This leaves students not knowing when and how they will receive feedback, which can cause anxiety. An inclusive assessment feedback practice is to ensure that information about when, how much and what type of feedback students will receive during the course is shared with students from the outset. For example, stating:

> You should expect to get formative feedback from me in the first 4 weeks of the course, in the form of written/audio/video comments. I would expect a response from you within one week of receiving it in the form of. ...

Unfortunately, often students ignore teachers' feedback comments and only look at the grade or outcome. This is very disheartening for academics who put much time and effort into providing meaningful comments. One way to ensure feedback is received, understood and acted upon is by shifting the emphasis from the end point to mid point(s)—offering it at key formative points during the course where students are eager to know how they are doing. By designing in formative and reflective interim assessment points that directly support the final summative assessment, we provide several opportunities for students to reflect on their progress. At those points we want to facilitate as much dialogue as possible around work in progress.

In terms of feedback timing:

> *Immediate*, formative feedback is particularly supportive when students are on task, applying new knowledge and need to know whether they are going in the right direction. Formative stages require more detailed formative feedback, while shorter comments work well for summative feedback.

> *Delayed* feedback provides some 'distance' from the learning event and the output, so it becomes more reflective. However, delayed must not turn into 'late'. Feedback should still be provided in advance of the next steps in the learning journey, making the links clear. Still, the usefulness of some feedback becomes clear as time passes.

As feedback has a strong emotional impact on students (Varlander 2008), what is the best way of providing it? To be truly inclusive, we need to check with students what feedback *mode* suits them best. The default, traditional mode is written comments, and there are advantages to this as they can be easily shared and are easy to refer back to. However, technology makes it possible to provide highly personalised feedback by using audio or video.

The next case study discusses screencast feedback as a more inclusive approach to providing tutorial-style feedback, even at scale. Notice why and how this feedback mode supports more *reflective* feedback.

Beyond telling—A clarion call for technology-mediated feedback conversations in online higher education

By Ameena L. Payne (Australia)

From mechanistic feedback

It is widely accepted that the commencing year of higher education (HE) is the most crucial time for engaging learners and equipping them with the skills to become independent in their learning and application throughout their qualification. It is also known that feedback can be a compelling learning process that instructors use to help students achieve these goals (Ajjawi et al. 2021). Yet, students consistently report that feedback is provided substandardly in HE (Boud and Molloy 2013).

Feedback is an inherently social process (Ajjawi et al. 2021). This is particularly true in online HE as students do not usually 'hang out' on institutional websites; their online subjects and instructors are their primary experience of university itself. Yet, with text feedback being the primary mode, feedback has been tantamount to 'telling'; it is unsurprising that a cost of this 'telling' has been that feedback is often not acted upon or is misinterpreted (Boud and Molloy 2013).

I contend that creating engaging, high-trust spaces (Payne et al. 2022) that are rich with relational and *formative encounters* can enhance the student experience of receiving, reflecting upon and actioning feedback. However, doing so requires practitioners to develop critical awareness of how to better shift feedback from one-way information transmission towards *experiences* that 'encourage, empathise [with] and engage' students (Payne 2021:96).

Towards reflective feedback

My application of video feedback began in 2019 and was met with much positivity from students and intrigue from the wider academic team. As shown in Figure 8.4, through video feedback, I found that I could express myself more easily—building rapport, establishing presence, showing appreciation and asking questions; this is in alignment with the findings of Borup et al. (2014). Further, the use of questions is deemed 'an integral part of effective teaching' (Steyn and Adendorff 2020). I found that feedback phrased as questions, rather than corrective comments, helped students become reflective and self-referential; video feedback coupled with questioning privileges cognitive, social and teaching presence (Payne 2021).

Figure 8.4 Video feedback simulates face-to-face, dialogic communication.

Given the increased enrolment to fully online HE, I feel it even more vital to re-evaluate assessment practices that may no longer be adequate. Strikingly, video feedback allowed me to be more human—expressive and nuanced. Rather than using feedback as information transmission, the use of video allowed me to more deeply consider and more easily incorporate questioning techniques that served to build rapport with students and encourage critical and reflective thinking. Video allowed me to transgress the constraints of text feedback.

> Ameena always gave great advice to myself and fellow learners and always made us think a little broader and outside the box. I found the video feedback for assignments was a lovely touch and made it more personal. I also found that the feedback received in these videos was clearer and left less room for confusion with the feedback.
> —Student, COM10011, Trimester 3, 2020

HEIs tend to be stuck in the traditional ways of doing things, and we, as educators, may never get permission to experiment, to take risks. I hope this case study can inspire instructors, especially those who teach first-year subjects, to continue to deeply consider their assessment practices. The inclusion of video feedback can return the focus onto more personable interactions in digital spaces. Sometimes we must dare to do things differently and stick our heads above the parapet and lead the way.

Bibliography

Ajjawi, R., Olson, R.E. and McNaughton, N. (2021). Emotion as Reflexive Practice: A New Discourse for Feedback Practice and Research. *Medical Education*. doi: 10.1111/medu.14700

Borup, J., West, R.E., Thomas, R.A. and Graham, C.R. (2014). Examining the Impact of Video Feedback on Instructor Social Presence in Blended Courses. *International Review of Research in Open and Distributed Learning*, 15(3), 232–256. doi: 10.19173/irrodl.v15i3.1821

Boud, D. and Molloy, E. (2013). Rethinking Models of Feedback for Learning: The Challenge of Design. *Assessment & Evaluation in Higher Education*, 38(6), 698–712. doi: 10.1080/02602938.2012.691462

Payne, A.L. (2021). A Resource for e-moderators on Fostering Participatory Engagement within Discussion Boards for Online Students in Higher Education. A Practice Report. *Student Success*, 12(1), 93–101. doi: 10.5204/ssj.1865

Payne, A.L., Stone, C. and Bennett, R. (2022). Conceptualising and Building Trust to Enhance the Engagement and Achievement of Under-served Students. *The Journal of Continuing Higher Education*, 1–18. doi: 10.1080/07377363.2021.2005759

Steyn, G. and Adendorff, S.A. (2020). Questioning Techniques Used by Foundation Phase Education Students Teaching Mathematical Problem-solving. *South African Journal of Childhood Education*, 10(1), 9. doi: 10.4102/sajce.v10i1.564

> **Inclusivity note**
>
> This case study shows that screencast feedback can be very supportive of students and help teachers connect with them. To be inclusive, and for audio-visually impaired students, we should ensure video feedback is accompanied by captions/transcripts, for instance using software which automatically caption videos. It is also important that we check with students whether this mode of feedback suits them—some students may prefer written feedback that they can more easily refer back to.
>
> Hybrid forms can also be very effective, such as a short, written feedback comment highlighting main strengths and areas for improvement accompanied by an audio-visual file with further details.
>
> As feedback needs to be sustainable for teachers, in large classes, it may be better to provide group feedback in one more generic video, highlighting common trends, and then add a shorter individualised comment for each student.

Audio-visual feedback could help teachers manage increased feedback workloads, while students welcome 'the relational dimensions of the medium' and usually report 'positive impacts on their feedback engagement' (Turnbull 2022). The case study shows the value of relationship building as part of the feedback process.

Head to the companion website inclusivelearningdesign.com (under Section 4) for a case study by Bonnie Amelia Dean (Australia) entitled: Personalised, connected feedback. You will read how to make written feedback comments (more) personal and linked to other learning. Such feedback helps students make connection to their future working lives. The case study includes a written feedback example.

For reflective and formative feedback to have maximum impact on student learning and to avoid one-way feedback, we should also include a mechanism where students:

1   *Collate* their feedback from multiple sources in a portfolio or other suitable (digital) space.
2   *Respond* to feedback wherever possible, saying how they intend to implement the feedback in their future learning and assessment.

This may sound like too much work for the students, but as Dylan (2015) says, 'feedback should be more work for the recipient than the donor'.

Collating and responding to feedback is useful at summative or end-point assessment of a module as well: at the start of the next module, students can be invited to review and reflect on the previous (collated) feedback they received and how it can inform their current studies.

Conclusion

This chapter has invited you to consider the importance of designing reflective and formative assessment and feedback as part of more inclusive assessment practices.

At the start of this chapter, I proposed these questions:

> **Activate your inner dialogue. ... How would you answer?**
>
> How can you design and implement a reflective and formative assessment and feedback regime on your course? How will this support more inclusive learning practices?

In a nutshell, in view of the ideas and case studies in this chapter, my provisional and evolving answers are:

Assessment needs to go beyond testing knowledge and skills, it needs to encourage students to reflect on their learning journey, more than once (formative assessment), not simply at the end (summative assessment). The case studies proposed assessment as learning, eportfolios and team learning charters as some possible ways to design more reflective and formative assessments.

This type of assessment goes hand in hand with reflective and formative feedback, provided in a supportive, developmental environment. Personalised/connected and screencast feedback are two ideas discussed in the case studies to design more inclusive, reflective and formative feedback.

Ultimately, if we apply the 'C', co-created, root-value here as well, we can design assessment and feedback modes that suit our students *together* with them, allowing them to have a say in how they are assessed and how we should provide them feedback.

Even when done well, teacher feedback (on assessment outputs) should not be the *only* type of feedback students receive. In the next chapter I discuss the key role of self and peer assessment and feedback in designing more inclusive learning assessment.

Bibliography

Bloxham, S. (2007). A System That is Wide Off the Mark. Times Higher Education Supplement, 26th October. Available at: https://www.timeshighereducation.com/news/a-system-that-is-wide-of-the-mark/310924.article

Boud, D. and Dawson, P. (2021). What Feedback Literate Teachers Do: An Empirically-derived Competency Framework. *Assessment & Evaluation in Higher Education.* doi: 10.1080/02602938.2021.1910928

Chan, C. and Lee, K. (2021). Reflection Literacy: A Multilevel Perspective on the Challenges of Using Reflections in Higher Education through a Comprehensive Literature Review. *Educational Research Review*, 32, 100376. ISSN 1747-938X. doi: 10.1016/j.edurev.2020.100376

Dylan, W. (2011). *Embedded Formative Assessment.* Bloomington, IN: Solution Tree Press.

Dylan, W. (2015). *Feedback for Learning: Make Time to Save Time.* Dylan William Center. Available at: https://www.dylanwiliamcenter.com/2015/01/06/feedback-for-learning-make-time-to-save-time/

Evans, C. (2021). Is Your Curriculum Design Limiting Students' Learning Potential? [online] THE. Available at: https://www.timeshighereducation.com/campus/your-curriculum-design-limiting-students-learning-potential

Kuh, G.D. (2008). *High-impact Educational Practices: What They Are, Who Has Access to Them, and Why They Matter.* Washington, DC: AAC&U.

Macfarlane, B. (2016). *Freedom to LEARN: The Threat to Student Academic Freedom and Why it Needs to be Reclaimed* (1st ed.). New York: Routledge. doi: 10.4324/9781315529455

Mackinney, R., Kelly, J. and Pulling, C. (2021). The Effect of Feedback Type on Academic Performance. *PESTLHE*, [online] 15(1). Available at: https://www.pestlhe.org/index.php/pestlhe/article/view/231

Nicol, D. (2019). Reconceptualising Feedback as an Internal Not an External Process. *Italian Journal of Educational Research*, Special Issue: 71–83. Available at: https://ojs.pensamultimedia.it/index.php/sird/article/view/3270

Shepard, L.A., Penuel, W.R. and Pellegrino, J.W. (2018). Using Learning and Motivation Theories to Coherently Link Formative Assessment, Grading Practices, and Large-scale Assessment. *Educational Measurement: Issues and Practice*, 37(1), 21–34. doi: 10.1111/emip.12189

Turnbull, A. (2022). Feeling Feedback: Screencasting Assessment Feedback for Tutor and Student Well-being. *The Law Teacher*, 56(1), 105–118. doi: 10.1080/03069400.2021.1968168

Varlander, S. (2008). The Role of Students' Emotions in Formal Feedback Situations. *Teaching in Higher Education*, 13(2), 145–156. doi: 10.1080/13562510801923195

Yan, Z. and Yang, L. (2022). *Assessment as Learning: Maximising Opportunities for Student Learning and Achievement*. New York: Routledge. doi: 10.4324/9781003052081.

Chapter 9

Self and peer assessment and feedback

> Self assessment is the first step to all assessment
>
> Enhance Dreams

Whereas in Chapter 8 I focussed on reflective and formative feedback from the part of the teachers, the focus of this chapter is on *who else* should give feedback. If you asked a student the question 'who should give you feedback on your learning?' chances are that the automatic response is going to be 'teachers'.

When it comes to formative, but especially in the case of summative assessment points, students typically submit their outputs to teachers and wait to hear the outcome, in the form of a grade or as feedback comments. Most students are not particularly aware of the success (assessment) criteria that will be applied to their submission, because although these might be listed somewhere in the official course paperwork, it is unlikely that they are discussed during the course and students do not usually have any practice *using* them.

This is because self and peer assessment are still considered relatively new pedagogical practices and are by no means the norm on university courses. Yet self and peer assessment are powerful amplifiers of learning particularly because they provide more formative feedback and develop students' self-regulation, which is a life asset for life-long, life-wide learning as well as for employment.

However, self and peer assessment and feedback are not simple pedagogical techniques, rather they advocate a *shared responsibility* for assessment and feedback. As Bovill et al. (2021) write: 'Students and educators need to set clear expectations and be open to negotiating students' and educators' roles in assessment and feedback, whilst acknowledging that this disrupts existing learner and teacher power dynamics and roles'.

> **Activate your inner dialogue. ... How would you answer?**
>
> In which ways do self and peer assessment promote more inclusive learning design and practices?
>
> How can you design and implement self and peer assessment on your course?

In keeping with the overall nature theme of the book's tree metaphor, I am going to use the metaphor of a *flower* (Figure 9.1) to represent a wide-angle view of inclusive feedback practices, to contextualise self and peer feedback.

DOI: 10.4324/9781003230144-15

Self and peer assessment and feedback 281

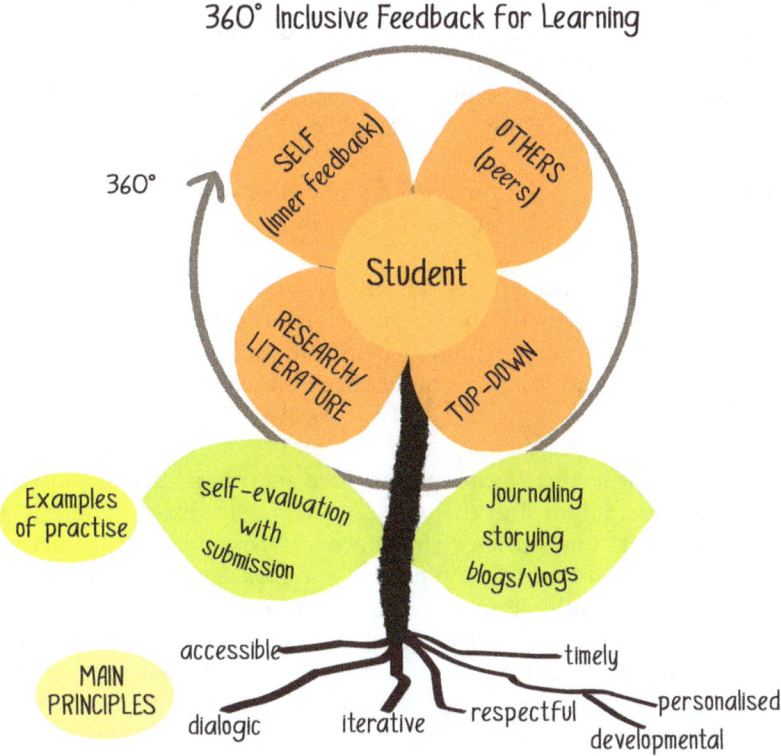

Figure 9.1 The 360-degree inclusive feedback for learning flower.

At the centre of the flower is the student. The roots of the feedback flower are the inclusive principles and values that underpin inclusive feedback practices such as:

- Accessible
- Dialogic
- Iterative
- Respectful
- Developmental
- Personalised
- Timely

To be **multidimensional**, feedback should come from a variety of sources. In the flower analogy, these are the four petals which form a 360° wide-angle view:

Self—Inner feedback is very valuable to develop self-efficacy. We 'talk to ourselves' about our learning, during the learning experience as well as once it is completed. Self-assessment and feedback considerably enhance students' self-regulation by clarifying success criteria and promoting metacognitive self-reflection.

- **Others**—This is to enhance peer-learning. For students the most meaningful 'others' are fellow students who can carry out peer assessment and feedback. The main benefits are enhanced 'ability to make evaluative judgements about work quality' but also 'navigating processes involved in feedback uptake' (Wood 2021). Alumni can also be part of 'others' by providing exemplars and assessment insights to current cohorts.
- **Top-down**—This is feedback from teachers and other educators such as librarians. It can be formal or informal, but it should be formative even when it is about summative assessment.
- **Research/literature**—This is the body of research of the discipline that students are studying: learning what the 'experts' in the field say—and discovering the present boundaries of the discipline—helps the students situate themselves within their field of study and is a form of feedback on where they are at in the road to mastery.

These are the main four feedback sources but there are others such as software.

The most notable paradigm shift that this 360-degree feedback highlights is the new role of teachers when it comes to feedback practices: from providers of better feedback to students to designers of effective and expansive *feedback systems* which allow students to receive feedback from multiple sources other than teachers.

Of the four feedback sources, self-feedback is underused and undervalued on most university courses, yet it is probably the most powerful one. Recent work by David Nicol (2022) has highlighted that what students need is many varied 'sources of comparison' (not just exemplars) *in order* to generate *their own* evaluative judgements.

How, in practice, can we promote self and peer assessment and feedback as part of a wide-angle inclusive feedback regime? I will briefly review three ways of doing this: (1) intentionally designating specific stages of the learning journey where self and peer assessment are required; (2) journaling and (3) students specifying which aspects of the submission they seek feedback on.

A key way to implement self-assessment is to design it into the life-cycle of the course at appropriate points 'where feedback can be encouraged in a more dialogical way' (Dawson et al. 2021) so that there is a clear expectation that each student submits a self-evaluation with *each* formative and summative assessment. Yan and Carless (2021) break down the self-assessment process into three steps: (1) determining and applying assessment criteria, (2) self-reflection, and (3) self-assessment judgement and calibration. Well-designed and prompted self-assessment benefits all three areas.

At the start of Chapter 8 I suggested a six-point possible assessment regime to enhance formative and reflective assessment *and feedback* which hinge on self and peer assessment and review (feedback). In all disciplines, learning (feedback) activities such as **journaling**, storying and blogs promote pausing and reflecting; they constitute a personal, safe space to articulate inner feedback; they are context rich; they help learners re-focus, articulate and *share* their learning experience. The journaling outputs can be part of formative and/or summative assessment submissions; or simply part of an ongoing (even life-long) learning portfolio. And they provide very rich feedback to the teachers. We could provide a focus for the journal entries such as: note three positive things about your learning—this can turn journaling into a gratitude exercise which supports resilience (Kukulska-Hulme et al. 2021).

For peer feedback, one way students can be proactive feedback seekers is by stating, in writing, 'which aspects of a particular assignment they would most like feedback on' from peers as well as from teachers; and 'this can be combined with some form of reflective self-evaluation' (Winstone and Carless 2019).

Self and peer feedback have pros and cons. We have Bloom to thank for showing us that formative feedback has a very big impact on learning (Guskey 2010) but, particularly in large cohorts, it is very difficult for teachers to have enough time to provide regular formative feedback to each student. By making fuller use of self and peer assessment and feedback, we increase the quantity and enhance the quality of feedback students receive during the learning cycle (Hughes 2001). Another main benefit students report about peer assessment is gaining different perspectives on their outputs. However, *providing* peer feedback is an even more developmental activity than receiving it (Double et al. 2020).

Having used peer assessment and feedback for many years, I can report that this approach has some disadvantages. Students can find participating in peer-assessment stressful both as assessors and recipients of peer-assessment feedback. Teachers need to allow enough time to provide appropriate scaffolds and practice of peer feedback, in order to get buy-in from the students and more meaningful peer feedback comments.

The following three case studies showcase various approaches to self and peer assessment and feedback: to deepen students' learning; to develop feedback literacy; and to assess individual contribution in group assignments.

The first case study, from the UK, discusses the critical role of self-assessment in enhancing and extending students' learning. Notice the careful, spiralling sequencing of self-assessment opportunities the students are afforded during their learning journey.

Supporting students to self-assess to deepen and develop their learning

By Kay Sambell and Linda Graham (UK)

Each year we teach a core module to first year Childhood Studies undergraduates who are in the first few weeks of transition into university. Cohort sizes range from 60 to 100 students. Our module introduces newcomers to the key theoretical ways in which childhood is studied and researched nowadays. This involves enabling students to grasp highly complex, abstract and transformative threshold concepts (Meyer and Land 2006) which they haven't encountered before. It entails helping students to see that, during their time with us, learning is not just about acquiring more knowledge, but is about changing the very way they see childhood. As with all threshold concepts, the process of grasping this new way of thinking and practicing is potentially exhilarating but also challenging and troublesome for learners. Hence, we do all we can to scaffold the learning experience as the module unfolds and to help our students to recognise and discuss the complexities this understanding opens up for them.

Our overall aim is to foster longer-term learning where learners realise they have the capacity to apply their childhood-related knowledge and skills to influence complex and ever-changing contexts by thinking and acting reflexively. We put this into practice by basing all our teaching and learning sessions around the idea of developing and honing students' capacity for self-assessment. To be clear, we don't see student self-assessment as a matter of getting them to guess their grades or assigning themselves marks (Sambell et al. n.d.). Instead, we see it as a *process* in which we design ongoing activities which support and encourage them to form a good idea *for themselves* about how their learning is going (Sadler 2013). Figure 9.2 illustrates the pedagogic process we have designed to enhance self-assessment.

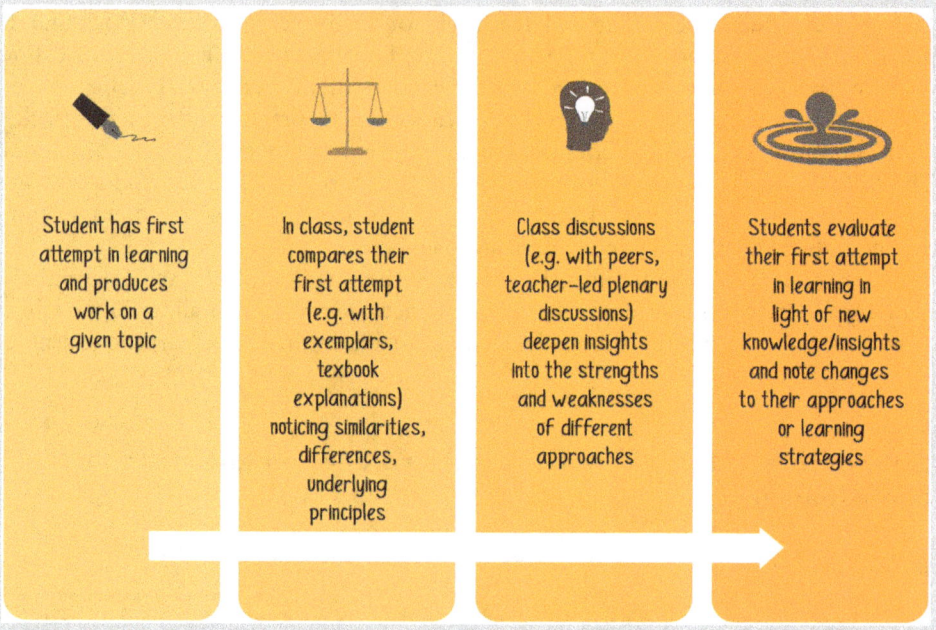

Figure 9.2 Pedagogic process to support all students to engage in self-assessment.

Each week students have an initial stab at a developmental low-stakes task, then (during the teaching session and working in a whole-group context) we design activities which enable everyone to interact with information (feedback) which helps them to reflect on their own first attempts in learning in relation to a specific learning goal, and to perceive the strengths and weaknesses of their initial steps.

While we use this process each week and encourage students to journal their developing insights in a self-assessment workbook, this mini case study will focus on just one of our recent teaching sessions (based on the use of exemplars) to illustrate our overall approach. In this instance students produced a 500-word response to a challenging conceptual task, which they brought along to the session. In the session itself we got them to compare their initial response with three samples of previous students' work, which illustrated strong, satisfactory and weak work.

First, we included the students in discussions about the criteria we would all use to evaluate the quality of each sample in relation to the learning goal. Next, working individually and journaling their thoughts in their assessment workbook, we asked students to evaluate each sample and generate feedback comments which would help the author of each sample to make their work even better. At this point we asked them to do the same on their own work.

After that, we facilitated an in-depth tutor-led discussion of the three samples with the whole class. Following all this, we asked all students once again to compare their *own* work against the samples and to write down the new insights or knowledge they had developed and anything else they might do to improve their own work yet further.

In our experience of using exemplars over many years (Sambell and Graham 2020), students respond enthusiastically to seeing concrete examples of how criteria and standards play out in practice, and they especially value seeing how else they might approach a task. We find that using exemplars as the focal point and encouraging students to create private learning journals to record their self-assessments on their first attempts in learning offer an inclusive, non-threatening approach which allows everyone to move forward from their own starting point and by learning, as most of us do, from making mistakes. Most importantly, we find that student feedback on such activities focuses on the change that flows from self-assessment activities:

- After that workshop I did change my work, but my frame of mind changed along with it as well. That was the first time I've seen examples of like, uni work. I thought: I'm capable of doing this and I'm even capable of doing the [best], but obviously, I've just got to get properly into it
- That was helpful because I discovered I'm on the right track but ... the wrong wavelength
- I'd got a bit confused ... so I need to read more, read thoroughly and make notes of what I read so that I understand what I'm reading

Effective learners engage 'naturally' and informally with self-assessment processes in an ongoing way behind the scenes, but most learners require explicit support to develop the capacity to make informed decisions about the quality of their own work and that of others (Tai et al. 2018), especially in the kinds of complex discipline-specific tasks they grapple with during higher education. Without this capacity they can't learn effectively whilst they are at university nor when they are in graduate professional practice. Hence, we continue to experiment, extend and evaluate the practical ways in which we can involve *all* our students in self-assessment processes, so that exercising evaluative judgment becomes second nature for all learners. Designing practices which embed this explicitly but informally in our teaching-learning interactions is important, not just because it is an effective and manageable way of engaging students in collective feedback dialogues but, more importantly, because rather than framing some students in deficit, it energetically seeks to level the playing field for everyone by creating multiple productive first attempts in learning.

Bibliography

Meyer, J. and Land, R. (2006). *Overcoming Barriers to Student Understanding: Threshold Concepts and Troublesome Knowledge*. New York: Routledge.

Sadler, D.R. (2013). Opening Up Feedback: Teaching Learners to See. In Merry, S., Price, M., Carless, D. and Taras, M. (Eds.) *Reconceptualising Feedback in Higher Education: Developing Dialogue with Students* (pp. 54–63). London: Routledge.

Sambell, K., Brown, S. and Race, P. (n.d.) Getting Students to Self Assess. Assessment and Feedback Resources, Quick Guide # 7, Heriot Watt University Learning & Teaching Academy. Available at: https://lta.hw.ac.uk/wp-content/uploads/GUIDE-NO7_Getting-students-to-self-assess.pdf

Sambell, K. and Graham, L. (2020). "We Need to Change What We're Doing." Using Pedagogic Action Research to Improve Teacher Management of Exemplars. *Practitioner Research in Higher Education*, 13(1), 3–17.

Tai, J., Ajjawi, R., Boud, D., Dawson, P. and Panadero, E. (2018). Developing Evaluative Judgement: Enabling Students to Make Decisions about the Quality of Work. *Higher Education*, 76(3), 467–481. doi: 10.1007/s10734-017-0220-3

Inclusivity note

This approach is inclusive as students develop a better understanding of the specific 'genre' they are writing about, of what quality looks like and of what they are aiming for—this is very supportive for students with specific learning needs.

Challenges are to do with obtaining suitable exemplars (because the brief might have changed) and having enough in-class time for this type of extended learning activity. It is possible to do something similar asynchronously and then discuss in class. Once the students have done their own assessment of the exemplars, the teacher can release their own feedback so students can clearly see how the criteria were applied to the output when they were submitted.

This case study exemplifies exactly the six-points assessment regime I mentioned earlier. It shows the value of using exemplars and taking the time to examine them *in class*. The variety of levels of the exemplars clearly shows to the students which ones have met a high quality standard and which ones haven't. In this way students become familiar with *using* rubrics and gauging the grades assigned to various outputs. This approach provides early opportunities for students to get onto the right track from the start, rather than waiting until students have produced a big final draft when it might be difficult to change the final output.

Head to the companion website inclusivelearningdesign.com (under Section 4) to read a case study by Chie Adachi and Jo Elliott from Australia, entitled: 'Developing feedback literacy in modelling professional practice—peer assessment among digital learning professionals'. The narrative shows how peer assessment to further assessment literacy can be integrated in an existing assessment regime, without altering the learning outcomes. Adding self and peer assessment and feedback to an existing course is a simple pedagogical tweak which increases the quantity and quality of peer learning and feedback each student is afforded. This is yet another no cost, easy to implement pedagogical strategy which supports more inclusive learning design and practice.

The last case study, from Spain, discusses the value of using rubrics for what is perceived as one of the most challenging assessment types: students' individual contribution in collaborative submissions. Notice the dimensions that make up the rubric and how these support a better understanding of the importance of self-regulation as an evolving professional competency.

Rubric to self and peer assess the students' individual contribution in group assignments

By Georgeta Ion, Anna Díaz-Vicario, Aleix Barrera-Corominas, Cristina Mercader and Cecilia Inés Suárez (Spain)

Self-assessment (SA) and peer-assessment (PA) processes are considered a learning opportunity (Carless and Boud 2018) since through these processes, students can get valuable information about their progress in learning. Furthermore, involving students in SA and PA processes helps to create a favourable environment for students to interact and put their prior knowledge into use (Ion et al. 2019) and to develop transversal competences such as communication, teamwork and self-regulation (Dochy and McDowell 1997), all key competences for future teachers.

We implemented SA and PA strategies with 400 students enrolled at the School of Education at the Autonomous University of Barcelona (Spain). For all subject specialisms, the assignments consisted of group tasks, and we formed groups of four to six teacher-students using different strategies (randomly, by friendship or by alphabetical order). During the task development, students worked in seminar sessions, receiving lecturers' guidance, and autonomously, outside the class. The assessment process required tasks for both teacher-students and lecturers. Lecturers assessed the final assignment, and the teacher-students assessed their contribution (SA) and their peers' contribution (PA) to the assignment, using a rubric especially designed for this purpose. The rubric, illustrated in Figure 9.3, enables the assessment of each teacher-student in the workgroup assignment and also allows lecturers to make a more personalised assessment in learning group settings.

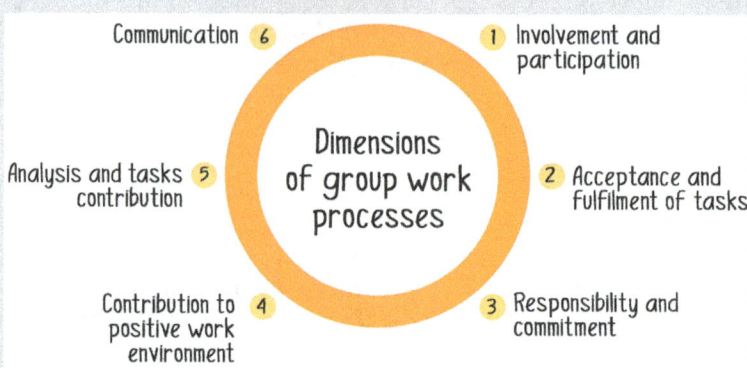

Figure 9.3 The dimensions considered to assess the individual contribution to the group assignment.

Considering the different purposes and benefits of SA and PA mentioned at the outset, the SA and PA rubric to assess the individual contribution to group assignments might be used in different ways, depending on: who fills the rubric (each teacher-student separately or the group itself); when the rubric is filled (during the live lessons or outside class); how the grades are established (each student individually, or the group agrees on the score for each item); what aim is pursued (initial diagnosis, formative or summative); and how the results are shared once the process is done (anonymously so nobody knows the individual grades; privately, so the teacher-student receives an average score of each of their grades; or publicly, so the teacher-student knows the details of their assessment and who assessed them).

Having used the rubric for many years, there are several lessons we have learnt: the rubric is an effective way to make students aware of the role of collaboration in group assignments and to democratise their participation as active agents in assessment; it provides an opportunity to (1) clarify with them what contributing to the group assignment means, (2) it reduces potential group conflicts and, (3) it empowers students to talk with their peers when they consider that someone is not acting professionally within the group. Moreover, it allows teacher-students to know in advance the criteria used to assess their contribution to the group assignment and to self-regulate their behaviour accordingly.

In order to maximise the benefit of the use of PA and SA, lecturers have to consider: 1) to share and clarify the rubric items from the beginning of the course, in order to make students aware of its importance and to set the students' expectations regarding the subject; 2) to give students time during the course to interact with the rubric and to apply it in different moments of the group's assignments, monitoring their progress; 3) to stimulate and motivate the students' engagement with the SA and PA, explaining their importance as valuable practices for their professional skills; 4) at the end of the process to discuss the SA and PA outcomes and to corroborate their findings with other assessment evidences (such as lecturer assessment or external assessments).

To understand the students' perception about this practice, we administrated a survey to the teacher-students participating in it. The responses showed that the experience had supported the students' development of collaborative learning and was useful to improve the participation in the group and to increase the commitment of each member in the group task. Furthermore, they felt that their judgement is taken into consideration by the lecturers and that, through this activity, the relationships between the group members improved. It is interesting to notice that students consider the process fairer when the PA is conducted individually.

To sum up, the application of the rubric of SA and PA: 1) contributes to the development of collaborative learning; 2) allows students' participation in the assessment process; and 3) contributes to develop their evaluative judgement and self-regulatory skills.

Bibliography

Carless, D. and Boud, D. (2018). The Development of Student Feedback Literacy: Enabling Uptake of Feedback. *Assessment & Evaluation in Higher Education*, 43(8), 1315–1325. doi: 10.1080/02602938.2018.1463354C

Dochy, F.J.R.C. and McDowell, L. (1997). Assessment as a Tool for Learning. *Studies in Educational Evaluation*, 23(4), 279–298.

Ion, G., Sanchez, A. and Agud, I. (2019). Giving or Receiving Feedback: Which Is More Beneficial to Students' Learning? *Assessment & Evaluation in Higher Education*, 44(1), 124–138. doi: 10.1080/02602938.2018.1484881

Inclusivity note

For neurodivergent students, having rubrics which clearly state what is expected of them and what group behaviours and social abilities will be part of the assessment outcome is very inclusive. Providing the rubric from the outset, discussing its purpose and meaning as well as using it in class for low-stake assessments are also inclusive practices which enhance feedback literacy.

Graded peer assessment has challenges to do with being honest in one's assessment of peers for fear of offending others, affecting friendship groups and even unfair retaliation in case of negative feedback comments or grades. Peer assessment needs to happen in a trusting mature environment, so it might be better to implement it only after the group is well integrated and there is a generally collaborative learning ethos.

This case study highlights the benefits of using a rubric to support formative, reflective, peer and self assessment and feedback processes. In this case the rubric was provided by the teachers and it helped students develop their assessment and feedback literacy in the context of an often difficult type of assessment: the contribution of individuals to group work. In other cases it may be possible for students and teachers to negotiate and co-create a rubric so students sharpen their sense of quality and of what counts in the outputs they are going to produce. Coupled with the team charter in a previous case study, rubrics are powerful allies to enhance these critical self-regulatory abilities.

Conclusion

This chapter has invited you to consider the critical role of self and peer assessment in promoting more inclusive assessment. The discussion and case studies make it clear that feedback should be seen as an ongoing dialogue, including among peers, hence a one-off self and peer feedback point is not enough and would not allow the students to reap the full benefits of peer review. From our part, as academics, we should 'scaffold support prior to and during episodes of peer feedback and peer assessment' (Pitt and Quinlan 2022).

At the start of this chapter, I proposed these questions:

> **Activate your inner dialogue. ... How would you answer?**
>
> In which ways do self and peer assessment promote more inclusive learning design and practices?
> How can you design and implement self and peer assessment on your course?

In a nutshell, in view of the ideas and case studies in this chapter, my provisional and evolving answer is that self and peer assessment are vital to promote self-regulation which is the ultimate goal of 'higher' education. They promote a more holistic educational experience and can be very supportive for neurodivergent students.

I propose you adopt and adapt this possible assessment regime to enhance formative and reflective self and peer assessment and feedback:

1. Towards the start of the course, once the assessment has been introduced, students, in groups and as a class, discuss exemplars and determine 'quality' criteria for the required outputs.
2. Students have multiple opportunities for smaller, scaffolded, low-stake, formative assessment tasks which build towards the final summative one.
3. Students have multiple opportunities for self and peer review of their work in progress at formative stage. Ideally, they use their own set of quality criteria to make evaluative judgements regarding their outputs.
4. At final submission, students attach their own self and peer feedback to the submission.
5. Teachers review the self and peer feedback and provide further feedback comments to refine (calibrate) the students' understanding of quality in relation to their outputs.

6   Students respond to the feedback with an action plan saying how they will implement it in future outputs. This is also used at the start of the next learning experience (module).

Not all the points might be possible in your context, but you may want to try a few of them with each iteration of your course and check how students' learning is affected to inform the next steps.

There is no doubt that more self and peer assessment and feedback increase students' self-regulation and assessment and feedback literacy, which will benefit them for the rest of their studies and in their daily life as well.

End note to Section 4

Section 1 was about the values at the roots of the inclusive learning design tree; Section 2 was about the context, environment and set-up; in Section 3 I addressed the course content (the design of input and practice activities) and in this section (4) I have addressed ways of making assessment and feedback more inclusive.

Through the chapters and the many case studies, I proposed ways in which we can make more inclusive assessment a reality on our courses.

In Chapter 7 I highlighted the role of giving student voice and choice and the benefits of designing more authentic outputs which are relevant and useful beyond the course; in Chapter 8 I discussed the benefits of reflective and formative assessment and feedback, promoting the adoption of an assessment as learning regime for more agentic students; in Chapter 9 I showed ways in which self and peer assessment and feedback can enhance the assessment experience for all involved by helping students become producers and seekers of varied feedback, beyond teachers' feedback.

> **Activate your inner dialogue. ... How would you answer?**
>
> What have your learnt in this section about learning assessment?
> What are your main take aways for more inclusive practice regarding the 'outputs and feedback' on your course?

Inclusive assessment by design can support the more flexible, hybrid teaching and learning many in academia would like and need to offer, especially in the wake of the changes provoked by the covid-19 pandemic.

All the ideas in this section promote a compassionate view of assessment, which should be about providing a space for students to showcase, peer review and discuss their learning in a variety of modes. This should be an integral part of an *overall* inclusive learning design.

The last step to design more inclusive learning is to design evaluation: why, when and how can we find out about the effectiveness of our learning design? I address these questions in the last section, which takes you around the symbolical learning design tree, in the outer circle.

Check the companion website to this book, inclusivelearningdesign.com for further resources about inclusive assessment.

Bibliography

Bovill, C., Matthews, K. and Hinchcliffe, T. (2021). *Student Partnerships in Assessment (SPiA)*. [online] AdvanceHE. Available at: https://www.advance-he.ac.uk/knowledge-hub/student-partnerships-assessment-spia

Dawson, P., Carless, D. and Pui Wah Lee, P. (2021). Authentic Feedback: Supporting Learners to Engage in Disciplinary Feedback Practices. *Assessment & Evaluation in Higher Education*, 46(2), 286–296. doi: 10.1080/02602938.2020.1769022

Double, K.S., McGrane, J.A. and Hopfenbeck, T.N. (2020). The Impact of Peer Assessment on Academic Performance: A Meta-analysis of Control Group Studies. *Educational Psychology Review*, 32, 481–509. doi: 10.1007/s10648-019-09510-3

Guskey, T. (2010). Formative Assessment: The Contributions of Benjamin S. Bloom. In Andrade, H.L. and Cizek, G.J. (Eds.) *Handbook of Formative Assessment* (pp. 106–124). New York: Taylor & Francis.

Haxton, K.J. (2019). Undergraduate Screencast Presentations with Self-, Peer-, and Tutor-assessment. In Seery, M. K. and Mc Donnell, C. (Eds.) *Teaching Chemistry in Higher Education: A Festschrift in Honour of Professor Tina Overton* (pp. 265–282). Dublin: Creathach Press. Available at: https://overtonfestschrift.files.wordpress.com/2020/04/overton-book-haxton.pdf

Hughes, I. (2001). But Isn't This What *You're* Paid For? The Pros and Cons of Peer and Self Assessment. *Planet*, 3(1), 20–23. doi: 10.11120/plan.2001.00030020

Kukulska-Hulme, A., Bossu, C., Coughlan, T., Ferguson, R., FitzGerald, E., Gaved, M., Herodotou, C., Rienties, B., Sargent, J., Scanlon, E., Tang, J., Wang, Q., Whitelock, D. and Zhang, S. (2021). *Innovating Pedagogy 2021: Open University Innovation Report 9*. Milton Keynes: The Open University.

Nicol, D. (2022). Turning Active Learning into Active Feedback. Introductory Guide from Active Feedback Toolkit. Adam Smith Business School, University of Glasgow. doi: 10.25416/NTR.19929290

Pitt, E. and Quinlan, K. (2022). *Impacts of Higher Education Assessment and Feedback Policy and Practice on Students: A Review of the Literature 2016–2021*. [online] AdvanceHE.

Winstone, N. and Carless, D. (2019). *Designing Effective Feedback Processes in Higher Education: A Learning-Focused Approach*. London: Routledge.

Wood, J. (2021). Making Peer Feedback Work: The Contribution of Technology-mediated Dialogic peer Feedback to Feedback Uptake and Literacy. *Assessment & Evaluation in Higher Education*. doi: 10.1080/02602938.2021.1914544

Yan, Z. and Carless, D. (2021). Self-assessment Is about More than Self: The Enabling Role of Feedback Literacy. *Assessment & Evaluation in Higher Education*. doi: 10.1080/02602938.2021.2001431

Section 5

Learning evaluation

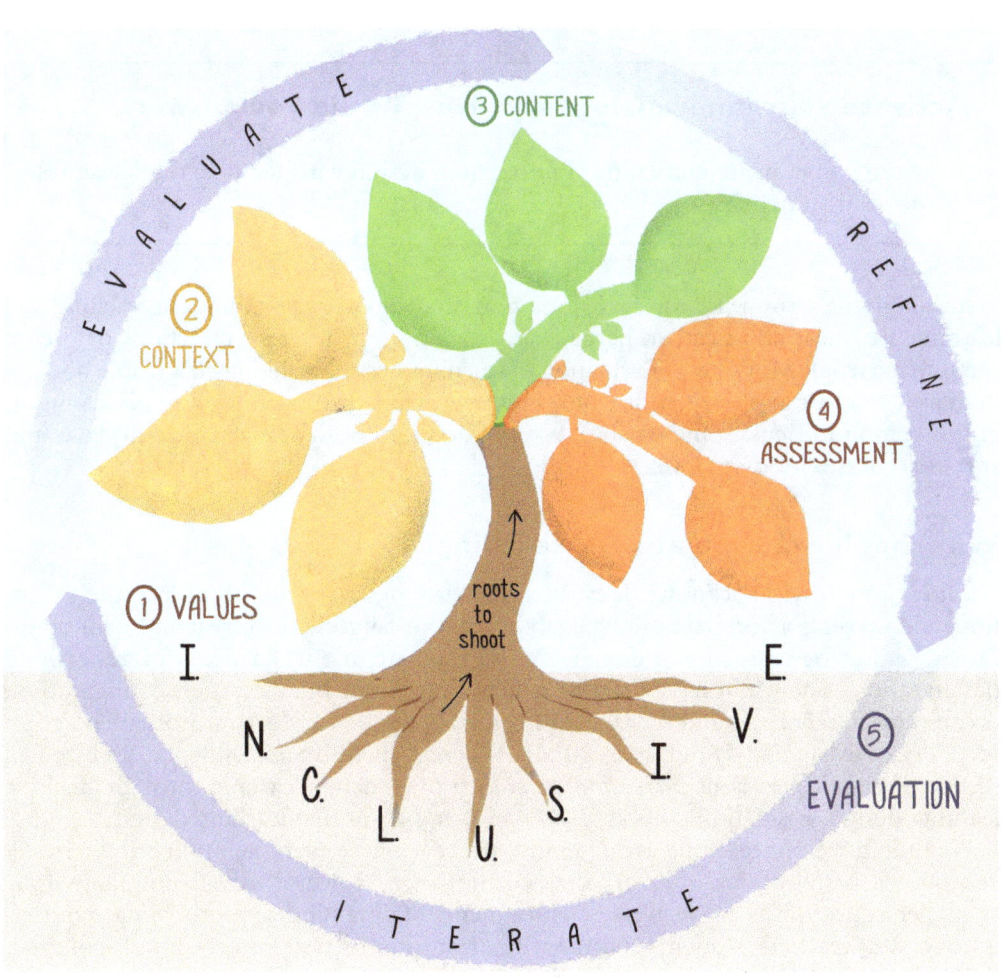

This section is about evaluation of learning, asking and checking whether 'what you are doing today is getting you closer to what you want to do tomorrow' (Coelho 2016). In this book I have taken you on a journey 'from roots to shoots': you read about the inclusivity values at the root of the symbolical learning design tree, then read about the setup, environment and engagement; the input and practice; and the outputs and feedback practices. However, the journey does not end there.

The tree image sits within three arrows which encircle it: this represents the fact that *learning design is an ongoing cycle* of evolving practice. The words on the arrows are: evaluate, refine, iterate. This section is about *evaluation*: capturing qualitative and quantitative data, reflecting on it and using it to *refine* the learning design for the next *iteration*. Our practice should evolve: 'we want to, with great care and intention, improve our practice, not just quickly jump from trend to trend but based on what our learners need' (Martin and Rowell 2022).

> **Activate your inner dialogue. ... How would you answer?**
>
> How can you evaluate and refine your learning design with the help of colleagues and your students?

Although the arrows and the circle look neat, in reality very few things in teaching and learning are linear and neat, so perhaps arrows going in different directions or even a spiral shape would work here. Evaluation of learning design would need a whole book in itself as it is a vast and deep endeavour. However, having to be concise in discussing it, in this section I discuss some practical ways of doing it, both at micro (lesson) level and at meso (course/module) level.

Why should we evaluate our teaching?

Because 'good design acknowledges the fact that redesign is the norm, not the exception, and that it is a correlate of sustainability, not of failure' (Goodyear and Dimitriadis 2013). Unless we evaluate our design, we will stagnate in our practice because learning design is not a one-off, it has a lifecycle which is not linear but 'considers configuration, orchestration, reflection and redesign as its main phases, with a forward-oriented design focus' (Goodyear and Dimitriadis 2013). Whereas inclusive assessment (discussed in section 4) should be about *increasing the quality* of students' learning through inclusive learning design, evaluation is about *judging the quality* of that learning design.

We should see our teaching as an iterative process where every iteration offers a better version, yet is still a *pilot, a draft, a work-in-progress*. However, this is not easily done as higher education is a risk-averse environment. Maintaining a 'prototyping mindset' is not easy as teachers, students and the wider institutional systems expect well-polished, finished course design, ready to be implemented.

On the other hand, I am not advocating that we adopt a *full-scale* continuous improvement mindset as this can eventually stifle innovation, can be taxing for teachers and is hard to sustain long term. It is not desirable to feel pressured to improve on *every* front, all the time. Still, in the context of this book, I think it is beneficial to view our design and implementation practices as *iterative* processes.

How can we evaluate our teaching, with particular attention to inclusive design and practice? Just as we discussed in Section 4 about self-assessment and feedback, we need a wide-angle view of our design and practice. The QAA quality code (2012) recognises that developing a programme is an iterative process based on reflection and critical self-assessment, drawing on the feedback and engagement of different departments, both academic and professional services. When it comes to learning evaluation, we need to apply, at a minimum, the (1) self, (2) students, (3) peers and (4) literature lenses to our evaluation.

Self-evaluation. Self-reflection should be every teacher's mindset. We should talk through our design and practice in our heads, on paper (or screen) and with words.
Students. We need systems in place to gather informal and formal student feedback. Students can evaluate individual classes, modules or entire courses. They are our most important stakeholders, hence theirs is the most important *voice* and perspective in the evaluation of the learning they experience with us.
Colleagues. Professional conversations and exchange classroom visits (observations with varying degrees of formality) are invaluable tools to stimulate dialogue about our design and practice.
Literature. Reading and research can provide a valuable 'lens' to scrutinise our design and practice and are a form of ongoing professional development.

When should we plan the evaluation of learning design? At design stage: for each course and for each lesson within that course, we should put mechanisms in place at the outset, to capture students' evaluation as well as our own and colleagues' feedback.

I will discuss lesson evaluation in Chapter 10 and course evaluation in Chapter 11.

Bibliography

Coelho, P. (2016). *The Spy.* London: Arrow Books, Penguin. Australia: Penguin Books Australia.
Goodyear, P. and Dimitriadis, Y. (2013). In Medias Res: Reframing Design for Learning. *Research in Learning Technology*, 21. doi: 10.3402/rlt.v21i3.19909
Martin, K. and Rowell, L. (2022). *Evolving through Connections, Feedback, and Relevancy.* [online] Getting Smart. Available at: https://www.gettingsmart.com/2022/03/03/evolving-through-connections-feedback-and-relevancy/
QAA (2012). The UK Quality Code for Higher Education. Available at: https://www.qaa.ac.uk/docs/qaa/quality-code/quality-code-overview-2015.pdf?sfvrsn=d309f781_6

Chapter 10

Lesson evaluation

The classroom is a place of opportunities. It is where we enact the designed curriculum. That's where the design gets tested and subsequently refined.

> **Activate your inner dialogue. ... How would you answer?**
>
> How can colleagues' and students' *lesson* evaluations inform your learning design and enactment?

Think about how you usually end your live lessons. Do you often run out of time and simply say 'that's it for today' or something on those lines? We have all been in that situation. But it is much better to design and plan for enough time at the end of a lesson, perhaps 10–15 minutes to stop and think about the learning that the lesson generated. What are the take aways for students? What feedback can you provide them? And, more importantly, what feedback can they provide to you?

We should have a system of varied ongoing, formal and informal evaluation activities, particularly at the *end* of every lesson. Lesson closure activities have an important cognitive function: they consolidate learning and prepare students for the next steps.

As you read the following case study about ways to purposefully close lessons, notice the practical ideas about how to gain evaluative feedback from students.

> **Inclusive lesson closures to evaluate learning**
>
> By Flower Darby (USA)
>
> One of the most impactful strategies we can implement to help all students learn more effectively is to end our lessons with an opportunity to process, evaluate and reflect on the new information they just learned. This strategy is equally effective and important in a real-time lesson that takes place in a videoconferencing platform, and in our lessons in an asynchronous format such as a module or

DOI: 10.4324/9781003230144-17

course in a Learning Management System (LMS). When we structure an opportunity for our students to think about and show us what they learned, we help them to consolidate their learning, which will in turn help students better retain and recall new concepts when needed. We also gain valuable feedback on our learning design and implementation.

Figure 10.1 captures the why, what and how of lesson closure and feedback.

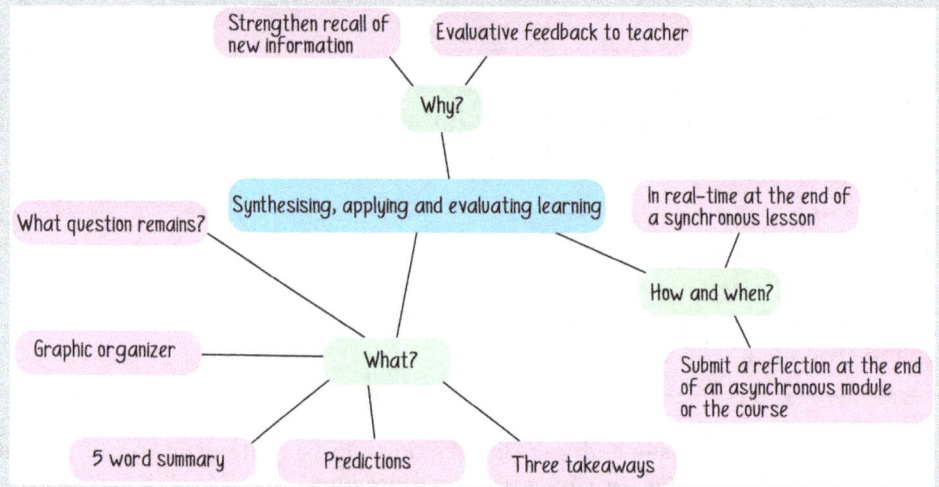

Figure 10.1 Overview of the 'why, 'how and when' and 'what' of end of lesson evaluative feedback.

There are many simple ways to do this, so you can plan something for your students that best fits your style, your subject matter, and your context. If you're teaching live, reserve a few minutes at the end of class to engage in a critical thinking and reflection exercise. This is a far better way to close class, far more supportive and inclusive, than allowing ourselves to run out of time and cut the lesson short. Intentionally reserving a few minutes at the end of the lesson communicates to your students that you care about them and value their learning. Online, students can draw or hand-write their evaluative reflection and hold it up to the camera, or take a picture with a smartphone and send it to you by email, or type their comments into the chat box—there's any number of ways students can engage in this closure activity in real time.

Or, if you're teaching in an asynchronous online format, create an activity that students submit as an assignment or a journal as the last thing they do before completing the module. This also works well at the end of the entire course. As above, students can create something on paper, snap a pic and upload the photo to the LMS, or they can type their response into an assignment submission text box, or they can record and share a 60-second smartphone video of themselves talking through and evaluating their learning. We should ask them to specifically comment on their muddiest point and on what support systems are working for them on the course, or that we should put in place.

So what should the lesson closure activity be? Here are some options to consider. You'll likely come up with your own ideas and variations that make sense for your students' age, your content, and the like.

You can ask students to write out three take aways from that lesson, three key points they want to remember and carry forward with them. Or have them anticipate what's coming up in the next lesson or module. Making predictions sparks curiosity and helps students focus and retain the actual content, having guessed what it might be. Some teachers have an end-of-lesson 'cliff hanger' to build anticipation for what is coming next. You can also ask students to write a five-word summary of the lesson where, as the name implies, students boil down the content of the lesson (or textbook section, or paragraph) into five concise words. This really requires careful analysis, evaluation and synthesis of new ideas. Other ideas include asking students to fill in a graphic organizer such as a table, chart or concept map, and finally, asking students to write or say a question that they have about the lesson's material.

What matters is that the lesson-close activity is not simply a facts recall, but prompts reflection and evaluation of the learning process and of the course (our learning design and enactment), so we can adjust our practice accordingly.

Once you get thinking about these approaches, you'll see that it doesn't take long to have students engage in an activity that results in a big impact on their ability to evaluate and remember new information. Show your students that you care about them, and support each one in their learning, by planning a purposeful lesson closure exercise.

Bibliography

Brown, P.C., Roediger, H.L. and McDaniel, M.A. (2014). *Make It Stick: The Science of Successful Learning*. Cambridge, MA: The Belknap Press of Harvard University Press.

Lang, J.M. (2016). *Small Teaching: Everyday Lessons from the Science of Learning* (pp. 32–34). San Francisco, CA: Jossey-Bass.

Inclusivity note

End of lesson evaluations can be particularly supportive for neurodivergent and non-native speakers as they help students make sense of the learning they just experienced and allow them to provide live feedback to the teacher.

However, some students need longer to think about it, so asynchronous evaluation works better for them.

The visual aid in the case study nicely illustrates the why, what and how of the end of lesson evaluation. Cognitively, having a regular habit of reviewing learning at the end of an 'episode', such as a lesson, can do much to help retain and make sense of learning by building meaningful connection with other, pre-existing understandings. It is also invaluable for teachers to have access to regular brief evaluative feedback to adjust their practice.

Head to the companion website inclusivelearningdesign.com (under Section 5) to read a case study by Xinli Wang (Canada) entitled *End of lesson student evaluative feedback*. It discusses three simple, inclusive, no-budget ways of closing the lesson to benefit the students and gather valuable feedback to inform our teaching.

Some additional ideas to carry out an end of lesson evaluation are:

- Video-record a live lesson and watch it (with students?) using some focus questions to prompt critical self-analysis.
- Plan an end of lesson evaluation raffle 'game' where students draw a ticket from a pool and answer evaluation questions in pairs before sharing their feedback with the rest of the group in a final plenary.
- Post-it evaluation wall: students jot down their evaluation of the lesson on sticky notes and put them on a wall on their way out of the classroom.
- Arrange for students to observe you teach a different class than theirs.
- Students (and you) journal about the learning for 5–10 minutes at the end of each lesson.

With this brief overview I hope you are convinced of the benefits of designing and planning an appropriate lesson closure for your live classes. According to your context and your preferences, you could implement one or more of these evaluation activities in order to support inclusive learning design.

Conclusion

This chapter has invited you to consider the benefits of designing an end of lesson closure. To make space and time for it, you may need to adjust the amount of learning activities or content allocated to each lesson.

At the start of this chapter, I proposed this question:

> **Activate your inner dialogue. … How would you answer?**
>
> How can colleagues' and students' *lesson* evaluations inform your learning design and enactment?

By making time and intentionally designing a regular (end of) lesson evaluation, we can get the pulse of the cohort, how their learning is progressing and what we should address next. The evaluative feedback we gather regularly can inform more inclusive learning design tailored to the needs of the cohort.

In the next chapter I discuss various ways of moving the evaluation to the next stage: course evaluation.

Chapter 11

Course evaluation

Besides designing lesson closures and lesson-level evaluative activities, we also need to make sure we intentionally design course-level evaluation activities.

> **Activate your inner dialogue. ... How would you answer?**
>
> How can colleagues' and students' course evaluation inform and refine future iterations of your course?

The typical end of course evaluation that universities send out by default to all the students enrolled on a course usually gets low response rates and does not provide teachers with rich qualitative data to support learning design enhancements. Depending on context, it is usually better for teachers to design a more tailored evaluation activity to gather qualitative data from each cohort.

As Winter (2022) puts it: 'The emphasis on Student Evaluation of Teaching (SET) instruments over those which capture learning gain, learning transfer, students' behavioural, emotional, and cognitive engagement, and subsequent engagement in life long and life wider learning, means that we do not often have the right data to answer our own question' about the impact we have had.

One of the most commonly used course evaluation methods is using feedback surveys. However, to avoid survey fatigue, we can use alternative, innovative evaluation activities such as:

- Annotated syllabus. Sharing with students a live syllabus, providing a space where we can annotate our self-evaluation on the go and students can anonymously add their comments is a very valuable collaborative activity.
- About one third into a course, students record a one-minute video (with their phone) talking about one or two prompt evaluation questions we provide. Students can post them on a shared platform.
- Students post *anonymous* feedback comments on a digital wall such as a Padlet.
- Set up 'dialogue days' to gather course feedback (Asghar 2012).
- Students write an evaluation in the form of a 'letter to my teacher' and add it to their final submission.

DOI: 10.4324/9781003230144-18

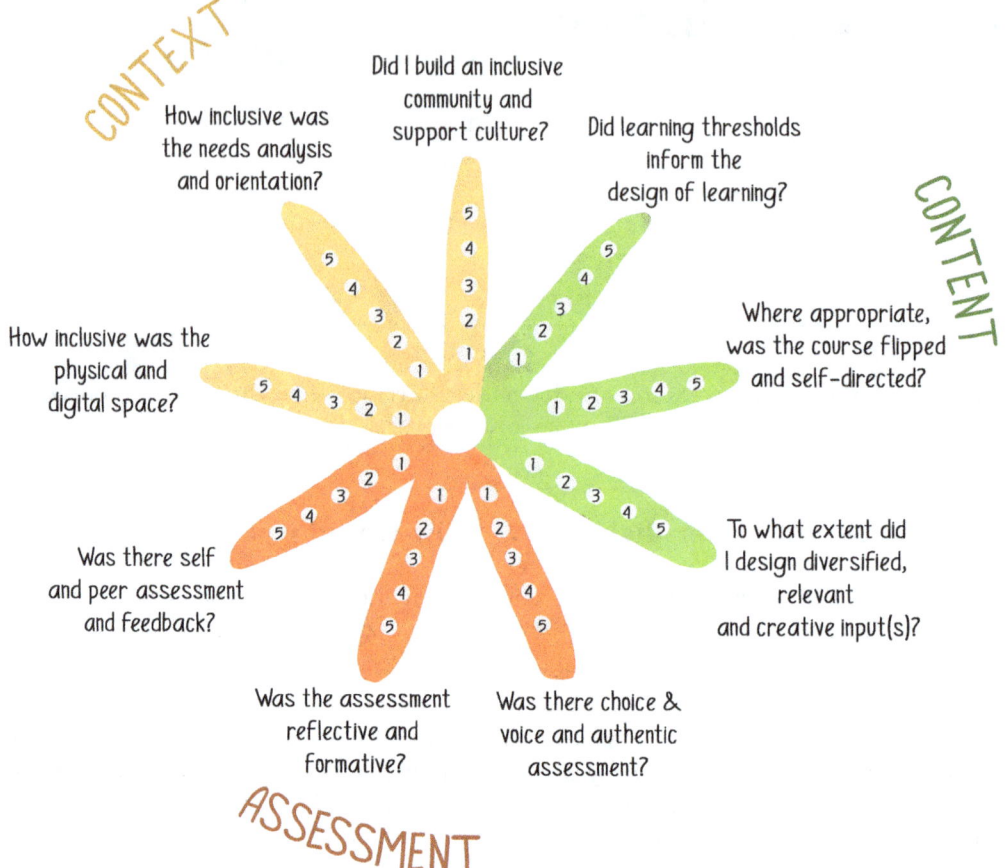

Figure 11.1 The inclusive star is a useful tool to design learning as well as to review and evaluate its enactment.

One way to receive more focussed feedback about how inclusive our learning design and enactment have been on a course is to use the prompts provided in the nine-point star (Figure 11.1) in Section 1 *at the end of a course*.

We can answer the questions ourselves, we can also discuss them with a critical friend such as a colleague and we can use them as prompts for our students to evaluate our course(s).

This star can be seen as a useful *checklist*, not in the sense of a tick box exercise, but as an example of how a complex job of designing learning (for instance a course) can be boiled down into a few meaningful steps/statements not to be overlooked in order to design and enact more inclusive learning. On the companion website there is a more detailed, downloadable checklist for your use, presented in a more linear table, based on the same elements.

You may know that even very experienced pilots are required to use flight preparation checklists, not because they are not competent, but simply because they are human and can make errors. The pilot's checklist is not simply a list of the order of operations, but it is underscored by values such as preparation, teamwork and accountability.

By routinely using the checklist before every flight, the pilot is reminded of key safety steps, develops a safety mindset and potentially saves lives by preventing human error to affect the flight.

Although our academic practice does not carry the same level of risk, we are still accountable for the academic and social development of the students under our care. Using the prompt questions of the star at design stage *as well as* at evaluation stage helps academics develop an inclusivity mindset in learning design and practice.

Another way to carry out an inclusive learning evaluation, is by asking students to come up with a rubric about what good and inclusive teaching should look like (the things they would like you to do as their teacher). This can be done in small-group discussion, and then in a plenary, so that the whole cohort agrees on what things should count and how they should be weighed. Then, anonymously, either with post-its or on a digital wall such as Padlet or Jamboard, students can actually rate our teaching. It is scary to expose ourselves so openly to students' judgement, but if we want to hear honest evaluative feedback on our practice, this is an excellent way to do it. It can be a real eye-opener in terms of what counts for students, and their candid feedback can inform future enhancements to our practice.

As mentioned under the root 'user-friendly', Universal Design for Learning (UDL) is a particularly useful approach to design more inclusive learning. We should of course use it **at the start** of the learning design process, to intentionally drive the process, ideally in collaboration with students. During the course, we should regularly signpost the UDL or design intentions of the curriculum. And UDL principles and practices can also be used as a **professional reflection and evaluation tool** during and after the learning event; once more, this would ideally involve the students. The following discussion and case study about UDL as an evaluation tool is adapted from my previous article on the INCLUDE website (Rossi 2021).

UDL principles as rear-view mirrors to review and evaluate our learning design

By Virna Rossi

As explained in Chapter 6, UDL has three key principles to guide learning design and make it more inclusive and accessible:

1. Multiple means of Engagement (Why of learning)
2. Multiple means of Action and Expression (How of learning)
3. Multiple means of Representation (What of learning)

A metaphor to illustrate the use of UDL three principles *as a tool for evaluation and reflection* is to see them as rear-view and side mirrors, as shown in Figure 11.2. The universal use of rear-view and side mirrors has changed the status of humans from a species only capable of perceiving the field of vision ahead, to one which can understand in a single glance two opposing visual fields. In cars, the inner rear-view mirror and the two side ones provide different angles of the same 'scene' behind, virtually eliminating blind spots. Each of the three mirrors informs the driver's driving decisions, with very little effort, *on the go*.

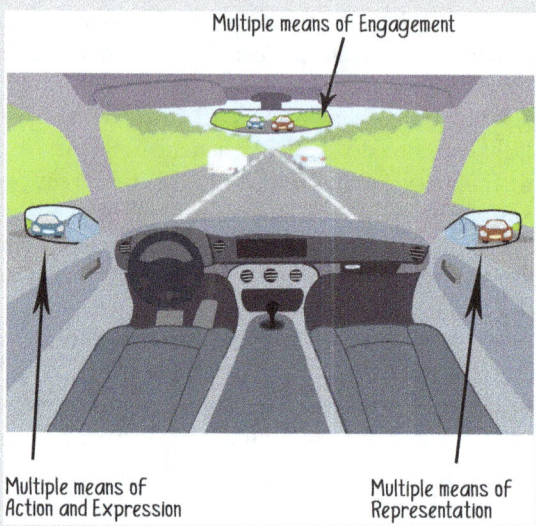

Figure 11.2 The three rear/side mirrors can be seen as the three UDL principles against which to gauge how inclusive our learning design is. The **three mirrors provide three perspectives** to evaluate our practice.

I am going to review: why, when and how we can 'glance' with these special UDL mirrors and how *students* benefit from this approach.

Why do we glance? We glance at the rear- and side-view mirrors to inform our driving, to avoid accidents, to check the state of the road, to situate ourselves, to change our trajectory. These are the same reasons why we should reflect 'on' and evaluate our teaching, in particular our learning design. This reflective and evaluative exercise provides us with a series of dynamic snapshots about our practice and the learning we are prompting.

At times there is a safety warning on the side mirrors: 'objects in mirror are closer than they appear'. In our metaphor this also has an equivalent: some situations may need attention as a priority because we might underestimate the closeness and relative importance of some aspects of our learning design. For instance, if we have dyslexic students—have we provided judicious output choices? How well equipped are they for their upcoming assessment? What study support systems are in place?

When do we glance? We do it *while* we drive. So, we can reflect on and evaluate our learning design while the learning experience is happening; we can indeed make it **part of the learning experience** itself. The three UDL rear-/side-mirrors can be used as a quick evaluative checkpoint, like a brief 'glance' while driving.

End-point course reviews are common practice, but as teachers we will not be able to action any feedback for that same cohort on that course at that point. In a way, it is like checking the rear-view mirror after a collision from behind which we could have avoided by checking earlier. For this reason, at least **one mid-term or mid-course** evaluation point is much more valuable in terms of informing our practice for that cohort.

Using our metaphor, as we drive and check the scene behind, some of the vehicles behind us at times overtake us or come alongside us (with thanks to David Baume for mentioning this point during an online event). So, in our metaphor, the reflection and evaluation exercise is not of a still image, but is one of a dynamic nature because we are dealing with a moving scene, with a living learning process. It is a learning journey in the making.

How do we glance? I will now discuss my case study of carrying out a mid-course evaluation on my Post-Graduate Certificate in Education (PGCert) course, using UDL principles and the pedagogical tool Ketso, discussed in Chapter 6.

I used UDL as the main learning design framework for our internal staff development course (PGCert) from the outset. I articulated this to the students even before the start of the course. But I also used the three lenses of UDL principles for mid-term review (the three rear-/side-view mirrors), during one of our live PGCert lessons to elicit evaluative feedback comments about my PGCert course design, from the users themselves, my teacher-students. I wanted to spark dialogue and to gain the student perspective. This was part of a 360-degree feedback approach, which invites the literature input, our own reflections and students' views as part of a wider-angle feedback view.

The literature view. I started by discussing with the cohort the theory underpinning UDL principles and guidelines, which provided the theoretical and current 'best practices' grounding.

The students' view. We used Ketso to represent our reflection and evaluation. For remote teaching, each student was sent their own pack at home to develop their ideas in their learning space. Students used the reusable, moveable pieces to represent their ideas, then arranged them on the felt workspace. The white shapes were used to label the UDL principles, and ideas for each principle were developed on the three different colour leaves (a colour for each principle). Students discussed their ideas in their study sets, in breakout rooms, and uploaded images of their Ketso representations onto a Padlet. The main question was: How are the three UDL principles evident on our PGCert course? How can UDL practices be enhanced on the PGCert?

My self-feedback. I also made a Ketso representation (at the same time as the students), shown in Figure 11.3, to highlight some of the ways I intentionally used UDL principles to drive my PGCert learning design process.

Figure 11.3 Using Ketso for my own mid-course self-evaluation.

The outcome of the exercise for me was gaining much needed insight into how the students were experiencing UDL on the course and where to improve. For instance, for Engagement many mentioned that using Ketso was a very good way to be engaged on the course. For Action & Expression some mentioned that they would welcome more 'debates' during the live lessons.

How do *students* benefit from glancing? What are the benefits for *students* in using the three rear-/side-view UDL lenses as a reflective and evaluative mid-course review? Firstly, this enhances students' meta-cognition and their ability to articulate their learning about learning. Secondly, understanding UDL principles can equip students with ideas and vocabulary to provide more meaningful feedback on *any* course design, not just on the PGCert. Thirdly, this exercise should inform immediate enhancements in course design and delivery. In our case, we discussed some of the suggested PGCert enhancements mentioned on the students' Ketsos, and I immediately implemented needed changes.

The three UDL rear-/side-view mirrors help us adjust our practice and inform better future learning design. Can students and colleagues suggest further ways to enhance our practice? This would be like adjusting or cleaning the mirrors so that we can better see how to evaluate our practice.

> **Inclusivity note**
>
> In this case, students provided evaluative mid-course feedback through Ketso and small group discussion. Although it is generally a highly inclusive tool, Ketso can be problematic for students with motor skill conditions or for those who cannot see the big picture through tactile means. An alternative is for students to draw or even just write their feedback on the three UDL principles.

Conclusion

This chapter has invited you to consider the value of setting up your own course evaluation, especially the mid-term one.

At the start of this chapter, I proposed this question:

> **Activate your inner dialogue. ... How would you answer?**
>
> How can colleagues' and students' course evaluation inform and refine future iterations of your course?

If we design an appropriate mid-course evaluation to gather data about students' learning, we can use the feedback to inform and adjust the remainder of the course. There are many practical ways of doing this, as long as students feel free to express themselves and we carefully choose the questions and tools we want to use. Undoubtedly, a well-designed course evaluation helps us enhance our teaching practice and promotes inclusivity by giving students voice in their learning.

End note to Section 5

Through the pages of this book I have prompted you to reflect on five dimensions of learning design, from roots to shoots: your values (Section 1), your context (Section 2), your content (Section 3), your assessment (Section 4) and your evaluation (Section 5).

In this section I briefly reviewed the value of designing micro (lesson) evaluations as well as meso (course/module) evaluations, especially mid-course evaluation. If you regularly evaluate your learning design, iterate and refine it, within a relatively short time you are likely to offer a considerably improved version of your course than you started off with.

> **Activate your inner dialogue. ... How would you answer?**
>
> What have you learnt in this section about learning evaluation?
> What are your main take aways for more inclusive practice regarding the evaluation of your course?

One of the most important ways to promote inclusivity at course evaluation stage is to make space for the students' voices, giving them multiple means of expressing their evaluative feedback on their learning experience. To 'close the feedback loop' it is vital to act on the evaluative feedback we receive and to let especially students know how we have incorporated their feedback into the current iteration of the course.

If the wealth of ideas and examples in this book seem intimidating, please read the conclusion for some practical ways to turn your good inclusivity intentions into good learning design and practice, by making small changes that require no budget.

Check the companion website to this book, inclusivelearningdesign.com for further resources about inclusive evaluation.

Bibliography

Asghar, M. (2012). Let's Talk! Using Dialogue Days as a Student Engagement Activity. *Educational Developments*, [online], 13(4), 18–20. Available at: https://www.seda.ac.uk/wp-content/uploads/2020/09/Educational-Developments-13.4.pdf

Rossi, V. (2021). Rear-view Mirror from a UK Perspective—Reflecting about Practice through the Lens of Universal Design for Learning Principles and Practices to Inform Learning Design. [Blog] INCLUDE Blog. Available at: https://include.wp.worc.ac.uk/rear-view-mirror-from-a-uk-perspective/

UCL (n.d.). Gathering Further Feedback. [online] Available at: https://www.ucl.ac.uk/teaching-learning/student-partnership/student-voice-and-surveys/gathering-further-feedback

Winter, J. (2022). Possibilities for Change—Evaluating Academic Development. [Blog] *The SEDA Blog*, Available at: https://thesedablog.wordpress.com/2022/03/02/possibilities-for-change-evaluating-academic-development/

Conclusion

> Inclusive teaching doesn't offer us a destination, but rather a path toward continuous attempts to align our practices with our values
>
> Bonni Stachowiak

The message of this book is that inclusivity is both a **duty and an opportunity**. As demonstrated through the many case studies and examples of practice, it is also a professional, pedagogical *competence* (Lawrence 2022), because inclusive learning design is **something to practice**, we are practitioners of it—striving for mastery. And finally, depending on many contextual factors, it can often be a *challenge* to implement.

I invite you to think back to the definition of inclusive learning design that I proposed at the start of the book:

> Inclusive learning design is design that considers the full range of human diversity with its complexity. It is designing learning environments, experiences, activities, tasks, assessment and feedback with students' voice and choice at its heart, so that students can grow academically, culturally and socially.

Now that you have read and interacted with the many ideas in this book, traveling from roots to shoots, you may have come up with your own inclusive learning design definition, suited to your context. If so, make note of it and keep it handy to refer back to anytime you design learning, from macro to micro level.

While the suggestions in this book are not silver bullets, they are ways to approach and change systemic cycles of exclusion in an attempt to *mainstream* inclusive practices. Inclusivity is an ongoing process of developing identities, clarifying our values, inquiry and learning through practice—processes in which all academics should engage. This one book will not 'fix' education's lack of inclusivity nor will this book necessarily *make* you a more inclusive teacher. But I hope it can challenge current thinking, inspire you to design more inclusive learning experiences and environments and provide a sense of hope.

By scrutinising practice through an inclusive lens, we should be able to *see* more clearly areas of improvement. As an example, you may know that you have an eyesight defect, but only when you use corrective lenses do you become fully aware of its degree as you realise the jump in quality to your vision. In a way, this book is an attempt to put inclusive, corrective glasses on our learning design and practice.

As mentioned in Section 1, the roots to shoots approach is a metaphor which works as a 'mediating artefact' (Conole 2008) to simplify the process of learning design while acknowledging the complex range of factors influencing it. By focusing in turn on the **five dimensions** of

1. Values
2. Context
3. Content
4. Assessment
5. Evaluation

I hope that you now have a wider repertoire to design or redesign your module(s) or course(s).

As one book cannot possibly address all the ways in which we can design more inclusive learning, what I have discussed here only scratches the surface of what currently works, most of the time in inclusive learning design and pedagogy. Take this book as a very big **meze meal**: you are invited to graze over the large board of small 'dishes' presented, to go back for some more, to taste and try new combinations and to create your own overall flavour of the meal. Even if you are doing most or even all of these things in your learning design and practice already, we have the challenge of catering for and adapting to each *new* cohort or setting, so inclusivity is an ongoing journey.

I propose these final reflective questions to support you to create your own inclusivity action plan:

Activate your inner dialogue. ... How would you answer?

What are your main take aways from this book?
How can you bridge the gap between your current inclusivity ambitions and your practice within your institution?
Going forward, what changes would you like to make to your learning design and practices to enhance inclusivity? Which of those changes are worth fighting for? Which internal and external allies can you make?
How will you keep growing as an (emergent) inclusive practitioner?

My main take aways are:

#Take away 1: Inclusive learning design starts by interrogating one's values (section 1) and carrying out a contextual analysis (section 2) which should inform the course input (section 3), output (section 4) and evaluation (section 5) stages.
#Take away 2: There is an urgent need to centre students' partnerships in all aspects of learning design, in the spirit of co-creation.
#Take away 3: Inclusivity is an opportunity *and a challenge*. This book has given you a menu of choices and 'warnings' to prompt you to start *your own* inclusive learning design journey.

You may not have thought about some of the barriers to inclusivity before, but now that you have, you probably feel you should do something about them. However, you may start to feel **overwhelmed** by the many things to consider and address for inclusive learning to be designed and enacted. I propose three ways to make inclusivity changes more feasible, linked to the three take aways above.

Firstly, use your contextual analysis (discussed in Section 2) to decide what makes sense in your context and with your cohort(s). Many of the case studies and ideas proposed by contributing colleagues are emerging and contingent. They worked in a particular context, with a particular cohort, on a particular course. In your quest for more inclusive ways of designing and enacting learning, use your professional judgement as you adopt and adapt the examples discussed to your context.

Second, identify areas of learning design and practices that would be easy for you to implement to enhance inclusivity on your course. Set yourself the goal of starting with those and then choose a few more as a future professional goal. Aim for quality of changes, rather than quantity. Most of all, remember that inclusive pedagogy is not simply an add on to what we already do. It is, rather, an opening up of our classrooms and our curricula. Our aim is to facilitate a greater sense of belonging and connection for all of our students.

Third, find 'allies' by networking within your institutions or elsewhere so you can start affecting change while getting some professional and emotional support yourself. Discuss the ideas with colleagues, set a realistic time frame and involve students in the process so as to make it a collaborative effort. As it takes a whole village to raise a child, not just one person: 'inclusion must cease to be about only who comes into university but what everyone within the university does' (McArthur 2021)—the more allies the better.

Additionally, it helps to be realistic about the scale and scope of the changes you can make but also to realise that they can have a greater effect than you may think. Inclusive learning design, which can be applied from activity and lesson level all the way to programme level, does not necessarily require complete overhauls. Many academics feel that things can and will only improve if truly big changes happen in our institutions. At times that is indeed the case, and we would all agree that systemic inequality issues and structural discrimination must be addressed. But as we make a case for those larger policy and cultural changes, we can commit to making our *own* learning design and practice, in our *own* sphere of influence (the cohorts we teach) more inclusive. Some of the examples in this book are likely to require only small adaptations to your practice design and no budget. But when many small changes take place, a synergy is created by these small aggregated gains which can eventually have considerable impacts on students' experience of accessibility and inclusion.

This compound effect of *small changes* has been called 'aggregation of marginal gains', an idea I first heard in connection with Sir Dave Brailsford (British Cycling performance director 2003–2014) and his coaching approach of the British cycling team which dominated the velodrome while he was directing it. It's a simple recipe: improve everything you do *by 1%*, and the compound effect will be remarkable. He looked at ways of improving little things to do with the cycling team—from pillows to hand soap. The culture of continual small improvements (also called kaizen) worked very well for his team, and he believed the principle can be applied to other fields as well. He said: 'Forget about perfection, focus on progression and compound the improvement' (Myer 2016). One useful takeaway from Sir Brailsford's approach is: look for *small things* that

Figure C.1 First know thyself (based on Roberts 2021).

you have control over in your learning design and make those as inclusive as possible. The overall, compound effect of these small changes can be remarkable.

Where should we start from? As discussed in Section 2, the first step of the contextual analysis that should inform our inclusive learning design is: First, know thyself (Figure C.1).

It is absolutely critical that we are honest with ourselves about our positionality, our values, our weaknesses in terms of inclusivity and where we need to improve. This self-analysis is likely to lead to a heightened awareness of the role we *can* play in initiating, 'sustaining or reducing inequality, exclusion and disabling practices' in our professional practice (Roberts 2021).

As part of your self-scrutiny, I invite you to use the 9-pointed star (Figure C.2) as a tool to (re-) design future modules or courses, using these prompts:

- What changes are easily implemented immediately? What long term changes can you make?
- How and when will the changes improve student experience?
- How will you check the ongoing progress?
- What resources can you draw on to support your action plan?

There is only a finite amount of examples and practices I could address in this book, but I acknowledge that there are other perfectly valid and inclusive practices that are not included in the tree (and the book). I have represented the unexplored possibilities in the tree image by adding smaller leaves on the branches, next to the three big leaves on each. This points to further unpredictable ways to develop inclusive environments, content and assessment. Seizing the serendipitous is vital to respond to students' needs and the changes in context. As Turner says (2020), 'While conscious design often plays a part in most of our systems, a level of organic evolution is often useful too, as all the "edge cases" of everyday working are often not picked up at the design stage'.

It may be that the analogy of the inclusive learning design tree will take me and you a fair distance at this time, but later be found to be missing some elements of inclusive education. In that case, I will be happy to change, adapt or review it as needed.

As discussed and demonstrated throughout this book, at times scrutinising our learning design and practice through an inclusivity lens may be challenging and

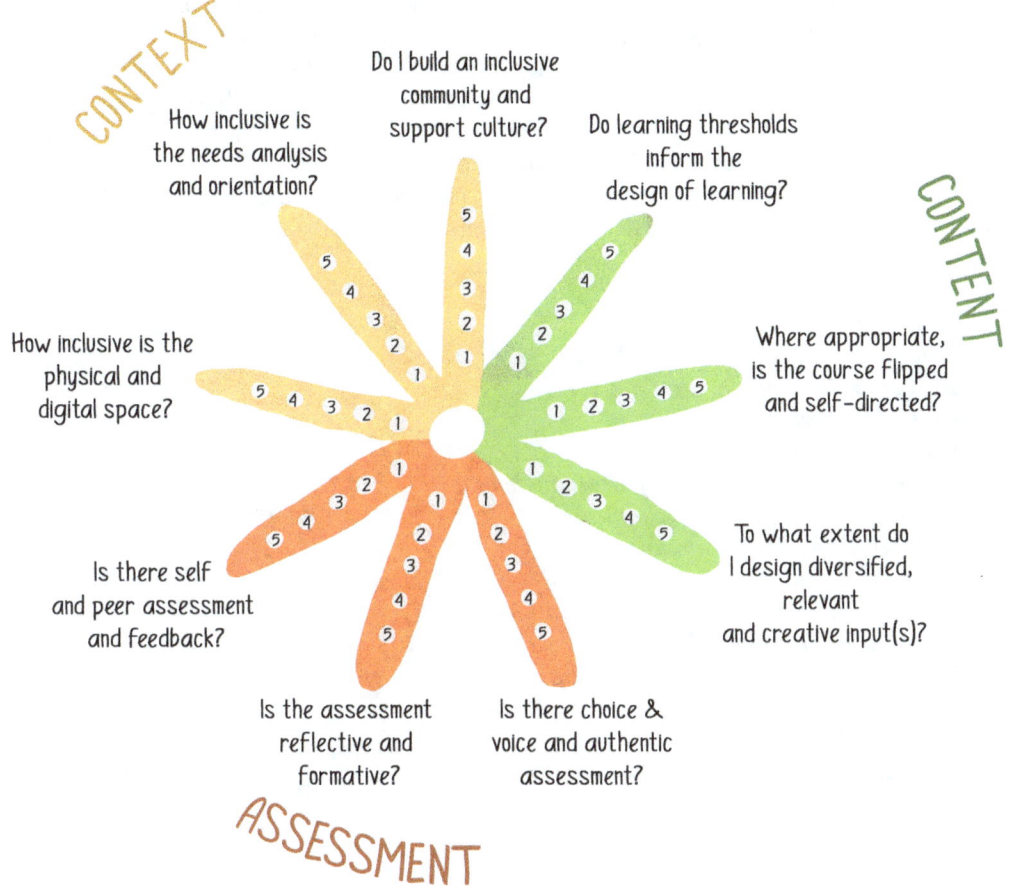

Figure C.2 The nine-point star to evaluate/refine/iterate our learning design.

uncomfortable, because it uncovers areas we need to address, requires extra work or is at odds with our biases. However, such scrutiny helps build confidence and skills, and prepares us for inclusivity-related work such as supporting learning across difference, supporting students with disabilities, facilitating a discussion where difficult feelings arise, or assessing and responding to calls for institutional change towards greater inclusion and equity. Ultimately the goal is not so much to create pockets of inclusive excellence (such as individual inclusive teachers) but to aim for inclusivity coalitions, or the creation of inclusivity communities of practice across departments (Crum 2022).

Once we have done all we can, in our sphere of influence, we are in a better position to make a case for more and better inclusivity at strategic level: governance, policies, financial commitment and institutional commitment (Roberts 2021). Inclusivity is an ongoing conversation that will only end when this type of book will not be needed because a truly inclusive educational system is in place everywhere. We are not there *yet*, so we should keep actioning incremental change, which prompts steady progress in the right direction.

Writing this book is part of my ongoing inclusivity journey. Mapping my understanding of inclusive learning design has been a very rewarding learning journey. Although it is classed as a monograph, in fact I feel this has been a crowdsourced, collaborative project from the start. The more than 60 case studies from so many different, global colleagues have inspired me with their practical wisdom. Books bind us as readers and authors, so I hope you feel connected to all the various authors who have contributed to this book and that you will feel free to reach out to them (for example through social media) for further professional dialogue and exchange.

To end this book, I propose we take 'Advice from a tree', which is the title of a poem by Ilan Shamir (n.d.), reprinted here with permission:

> *Dear Friend,*
> *Stand Tall and Proud*
> *Sink your roots deeply into the Earth*
> *Reflect the light of a greater source*
> *Think long term*
> *Go out on a limb*
> *Remember your place among all living beings*
> *Embrace with joy the changing seasons*
> *For each yields its own abundance*
> *The Energy and Birth of Spring*
> *The Growth and Contentment of Summer*
> *The Wisdom to let go of leaves in the Fall*
> *The Rest and Quiet Renewal of Winter*
> *Feel the wind and the sun*
> *And delight in their presence*
> *Look up at the moon that shines down upon you*
> *And the mystery of the stars at night.*
> *Seek nourishment from the good things in life*
> *Simple pleasures*
> *Earth, fresh air, light*
> *Be content with your natural beauty*
> *Drink plenty of water*
> *Let your limbs sway and dance in the breezes*
> *Be flexible*
> *Remember your roots*
> *Enjoy the view!*

The last two lines directly support the key message of this book. It is my hope that my 'roots to shoots' approach will make you more rooted and will help your students blossom thanks to the more inclusive learning that you design and implement.

Bibliography

Conole, G. (2008). The Role of Mediating Artefacts in Learning Design. In *Handbook of Research on Learning Design and Learning Objects: Issues, Applications and Technologies*. doi: 10.4018/9781599048611.ch008

Crum, A. (2022). What Does Inclusive Education Look Like at a Subject Level? [blog] WonkHE. Available at: https://wonkhe.com/blogs/what-does-inclusive-education-look-like-at-a-subject-level/

Lawrence, J. (2022). Inclusive Academic Practice as Pedagogic Competence. [Blog] The SEDA Blog. Available at: https://thesedablog.wordpress.com/2022/05/12/inclusive-academic-practice-as-pedagogic-competence/comment-page-1/#comment-7187

McArthur, J. (2021). The Inclusive University: A Critical Theory Perspective Using a Recognition-Based Approach. *Social Inclusion*, 9(3), 6–15. Available at: https://www.cogitatiopress.com/socialinclusion/article/view/4122/4122

Myer, J. (2016). This Coach Improved Everything by 1%, Putting Britain on the Road to Rio Olympic Glory. [online] World Economic Forum. Available at: https://www.weforum.org/agenda/2016/08/this-coach-improved-everything-by-1-this-is-the-remarkable-difference-it-s-made/

Roberts, D. (2021). EDI: A Seat at the Table, Not Crumbs from the Floor. Racism and Discrimination are Structural; Approaches to EDI Must Be Too [blog] Available at: https://blog.lboro.ac.uk/edi/2021/05/14/edi-a-seat-at-the-table-not-crumbs-from-the-floor/

Shamir, I. (n.d.). Advice From A Tree. [online] Awakin.org. Available at: https://www.awakin.org/v2/read/view.php?tid=2237

Index

access 6, 20–25, 62, 65, 67, 71, 73, 74, 77, 78, 80–88, 96, 165, 166, 187, 189, 198, 212, 225, 255, 256, 269
accessibility 21, 65, 77, 78, 80–88, 138, 172, 187–190, 217, 242, 311
accommodations 5, 22, 188, 192
active learning 69, 79, 198, 199
activities 3, 11, 12, 28, 41, 43, 48, 52, 63, 66, 67, 71, 72, 75, 76, 91, 97, 98, 100, 103, 106, 107, 110, 119, 126, 130, 148, 151, 153, 155, 157, 162, 163, 165, 172, 173, 175, 180, 181, 186–188, 194, 198, 199–201, 205, 207, 211, 213, 221, 224, 227, 239, 265, 266, 282, 284, 285, 291, 297, 300, 301, 309
agency 7, 8, 20, 51, 132, 162, 165, 175, 180, 183, 184, 215, 218, 234, 237, 246, 247
annotated 250, 301
art integrated learning (AIL) 217, 220–223, 226
assessment as learning 263–266, 278
asynchronous 71, 72, 87–89, 106, 148, 169, 175, 253, 272, 297–299
audio-visual 107, 160, 186, 200, 267, 277
authentic 87, 95, 97, 151, 167, 168, 210, 211, 216, 220, 234, 237, 238, 242, 243, 245, 247, 249–252, 255, 258, 259, 264, 266, 291

BAME 173
belonging 10, 15, 71, 101–103, 105, 107, 109–111, 127, 311
big ideas 119, 132, 136, 138, 144–148, 156–161
blended 7, 68, 71–73, 75, 76, 87, 93, 94, 170
blogs 165–169, 182, 203, 241, 282

choice 3, 6, 8, 11, 21, 22, 23, 44, 73, 74, 106, 117, 162, 165, 166, 169, 174, 177, 180, 181, 183, 184, 187, 188, 210, 222, 225, 233, 237–245, 249, 252, 258, 259, 270, 291, 309
choose-your-own 183

chunked 168
closure 297–300
cognitive load 76, 102, 163, 191–194
communities of practice 66, 67, 313
creative 37, 67, 68, 132, 158, 160, 169, 176, 184, 186, 198, 215, 216, 220, 221, 223, 226, 239, 251, 267
cultural wealth 93, 94, 96
culturally responsive 5, 93–96, 107, 120, 132, 202, 212
curating 190

decolonising 18, 21, 36, 37, 85, 132, 141, 202, 203
dialogical 164, 195, 210, 282
differentiation 137, 163, 169, 199, 218, 241, 245
digital literacy 67, 83–85, 164, 242, 259
diversity 3, 9, 10, 18, 21, 29, 33, 39, 43, 45, 47, 68, 80, 93, 94, 100, 115, 119, 181, 187, 202, 203, 206, 267, 309

ecological 38–41, 131, 179, 217, 234
emotional 11, 12, 23, 87, 88, 91, 97, 99, 106, 111–113, 118, 124, 126, 181, 205, 208, 263, 274, 301, 311
employability 215, 249, 267, 268, 272
engagement 22, 25, 27, 28, 31, 46, 62, 64, 68, 73, 77, 78, 87, 88, 95, 97, 98, 112, 113, 118, 124, 128, 155, 164, 166–168, 180, 181, 187, 188, 200, 211, 224, 226, 239, 240, 251, 253, 256, 264, 268, 277, 288, 294, 295, 301, 303
enquiry-based learning 175, 183
environment(s) 2, 3, 9–12, 15, 24, 27, 35, 36, 40, 41, 46, 51, 62–70, 74, 75, 77–84, 88, 107, 110, 118, 119, 128, 132, 149, 150, 162, 163, 169, 174, 176, 198, 200, 203, 215, 216, 223, 227, 231, 256, 271, 272, 278, 289, 291, 294
eportfolio 267–270
equity 5–8, 21, 26, 27, 89, 93, 95, 111, 222, 233, 313

flexible 11, 45, 66, 72–74, 76, 78, 81, 113, 154, 170, 180, 190, 233, 237, 238, 258, 268, 291, 314
flipped 161–166, 168, 169, 171–173, 175, 183, 184, 186, 227, 238
formative assessment 232, 240, 242, 261–263, 266, 270, 273, 277, 278, 290, 291
formative feedback 173, 262, 273, 274, 277, 278, 280, 283

games 113, 201, 216–220, 226, 228, 240
Global South 85, 202
ground rules 76, 77, 171, 273
group work 163, 174, 213, 222, 255, 290
group learning 68, 149, 151, 162

holistic 9–12, 17, 32, 45, 52, 62, 64, 93, 104, 128, 144, 186, 223, 233, 267, 290
hybrid 68, 71–76, 89, 97, 200, 291

independent 162, 165, 175, 274
induction 91, 92, 100–104, 108, 164
inquiry 14, 17, 131, 176, 195, 198, 210, 309
integrated learning 30, 31, 97, 211, 217, 220, 221, 223, 226, 259
intercultural learning 52, 120–123
interdisciplinarity 30–34
intersectionality 6, 21, 104, 202

kinaesthetic 186, 199–201, 226

learning outcomes 95, 124, 130, 136–140, 142–144, 146–148, 152, 154–156, 161, 173, 176, 181, 193, 207, 216, 224, 227, 232, 239, 240–242, 254, 267, 287
learning thresholds 130, 132, 136, 138, 141–148, 156, 160, 161, 186, 190, 197, 198, 206, 223, 226, 227, 242
liberating 17, 18, 62, 131, 186, 203, 233

macro level 17, 40, 136, 162
mattering 110
metacognition 177, 198, 234
micro level 34, 136, 162, 175, 309
mobile learning 81–87
motivation 48, 78, 81, 86, 130, 132, 216, 242, 251, 253

needs analysis 62, 63, 70, 88, 91, 92, 93, 96, 99, 103, 107, 128, 194

online learning 71, 76–78, 81, 118, 180, 200
outputs 2, 14, 21, 22, 41, 51, 72, 87, 95, 117, 125, 148, 168, 175, 176, 213, 225, 227, 232–234, 238, 239, 242, 245, 249–251, 255, 258, 259, 262, 273, 278, 280, 282, 283, 286, 290, 291, 294

peer assessment 98, 244, 261, 265, 268, 278, 280, 282, 283, 287, 289–291
peer mentoring 100, 110, 111, 114
personal tutoring 110, 111, 117
play 37, 157, 215–219
positionality 2, 63, 258, 312
projects 27, 28, 34, 45, 46, 48, 49, 125, 163, 180, 200, 215, 242, 244, 245, 253, 255, 256, 264

QAA 2, 43, 232, 233, 295

race 6, 32, 203, 204
reading list 87, 202, 203
reflective 11, 19, 94, 141, 153, 166, 252, 253, 259, 261–265, 267, 268, 270, 271, 273–278, 280, 282, 290, 291, 304, 306, 310
restorative practice 5
rubrics 222, 233, 240, 242, 262, 268, 286, 287, 289, 290

scaffolding 104, 183, 191–194, 208, 251, 262, 264, 268
screencast 22, 274, 277, 278
SDGs 27, 39, 42, 179
self-assessment 60, 244, 264, 281–285, 295
self-directed 8, 94, 132, 149, 161, 162, 165, 175–177, 180, 183, 184, 186, 227, 238
self-regulation 166, 234, 259, 261, 264, 266, 267, 273, 280, 281, 287, 290, 291
socially responsible 27, 28, 63, 131, 198
standards 2, 177, 232, 240, 263, 285
success criteria 175, 263, 281
sustainability 38–42, 57, 234, 294

teamwork 215, 243, 253, 270–273, 287, 302
technology 28, 32, 46, 66, 74, 76, 77, 81, 82, 84, 86, 87, 101–103, 131, 193, 197, 209, 225, 250, 254, 255, 256, 274
threshold concepts 136, 138–142, 144, 148–153, 155, 156, 158–160, 225, 283
transition 10, 91, 94, 99, 100, 103–107, 159, 207, 283
trauma-informed 111, 113, 114, 118, 126, 127

UDL 21–23, 25, 26, 55, 78, 180, 181, 183, 187–190, 238, 267, 303–307
underserved 6, 17, 67, 100, 173, 179

videos 23, 25, 70, 72, 81, 163–166, 169–173, 189, 276, 277
voice and choice 3, 6, 117, 180, 187, 233, 237, 243, 244, 259, 291, 309
VLE 62, 77, 79–81, 118–120, 126, 188

well-being 9, 10, 12, 46, 68, 86, 101–103, 109–111, 113, 118, 126, 127, 233

For Product Safety Concerns and Information please contact our EU
representative GPSR@taylorandfrancis.com
Taylor & Francis Verlag GmbH, Kaufingerstraße 24, 80331 München, Germany

www.ingramcontent.com/pod-product-compliance
Lightning Source LLC
Chambersburg PA
CBHW080923300426
44115CB00018B/2922